The Harmonial Philosophy

The Eight Books of Hermetic Science, Tradition, Astrology, Philosophy and Laws – Complete and Unabridged

By Andrew Jackson Davis

PANTIANOS
CLASSICS

Published by Pantianos Classics

ISBN-13: 9781986930680

First published in 1917

Contents

Preface

The seership of Andrew Jackson Davis was attracting wide attention in America, and in a more restricted sense was known also in England, some few years before the Rochester Knockings inaugurated the epoch of modern Spiritualism. By the hypothesis, it gave forth — like the latter — a revelation from the world beyond, and was to all intents and purposes an early example of trance mediumship, though Davis never claimed to speak under the influence of specific personal controls, like the long line of psychic orators who came after him and were, for the better part, his contemporaries. As he was, on the one hand, so much the most important of all that there is no person who could be placed in the second rank beneath him, so he has been of all the most popular. The Principles of Nature, his first book of revelations, and the only one which claims to have been dictated by him in the "magnetic" state, has passed through at the least forty-four American editions, and as there is no question that it is still in demand, it is likely to be reprinted again — perhaps many times over. It is the most comprehensive of all his writings. He wrote and published continuously during a long period of years, and his readers seem to have been no less eager than he was himself untiring, the demand for his successive volumes being always large. His collected works have been issued on several occasions, available sometimes in single volumes separately, sometimes in complete sets only.

The reason of this popularity is not far to seek. In The Principles of Nature a philosophy of modern Spiritualism preceded Spiritualism itself, and so also a doctrine concerning the world beyond in that sphere which was held to be in immediate contiguity with the life of earth was put forward as the result of personal knowledge in seership, while later on a thousand voices coming from that sphere and, according to the claim of Spiritualism, speaking through a thousand mediums, testified to its general truth. There is no seer of the past — and there is no prophet — who had such a cloud of witnesses. The effect was greater and stronger because they did not set out to testify in favour of Davis; he was not for them the precursor of all those voices, but that which he affirmed was by them verified without reference to him. The doctrine, in a word, was that the world beyond is as natural as this world of ours; that it is neither the heaven nor hell of official Christianity; that it is simply this world spiritualised, and that men and women in their psychic bodies are as men and women here in the bodies of flesh, but with better opportunities of progress and a far better environment. They are encompassed by helpers innumerable, so that those even who pass from the life of earth in a state of hardened criminality have every encouragement to amend and ultimately never fail to do so. In a word, the gospel of Davis, in common with that of Spiritualism, cast out all fear concerning the life to come. The prototype of Davis is a still greater seer in the person of Emanuel Swedenborg; but whatever Its claims and merits — about which much yet remains to be said after a new manner — the doctrine of the New Jerusalem, according to the Swedish prophet, will bear no comparison on the ground of popular appeal with the "Divine Revelations" of him who was the Poughkeepsie seer and the exponent of Harmonial Philosophy. It is obvious that this is put forward in the only reasonable and therefore possible sense, not as a test of truth or even a title of excellence, but as a purely explanatory statement concerning a great vogue.

Whatever their deserts or defects otherwise, the postulated principles of Nature are embodied in a work which marks an epoch, and it gave a status to Spiritualism when that movement and all its host of phenomena were still in the womb of time. Later on it is evident abundantly that this movement and the revelations involved therein reacted on Davis, quite naturally and quite of necessity too. They led of course to no change of ground, for essentially they belonged to one another, but he was stimulated under their influence, and they gave him, moreover, a field, an audience, an opportunity which he could scarcely have had in their absence.

This was the position at the beginning of the new movement, and speaking as one who is acquainted with all the activities and nearly the whole literature of modern psychological and occult schools, it remains to be said that — so far as English-speaking countries are concerned — the seer and prophet of Spiritualism in its first days is even now par excellence — but I speak of excellence as judged within the limits of the schools — the prophet and philosopher, if not also the seer, of the present moment. Time has changed otherwise the actual modus videndi in many important respects. No one speaks of a rainbow-belt among the star-clouds of the Milky Way as the world of disembodied souls. No one expresses or owns to any special view or concern about humanities of other planets and whether they proceed at death to that Second Sphere which receives souls from earth. No one accepts or denies the Davis classification of six spheres of intelligent being, with a seventh which is a Central Sun and the more particular abode of the Godhead. But of the general philosophy of Spiritualism, and of all that is weak as of all that is strong therein, Davis is the general exponent, if only because there is — practically speaking — no other who has arisen. It is difficult even now to take up a current number of any periodical devoted to the concerns of the subject and not find that he is quoted. His classification of mediumship was in all probability a matter of suspicion from the beginning, and it might be derided now, while there are many other views of his which have passed into utter desuetude; but he himself remains the spokesman at large of the subject, so far as man's place in the universe, the contiguity and interpenetration of the two worlds are concerned. On the other hand, in so far as he came forward in the guise of a scientific teacher — under "control" or psychic influence — he probably convinced few or none, even at the beginning, and he reflects now the most primitive side of the most exploded authorities. His titles to consideration are those of a seer; his visions of the world beyond are the appealing side of his seership; and for persons who accept the possibility of such experiences, there is nothing in all the annals of psychism to compare with his Summer Land. The ten thousand controls of later mediumship — except in so far as they reflect his revelations — tell us little or nothing concerning the phenomena of physically disembodied life. He has set out all its phases, all its topography, all concerns therein, and we shall doubtless have to await the advent of another prophet before anything substantial is added thereto or altered substantially therein. Meanwhile the important investigations of psychical research, apart from professed Spiritualism, remove us by the nature of things from the philosophy of the subject, being concerned with the facts of manifestations and with tolerable deductions from these, not with the nature and pursuits of the spiritual spheres of being.

Now, the collected writings of Andrew Jackson Davis fill twenty-seven volumes, full of repetitions, verbosities and extraneous material. On account of the position which he has occupied for a period of seventy years in a movement which numbers at this day many thousands of adherents in Great Britain and the Colonies alone, it has seemed to the present editor that it would be serviceable to them and others to present — in the form of a digest — the essential parts of his doctrine, philosophy and testimony to the world of spirits and the natural law therein. The result of that undertaking is offered in this volume. As regards all that is incorporated and all that is excluded, it represents of course the personal views of the editor in respect of presumptive values, and he makes no claim to the possession of a final criterion. The work has been done with sincerity; nothing has been inserted because it appeals to him personally, apart from other considerations; nothing has been omitted because it opposes his views. Except upon points of fact those views are obtruded nowhere, and as far as possible they enter into expression nowhere. The object has been to present the essence of Davis, and though the task as a whole has been anxious rather than easy, there has been throughout a singular satisfaction in observing how that essence has been extracted in the process of condensation without diminution of any kind, though many original pages may be represented occasionally by a single paragraph. There is no need to say that the process has involved re-expression — as it is believed, to the advantage of Davis and never to the sacrifice of the meaning which he designed to convey. [1] A few among those who know him may think that his anti-theological views should have been represented more fully; but enough has been given to show how he stood as to this subject. The particular circumstances under which he was born and lived denied him qualifications for judgment thereupon; even at his own period he did not represent the real difficulties of doctrine, and at the present day we are dealing with different and perhaps greater difficulties. In any case the ground has changed, and the animadversions of Davis, both in and out of season, but too often sacrificing the logical sequence of his text, were of less moment at their period than the discourses of Bradlaugh or Ingersoll and are of no consequence now. There are a few others who may feel that an undue space has been given to descriptions of the Summer Land, as Davis claims to have seen it in his "superior condition"; but without attempting to pronounce on their value, it is believed that they have been always the chief attraction of his "revelations," and that his "harmonial philosophy," apart from these as a title or warrant in seership, would scarcely demand presentation in a new form, its great occasional insight and suggestion notwithstanding. It is in connection with these more especially that this work has been undertaken, and to mark the philosophical aspects of the claim respecting intervention between the physical and spiritual worlds.

To sum up, the message of Davis, as here presented, stands in the editor's opinion for the spirit or essence of the whole, liberated only from unwieldy accretions into which the essence does not enter, and of course separated from other extraneous matter — as, e.g. things which belong to the domain of medical formulae. It is very curious, in conclusion, to note the various points at which the Harmonial Philosophy of Davis is in quite unconscious harmony with the Hermetic Science, of which the editor claims to be a student, as also with the later theory of evolution. A few instances belonging to the first case have been cited in the notes, the most striking of all being his theory of a universal fluid, which corresponds to the Astral Light of the Martinists and to the Kabalistic so-called "light of glory." These analogies could have been traced further, but it exceeded the present undertaking, which appeals to a class of minds whose acquaintance with occult lore cannot be presupposed.

[1] It has not of course been possible to rectify reasoning, where this must be regarded as defective.

Biographical Introduction

Being Episodes in the Life of a Seer

ANDREW JACKSON DAVIS was born on the 11th of August, 1826, at Bloomingrove, Orange County, in the State of New York. His father, Samuel Davis, described as a simple-hearted, unsophisticated man, followed the trade of a shoemaker and weaver, varied by haymaking and harvesting at their proper seasons. There was a moderately numerous family, the general characteristic of which was extreme poverty. Both father and mother are said — in the first autobiographical record of Andrew Jackson — to have been "destitute of the commonest education," [1] meaning presumably that they could neither read nor write. Occasional intemperance — for it does not seem to have been a rooted and continuous habit — was the chief weakness of the former, in the boy's earlier days; but he worked hard, as his opportunities offered, and tried various humble schemes to improve his position, frequent migrations included. As delineated by her son, the mother "possessed a spirit of meekness and quiet, unqualified by any really positive element of character." [2] Davis was two years old when there was a hurried sale of effects and a removal to Staatsburgh, followed in 1832 by a second exodus, this time to Hyde Park in Dutchess County, also in the State of New York. Here the family was stationary for about six years, when it proceeded to Poughkeepsie, where occurred those events which were to shape the future life of Davis, and in consequence of which he became and has continued to be known as the Poughkeepsie seer. His first tuition was obtained at Hyde Park village in a species of dame's school, but presently under other auspices. The experiment was highly unsuccessful and is said to have been dropped speedily, though resumed in his twelfth year — as he says — for a few weeks only, and again at Poughkeepsie, apparently in the closing weeks of 1839 and the beginning of the following year. He confesses altogether to five months of education, by the help of which he acquired some rudiments of reading, writing and ciphering. The schooling was interspersed with various humble employments, humiliating in their results as the teaching — for, according to his own description, he was dull, backward and clumsy, not to speak of timidity and an over-sensitive nature. Such as it was, his religious training was also of a haphazard kind, picked up between church and meeting-house, with little regularity at either. His mother — who shines through his early life with much patience and sweetness amidst her incessant difficulties — had, however, some elements of piety after a crude manner, and, speaking generally, he responded to her good influence, partly by sympathy and partly through natural goodness in his own character. In the early part of 1841 her death put an end to their companionship. The main points of his record during the period which followed this loss, as indeed previously, are concerned with miscellaneous and mostly abortive efforts to retain such employment as came in his way.

There is no reason for reciting them in this place, and the narrative may pass therefore to that period and occurrence which was to influence his entire life and reveal his future vocation

At the close of 1843, Andrew Jackson Davis being seventeen years of age, an itinerant phrenologist and mesmerist, named Grimes, appeared at Poughkeepsie and lectured on Animal Magnetism. Davis attended and was one of the subjects on whom the "professor" tried certain experiments, but in this case unsuccessfully. There was, however, a tailor in the village, by name William Levingston, who — as the result of Grimes' visit — made a trial of his own powers in producing magnetic phenomena. He appears to have achieved considerable success, and Davis came at length into his hands. On the very first occasion it is affirmed that "the boy exhibited powers of clairvoyance which were truly surprising." This is on the authority of William Fishbough, whose introduction appears in every edition of The Principles of Nature. Davis, on his part, records the circumstances and his recollected experience at length in the work already quoted. [3] He describes his first sensations when the operator's hands passed and repassed over his head, the momentary illumination which followed, the intense darkness thereafter, a conviction of actual dissolution, the transitory and vain struggle against the whole operation, and the consciousness that he was lying supine — incapable of all physical motion. Thereafter, as he tells us, consciousness was itself suspended and the rest of his account embodies that which he heard from others. In the presence of witnesses, and with eyes bandaged, he had read from a newspaper, told the time by a watch, described the complaints from which certain spectators were suffering — in all cases with accuracy. This experiment took place on December 1st, 1843.

Davis frequented Levingston's parlour night after night, not without "inexpressible apprehensions," but with uniformly successful results. "At each session some new truth or interesting wonder would make its appearance," [4] the operator freely admitting all whom curiosity or expectation drew towards the new prodigy, thus manifesting in the little community. The result was an exceedingly mixed audience, with considerable notoriety for the subject, not unmixed with hostility and even persecution. On January 1st, 1844, Davis, according to his story, made his first psychic "flight through space," [5] though his recollection concerning it appears to have come long after the event. He describes himself as "born again" in the spirit. "It seemed that the whole earth, with all its inhabitants, had been suddenly translated into some Elysium." He saw not only the encompassing auras of the various spectators, but their physical bodies became "transparent as a sheet of glass" and "invested with a strange, rich, spiritual beauty." He beheld within the veil every separate material organ and the peculiar emanations by which each was surrounded. It is claimed also that behind the "real physical structures," he became conscious of the "indwelling essences and vitalic elements." This was the first stage of his vision, and the second brought within his field of consciousness the furniture in the room about him and the walls by which it was enclosed. The walls dissolved, and he could see into the adjoining house. This was the second stage, and he passed thereafter into what he terms a deeper sleep, in which, "by a process of interpenetration," he was "placed en rapport with Nature." He became aware of "a high and eternal communion," as between that which was within him and that which is alive in the world. The earth opened to his view, and he explored the mineral kingdom, the properties and essences of plants, and the internal physiology of the animal creation. He saw something also of man, in the sense that all animate nature was working up towards humanity. [6]

On another occasion, the date being March 6 of the same year, the magnetic condition was induced as usual, but experiencing a painful impression from what is termed the "spheres" of the sitters, he quitted the operator's premises, and being still in the subjective state, called at the house of a clergyman, proceeding thence to the operator's private residence — where he was staying at the time — and there going straight to bed. He awakened, still under the magnetic influence, dressed and went out into the street, passing from point to point "with a fleetness indescribable." It was still night, and "under the heavenly archway" he appeared to stand alone, "unseen by any save the eye of the Eternal Being." An allegorical vision followed, concerning "a shadowy congregation of clean and beautiful sheep" and their shepherd — "a kind and gentle being, endowed with physical and spiritual perfection." The flock represented humanity and the herdsman was a reformer among it whose mission was to overcome ignorance and confusion therein. The part of Davis in the vision was to help the shepherd in his tending, which was at length accomplished, after which the flock and its guide proceeded onward and vanished in the distance. The scene changed presently, and he was across the river Hudson, now overcome with fatigue, again restored inwardly, now in storm and darkness, again under a clear sky in the daylight, now conscious of sleeping, then of awaking, and finally finding himself in an utterly strange region. Once more he beheld a scattered crowd of sheep, striving to climb a hill, and a shepherd like the former one, whom he was also called to help, with similar results. At a later period teachers came to himself, and between their visits he inquired of a person in a farmer's dress how far it was to Poughkeepsie. He was told that it was about forty miles. He began travelling homeward, alternately sleeping and running. Part of his instructions were concerned with the art of healing, but this also was conveyed figuratively; and part told him that through his mediation new light would come to mankind. All this time he was travelling in the physical body, though only conscious in the spirit. At length he reached Poughkeepsie and returned to the house of Levingston, having been absent since the previous night. It was not until he had eaten a hearty meal that he regained his normal sensibility.

He was magnetised as usual on the following evening, and then proceeded to explain the moral of his recent visions. They signified a complete change, an end to the gratification of curiosity and the advancement of magnetic science by devoting the clairvoyant faculties of the seer exclusively to the healing of the sick. The limits of sittings were fixed, the manner of conducting the magnetic process was prescribed, and it was laid down that there should be no charge for consultation except to those who were in "easy circumstances." Davis represents his operator — the tailor, Levingston — as having an abundant and profitable business; but he was a man inspired with the love of humanity, and this to such an extent that, encouraged by his wife, he gave up his trade to follow the course outlined by the young seer. A clairvoyant clinic was opened accordingly, beginning at Poughkeepsie and extended afterwards to Bridgeport, Connecticut, operator and subject living as they could upon the proceeds which came into the common coffer. But as the days drew towards the summer of 1845, Davis was in labour with the undetermined sense of another mission, a wider and more important field of labour, concurrently with which he became acquainted with Dr. S. S. Lyon of Bridgeport, apparently an ordinary medical practitioner, whom he convinced of the truth of clairvoyance. Now, Davis in his entranced condition had delivered already some two or three lectures, and as the horizon cleared inwardly before him he saw that his coming work lay in this direction, or to put it quite plainly and boldly, a book was to be delivered in sections, in the magnetic state, and reduced into writing by a scribe present on the occasions. There was to be one magnetiser and there was to be one scribe only. So did Davis, something less at the date in question than twenty years old, enter upon a new phase of his career, and the connection with his previous operator came to an end abruptly, for, while in the clairvoyant state, he "voluntarily chose Dr. Lyon to be his magnetiser during the delivery of this book," [7] the reporter — similarly selected — being the Rev. William Fishbough, of New Haven, Connecticut — probably a universalist minister. As the seer decided further that the "revelations" must take place in New York, rather than Bridgeport, Dr. Lyon relinquished "a remunerative and increasing practice," with the result that another clairvoyant clinic had to be opened at the new centre as a visible means of subsistence for operator and subject during the long course of the lectures.

In addition to operator and scribe, three permanent witnesses were selected, "so that the world through them might know from what source these revelations flow." [8] They were the Rev. J. N. Parker, Theron A. Lapham and Dr. T. Lea Smith — of whom little or nothing is known at this day, beyond the brief references of Davis. The lectures, to the number of one hundred and fifty-seven, were delivered at 92 Greene Street, Manhattan, from November 28th, 1845, to January 25th, 1847, apart from any public announcement, a few persons being privately notified from time to time. The remarkable scheme had therefore no financial aspect, so far as its chief actors were concerned. As regards procedure, it will be sufficient to state (a) that the subject was hoodwinked, as was the case also in the previous experiments and throughout the diagnoses generally; (b) that he was put invariably into the magnetic condition; and (c) that the seer dictated to the operator slowly and in a low voice, the operator repeating the words aloud, making sure that they had been heard correctly, after which they were written down by the scribe. The source of information was claimed to be "the spiritual world," but apart from any special personality, thus constituting — at whatever may be its importance and value — one salient distinction between the Davis communications and a considerable proportion of those which characterised the séance through many subsequent years. In a word, the Manhattan orations were the first to be delivered in trance, the inspirational poems of Thomas Lake Harris coming probably next in time, as they do certainly in importance.

In the digest which follows, The Principles of Nature — into which the lectures developed — will speak adequately for itself. Here it will be sufficient to add a word only on two external facts. The means for its publication came at the right moment — as they seem to come always in cases of this kind — through the munificence of private sources; and the work was prepared for the press by William Fishbough, who gives a scrupulous account as to his hand therein. The following heads of particulars are worth noting, as indications of his personal good faith. He made needful corrections in grammar, pruned certain verbal redundancies and elucidated some obscure sentences. He altered nothing in respect of ideas and, moreover, added nothing. With these unimportant qualifications, he bears witness that the work, in its published form, "may be considered as paragraph for paragraph, sentence for sentence, and word for word, as it was delivered by the author." With one exception, the appended annotations were those of Fishbough; but they were very few and unimportant, and have not been reproduced here.

A little prior to the publication of this work, Davis felt that what he terms the second magnetic crisis of his life was on the threshold or within the door. As a fact, he was put to sleep by Dr. Lyon for the last time on April 10th, 1847, and he looked in other directions for the "further development of his powers." Such at least was the testimony of Thomas Lake Harris, the inspirational poet, who had become acquainted with him at this time and is claimed to have looked for his guidance during a brief period. On August 11th, Davis attained his twenty-first year, when it was proposed to establish a "reform paper," to be entitled The Univercoelum with Dr. S. B. Brittan as editor-in-chief. He was another friend of that season and well known in the circles of liberal thinking, as he was subsequently in the spiritualistic movement for a considerable number of years. The project was brought to birth, and Davis was one of the contributors; but adequate capital was wanting for such a venture, and its struggle for existence ceased at the end of 1848. In the meantime, or specifically on July 1st, 1848, Davis was married to the woman whose generosity had mainly made possible the publication of The Principles of Nature. She was much older than himself and had occasion to secure a divorce from her first husband before the union could take place.

The history of this period is really that of the liberation of Davis from the leading strings of magnetic operators. He was conscious and has put on record the fact that he could enter "the superior state" whenever circumstances and his own will demanded it. [9] Under these circumstances, and without — as he tells us — the aid of any scribe or help from other books, he began writing the first volume of his next most considerable work, The Great Harmonia. This was during the autumn of 1849 and the spring of the following year. In this manner there passes into record the beginning of that psychic, intellectual and literary life which Davis was to lead henceforward. His books are its landmarks, and to all intents and purposes they represent it so fully that the bibliography of his writings at the end of the present volume might be taken as a sufficient supplement to the present biographical note. Everything else is transitory and its interest has perished long ago, as those who at this day may undertake the experiment of reading The Magic Staff and Beyond the Valley, which are his memoirs very much at large, are likely to find to their cost.

Here it will be sufficient to say that she who was his first wife died on November 2nd, 1853, and on May 15th, 1855, he was married for a second time. As Mrs. Katie Dodge secured a divorce with the intention of marrying Davis if and when it was obtained, so Mrs. May Love was moving for similar liberation when that which Davis terms his "clairvoyant penetration" had discovered a "genuine fitness" between her soul and his. The second union continued for something like twenty-nine years, when it was terminated on November 18th, 1884, in a letter which Davis wrote to his wife, addressing her as "my companion in the work," and this course was subsequently clinched by a nullity decree, on the ground that the divorce obtained from Mr. Love in 1854 by Mary Love "was not sufficiently valid in the State of New York," where Davis married her subsequently. [10] Mary Davis raised no plea against the proceedings and — apparently with a broken heart — reassumed her maiden name of Mary Fennell. This is enough to register in the present place concerning a particularly painful business.

Davis appears to have entered the married state for a third time, as it has been stated that "his beloved wife," Delia, "ministered to his last earthly needs" at the time of his death. For the rest, he was an active and ready lecturer on the Harmonial Philosophy. He was connected, editorially and otherwise, with several periodicals, among others The Herald of Progress, and, generally speaking, with a number of "reform" movements. Moreover, in or about the year 1886, having taken up the study of medicine through the authorised channels, he earned and received his diploma of M.D. from the United States Medical College of New York. Though he claimed always to be guided by an inward light and to possess, as we have seen, the power to pass continually and voluntarily into higher psychic conditions, in which the unseen world opened its vistas before him, The Principles of Nature is the only work which he dictated in an entranced state, so that it stands in a category by itself when compared with his later writings. It has certain manifest resemblances with the revelations of Swedenborg, and it may be noted that Davis claimed the Swedish seer as one of his early "guides." He took exception, however, as we have seen, to the notion that he occupied the position of a medium in relation to any spirit, "as if my mind — while in the superior condition — were an insensible, unintelligent and passive substance or spout, through which disembodied personages express or promulgate their own specific opinions." The remark has reference to The Principles of Nature, and Davis describes with considerable detail his mental state as one of "watching and analysing" on the night that its dictation began and when he was like a "conscious mirror . . . on which were reflected and in which were focalised the principles and properties of the System of Nature." His magnetisation or entrancement produced therefore only a suspension of physical faculties which — ex hypothesi — liberated and extended his interior powers. No seer of ancient or modern times has given so lucid an account of his psychic states, as remembered subsequently.

While *The Principles of Nature* is accurately described in the preface to the present volume as the most comprehensive of all his writings, it is of course not the most mature. Personally Davis preferred Penetralia to any of his other books, on the ground that it was "the wisest," an opinion probably endorsed by very few of his readers. In any case it is believed that he is represented at his best by no one work but rather by that harmony and digest of all which is presented here. "The Poughkeepsie seer" departed this life on January 13th, 1910, and since his entrance into the Summer Land there seems no evidence of his communication with "the first sphere."

[1] *See The Magic Staff, edition of 1885, p. 38.*
[2] *Ibid.*
[3] *Ibid. c. 32.*
[4] *Ibid., pp. 211, 212.*
[5] *See ibid., c. xxxiii, passim.*
[6] *It calls to be said that this vision is intincted with the considered opinions and expe-riences of Davis in his later years. It took him four years to recollect anything concern-ing it, and as, according to his own quite sincere statement, it was when writing The Magic Staff in 1857 — after a space of thirteen years — that the vast scene unrolled before his memory, we shall be justified in making certain allowances for the very probable intermixture of earlier and later seership in the narrative, taken as a whole,*
[7] *See William Fishbough's introduction to The Principles of Nature, original edition, p. 18. This memorial states that the choice mentioned above was neither solicited nor an-ticipated by Dr. Lyon until it was actually announced. Davis, however, gives a different account. He had called upon his future operator when in dejection over the inability of Levingston to develop his clairvoyance further and told him that he would present him-self at the proper time if he — Dr. Lyon — was to replace the first operator. He called again — to communicate the fact — when he had decided affirmatively as the result of meditation in solitude; and so far as it is possible to judge from the words of his narra-tive, Davis was not then in a state of induced clairvoyance. See The Magic Staff, c. xxxix.*
[8] *See An Address to the World, prefixed to The Principles of Nature, p. 2.*
[9] *See The Magic Staff, c. xlix.*
[10] *See "In Memoriam — Mary Fenn Davis," by Hester K. Poole, reprinted from The Religio-Philosophical Journal by Light of August 21st, 1886. So the lady did not long survive her enforced separation.*

Book One - Revelations of Divine Being

Chapter One - What and Where Is God? [1]

The mind is incarnated in a physical temple of which the dome is measured by inches, but its thoughts and affections expand into greater dimensions. Earth is too limited, and its materiality is too obvious for the soul. It seeks those living orbs that roll through infinitude. Star after star is counted; constellations are mapped out, like milestones along familiar roads. Still the mind goes on. It reaches the ineffable mysteries of the sidereal heavens, those invisible worlds of grandeur beyond the most distant stars. Amazed at the splendours and harmony, pulsating with joy and the desire to know yet more, the soul demands: what and where is God? The fields of science have been traversed, the beauties of art have been displayed for our contemplation; the religious works of all nations have been searched, that the soul might comprehend and gaze upon the Supernal Ruler of the universe; but He remains the unseen, uncomprehended Father of all spirits—pure, holy, everlasting, infinite. Belief in God, or in a superior power, is indigenous to the soul and consequently to all nations and tribes on the surface of the earth. While individual conceptions of God reflect prevailing beliefs for the vast majority, to the mind which thinks independently such notions will be representative of the person himself, and to this extent God is in our likeness. They may be scientific, philosophical or theological. God considered scientifically is the greatest fact in the universe—the greatest Principle and Reality. He is the active or moving Principle, contrasted with which Nature is moved or passive. He is Being, of absolute necessity. Vitalising all things, He dwells with all substances and elements, and individualises His motion, life, sensation and intelligence therein.[2] It is true therefore that God is Nature. [3] Being substance in and of Himself, and exerting an active and moving power continually in the empire of matter, it is reasonable to conclude that His attributes and elements are also matter or substance. All His modes of motion may be generalised under attraction and repulsion or—in the language of Harmonial Philosophy—as association, progression and development. But a scientific inquiry into the nature and mode of God is the first and most inferior effort of human reason, and its conclusions are of an external kind, true only so far as they go.

Philosophy, on the other hand, considers God in reference to principles, causes and designs, instead of things, effects and phenomena, which are the province of science. He is for philosophy the Great Central Source of life, love, order and form. Nature exists and operates between God and His designs, while the end or issue of such design must correspond to the magnitude and majesty of the Inventor. Contemplate that Eternal Centre from which proceeded the innumerable worlds of immensity, and reason will confess that God is positive but all else negative. Spirit and matter must not be confounded nor separated. When defining spirit I have been compelled to employ the term matter, in the absence of a better word, because it is expressive of substance, and such is spirit. So also the Positive Mind must not be confounded with Nature, nor separated therefrom. God is as distinct from Nature as is the human soul from its body. [4] He is personal in the sense that He contains the principles of perception, and all other principles; yet is He not separate from or outside Nature. His mode of being and action is determined by that inevitable constitution of things, of which He is the Unfolder, Sustainer and Co-essential.

Theologically considered, God is the Great Father, Spirit of all spirits. The essential qualities and properties of His Infinite Soul penetrate all Nature and all intelligent essences. These qualities and properties are love, understood fundamentally, and thus God is love. Theologically we think of the inexhaustible sweetness of this love; we think of God's close and unchangeable relation to our most interior selves; we feel a particular providence in our existence, a protection from multifarious temptations and accidents in the doing of His will willingly. When this view rests, as it should rest always, upon a scientific and philosophical foundation, divested of mystery and supernaturalism, it is a source of unfailing consolation. If God is apprehended as an organised principle, [5] operating according to eternally established laws—so surpassingly righteous that they produce a kind of necessary freedom or independence—then will our spirits bow with intellectual obedience to the Will of our Father and experience a beautiful liberty in moving harmoniously with universal Nature. It follows that, viewed with scientific eyes, God is a Great Fact, philosophically a Great Positive Mind and theologically a Great Spirit Father. The executive element of the Great Positive Mind is will, and the essential element is love. Divine Love and Divine Will, in their governing and directing principle, constitute Divine Wisdom—eternal, infinite, spread throughout the length and breadth of the universe.

In accordance with the rules of analogical reasoning, it is easy to comprehend what God is, and where and how He dwells in the universe. He is the sublimation of all substantial qualities, essences, elements, principles, in the highest concentration of unity, the crystallisation of all that is refined, pure, bright and harmonious. [6] He resides especially in the vortical encephalon or cerebrum of the universe. The analogy which exists between the Divine Mind and the universe is therefore established. As the human mind is organised on a finite plane, so is the Divine Mind organised on an infinite plane. As the seat of human sensation, affection, sentiment, intelligence and voluntary power is in the brain, so are the qualities, essences, principles, omnipotent power and eternal omniscience in the sensorium of the universe. The outer universe is a visible manifestation of the Indwelling Deity. Nature is the body, God is the soul. Nature is the dormitory of all that is unfolded in the great sensorium. God is the Cause, Nature is the effect; God is the spiritual, Nature the material; Nature is finite, God is infinite. The two are joined indissolubly and harmoniously—matrimonially, so to speak—and can never fall asunder. The highest conception which the human mind can attain of the Infinite is essentially theological; but the relations which the Infinite sustains to the finite, [7] which God sustains to Nature, can be comprehended only by a philosophical intellect, and hence such terms as our Heavenly Father and the Great First Cause will be understood readily, but the Organised Principle and the Great Sensorium of the universe make a deeper call on minds. The Great Positive Mind is love, will, wisdom; Nature is substance, aggregation, universe; and the laws which flow from God into the organism of Nature are those of association, progression and development. God acts upon the universe anatomically. In the structure of planets and in the forms of solar systems there are manifold indications of a great anatomical law; and inasmuch as spirit is a substance superior to matter, which it moves, the formative principle which lies back of and beneath all visible combinations of matter must of necessity contain whatsoever the externals of Nature manifest to sense. The series, degrees, associations of structures in Nature are expressive of principles contained in the One Great Principle. God also acts physiologically on the universe. As the acorn develops into an oak, as the germ of all forms produces an ultimate development in its own image and likeness, so the Divine Mind begets Its image and likeness in the human soul.

So also it expands and unfolds its celestial and immutable principles into mineral, vegetable and all animate forms. A great functional or physiological law flows through the labyrinths of immensity. Nothing which manifests life is without functions to perform in the great body of causation, and the forms and functions of material organisms in Nature are demonstrations that the Great Motive Power of the universe contains principles of structure and function, which in these attain their ultimate. In the third place, God acts on the universe mechanically, for there is a certain sense in which Nature is a vast mechanism, of which God is the Great Inventor; and in its sublime workings the true mechanic on earth can learn of God. From the lowest to the highest he can discern the constant evolution of principles, motives and forces. The centrifugal and centripetal tendencies of human mechanics imitate, on an imperfect scale, corresponding tendencies and motions among planetary bodies. Once more, Nature indicates the modes of Divine Existence. [8] As the spirit of man acts on his body so does the Spirit of God act upon the universe. But, in the fourth place, God acts on the universe chemically, and this Divine Chemistry is the harmony and perfection of those laws which interrelate the Great Vital Principle and its physical organism— that is to say, the boundless universe. The principle of association, which is the primary manifestation of Divine Love, flows forth into all branches of organic life, and chemical action is its sequence or companion. Such action is indeed one mode of creation. In the fifth place, God acts upon the universe electrically. The Divine Mind employs electricity as a medium of communication to all parts and particles of the universe, an expression of the unchanging pulsations of His Eternal Soul. He acts also magnetically. The Eternal Mind is surrounded by a Great Spiritual Sun, resplendent with emanations of immortal life and beauty. Its essences, principles and harmonies flow through the whole organism of Nature, as the blood and principles of life and sensation flow through man's body. But in fine God acts upon the universe spiritually, as the Great Spiritual Principle, totality of being and crown of all.

[1] See The Great Harmonia, Vol. II, p. 255 et seg,, summarised and collated.

[2] According to The Great Harmonia, the universal empire of worlds about us is actuated and governed by a Divine Mind, which is the Cause of all that feels or exhibits life. It is likewise the Source of all power, and is Itself actual substance, because it requires substance to move substance. The affirmation recurs continually. See op. cit., Vol. I, p. 46. See also the annotation on p. 112 of the present work. Meanwhile, it is sufficient to mention that—whatever may appear on the surface—Davis does not really intend to confuse phenomena with noumena or matter with substance.

[3] Nature is elsewhere described as the body of God, meaning the Divine Vehicle or Vesture.

[4] At a much, later period Davis re-expressed the position thus: The Father-God is one universe and the Mother-Nature is another universe. In heart, in brain, in essence and in spirit, the twain are perfect counterparts; and their duality is a living oneness which is called truly Eternal Harmony. Views of our Heavenly Home, p. 109. The word eternal does not appear to be used in any rigid sense, for Davis recognised elsewhere that the present cosmic order may be dissolved and be replaced afterwards by another. So also the comparison in the text above, respecting soul and body, is subject to the transitory nature of the latter.

[5] The argument is that God must be Himself organised before He can "breathe forth"—that is create, produce, beget or emanate—organisations, and that He must embody within Himself the principles of all modes of action before there can be such processes or activities in Nature as are found everywhere therein. Hence God is regarded as the Principle of sensation, not less than of motion, life and intelligence. They are parts or aspects of the organisation postulated. See The Great Harmonia, Vol. I, pp. 48, 49.

[6] Above all, God is love, for Davis as well as the Hebrew and Christian Scriptures. It is necessary to reiterate this, for on account of it he regards the Divine Being as a principle rather than a person, though also affirming personality, as we have seen, and sometimes at the expense of occasional confusion in the minds of his readers. The truth is that he speaks very often as one carried away by the rush of a particular notion. A certain order can be extracted, however, from the confusion in the present case, for it is said also that love is a principle by which all things are filled with vitality, expanded and made beautiful. If love is God and God is love, then God is a principle, and the Divine Personality dissolves in the immensity of this conception.—Morning Lectures, p. 256. It dissolves—that is to say, in the mind of the thinker, but remains in the Divine Being, to Whom is otherwise attributed that consciousness which is impossible apart from personality.

[7] In considering the question whether the universe is boundless, it is stated in Penetralia, p. 76, that boundlessness is a comparative term applicable only to infinity, not to the organic or inorganic contents thereof. That which men term infinity is the. shoreless space wherein the universe revolves. The contents of such infinity are not fixed eternally, because this can be predicated only of principles. Infinity is something containing something. Boundless space is filled with matter and motion, and no space is unoccupied, while nothing is capable of annihilation in the realms of infinitude. The reason is

21

that nothing is brought into being without embodying Divine Ideas and subserving eternal uses—meaning that the purpose of God is within and behind all that is. It will be seen that Davis looks perilously near the affirmation of two infinities, and as there are other instances of this in his writings, we may note in the present case a certain qualification, when he speaks of space as that which men term infinity. The true way of escape is to realise that God is the one only infinite being and that space is the distance be tween cognisable or imaginable objects in that creation which moves and has conditioned being in Him. But this was not clear to Davis, and though he states categorically in the text that Nature is finite, he testifies differently in several later places.

[8] Nature is also—according to one of many definitions offered by Davis—the internal love-source of all being. According to its common signification, it is the fixed order of things, but according to the interior meaning it is the fountain-heart of the life of things. The physical universe, or objective sphere of matter, is not Nature. The phenomenal universe is a physical organisation, and the spiritual universe is a spiritual organisation. The two are expressions of the male and female principles, which are interior and invisible. Nature—the infinite heart—and God—the positive soul—like soul and brain married indissolubly, propagate both the physical and spiritual universe, which are related to "summer spheres." Objects in the physical worlds and human beings, including the higher grades of intelligence, are children born from that beautiful central marriage of the Father and Mother—the union of the Eternal Heart with the Eternal Head, the conjunction of Love and Wisdom. As we behold in our children our own tendencies, attributes, habits and external likeness, so in the physical universe we may discern the attributes, elements and principles of the Infinite Father and Mother.— Morning Lectures, pp. 215, 216. I commend this to the notice of my readers, because Davis speaks frequently as if he had forgotten the point. It may also be true to say that some of his views had ripened in his later works—of which here is one instance—and some had been outgrown, consciously or otherwise.

Chapter Two - God Revealed to Intellect [1]

The true nature of causation must be regarded as the fundamental problem of science, for we can never know anything but causes and effects. They are correlatives in language and in thought. To the question—What is causation?— four answers can be given: (1) the sceptical, (2) the material, (3) the pantheistic, (4) the rational or Christian. To assert that man is utterly ignorant of the true nature of causation is total scepticism. To predicate the doctrine of invariable sequence, as did Hume and Brown, presents the formula of materialism, of which idealism is another phase. Idealism and materialism are identical at the root. [2] Both take it for granted that all Nature is but a dream-show, where phenomena are interlinked only by the bond of antecedent and consequent. If we answer that emanation is the only causation, we are landed in pantheism, where all individual existence vanishes, all notion of right and wrong, truth and falsehood. The remaining answer is that which I deem rational, Christian and true—that causation resides in mind, that matter can never be a cause, and that every phenomenon is the effect of intellectual force exerted by pure volition. This view it is now proposed to demonstrate after the rigorous method of geometricians. It may be laid down as a general proposition that the perception of mathematical truth is essentially an attribute of intellect. It follows that to work mathematically evinces mind. Now, all motions of the material universe, in their wondrous variety and unity, are strictly mathematical. I will begin with my own organism. I survey my right hand: it has five fingers. I look at my left: this has five also. I turn to each foot and on each behold five toes. I think of my bodily senses: these are five again. Throughout all members of my body there runs also a wondrous duality— in my eyes, arms, hands, feet, ribs and the convolutions of my brain, where equal members balance each other. If the Cause which arranged the relations of my several organs understand mathematical harmonies, all is luminous. There is no chance to be calculated against their production, since He who comprehends the relations of number can involve them indefinitely and even infinitely, supposing that He is Himself infinite. But if the Cause which produces the combinations be not mathematical mind, what are the chances against a single combination of fives in a pair? And what are they in respect of the millions now living, as of all that have lived and passed away? The algebra of an archangel, with infinite space for his sheet and eternity for the period of solution, might be insufficient for the overwhelming computation. The question therefore recurs: could any Cause without intellect to perceive and reason to count produce these invariable equations?

We can, however, carry the demonstration that all motions in Nature are mathematical through the whole field of phenomena. We may take the invariable ratio between the hydrogen and oxygen in water, of oxygen and nitrogen in atmospheric air, of oxygen and carbon in carbonic acid. Here are a few fragments of the evidence drawn from chemistry. In botany we may take the first two classes of Linnaeus, arranged according to the number of stamens in each flower. We may analyse a flower of the tobacco plant. It is of the fifth class and has therefore five stamens; its corolla has five parts and its calyx five points. It is so with every tobacco flower on earth: so it has ever been and so will remain always. We may appeal to the phenomena of light, that wonderful agent which plays so important a part in the processes of creation. We may confine ourselves to the strict algebraic formula of its first law—that the intensity of light decreases as the square of its distance increases, and vice versa. So also the second law, that the angles of incidence and reflection are always equal. Is it possible that the Cause which thus geometrises is devoid of all knowledge of geometry? Were there no other proof of the existence of Deity, there is one other consideration in the domain of light which should settle the question for ever. It is this—that every rainbow is an exact mathematical equation of every other rainbow in the universe. [3] But there is finally the science of astronomy, which is another name for sublimity itself, and there are the three great laws of Kepler: (1) That all planetary orbits are regular ellipses, in the lower focus of which the sun is placed; (2) that the times occupied by any planet, in describing any given arcs of its orbit, are always as the areas of sectors, formed by straight lines drawn from the beginning and end of the arcs to the sun, as a centre; (3) that the squares of the periods of the planet's revolutions vary, as the cubes of their distance from the sun. We are taught in this manner that nothing but mathematical harmony obtains in all motions within our own sphere. We can conceive of nothing but mathematical harmony in any other region, and as nothing but mind can work mathematically, we behold, everywhere about us, the unequivocal footsteps of a God. It follows that every effect in the universe is produced by the immediate agency of Mind. Matter and Mind are two logical categories which encompass all thought and exhaust all Nature. But matter being passive and unable therefore to originate its own motions, without which no effect can occur in Nature, our search after causal force must be carried into the domain of mind. [4] That it is found there is confirmed by our inner consciousness, in the motions of its voluntary activity. Our argument is directed to the present, to things as they now are, to the sublime evolutions manifested before our eyes, and it is proved to us that God is. But it is directed also to the past, and it is demonstrated that He was then, while the eternal uniformity of Nature leads us to a not less certain inference—that He will continue for ever. There is indeed no past or future. The faith that asserts God proclaims all things present to the soul. We repose on the bosom of our Father with a confidence that nothing can shake. Friends may grow cold and change around us; enemies may combine for our destruction; but we have our immortal Friend, encircling our souls in arms of everlasting love. Then "will I trust Him, though He slay me." On the summit of this exalted faith, which is certainty, I rest secure. Nothing can move me more. The sensuous world has vanished from beneath my feet. I live already in the Spirit Land. The immortal dead are around me. I hear them holding high converse in translucent clouds. It is no night's vision, though brighter than all dreams. I am son and heir of universal empire. I have found God, Who owneth all. The vessel in which I have embarked may drift whithersoever it will on the immeasurable sea of being. Impenetrable clouds may hide the stars of heaven; but God guides the storm. Lightnings may rend my sails, but on whatsoever shore the wreck of my barque is strewn, He is sure to be there, with all my love and all my hopes around Him. There where He is it is an open gate of heaven, for there is the Everlasting Love, and love is heaven.

[1] See the volume entitled Arabula, or The Divine Guest.
[2] The statement as made is after the manner of an intellectual puzzle, and one is left wondering, here as in other places, about the sense in which certain words interpreted themselves to the mind of the author. If there is a contrast anywhere in the world of speculative thought it would be obviously between idealism and materialism, or between Berkeley and e.g. Condorcet, while the suggestion that materialism regards Nature as a dream-show would be scouted by every one who has suffered himself to rank in that class. The bond between antecedent and consequent has nothing to do with the interpretation of Nature as a visionary pageant, and as one who—by his own hypothesis—was a man of vision, Davis should have known, like Emerson, that Nature as it communicates with us through the channels of the senses is an omen and a sign, because that which passes through these media cannot be known at first hand but by derivation only. The senses are a mode of adjustment, a contrivance for communication,

and that which passes through them has—in respect of its external source—the relation of type to antitype.

It is therefore figurative, emblematic, and the world at large is for us therefore, and inevitably, a sacramental world—that is to say, phenomenal, having the noumenal behind it in the hiddenness.

[3] The infidel Diderot—who did not understand mathematics and hated it when he was confronted with them—fled the Russian Court because one who knew his weakness said to him in a large assembly at the palace: Monsieur Diderot, a+b multiplied by a+b =a2 + 2ab +b2, and it follows that there is a God. The argument is not convincing and would frighten no one but Diderot. It is comparable to the famous: God geometrises. All such reasoning is at most a re-statement of the truth that the modes of manifestation are interpreted to our minds as law, and hence in the search after God must be transferred in the last resource from all whatsoever that is without us to the mind itself.

[4] It is satisfactory to see that Davis recognises in his own manner the cogency of this view, and also that the true witness is our inner consciousness. He makes use of it, however, to establish the fact of causation in the world without rather than to discover its evidences by exploring the inward world. There are sound suggestions notwithstanding in several points that follow, for the last tribunal is within us and whatsoever may testify to us in the world without—whether that world be one of physics or of spirit—makes appeal to our invisible judge and so stands or falls. Moreover, because of that judge, it is true to say that we live already in the spirit world, for the judge is spirit. It is true also that we are sons and heirs of universal empire, for therein we move and have our being, and by the spirit of inward grace and truth we find God Who is within.

Chapter Three - The Central Sun [1]

The original, self-existent, omniscient, omnipresent, omnipotent productive power, the soul of all existences, is throned in a central sphere, the circumference of which is the boundless universe, and around this the sidereal systems revolve in silent sublimity and harmony. [2] This power is what mankind call Deity, whose attributes are love and wisdom, corresponding with the principles of male and female, positive and negative, creative and sustaining. The first goings forth or outbirths from the Great Celestial Centre are spiritual or vital suns, which give birth to natural suns, being those that are cognisable by the outward senses of man. These again become centres, or mothers, from which earths are born, each minutest particle of which is infused with the vivifying spirit of the parent formator. The essences of heat or fire—electricity, galvanism, magnetism—are natural manifestations of that productive energy which is the vitalising Cause of all existences. It pervades all substances and animates all forms.

The great spiritual and eternal truth which it is necessary for man to know and realise before he can know himself and be happy is that all manifest substances are expressions of an interior productive cause, which is the spiritual essence. The mineral kingdom is an expression of motion, the vegetable an expression of life, the animal an expression of sensation, while man is an expression of intelligence. The planets in our solar system are a perfect expression of the sun from which they sprang. The various combined bodies and planetary systems in the universe are a perfect expression of the Great Sun of the Univercoelum. The Great Sun is a perfect expression of the Spiritual Sun within it; and the Spiritual Sun is a perfect expression of the Divine Mind, Love, or Essence. [3] The Spiritual Sun is thus the centre and cause of all material things. It is a radiating sphere or atmosphere of the Great Eternal Cause, an aroma, a garment of the more interior essence—the Divine, Creative Soul. [4] The material universe is a perfect representation of the spiritual universe, in which nothing exists but what is everlasting and infinite. The whole material system is the body of the Creative Soul, and the Spiritual Essence has unfolded and manifested itself in a material form. This form is the order and wisdom of the Divine Mind.

Light and Love constituted the first development of the Spiritual Sun, and That was Light and Life inconceivable, which became illuminated space itself. [5] Yet space is not limited, neither could it transcend the expansive illuminations of the Great Spiritual Sun. When the universe was completed, order and form reigned omnipresent throughout the whole Univercoelum. Such was the grand and stupendous development of the Great Spiritual Sun—this having developed the material Sun, and this the expanded universe. So therefore—far and beyond the countless constellations—throbs the heart of life and animation. Its pulses flow to the circumference of all planetary existence. This Heart is God, the centre of all that is.

Previous to the present structure of the universe—when inconceivable realms of immensity were channels through which flowed an ocean of formless materials—the Infinite Spirit was manifested only as a principle of motion. Incessant, unrestrained, unchangeable, omnipotent action was the first manifestation of Deity. It must not be apprehended that God was otherwise then than organised Intelligence, but there were no media sufficiently unfolded for a higher operation of the creative principle, except motion only. Nor must it be inferred that God is subject to the identical laws of association, progression and development which proceed from Him and operate in all things. These laws are expressions of the Creator's habits, the constitutional tendencies of His Divine Nature. The God of the universe is not a being of development or growth. He is a fixed Fact; a fixed Principle, a fixed Heart of perfection and infinite Intelligence; but He displays the attributes of His being in successive and endless series and degrees, each unfolded in progressive and harmonious order.

The great vortex of Celestial Intelligence—nucleus of omnipotence, centre of love, flower of wisdom—is the irresistible magnet which draws upward the human soul. It is the sensorium of the Divine Mind, the central spring of all action and vitality, the fount of magnificence and perfection. He lives through all things, but more especially in the Great Spiritual Sphere [6] or Sun of the universe. God is the Soul of that universe, which is therefore the body of God and a perfect representative, or bold and clear expression of the interior Divine Mind, even as the human form is an express likeness of the quality of its interior soul. [7]

26

[1] See Discourse entitled The End of the World in Morning Lectures, 1865, p. 59 et seq.

[2] In another place, and referring presumably to Divine Prototypes, it is said that the Central Sun contains inconceivably vast universes. While the highest angelic intelligence can never hope to comprehend the infinite wealth of Divine Perfections, it is possible to understand analogically the constitution and operations of the Great Centre by the study of other centres nearer to our own situation. The fact of a physical sun—originating, actuating and governing all around it—is an illustration, within its own measures, of the Spiritual Central Sun.—Views of our Heavenly Home, p. 118.

[3] Once more therefore love is the centre of the universe, as it is said elsewhere to be the centre of man's own inner life, described as a substantial principle, an element as real as light or electricity—the seed-fountain of affection, volition and intellect.—The Great Harmonia, Vol. V, pp. 27, 28.

[4] This paragraph to the end of the sentence here indicated is taken from A Stellar Key to the Summer Land, pp. 118, 119.

[5] The manifestation of light and life of course postulates space, and so also does any process of becoming, but it will be understood that the seership of Davis was apart from any training in philosophy.

[6] In the first testimony of Davis the Central Sun is identified with the Great Positive Mind, and is termed the Fountain, the Great Illuminator, unchangeable and eternal, governing all existence. Whatsoever is subordinate to this Mind is negative in respect thereof, the manifest creation included.—See The Principles of Nature, p. 40. It is on the basis of this sentiment that Davis speaks frequently of Nature—understood, however, in a certain archetypal sense—as a Divine Mother, the Deity being Divine Father, thus postulating an ineffable state of spiritual marriage between them.

[7] It is said also that the Centre of the Universe is a Sun around which all spirits revolve, as planets about their primary.—Answers to Ever-Recurring Questions from the People, p. 93.

Book Two - The Principles of Nature

Chapter One - The Great Cosmos

[1]

In the beginning the Univercoelum was a boundless, undefinable ocean of liquid fire, understood as the original condition of matter. It was an undifferentiated eternity of motion, without beginning or end. Matter and force existed as one inseparable whole, an Eternal Sun, a vortex the power wherein was the Great Positive Mind, of which that vortex was the perfect and spontaneous substance. It was impossible for matter to exist without a principle of inherent production; it was impossible for this Internal Positive Power to subsist without matter as its vehicle; and in order that matter might pass from the formless to the state of forms there was action necessary on the part of the Great Positive Power. Matter was developed thereby until it became an external negative to the Positive Power within it; and thus positive and negative were established in matter. Thus was inaugurated the law of universal motion, and so also in the beginning God created the forms that are now manifested universally.

The great ocean of matter and movement constituted a mighty sun or vast centre of worlds, which emanated heat and light, producing a nebulous zone in the immensity of space. The laws of attraction, repulsion and condensation at work herein set up in their turn an incalculable number of local centres or suns, from which were created [2] planetary systems, each revolving about its particular controlling centre. The first ring of converging formations so commenced and was so at last completed. But incessant evolution from the great centre produced a second orbit or circle of corresponding suns and systems. A third, fourth and fifth zone appeared in succession, all consisting of solar and planetary worlds. There was in fine a sixth circle of formations, the constituents of which, not being as yet consolidated, are suns only, pursuing their various orbits in the form of blazing comets.

The great centre from which all these systems of systems emanated remains an inexhaustible fountain, the everlasting parent of all things. It is still an ocean of undulated and indefinable fire, the holy emblem of perfection. It displays, throughout the immensity of space, correspondences of its inherent nature and breathes forth worlds unnumbered with an everlasting spontaneousness, developing its attributes in successive degrees and orders throughout the vast Univercoelum and the boundless duration of eternity. It should be understood also that the nebulous zone—formed in time unimaginable by incessant emanation of light and heat from the Great Sun—not only approximates to that which produced it originally but expands through infinite space far beyond the sixth circle of suns. The suns of the first circle, being fire inconceivable, were too light and undifferentiated to consolidate like other centres; but the light thrown forth by them was capable of becoming less rare than their own composition, and thus a hardened or consolidated combination was produced in each of their planets, though their interior constitution is still fiery. The suns of the second circle are yet more rare than the first but have less fire and greater heat, and their planets condensed gradually into earthy compositions, though unlike anything that we understand as terrestrial in nature. The suns and planets of the second circle are immeasurably vaster than those appertaining to the fifth, to which our own system belongs, while those of the first circle are of still more inconceivable dimensions. The suns of the third circle have less heat and more light than the former. While they are nearer to a state of condensation, they are not actually condensed. The material formation of their planets is still so refined that no substance known on earth bears any resemblance thereto. The suns of the fourth circle have still less heat and light than those of the former, while their planetary worlds are less numerous and less also in magnitude, though they cannot be calculated or comprehended. They are also of denser constitution than any so far described, and some of their formations begin to resemble the appearance of our own globe. The fifth circle of suns has relatively less heat and light. They have brought into existence an immense number of planets and satellites, and our own solar system may stand as a general representative of all included herein. As regards the sixth circle, it contains no fire, less light and more electricity than all others. The orbits of its various suns embrace space incalculable.

As the suns of the first circle came forth from the Great Sun, so were the succeeding circles evolved one from another in perfect harmony. It follows that there is one only general evolution, one infinite production from one eternal origin. The vast deep of materials—in ceaseless motion and activity—out of which all systems were developed, bears testimony to future corresponding emanations from the same inexhaustible fountain. That which has been so far produced from this living vortex is comparable in its totality to a single atom in comparison with that which is yet to be. The Great Sun of all suns emanated heat, light and electricity, evolved one from another, as three principles that are mediums and connecting links of universal motion and activity. The fountain from which they sprang into existence was an emanation from the interior—and from qualities existing therein. The great body was an atmosphere surrounding the centre or sun within. The ever-controlling influence and active energies of the Divine Positive Mind brought all effects into being, as parts of one vast whole. It will continue to create new worlds until every particle that composes the cosmic world has become the very essence of organic life; until this has attained in man the perfection of spiritual essence; and until the influence of man upon all that is below humanity has brought all into that state which is celestial. Then will the Grand Mind be the positive to that great negative formed by the perfection of all things else in being; and then Deity and Spirit will subsist only. [3] Thereafter, between these two, will be brought forth new worlds, in the epoch of another beginning.

It becomes evident in this manner that the internal and invisible is the one reality and that this is eternal truth, essential nature of Eternal Mind, the attributes of which, expressed in the cosmos and its harmony, are wisdom, goodness, justice, equity and mercy. Within and without, principle and form of being, Infinite Mind and its vesture, which is the cosmic world—these are the two modes of universal being. As the outer must be and is an emanation from the inner or centre, so that which encompasses the centre is not opposed thereto. Disorder and confusion may seem to reign everywhere, but in reality there are perfect harmony, union and reciprocity. There is correspondence everywhere, in virtue of an immutable law, affording to the human mind an indestructible basis on which to rest a correct understanding of the nature of all effects and from which to behold the unspeakable grandeur of the end—of that end where the cosmic world, by virtue of inherent powers, shall be so refined and perfected as to be a counterpart of the Great Power which brought all things into being.

As parts of the great whole, humanity should be actuated by those perfect principles shown forth in the law of the universe, conforming to which it would be truly in correspondence therewith. All motion would be such as to produce good results; all parts would work together; and harmony would reign in all. The whole, thus existing, would receive the tranquillising influence of Divine Law, the essence of which is the perfection of goodness and truth. Opposites would be henceforth unknown, for real knowledge would cast out their false appearance and destructive influence for ever. The truth of all truths, the reality of all realities, the foundations of happiness and peace would be medicine for all souls. The human race would be itself as a great sun, like the Central Sun of the cosmos, the vesture of its Eternal Parent and a reflection of His Divine attributes. Then would all be filled with that spontaneous reciprocity which would banish from the face of the earth the strife of exclusive interests, with every quality and principle which responds to the name of antagonism. By their expulsion from within our own selves there would manifest the truth of that which has been affirmed already, that true opposites do not exist in Nature, while their very appearances would be swallowed up in the flood of light and knowledge.

There is one thing more that should be understood in respect of the cosmos, and it is this—that the term boundless is not applicable to the universe of organised matter, [4] when this is taken by itself, but only to the unorganised universe, the ocean of perpetually forming material, which is indeed infinite. The Divine Sensorium is the centre of the organised cosmos.

[1] See The Principles of Nature, Part II, pp. 121-157, extracted as to their essence and harmonised.
[2] As occasionally in this section, so elsewhere in the same work, Davis appears to speak vaguely of the manifested universe as created by God. The use of this expression recurs, and that indeed somewhat obtrusively, throughout The Principles of Nature, nor is it absent from some of the later works. This notwithstanding, we see that the boundless "ocean of liquid fire," or "original condition of matter" is described also as "an eternity of motion," and redundantly as "without beginning or end." Now, the proper sense of the word "create" in connection with the making of worlds is "to bring into being out

of nothing "—as any dictionary will tell us—and this does not agree with a notion of the eternity of matter, whether in a solid or an incandescent form. Elsewhere Davis unfolds the view that there was no creation at all but formation only, because the Harmonial Philosophy affirms the eternity of matter. He must therefore have used the word creation in a very loose sense from the beginning, even when he seems to use it clearly and categorically according to its normal significance. His case against creation in his later work is that it implies the certainty of an end; but it is clear from the present section that he looked in the far future to a term of material manifestation in respect of its present mode, or a kind of substituted end. As regards formation, its ever-changing processes are the organised phenomena of this external world.—Op, cit., pp. 52, 53.

[3] This statement contains in a brief summary the root-matter of what Davis calls his Divine Revelations of Nature; and though here and there in his writings we come across unacknowledged, and perhaps unrealised changes—as his psychic reflections developed through the later years—he never moved from this ground. It is of considerable interest and importance for reasons of which he could personally have known nothing, and among others for its independent analogies with high metaphysical speculations of the later Hermetic School, more especially that of L. C. de Saint-Martin, at the end of the eighteenth century. For the French mystic a great vocation was imposed on humanity from the beginning—to lead all creation back into that Divine Order and Union which had been wrecked by the fall of Lucifer, regarded as prince of this world. For Davis, who recognises no hierarchies save that of immortal humanity and for whom the fall of man is a dream, the cosmos came into being for no other purpose than to develop and perfect individualised self-conscious spirits (A Stellar Key to the Summer Land, p. 195). As said in the text above, it is designed to attain in him and having thus served its purpose it will be dissolved in a sense. That is to say, its essence will have been incorporated in the grand body general of humanity, and then there will be God the Spirit only, plus the Universal Soul of all intelligent created beings integrated in an ineffable union. There is no doubt that this is a sublime dream, having analogies with Indian theosophies, Zoharic Kabalism and even Christian Mysticism, for it re-expresses on a cosmic scale that which the latter conceives as a possible and actual attainment in sanctity for the individual souls of men.

[4] See Answers to Ever-Recurring Questions from the People, p. 16.

Chapter Two - The Solar System

[1]

The sun or centre to which our solar system belongs is a remote orb of another system existing prior to its formation. The planets of our solar system may be considered as satellites belonging to a planet, which planet belongs itself to a sun. The materials constituting our sun were thrown off from other bodies during revolutions round their common centre, owing to centrifugal force; and by the gravitation of such materials the sun assumed its form. It has the same dual motion as all celestial spheres—one upon its axis and the other in its orbit round the centre to which it belongs. Its internal portion is a mass of liquid fire, evolving heat, light and electricity, extending—like an atmosphere—to the orbit of the last planet comprised in the system. [2] This last is the ninth in number and the first which came into being, moving in the same plane as the parent sun. The eighth was evolved next and was situated within the orbit of the former, in harmony with established principles of gravitation and of orbicular and rotary motion. The eighth and ninth planets are not yet recognised as bodies belonging to the solar system, but it can be affirmed in respect of the eighth that its density is four- fifths that of water and that its atmosphere is exceedingly rare, containing little oxygen and composed mostly of fluorine and hydrogen. No organic constitution corresponding to anything on earth could exist there. The human eye would be useless, for light is there of such a nature as to render the planet's darkness, at its darkest period, several hundred degrees lighter than the light which is received on earth from the sun. Like Uranus, it has six satellites, the farthest from the primary being the original extension of this, while the nearest is an accumulation of denser atoms from the planet. The planet itself is denser than any of its satellites, and their respective distances therefrom, with their diameters and periods of revolution, are determined by their respective constituents and the relations which they bear to each other.

The next planet in the order of evolution was Uranus. During its first stages it was an accumulation of igneous particles, the rarity of which unfitted them for any other sphere of association. By virtue of inherent motion, its six satellites were developed successively. The harmony and magnificence displayed by this planet and its attendants are unsurpassed by any other body as yet discovered. Its atmosphere has a light reddish appearance, with a density in proportion to that of the planet itself, which is a little greater than the density of water. No life exists thereon, nor will life be possible until further condensation and development occur. Its atmosphere is igneous and carbonaceous, having one three hundred and sixtieth part of carbon to one of oxygen. The carbon is, however, unlike any element or gas known on earth. The satellites apparently observe a different direction in their orbicular movements from that of any other body or its appendages. The planet is also less in magnitude relatively than others, according to the law of progression.

The planet next developed was the sixth, named Saturn. Its original composition was extremely igneous, but a gradual accumulation of particles emanating from the sun organised it ultimately into denser matter than that of Uranus. The igneous composition being very active, the planet's emanations produced the nebulous zones or belts which now surround the primary. These zones, like the planet itself, existed for many ages in the form of a fiery atmosphere, at a distance from the primary in correspondence with the law of association and centrifugal force. The centre of Saturn is still an igneous, unstratified substance, the surface having become condensed chemically by the escape of internal heat and by the production of organising and vivifying gases. Such also are its rings, which show many seemingly uneven portions, appearances produced by the reflection of its satellites upon various parts of these belts during their revolutions and by frequent eclipses, as well as by their own situation, which is unfavourable at times to proper observation. [3] The rings will be resolved ultimately into one sphere, which will produce another planet. The geography of Saturn is very beautiful. It is divided into two-thirds water and one-third earth, and, being free from volcanic disturbances, it presents an even surface. There are few prominences, and these are near the poles. The equator has only certain promontories, connected with still higher land, the dividing chasm of which forms the bed of a great body of water. Organic beings inhabited this planet for many thousands of years before our earth came into being, for which reason they have attained a higher development. There are four general classes of vegetable natures: (1) gigantic tree forms, produced near the poles, where light and heat are at a minimum; (2) trees similar to the Upas, but in appearance, not quality, for they bear delicious fruit of elongated shape, white internally and encompassed with a thick coating; (3) more perfect growths, rising a few feet only above the surface and yielding a kind of pulse-fruit which is exceedingly pleasant; (4) the most useful vegetable upon the surface of Saturn, of no great height but exceeding spontaneity, with long and slender roots and trunk, the fruit being fitted for the uses of the animal economy. It is produced at the equator twice in one of the planet's years. Of various intermediate formations it would be impossible to speak. There are five general classes of animal existence. The first is well organised, having fine vascular and muscular tissues. It is very large and strong, with joints in the hind legs only. The fore legs, composed of strong muscular and osseous substances, are elastic and pliable at need but immovable also at will. Being of great power, this animal genus is most useful to its masters. The eyes are small; the ears short and narrow; the head is wide and high; the mouth and proboscis are closely connected, the latter serving not only as a nasal organ but for drinking and transferring to the mouth the hard-shelled fruit, produced by the fourth vegetable form already mentioned. The disposition of the genus is firm and yet submissive. It constructs large caves to dwell in during the long night experienced at the pole, and during the correspondingly long day it roams about the seashore or seeks those places where the fruit on which it subsists grows in greatest abundance. The second class is not so graceful but is a degree more perfect. It associates with the former but is amphibious. Owing to a highly developed muscular and vascular system, it is irritable and excitable in disposition. It is saurian in form, but not in other respects. The third class is still finer in organisation, with great muscular power and celerity. It has four legs, the two hinder having feet resembling the human, while the foremost recall the limbs of the seal. In length and height it resembles the iguanodon. Though master naturally over all that ranks below it and repulsive in appearance, it is not antagonistic or destructive. The flesh is very tender in comparison with that of the former class, but the osseous skin—like a complex network of scales—would be impenetrable by any instrument known on earth. The fourth class is broadly typical of the natural man. [4] Two of its four limbs serve as organs of locomotion and the others answer to arms. It is more highly vertebrated, and has greater elasticity of muscles than those below it. The body is rather wide and not perfectly rounded, but the sacral bone and hips—being much distended—give great muscular power. Owing to the high shoulders and neck of corresponding length, there is conspicuous elasticity in the movements of the trunk. The mental organisation corresponds nearly to that of the human being, but the exterior understanding and knowledge surpass those of our race on earth. The head is round and long, indicating a wider scope of mental comprehension. The general disposition is one of strong attachments and social desires. To great concentration is added keen sense of natural right and justice. But the head is not very high in proportion to size, and there is consequently an absence of veneration for things unseen, though it obtains for those attested by the senses. The memory is retentive; intellectual faculties are strong; mechanical ingenuity gives rule over lower beings; while the sense of humour and a passion for pleasurable emotions render communications more subtle than those of our own race. While this class is a perfect example of animal intellectual being, the fifth and ultimate race of Saturn is alone truly man. The limbs are straight and round; joints and appendages display perfect adaptation; and the symmetry of body is unequalled by any other creature on that planet. [5] The sternum is oval and full, joining the costals with a kind of bracework, which gives full space and free action to the visceral system. The lungs—divided into two hemispheres—are of an adipose, elastic, active substance. The heart also has two divisions and movements corresponding with those of the lungs. The ganglionic system is spread throughout the body, giving almost imperceptible motions to the motor nerves thereof. Not being composed of thick and heavy substance, the cranium imparts great activity to the senses in respect of external objects. The cerebrum is large and full, while the cerebellum and its divisions are still larger.

The restiform, medulla oblangata and medulla spinalis are composed of such sensitive substances that a perfect system of motion and sensation results. The brain is exceedingly active, sending a refined ether of sensation throughout the nervous system. The brain is composed of innumerable cortical glands, each of which attracts and repels, performing systolic and diastolic motions. These glands are reservoirs from which proceed the fibres and nerves of sensation, conceived and produced thereby. Thus the nerves of sensation are connected with the corcula of the brain, as the veins and arteries are connected with the ventricles of the heart. The contraction and expansion of these cortical glands produce the involuntary motions of the system, while—by the same forces—the heart presses the blood throughout the body. The motions of lungs and heart are very powerful; the motion of the brain corresponds; and that of the whole illustrates the gigantic strength of all. The form is of singular beauty and the surface so fine that it is almost transparent. The external movements are of greater precision and governed by more decided judgment than our own. Physically and mentally, the organisation is most perfect, while the intellect is expansive and powerful, so that judgment controls entirely and weakness or disease is unknown. The prominent mental qualities are moral and intellectual; strong social attachments are governed by intellect; and great force of character is under the guidance of reason. The will is firm, though generally submissive; veneration is deep for that which judgment pronounces to be true. Causality is not developed so fully as comparison or analogical power. Perception is extremely vivid and penetrating. Reasoning is from the internal, truth being received through highly sanctioned convictions of interior principles. With telescopic mind these beings familiarise themselves with the earths between them and the sun and with their inhabitants. Their minds being free from imperfection, from all that is opposed to righteousness, they associate with that which is pure and good. The perfection of their internal principle exceeds that of other human beings in our solar system. They associate with the knowledge of the Second Sphere, and receive no impressions but those which flow from internal realities. They inhabit buildings of ingenious, beautiful and peculiar structure. They form associations according to internal desire, and—not being governed by the inclinations of natural man— they take mates according to mutual inward approbation and are thus united in bonds of spiritual happiness and peace. Their minds are sufficiently expansive to comprehend at a glance the whole surface of their planet and the movements of the entire nation, which is united as one brotherhood. Such are the inhabitants of Saturn—an illustration of purity and goodness manifested as the result of perfected knowledge and highly unfolded powers.

The next planet evolved from the sun was Jupiter, [6] which—together with its satellites—was denser than former developments, for the materials composing the sun had themselves condensed with the increase of the planets thrown off from the parent mass. The vegetable productions of Jupiter are more extensive than those of Saturn, and five classifications are possible: (1) An exceedingly large and bulky fruit-bearing tree, which is edible by the lower animals only; (2) trees which exude juice, flowing freely from cup-shaped growths, and very nourishing and invigorating; (3) a cereal having the character of wheat; (4) a class with variegated foliage, the extracts from which enter into the forms of the first animals; (5) a species of zoophyte, partaking of vegetable and animal life. Jupiter contains altogether about 300,000 species of plants. The animal developments are a degree less perfect than those of Saturn, and though there are a great many species they are not so generally disseminated as those of the vegetable kingdom. They admit of four general classifications: (1) Those which are rodent and ruminating, corresponding to Class I of Saturn, but dissimilar in disposition and habits. (2) A class which is nearly digitigrade and similar to the seal, being also amphibious. Its disposition is secretive, retiring and apparently submissive, but it is tyrannical over animals within its power. (3) A class answering in size to the natural man, and of incredible strength. It is at once ingenious and retiring, active when occasion requires, and it constitutes a connecting link between animal and human organisation. It is combative and secretive, has great firmness and self-will, possesses quick intuitive perceptions and a retentive memory, while its affections are as pure as the form would indicate. It associates with all things agreeable to its inclination, the latter being qualified by its sense of refinement. It is governed by natural instincts and reasons from things seen. (4) The human inhabitants of Jupiter are in closer relation to our conception of a perfect being than those of Saturn. Size, symmetry and beauty of form exceed those of earth, and they are well sustained by inward and physical forces, while mental organisation corresponds to material development. General contour is characterised by smoothness and evenness. The lower extremities are rather shorter than the upper, and walking is in an inclined position, using both hands and arms. [7] The main characteristics are mechanical and intellectual, accompanied by strong affections and interior love for each other. The intelligence of these beings greatly excels those of earth, and they comprehend the laws and relations of their nature by one concentrated thought. They discern the uses of all things and their original adaptations. They reason perfectly by induction and from correspondences. Affections are breathed forth from their interiors, and the external expression is emblematic of love and purity. It is impossible for them to think one thing and speak another, to have more self-love than universal affection, or to conceive impure and unrighteous thoughts. Being thus free from all imperfections of this and other earths, they are open to the reception of light and truth, which correspond to the fire of spiritual purification. Their associations one with another are according to inward affinity, and they form a united, harmonious, spiritual brotherhood, regarding the internal of all things as the only reality in the universe. They observe great care in producing their offspring and in preserving their health. Disease is not known, and freedom from this imperfection enables them to generate rapidly. They are composed of finer elements than the man of earth and remain in their physical forms for a short period only—an average of thirty years. They do not die, but rather sink into repose by an expansion of their interiors, which seek still more agreeable spheres. In knowledge and refinement they occupy an intermediate position between the First and Second Spheres. They inhabit well-constructed edifices corresponding to a tent rather than a house on earth, and impervious alike to cold, water and light. As regards solar light, they receive only one twenty-fifth of that which the earth enjoys, but it strikes vertically on the equator, where their habitations are located. Jupiter abounds in all that enlists the affections of man, as objects of his deepest yearning, while aspiring to higher states of purity and peace.

Approaching nearer to the sun, four spheroidal bodies exist between Jupiter and Mars. [8] They have been discovered within the present century and have been named, Ceres, Pallas, Juno and Vesta. The fact that their orbits are exceedingly elliptic and constantly intersecting the planes of each other has suggested the hypothesis that they are formed from a comet which appeared in 1770. This is incorrect, and their true origin follows. When the atmospheric emanation of the sun terminated in that region now occupied by the orbit of Pallas the association of particles produced an igneous mass, according to principles previously established. Had this aggregation condensed properly, like other planets, there would have been produced a single sphere of lesser magnitude than Jupiter, though greater than that of Mars. It would have corresponded to the combined dimensions of the present four bodies. But there was not a perfect association of interior materials, and great convulsions were going on constantly throughout its composition. The interior heat was excessive, and evaporation could not take place with sufficient rapidity to relieve the expanding elements. The elements, moreover, could not associate chemically, nor could unity exist in the partly stratified exterior. Being thus internally divided and not perfectly under the influence of attraction and repulsion, an expansion of interior constituents rent the whole asunder, producing the present four asteroids. Under the direct influence of Jupiter and Mars—which had then nearly assumed their actual forms—uniformity of motion was imposed upon them, which motion obtained in the primary body. One being denser than another and the whole being denser than Jupiter prevented any nearer approach toward that planet. Movements and revolutions were, however, somewhat modified by foreign causes. The orbit of Pallas inclines most to the ecliptic, this body sustaining the highest position, with poles much flattened and equator bulged. Such is the origin of these asteroids, which—combined—make one planet, as may and will be confirmed by astronomical research. They have not developed anything beyond the vegetable kingdom, though the era is now approaching which will call a class of zoophytes into existence.

Being beyond the orbit of our own earth, the planet Mars is of superior quality and constitution. [9] It abounds with vegetable productions, more numerous than those of Jupiter but less perfect, though again superior to ours. Animal formations are less extensive, but ascending from the lowest to man in successive modifications of form corresponding to interior principles. As regards man, he is in a much more exalted state than the humanity of this planet, both physically and mentally, without attaining the perfection and refinement which characterise the inhabitants of spheres already enumerated. Among vegetable products there may be noted: (1) A tree having a bulky, spiral trunk, long branches and broad leaves, in which green is combined with a bluish and reddish colour. The blossoms are very beautiful, and the round fruit recalls the cocoanut. It is the most useful tree upon the planet, and is used as a kind of bread, which is invigorating to the system. The bark is adapted for the manufacture of garments and in the building of habitations. (2) A vegetable growth, attaining no great height, and producing beautiful fine fibres, the staple material for apparel. The inhabitants are divided into three great associated families or nations, governed by common principles, the result of superior knowledge and keen sense of justice. [10] There is a peculiar prominence of the top of the head, indicative of high veneration. Cerebrum and cerebellum correspond in form and size, the latter extending upward at the junction of the two brains, rendering them highly susceptible of interior and true affection. Their form nearly approaches that of man on earth, but is of more perfect symmetry. Their movements exhibit a peculiar dignity and air of exaltation—reflections of an inward reality. The upper part of the face has a peculiar yellowish cast, with radiations from forehead and eyes, as also from the blush of the cheeks. The lower part is of different colour, being rather dark, though suffused by the radiations mentioned. There is no beard, but the dark tinge also encompasses neck and ears, extending backwards and joining with the hair on the neck. The top of the head is free from any such appearances. The structure is not tall, and as to physical appearance that which is beauty to them would be to us highly repellent, the standard in both cases resulting from habitual modes of thought rather than from knowledge of that which is intrinsically perfect. The only standard of beauty on any earth in the universe is that which obtains the general approbation of society. The attitude of these humanities is modest, and the female form is characterised by great delicacy, symmetry and straightness, accompanied by affability and courtesy. The settlements and habitations of the race are situated near the equator and a high degree of harmony obtains throughout; but as they have digressed a little from natural law there is some imperfection among them. Neither moral nor physical disease are, however, known. There are no arbitrary laws and hence none of the inequalities which result therefrom. Possessing a high moral principle, they are obedient to that which it dictates, such obedience being insured by union of interests and by affections and desires being centred in the workings of good and righteousness. Their minds are constantly open to the reception of all high things—light, life and purity. The science of correspondences gives them knowledge of internal truths. The light which they receive from the sun testifies to them concerning the light of celestial love. From the materials and form of their planet they infer a principle of motion; from the vegetable they infer motion and life; from animal existences they infer sensation; while from the organisation of man they conceive motion, life, sensation, in the union of these with intelligence. From such data they endeavour to understand their spiritual principle, which, however, is incapable of self-comprehension and is obscure to them as to us. Their knowledge, being pure and truthful, begets affection; their aspirations are high and pure; and our loftiest conceptions cannot transcend the peace that dwells among them. Sentiments arising in their minds become impressed instantly upon their countenances. Their soft blue eyes are their most powerful agents in conversation, eye speaking to eye. In their social relations they display the deepest attachment. Thus do peace, truth and love abound with them universally; light, life and knowledge serve as an index of higher and more perfect spheres. Such is the condition of dwellers on the fourth planet.

The earth stands next in order, but the story of its creation and progression is held over until the description of other parts of the solar system has been completed.

In approaching the sun Venus is the next planet evolved from the central mass. Its physical appearance is less beautiful than that of other spheres which have been treated heretofore. [11] There are very high mountains, and a great portion of the sphere is covered with water. The atmosphere is nearly like that which encompasses earth, though less rarefied, and it receives much more light from the sun than any planet receding therefrom. The trees are generally rather low, thick and extensively branched. There is much variegated foliage, and many useful plants exist on the surface. The animals are not so highly developed as those of remoter spheres. They are, however, very numerous, some strong and ferocious, corresponding to the lion, though of different form and aspect. The human inhabitants are like those of earth, with breasts wide and full, great activity and strength of the viscera and excellent general constitution. Mental dispositions are dissimilar. One race has a mild and gentle countenance, the index of inward purity; their conjugal affections are good; they reason principally from externals and are enlightened therein, but they have no high conceptions of things in the universe. Male and female are usually associated purely; the general disposition is that of affection one for another; but there are manifest imperfections in customs and national privileges. Mental organisation, as a whole, corresponds to that of earth. But there is another race—very tall, stout and physically energetic—which is inferior to our own. Those who constitute it are of savage and ferocious disposition, having no conception of right or the beauty of goodness and refinement, and receiving no spontaneous promptings from spiritual principles in man. They form themselves into armies, go forth to plunder the stores of other nations, and when they return from these barbarous expeditions they rejoice in devouring the booty, which includes living children. Thus there are two distinct nations inhabiting the surface of Venus, but the beauty and magnificence of other planets are not by them imagined. The institutions and forms of government which prevail among the superior race far exceed those of earth, because they are in closer agreement with the laws of their nature and the universe. But though they are surrounded with many beauties and clean associations they are not in a happy condition, having little knowledge of higher spheres, for the materials of Venus are less perfect than those of the further planets and so also must be the composition and situation of all its ultimates.

The atmosphere surrounding Mercury is exceedingly luminous, though the light and heat derived from the sun are not so excessive as might be supposed, for the materials of this planet have not much affinity either for light or heat. It rejects therefore that which would be otherwise received and retains what is suitable to sustain life and action among the forms upon its surface. Some portions of the planet are very uneven, while others are smooth and beautiful. The vegetable productions are neither so refined nor so numerous as those of other spheres. There are only three general classes of plants, of which the highest are but a few inches. All are full and gross, and there are neither flowers nor trees. Two barren deserts cover almost one-third of the planet, while excessive subterranean heat produces commotion of water near the desert borders. A corresponding excitement of atmospheric elements causes great winds in the same vicinity, driving hot sand and water before them, and causing much destruction of life. The animals are imperfectly formed; species are few, and they would be repulsive if seen by us. They are combatant and prey upon each other. Their chief classes are amphibious and digitigrade. The human inhabitants are also not numerous, compared with those of other spheres, and are imperfect in physical organisation. [12] They manifest the same incessant activity as the other animals. Their mental constitution is peculiar, combining strong attachments, concentration and memory. Each desires to be thought more enlightened than any other being in existence, and all presume upon their memory to sustain pretensions in respect of superior intelligence. They do not investigate causes but rather the uses of things. Moreover, they do not depend upon their sensualities or inclinations as a source of knowledge, but seek the internal. A person endeavouring to display elegance and beauty in his speech would be disregarded altogether, since they dislike having their ears addressed instead of their understanding. Hence the shades of meaning that are thrown upon any subject by skill of this kind are rejected, and there is retained only the substance of conversation. They regard words and technicalities as too often mere false sheaths concealing a corrupt interior. They admire truth and the goods of truth, excelling to this extent the dwellers of earth and Venus; but—like the situation of their planet—they are imperfect in all other respects. They have no well-organised communities, being governed by an ignorant arbitration which prevails among them. It should be remembered, however, that Venus has not been peopled by human beings for more than about eight thousand years, in place of the innumerable ages of other habitable spheres. War and persecution prevail to an extreme extent, malice and all things belonging to ignorance and folly. There are all characters of ferocious animals. The implements of destruction are curiously hewn stones, thrown from a sling and causing horrible incisions. At the present time a violent battle is about to be waged. The countenance of this people is full and dark, the body is covered with a kind of hair, and the whole appearance is repellent, recalling the orang-outang. As now existing, there are displayed all results arising from degraded situation and depressed intellect. Conditions are more unfavourable than those of dwellers on any other planet; and yet they are instruments for the accomplishment of more perfect ends, rudimentary materials ascending to higher stages gradually. Only as the highest elements are separated from the lowest do they rise to assume newer and more perfect forms. Thus human dwellers in Venus and Mercury are in some particulars superior to those of the earth, but—speaking generally—they are much more gross and imperfect.

Concerning that luminous centre of our solar system from which all the planets and their satellites have been formed, it is yet incessantly giving off rarefied particles and exerting an orderly influence upon all under its rule. [13] It cannot decrease in magnitude, for it has attained the degree of density belonging to a more interior centre. It is counterbalanced by the magnitude of its whole planetary system, has formed all that its substance can well produce, and the whole is conjoined harmoniously, having motions in accordance with the established law of gravitation, and order and uniformity manifested from first to last. An ascending degree of refinement is evident throughout, from the first evolved body even to the last. Mercury, the last in formation, is composed of denser materials than any other planet, whence it takes the lowest point and observes the greatest velocity of motion. As we recede therefrom a superior refinement is observed in each planet successively and a corresponding modification in motions and relations to each other. The law of progression is established also, though in comparison with Jupiter and Saturn retrogression may seem to be indicated by the less perfect planets which were formed subsequently. But it must be remembered that the lowest contains the highest undeveloped, while the highest pervades the lowest. The composition of Mercury includes in an undeveloped state all that Saturn manifests, and therefore typifies a higher formation. Nothing is too low in the universe to represent something above it, nor is anything so advanced that it is not the lowest degree of that which is still more perfect. It follows that there is unceasing progression as there is transformation everywhere. The sun itself is a never failing symbol of all material formations, the vortex, the centre, containing all that has been since brought into existence, as connected with our planetary system. The materials therein became impregnated and active by virtue of inherent forces, resulting in the teeming productions now manifested. It is therefore a body corresponding to the Sun of the Universe, while all its offspring are in analogy with those greater planets which that Sun brought into being. The satellites on their part correspond to those planets which the greater planets—or rather suns—produced. Thus our solar system typifies that of the Univercoelum.

The vegetable formations of each planet indicate the character of those primary particles which produced them. They represent also higher stages of formation. We have seen how this movement and life lead us on to conceive sensation, which itself leads us on to instinct, that is, to the animal kingdom, between which and man an unbroken connection exists. Man stands as the ultimate of all, combining motion, life, sensation and intelligence. The humanity of Mercury is indicative of higher forms existing otherwise, and an unbroken chain connects the dwellers in the lowest planet with those comparatively spiritual beings whose place is in the highest. So also vegetable forms give true conceptions of uses leading to more perfect ends. Plants receive nourishment from the mineral kingdom as well as the atmosphere. The animal kingdom receives nourishment from the vegetable. So is one necessary to the other. But without general principles, putting forth general uses, none of these forms would have existed. Cause and effect are in fine inseparable, and this truth establishes a link between every particle in the universe, while it offers to our thought the highest representation of the original design conceived by the Great Positive Mind.

So in our solar system [14] are all things in the universe represented; and as it is impossible for the mind to form an adequate conception of anything beyond the harmonious system to which we belong, here is the appropriate field for present investigation. Thought is unlimited, but thought is not knowledge. Within our comprehension, however, lies the great law of correspondence, the knowledge of which leads to peace and happiness.

[1] See The Principles of Nature, p. 159 et seq., collated and compared.
[2] The origin of planets from their parent sun is described elsewhere as follows: Within the circumference of the sun elementary particles of matter gather about a nucleus, which continues to increase in dimensions and variety of parts, gradually advancing in its endless revolutions toward the outer surface of this fiery orb, till it approaches the extreme verge. It has increased in density and consequent specific gravity, till at length it breaks loose from its parent and flies off at a tangent into illimitable space. It has at first the eccentric movement of a comet, which is—in fact—a newborn earth or planet. The extreme fluidity and rarefaction of its particles, their feeble cohesive attraction, together with the irregular orbital and axillary movements, give the new body a curious elongated form. It happens sometimes that the caudal extremity is so long drawn out and consequently so remote from its centre of gravity that a part or parts may become detached. These are henceforward satellites or moons, which continue to revolve around and within the orbit of the new earth. In the lapse of ages, the attractive and repulsive, or centripetal and centrifugal forces become equalised; the outer surfaces have locked up a large portion of the free caloric within the embrace of their own substance and have thus condensed and hardened; a globular form has succeeded the oblate sphere and a regular orbit is defined and maintained. Oxygen and nitrogen have

united in proper proportions to produce an atmosphere; oxygen and hydrogen have combined to constitute water; numerous other combinations have brought solid and permanent forms out of the amorphous mass of elementary materials. In all this beautiful, harmonious and ever-progressive development, oxygen has played a conspicuous part as a positive, energising, vitalising principle. It appears to have grasped and held fast in its embrace the very germs of vitality. Phosphorus is another form of its tangible development, not yet understood by chemists or physiologists. As no living plant or animal can exist in its absence, it is always found in the seeds and germinal principles, in the substance of bone, brain and nerves, and in yet other parts of organised and animated natures.—See Morning Lectures, pp. 60-63. It is an interesting fact that the enumeration of nine planets by Davis anteceded the discovery of Neptune.

[3] Compare Camille Flammarion: Les Monies Imaginaires et les Mondes Reels, 1865. There is a very curious account of the possible state of astronomy on the planet Saturn, supposing that it is inhabited by intelligent observers. The effect is heightened by a hypothetical picture of the planet at midnight in the middle summer, 20th degree of latitude. The rings and moons are shining over a rocky promontory jutting out into the sea. An unversed reader will be astonished at the literature concerning the possible habitation of planets, from the days of Athanasius Kircher and his Iter Ecstaticum. According to this learned Jesuit of the seventeenth century, Saturn is a mournful domain; its angels have a scythe in the left hand, poisons in the right, and with these they deal vengeance upon the unjust and oppressors of earth.

[4] It is said in another revelation—which, at least substantially, applies also to Jupiter—that the people of Saturn, owing to their exceeding refinement, purity and inwardness, are in constant fellowship with those who have passed on through the gate of death. The rarefaction of the atmosphere, compared with that of earth, conduces to this end. The social elements and enjoyments are as high and harmonious as in many portions of the Summer Land, on that side of it which looks toward the solar system. There is also a spiritual—meaning a disembodied—population associating with the almost spiritual but embodied inhabitants. The fact offers to those who can see an illustration of that which, in times to come, will be an experience also on earth. It is affirmed further—presumably as a collateral explanation of the communion under notice—that the orbits of Saturn, Jupiter and Mars pass through the heavens above the northern edge of the spiritual zone.—Views of our Heavenly Home, pp. 144, 145.

[5] In his psychic descriptions of earths in the solar systems Davis was preceded by Swedenborg, with occasionally different findings as to their inhabitants. According to the Swedish seer, the people of Saturn are upright and modest, having little solicitude about food or raiment. They subsist on fruits and pulse, wearing light clothing only, with a coarse upper garment to keep out the cold. Each family lives by itself and consists of husband and wife, with their children. When the latter marry they are separated from the house of their parents and have no further care about it. All the Saturnians know that they will live after death, and they set therefore but little store by their bodies, beyond what is needful for life, the great object of which is to serve the Lord. They do not bury the bodies of the dead, but merely cover them with branches of trees. In respect of religion, the majority are worshippers of the Lord—that is to say, of Christ—according to the doctrines revealed by Swedenborg. They regard Him as the only God, and the Lord appears to them under an angelic form, meaning the form of a man. They have also communications with spirits, who instruct them concerning the Lord. There

is, however, a certain sect which worships the nocturnal light of the Saturnian belt and regards this as the Lord, but they are not tolerated by the others and live in separation from these.—See *Earths in the Universe* and *Earths in the Starry Heavens*.

[6] Swedenborg testifies that he was permitted to enjoy longer social intercourse with the spirits and angels of Jupiter than with those of any other planet. He found more to admire in their character than was the case with those of most other earths in the solar system. As he beheld them, they had beautiful faces, beaming with modesty and sincerity; but it should be understood that he did not see them as they dwelt in flesh on their particular planets, but rather their spirits when the bodies had been laid aside in death. The distinction applies to all his planetary visions. He learned that Jupiter is fertile and thickly populated—the inhabitants being divided into nations, families and houses. Wars, depredations, murders, covetousness are unknown among them, for they are gentle and sweet in disposition. They do not walk erect but assist themselves with their hands as they advance—or as stated in the text above. In the warm zones they wear nothing but a covering about the loins. Their faces are eloquent in manifestation of thought, and this is one kind of their language, but they have also spoken words. As Davis says of our own earth, so Swedenborg testifies of all the planets—that the first language of human beings has ever been expressed by the face, as a likeness and index of the mind. It is the tongue of sincerity and belongs to the period when man had no thought which he was unwilling should appear on his countenance. This kind of language is as much superior to words as sight is superior to hearing, and it is in agreement with the speech of angels. When man began to think one thing and express another vocal language was developed. The inhabitants of Jupiter regard good and just thinking on all occurrences of life as constituting the sum of wisdom. They acknowledge the Lord as supreme; they worship Him during their life and seek and find Him in death. He is seen by many in the form of a man; He instructs them concerning the truth and gives eternal life to those who worship Him. For them death is the process of being heaven-made. Their mortal period is for the most part thirty years—according to our years on earth; and those who have lived well do not die of disease, but fall tranquilly asleep and so pass into heaven. They mature more rapidly than ourselves and marry in the first flower of youth. Their greatest care is the education of their children, whom they love tenderly. Their houses are constructed of wood, lined with pale blue bark, having walls and ceilings perforated as with little stars, to imitate the sky. They regard the stars as abodes of angels. They use tents also as a refuge from noonday heat.—*Earths in the Universe*. It is difficult to think that Davis did not owe anything to his illustrious predecessor.

[7] It is on record that Davis received a multitude of communications, urging that some explanation of this passage was desirable, or alternatively dwelling on its absurdity; but he never altered or expunged anything until he had acquired some explicit and comprehensible reason for so doing. After many years he received, however, another revelation or vision, in which he learned that the above posture represented an attitude assumed in the religious ceremonies of a peculiar brotherhood.—*Views of our Heavenly Home*, p. 134. Compare, however, the revelation of Swedenborg, just quoted.

[8] The clairvoyance of Davis did not lead him to perceive or conjecture the existence of other asteroids. It may be mentioned that the discovery of Astraea was almost coincident with the publication of *The Principles of Nature*. The hypothesis of Davis concerning the origin of the minor planets has no foundation.

43

[9] It is said to be a peer and representative of the earth in many particulars.—Views of our Heavenly Home, p. 141. Mars moves in an orbit which, at its greatest distance from earth, is directly above the extremity of the spiritual zone—on that side which is nearest to earth. The people of Mars would see the Summer Land stretching like a great belt. Jupiter and Saturn would be visible also, in appearance like suns, when in the aphelion of their orbits, and so also would their more remote and volatile relatives (see p. 166 of the present work). To all people of the habitable planets the Summer Land is like sunny Italy to an American, but more accessible in point of time.—Ibid.

[10] Swedenborg says that the people of Mars are the best of all spirits on the earths of the solar system, being for the most part celestial men. Their speech insinuates itself into the interior hearing and is thus more perfect than ours. Ideas are more numerous and altogether language in Mars is nearer to that of angels. Emotion shines upon the face and thought in the eyes. Hypocrisy, pretence and deceit are unknown. There are no Governments, but there is division into district societies, being associations of congenial minds. Some have open communication with the angels of heaven, while any who think perversely or plan evil are ostracised from the rest. In regard to Divine Worship, the Lord is acknowledged as the only God and Governor of the universe, from Whom is every good. He leads and directs the people, appearing often among them. External characteristics are described much after the manner of Davis. In the picture of one Martian, the lower part of the face is described as black, although there is no beard. The tinge extends on both sides under the ears, and the upper part of the face is tawny. The food used is fruit, pulse and a globular fruit which springs out of the ground. Garments are woven from the fibrous bark of certain trees.—Earths in the Universe. Once more and obviously, Swedenborg and Davis used the same glass of vision.

[11] Humanity in Venus is distinguished by Swedenborg into two races, still much after the manner of Davis. The first is mild and human; they acknowledge the Lord and affirm that they have seen Him on their planet. These people are on the side of Venus which looks away from the earth. But on the side which looks hither the people are savage and almost brutal, delighting in rapine and feeding on the spoils which they take in battle. They are giants for the most part and are stupid creatures, thinking nothing of eternal life and caring only for things relating to their land and cattle.—Earths in the Universe.

[12] Swedenborg, on the contrary, says that the women are beautiful, but smaller than those on earth, though their height is about the same. The men also are slighter. The latter are clothed in raiment of dark blue, fitting close to the body. The women wear linen caps, which are at once artless and graceful. We hear nothing of their draperies. The people generally count little on things corporeal and terrestrial, for—knowing that there is a life after death—they are concerned with those that are heavenly. They have knowledge of the solar system and of the earths in the starry heavens. They are averse to verbal discourse, because it is material, and when the Swedish seer conversed with them—apart from intermediate spirits—it was by a kind of active thought. They are not distinguished by judgment but are engrossed in matters of simple knowledge. They do not look at the husk but at that which lies within. There are oxen on Mercury, not differing specifically from those on our planet, except that they are smaller. The temperature is medium—neither excessively hot nor cold, and Swedenborg explains here that heat does not arise from proximity to the sun, but from altitude and density of at-

mosphere and from the direct or oblique incidence of the solar rays.—Earths in the Universe.

[13] Swedenborg, like Davis, does not venture to suggest that the sun is itself a habitable and inhabited globe. It is otherwise with some makers of imaginary voyages through the solar system, and a notable instance is the Voyages de Ceton dans les Sept Planetes, by Marie-Anne de Roumier, which appeared at the Hague in seven volumes, 1765. I do not know whether it has any bibliographical value, but it is at least very difficult to find. According to this romance, the sun is the abode of those who have been great on earth. Astronomers who have penetrated the mysteries of the universe find rest therein, from Thales to Isaac Newton. But there are those who are native to the day-star, and these have diaphanous bodies, so that their thoughts are visible in their heads and their emotions in their hearts. No material interest clouds the nobility of their sentiments; they are entirely devoted to the pursuit of knowledge, for which they have excellent opportunities, as their span of life is nine thousand years.

[14] In a chapter on the beauty and glory of the planets, it is stated that our particular solar system is comparatively a young formation and that many of its operations are as yet crude and deficient, when contrasted with those of similar but older systems which move through the firmament. The surfaces and climates of the earth appear to be notable instances of crudity in form and operation.—Views of our Heavenly Home, pp. 129, 130, edition of 1878.

Chapter Three - The Days of Creation

[1]

The first day of creation unfolded one of the laws or attributes belonging to the cosmic totality, being that of power manifested in motion. The developments of the second day brought forth the attribute of wisdom. [2] Goodness was manifested on the third day in the arrangement and adaptation of all things. Those peculiar conditions and circumstances which characterised the fourth day and their results—which were very good—developed justice and reciprocity, as further aspects of wisdom. The fifth day produced a new order of beings, possessing faculties and sensibility not existing previously and capable therefore of estimating the distinction between higher and lower forms. In this manner forbearance came into expression, and a spirit of mercy was established in the animated tribes. The beauties which were unfolded on the sixth day, connected as they are with all previous forms and being a development of their interior qualities, correspond to the ultimate ascension of all parts and principles, the unfolding of all attributes latent in the first type, or the germ of all subsequent developments. The attribute of the sixth day is, in a word, immortal truth—at once in relation to all others, because it is the root of all and is exalted above all. [3] It comprehends that which is below and contains that which is beyond, being qualities which will unfold eternally in the future of worlds. It is the medium of association between all spiritually expanded minds and encompasses all Nature. It is that which is to be admired and adored above every other thing; it should illuminate the interior constitution of every being, and should lead the mind from that which is without, the understanding of things present, to that which is within, the term of all and the ultimate. It is an index to the whole creation of the sixth day. It will yet prepare the mind for the corresponding future day of a more perfect creation.

Looking in this direction and to that which unfolds therefrom, looking also behind and discerning in past epochs the germ of those which are to come, we enter into a world of knowledge which has righteousness as its higher name. The field of truth expands; and there expand also within us the spirit of goodness and benevolence, of justice and reciprocity, the gifts of wisdom and the meaning of beauty. A pure and reverential regard for truth makes order in the whole mind, and from that which is mind in humanity we pass on to contemplate in its stupendous operations the Fountain of Omnipotent Mind.

[1] See The Principles of Nature, Part II, pp. 294, 295.
[2] It should be observed that this is a moral apologue arising in the mind of the seer after the pageant of creation had passed before the eyes of his vision. But as the universe for Davis exemplified the Divine Perfections, there is a sense in which it can be understood—as one might say—literally. A poet has said that "God reveals Himself in many ways," and hence the world is God's Gospel. His beneflacitum termino carens—as the Hermetists call it—abounds everywhere.
[3] It will be seen that this is a figurative delineation of the creative days, and there is an analogous presentation by Swedenborg, though Davis is concerned with the cosmic order and its development, while the author of Arcana Coelestia deals more especially with the microcosm. Both, without knowing it, reflect the Zohar, for which also man is the great intent of creation, and the story of creation unfolding, as given in Genesis, is that of the macrocosm certainly, but its vital import is as the spiritual history of Israel. According to Swedenborg, the six days or periods are successive states of human regeneration: (1) The spirit of God moving over the face of the waters of the soul; (2) The division between those things which are the Lord's and those that belong to man; (3) The state of repentance, which brings forth tender herbs, the herb yielding seed and the tree bearing fruit; (4) The state of love enlightened by faith, or the sun and moon; (5) The state of being confirmed in faith and goodness, producing living consequences—typified by fishes of the sea and birds of heaven; (6) The state of truth in its expression and deeds done from faith—typified by the living soul and the beast. So does the regenerate become a spiritual man in the image of God.—Arcana Coelestia, Nos. 6-13. There is nothing more arbitrary than this, and the moralities of Davis are to the manner born of Nature in comparison.

Chapter Four - The Earth and Its Story

[1]

A glance at the progress of creation in the production of our earth and its inhabitants might serve for an illustration of the same process and progress of worlds in the vast expanse of the universe, as these are continually brought into existence. The object is one throughout, being—as we shall see fully elsewhere—

to develop and perfect individualised, self-conscious, immortal spirits, manifested in the image and likeness of the Central Cause and destined for the Summer Spheres. The process of formation is always from lower to higher, from crude to refined, from simple to complicated, from imperfect to perfect—but in distinct degrees or congeries. Thus, after the sun gave birth to our planet—and it was the same with all other earths—the action of vitality within the particles of matter, and its constant emanation in the form of heat, light, electricity, etc., produced new compounds, possessing the vital principle in sufficient quantities to give definite forms, from those of crystallisation up to sensation and intelligence. The last is the highest or ultimate attribute of things on earth, and is possessed or attained in perfection by man alone. [2]

In the course of time, when "the waters had subsided," the heat and light emanating from the sun acted upon the surfaces of rocks, abrading, decomposing and uniting with their elements, and with the waters of the seas, as also with rain and mist, to produce other compounds of more perfect nature. Thus large beds of gelatinous matter were formed beneath the water level. Thus soil was first formed, a combination of material susceptible of developing vegetable life, both marine and terrestrial. The first vegetable forms, springing from slimy rocks, were simple in their structure—lichens or cryptogamous plants. They elaborated from their own substance a germ or nucleus of vitality, enclosed within a receptacle capable of preserving and sustaining it, till the favourable action of the elements could bring forth from each an image or likeness of its parent. Thereafter the organised substance or body of the original plant died—having fulfilled its object of existence—and the elements of which it was composed mingled with the thin soil on the surface of the rocks, adding to its substance, increasing its complexity and refining its particles, so that with the return of the vernal equinox—and the genial rays of the sun—not only the seeds of the old lichen unfolded but a new and more complicated plant made its appearance. Thus the ever-present and working principle of vitality and creative energy, acting and reacting upon the materials of our globe, started the kingdoms of Nature, each new type being dependent upon all that preceded it for existence and being yet distinct from its predecessors.

Certain conditions, proportions and combinations of elementary inorganic substances are required to produce a vegetable, and vegetable growth is dependent upon elementary regimen, while animals—which cannot be produced or sustained thereby—depend in their turn upon the vegetable kingdom, and this must therefore have preceded them. Were it possible for vegetation to be blotted out from the face of the earth, the animal kingdom would soon be annihilated also. So are all types in the endless chain of organic and inorganic substances the links in one system of cause and effect; so fixed and unvarying are those laws of the Father which regulate all His works.

In this manner vegetation has been traced to its beginnings; but in the depths of the warm seas there were slowly developed other points of life, till minute fishes flourished in myriads therein. On the face of the solid earth, the first animals were huge in physical organisation, mere gastric receptacles for the digestion of dense forms of vegetable matter. They were steps in a flight of stairs for laws and materials to walk upward to the plane of finer organisations.

[1] See Morning Lectures, pp. 60, 63. The account is also reproduced substantially in A Stellar Key to the Summer Land, c. xviii. It is a recurring example of the loose literary methods adopted by Davis, though he mentions on one occasion that he dislikes repeating himself.

[2] It is also, according to Davis, the highest and the ultimate in creation, taken at large, as it is the sole purpose. Herein the seer of Poughkeepsie reflected the Swedish seer. Swedenborg says that the end of the universe is that there may be an angelic heaven—comparable to the Sixth Sphere of Davis, which is on the threshold of Deity. But to say that an angelic heaven is the end of creation is to say that man is the end, because heaven consists of the human race. "Hence all things that are created are mediate ends and uses, in the order, degree and respect that they have relation to man, and by man to the Lord."—See Divine Love and Wisdom, No. 329.

Chapter Five - The Origin of Man

[1]

Prior to the present structure of the universe, the immeasurable realms of immensity were seas of unformed materials, filled with elements of Divine Power, with essences of progressive and eternal tendency. At once in the centre and spreading to the unimaginable circumference was the Holy Artisan, the Divine Architect, the Great Positive Mind. A sacred embodiment of celestial principles, a sublime creation, was conceived in the depths of His being. Having perfected the plan of the universe, God said—with full co-operation on the part of His indwelling love—" Let us make man." Thereupon, the first attribute of wisdom, which is use, said: "Man shall be a culmination of universal Nature, so organised in his body as to receive and elaborate the animating elements of Nature into an unchangeable soul, which soul shall possess and obey the tendency to unfold for ever." But the second attribute of wisdom, which is justice, said: "He shall occupy such a position as will secure to all things, organised and unorganised, visible or invisible, a permanent equilibrium of power, possession and demand." And power, which is the third attribute, said: "Man shall be created through the instrumentality of the suns and planets, through regular and harmonious development of minerals, vegetables and animals, each of which shall correspond to and embody some portion of his organism." Then said beauty, which is the fourth attribute of wisdom: "He shall embrace all suns and planets, minerals and vegetables, with the strength and symmetry of all animals in his form, organs and functions." The fifth attribute of wisdom, which is aspiration, said: "Man shall know himself immortal, lord and crown of Nature, seeking to become an angel, a seraph, even a god." In fine, the sixth and highest attribute of Nature, which is harmony, said: "He shall be an exact embodiment of that Great Spirit Who creates him, shall represent in a finite degree the attributes of the infinite, shall desire and enjoy ineffable beatitude, shall unfold and maintain harmony, and shall be a complete embodiment of Nature."

Thereafter was the universe organised for the ultimate purpose of producing man therein, by a focal concentration of all elements, essences, substances, under the most perfect conditions and influences which exist in Nature. [2] As the growing plant reaches that stage when branches are unfolded, and another when buds burst forth, but a third, lastly, when fruit is matured, so the macrocosmic scheme, under workings of Divine Law, [3] arrived at a period when minerals came into being, a second when vegetables appeared, a third when animals developed, and that, lastly, when all conditions united for the organisation of man. It follows that the ultimate use of Nature is to individualise and immortalise the human spiritual principle, as a mighty and magnificent machine adapted to this end by the omnipotent and omniscient Artisan.

The progressive development of the animal kingdom up to man may be traced from its very beginnings, when—as the result of a marriage between the highest forms and essences in the vegetable kingdom—there arose the first form of animal life—the inferior order of radiata. At a later era the pisces or saurian kingdom was unfolded, followed by that of the birds. The marsupial was next in order, and then came the mammalian, with all its classes and genera, including quadrumana. The primary change from this last into inferior types of human organism is so easy that the anatomical and physiological transformation is scarcely perceptible. Each atom, element and essence, every mineral, animal and vegetable substance aspired to be man. Thereafter strove the vast ascending spiral of forms in creation, for man was the grand end which they were designed originally to accomplish. When every mode of organic life reached the fulness of its development, when Nature was adorned with beauty, with fitting atmospheric and geographical conditions, then earth was prepared for man. By a universal combination of tendencies and efforts on the part of each, he was in fine unfolded, and though at first huge and coarse, resembling quadrumana more than other types of animal creation, his tendency was toward perfection, until he became that which he now is. [4]

Such then is the sequence of creation—that things of the mineral kingdom lose themselves actually and constantly in vegetable organisations and the latter in the animal kingdom, culminating in the development of man. But man never loses his identity in subordinate forms, for he is the grand concentrated product and union of all. [5] Thus in planet, mineral, vegetable, but especially in the higher animal forms, we behold in their workings the laws of association, progression and development, or of the universal predisposition of all matter and vitality toward a homocentric unity and individualisation. All forms inferior and subordinate to man are but parts of him, and his own use—considered as a physical being—is to individualise the spirit. [6] To this end the human brain possesses the concentrated power and beauty of all cerebral organisations in Nature, and is endowed with three great functions: (1) To receive the omnipresent moving essence of the Great Divine Spirit; (2) To concentrate and dispense it to all parts of the dependent system; (3) To give it indestructible organisation, connecting it with elements and substances in the outer world and enabling this interior and divine life to manifest intelligence in reference to itself and external things.

As regards the individualisation of the spirit, the soul's sublime destiny, as the spiritual ultimate of material creation, the concentrated centre of Divine Love, Will and Wisdom, our knowledge of the Creator's goodness enables us to know that which our experience has taught us also to believe—that every human desire is provided with appropriate means of gratification. Each has been given us for wise ends; but the strongest, deepest, most interior of all desires are for immortality, happiness and eternal progression. They proclaim the truth that we are immortal and are approaching a period of unity which will satisfy our highest conceptions of eternal happiness and development. It is for us therefore to unfold the beauties of the spirit, study its immense possessions, and so attain just conceptions of our mission and destiny. Mind must familiarise itself with the principles of justice and order, must unfold its internal capacities, its spiritual perceptions and intuitions, must explore the relations which subsist between man and man, between the natural and spiritual world, between the widespread universe and that Super-Celestial Principle which enlivens and sanctifies the whole. Each human soul must attain a full comprehension of the many and glorious affinities which interlink its destiny and experience with the experiences and the destinies of universal humanity.

It is good to know that there is an omnipotent, purifying and fraternal principle permeating the natural, spiritual and celestial departments of God's most high temple, a principle which unites atoms and planets into one stupendous system, which unfolds spirits and angels [7] as immortal flowers, which is the divinely inherited treasure of the human soul; and this principle is called the Great Harmonia.

[1] See The Great Harmonia, Vol. I, p. 15 et seq., and compare The Principles of Nature, as summarised in the next section.
[2] See also The Great Harmonia, Vol. V, pp. 407, 408: The soul is composed of imperishable materials, with an immortal form. The anatomical and physiological man is the ultimate flower of all material primates and spermatic essences. His silver lining or soul is the culmination of all refined substances and vital forces. When body and soul are perfectly wedded, they discharge the sacred mission of developing a permanently individualised and self-centred existence. This is an interior and beautiful truth.
[3] It may be noted that, according to Davis, the laws of Nature are not creations or institutions but emanations and inherents. They tell us not what God thinks or wills but how He lives and how He must act inevitably. Could a single law of His constitution be violated or suspended there would follow the disaster of utter chaos—as much in the Divine Being Himself as in the world which comes from Him.—The Great Harmonia, Vol. IV, p. 15. This is another way of saying that law is the mode under which existences came into manifestation and is not imposed from without, and that the root of all law is in God.
[4] Compare Morning Lectures, p. 9, where Davis says: I accept the doctrine that man is the ultimate image of a Divine Plan, and that he is destined to be symmetrically developed in body and caused to ripen in spirit.

[5]
Man doth usurp all space,
Stares thee, in rock, bush, river, in the face.
Never yet thine eyes behold a tree;
'Tis no sea thou seest in the sea,
'Tis but a disguised humanity.—Henry Sutton.
All Kabalism acclaims both poet and seer.

[6] This method of expression—which recurs many times in the writings of Davis—is a figurative method of speaking, and while it is liable to be misunderstood by the reader it is not possible to say that the sense in which it was used has been consistently explained anywhere. Within the measures of the symbolism, the Divine Being is, as one might say, a vast ocean and man is an unlimited multiplicity of vessels so organised that they can receive a portion of this water of life and being, which becomes therefore individualised in them. So far the emblem is clear, whatever its value. But the Divine Being of Davis is infinite, which means that He is outside all measures and cannot therefore be divided or separated into parts. Moreover, as the Infinite and Eternal Unity, He is ineffably individual and cannot therefore so become when incorporated with humanity. That which Davis is trying to expound for himself and to others is a particular aspect of the Divine immanent in the universe and transcendent beyond it, as to which an intelligible thesis would be that man by self-adjustment or unification with that Immanence becomes immortal therein. There are difficulties attached to this, and indeed they are grave and many, but the proposition is at least thinkable.

[7] As Davis speaks frequently of angels and sometimes even of seraphs, it is desirable to say that he recognised no hierarchies of spiritual intelligence which had not at some period and on some earth in the universe begun their progress as human beings. Moreover, his hypothesis of the spiritual universe did not admit either pre-existence or reincarnation.

Chapter Six - Primitive History of Man from Psychic Sources

[1]

As all mythological traditions truly indicate, Asia cradled the first-born of the human species, sustaining them from the lowest stages of infant innocence to the extension of their powers and faculties, and until the change of their local habitations to other parts of the earth. The place was the interior of Asia, [2] and the people therein were a kind of primitive association or family. On a parallel herewith there was located subsequently a second family, of similar type but of weaker and more effeminate nature—neither so large in stature nor so considerable in number. The two became acquainted gradually and sought association with each other. The explanation is that there were originally two distinct moulds or forms of mammiferous species, ascending concurrently toward the human type of organisation. One had existed in the arctic regions of Asia since the great revolution in animal types at the close of the fifth day of creation. It was this which developed the human form characteristic of those who existed in the interior of eastern Asia. By a corresponding modification, the mammiferae in the interior portion of western Asia ascended to the effeminate type already mentioned. They did not discover one another till industry had accumulated social wealth in abundance. It was the undeveloped and effeminate race which established communication with the older and more matured inhabitants of eastern Asia. As already seen, the two ultimately formed one family.

Two branches sprang afterwards herefrom, one emigrating into the lower portion of Asia now known as Egypt,[1] the other into the interior of Africa. They developed into large families and one of them into a powerful nation. Those in Egypt sprang from a somewhat more matured stock of the primitive association, retaining the peculiar characteristics of their gross and powerful constitutions. They possessed also great nervous force, sustained by strict adherence to bodily requirements, with abstinence from organic violation. They were not subject to disease. On the other hand, those who settled in Africa continued to possess the imperfect and delicate characteristics of the less developed members of the original family. There came a time when the dwellers in Egypt rose against the weaker nation, destroying nearly three-fourths of their number and dispersing the rest through various parts of Africa. Of these remnants all trace is lost, and it is evident that they became extinct.

There were thus left two nations on the face of the earth—in Egypt and eastern Asia. The former migrated into the southern part of Europe and were so far advanced in civilised life that they built a beautiful city of eccentric form. This new nation increased greatly in numbers, but the people, incapable of self-direction, became disunited again. There were further migrations, and later on two branches established, in Central and South America, two yet more beautiful cities. Those meanwhile who dwelt in Asia set out on another voyage of discovery. At this period the Pacific Ocean was unformed, so that it was possible for them to pass from the eastern to the western hemisphere and gain the upper portions of America. By then the southern portion contained an advanced nation of the original family, whose migrations extended in one direction to Spain, in another to Yucatan, to the region now occupied by the Gulf of Mexico, and also to Brazil and Buenos Aires—as these places are now known to us. They constructed here their cities of stone and other durable materials, becoming very much advanced in science and hieroglyphical architecture. But for a period of about five centuries portions of South America suffered much from volcanic catastrophes, which formed the Mexican Gulf, Caribbean Sea and Pacific Ocean. During these appalling occurrences, nation after nation was destroyed. The inhabitants of Yucatan had, however, extended their possessions almost to those islands now denominated the West Indies, a portion of the same nation being established in the region afterwards called Herculaneum. A city was built there and so also in the region of Pompeii, which was a place of grandeur, pride and arrogance; but then, as later, it was subject to volcanic action. Yucatan continued to flourish— altogether for nearly seven centuries. Other branches of the human family passed toward America from Asia, some reaching that destination, while some settled in intermediate fertile places. Of those who remained in Europe a certain proportion settled in Northern France.

Century followed upon century, and Egypt became founded, as known to historians subsequently. A branch or tribe from Egypt settled in Jerusalem and Jericho. From thence and from Egypt sprang a colony which discovered Greece, and from Greece other portions of Europe were peopled permanently, including Britain. It was owing to dissimilarity of constitution, as adapted to climate and food, to difference in habits and modes of life, to variations of advancement in science and art, to different kinds of ambition that the inhabitants of the whole earth became thus distributed. They were subsequently classified and reclassified according to each modification of original type. It is to be noted in the above account that as America was colonised from Asia, so its southern people migrated to Egypt, and there became a large and advanced nation.

As regards the origin of language, men began first to express their thoughts by the configurations of their countenances, and while this form of communication remained unchanged they were united peacefully; but when artificial signs assumed ascendency the new mode of expression proved deceptive and unreal; unity of thought and harmonious social relations were therefore disturbed. [4] Objects corresponding to ideas were constructed in like manner, being figures and symbolical representations to express general thoughts. Thus language proceeded from manual and corporeal to instrumental formulation. But men experienced inconvenience through the want of a more perfect mode, more especially for the expression of minutiae; and these began to be represented by certain distinct sounds, governed by the natural suggestion of the thought intended to be impressed; and in order that the same sounds might convey uniformly the same idea, the beginnings of a rule were established to govern vocal expression. At a later period sounds were represented by hieroglyphic al characters, or minute figures and strokes. Such was the condition of language at the time of the settlement of Yucatan and the adjoining districts. For an indefinite period symbolical and correspondential language remained unchanged among the inhabitants of earth. The next developments took place in Spain and Asia. The first invented more perfect hieroglyphic al forms, which became ultimately a picture-language. Asia improved the verbal and grammatical forms and placed upon these a certain seal of permanence which still persists therein. The monosyllabic form became, however, confirmed in China, where every character is the substantial representative of a thought, contrary to the other tongues, in which compound figures are employed. Primitive history conveys nothing reliable in respect of language anterior to that of which Chinese is the development.

While language is connected inseparably with the origin of thought, it is still an external, artificial invention, as such misleading and as such also injurious to the human race. All present languages and dialects have arisen in consequence of a misdirection of the sentient faculties and judgment which befell the first-born of the human species. So long as they observed the natural language of the principle within, by means of figures, motions, gesticulations and configurations of countenance, as already seen, they abode together in harmony, while the thoughts and affections of the mind had a real method of expression. [5] But when they discovered their ability to produce intelligible vocal sounds, they lost their primitive habit of radiated expression, and with it the perfect purity of their interior thoughts. Misunderstanding each other's thoughts and intentions through the uncertainty of sound, they became cruel, deceptive, envious. In a word, sounds were not true symbolical representations of the thoughts designed to be conveyed thereby.

[1] *See The Principles of Nature, original edition, p. 351 et seq., selected and collated throughout.*

[2] *An alternative account, which is not in complete accord with the text above, states that the cradle of humanity—as the term is strictly understood—was within and near that portion of Asia which has since been named Turkey, extending to the region of the Euphrates and Tigris, and joining in two distinct lines to the locality where Jerusalem was built in after ages. A lower type existed in some portions of Africa. Those who dwelt upon the borders and in the interior of Asia were very large of form, having strength in proportion to the great density of their osseous composition, and motions governed by the peculiar plan of their anatomical structure. They were marked by gentleness and humility and were social rather than intellectual but with great power of perception and memory—apart, however, from any noble moral qualities. Male and female differed only in stature and comparative strength. This was the first class of beings that could properly be termed mankind, and it has been designated by the comprehensive term of Adam, which included lower and kindred races developing from the animal to the human type in Europe and Africa. An associate tribe, being presumably that which is described as effeminate in the text above, was designated by the term Eve in the primitive records. Asia was thus peopled for many ages, but there was no vestige of art or science. The place where they dwelt was exceedingly fertile, yielding many kinds of vegetation. Being free from all cupidity and absolute deception, the people abode in unity, innocence and purity. But under circumstances narrated in the text they sank into a state of depravity—not because they had violated any physical or mental faculty, but because these had developed wrongly. Misery and impure associations arose herefrom, and misery and vice increased as the ill-directed development continued. At the period when this wretchedness prevailed most extensively the people were obliged to leave the happy associations of their former days—the beautiful earthly Eden—and they were dispersed through other lands. Three distinct nations became established ultimately— one of them in the interior of Asia, one upon its eastern borders and a third in the lower part of Africa. The inhabitants of Asia, divided into two nations—the original and the branch—sustained close relations with each other and with the people in Africa. They were all the legitimate children of the original stock, but, differing in constitutions and tendencies, they did not harmonise together. One of them was inclined to peace and unity of action; they were kind to one another and to the neighbouring nation; they are classified therefore in the old record under the name of Abel, an amiable and good man who followed a shepherd's calling. The rival nation, which dwelt upon the borders of Asia, possessed the dispositions of the primary inhabitants, manifesting envy, retaliation, deception, tyranny and selfishness. They were compared by the primitive history to an unholy man, termed Cain. After maintaining relations for a period, the two nations warred together, but the combat was soon ended, and Cain—the overbearing and con-*

quering people—usurped the wide dominion of the whole earth.—The Principles of Nature, pp. 328-334, and p. 227 of this digest.

[3] Sic in the original text.

[4] The alternative account, summarised in the previous note, allocates the communication of ideas by expressions of the countenance and outward physical signs to a single stage or period, being that of innocence and candour. The stage of deception and depravity supervened when primitive men advanced in artful attainments and began to exchange thoughts through the medium of vocal monosyllabic sounds. They became by this means the possessors of a new power, consequent upon the unfolding of their mental faculties. The misconceptions and deceptions which followed are said to have been an opening of the eyes by which they recognised the condition into which they had fallen. Having a new power of communicating one with another, they clothed their real thoughts in false sheaths or deceptive aprons of obscurity.—Ibid., pp. 330, 332.

[5] Without pursuing the subject, it is intimated in the alternative account that the age of innocence was that period, described by Genesis, when "the whole earth was of one language, and of one speech" (xi. i), which speech and language was by means of facial and other physical signs. The use of vocal sounds is veiled in the sacred text as a confusion of tongues, as the result of which men no longer understood one another's speech and were consequently scattered abroad "upon the face of all the earth."—The Principles of Nature, p. 342. When discussing the true origin of evil in The Approaching Crisis, Davis produced yet another variation, not only as to the origin of man but to the genesis of language. It is based largely on the text above, as usual without reference thereto. The original language of gesture is said to have been assisted by a crude form of hieroglyphical language—derived apparently from vegetables, animals, birds, mud images and objects worked out of stone. When vocal expressions came into use the misunderstandings which followed are referred to the absence of grammatical order and intelligent sounds. The discords led to separation and the race was scattered over the earth. The wandering tribes grew into nations gradually, each developing a different language. It must be said that the seership of Davis was not competent to grapple with the problem of intelligible speech in its origin, and the product of his attempt is pure fantasy. It is adopted in the present case to eke out a speculation concerning early ideas of evil by supposing a mythical chieftain who instructed his people about the doings of a wicked spirit of the air.

Book Three - Revelations of Mind and Soul

Chapter One - The Outward and Inward

[1]

The body of man is a form and as such is transient and changeable; the internal does not change. The true man is inward; that which is outward—his form—is an effect. Mind acts upon body, not body upon mind. The reality is that which is within, and that upon which it acts is visible and mortal, like other appearances. The visible is not the real, and that which is unseen is that also which is eternal. Yet outward searching after truth and inductions drawn from the appearances of external substances have been regarded as the only way to demonstrate tangible realities. So also the external and manifest have been made the test of inward truth. The generality of men are convinced of the reality of things only in proportion as evidence appeals to their senses. Whatsoever is invisible and imperceptible is for them doubtful or visionary. The external tests of truth and reality are, however, invariably deceptive. Reasoning from cause to effect is the one sure guide to truth; and then analogy and association may follow, as carrying direct evidence to the mind of that which is beyond the senses. Cause and reality are within; without are effects and ultimates: prove therefore the visible by the invisible; and if this should seem at first sight a reversal of the usual process followed in reasoning—which is inductive or upward from effect to cause, rather than from cause to effect downward—its justification will be found where few only might expect it, namely, in a philosophical consideration of ideas. Here above all it may seem that the mind of man is dependent on impressions received from without, but such impressions are occasions only for the generation of activity on the part of that which is within and invisible, being the mind itself. Every thought is an unrestrained production of a mind—acted upon by forms, reflections, sounds, associations and so forth. [2] The cause of all such is invisible. It is not the form, substance, sound or word that produces thought, but the irresistible impression which these produce upon the mind. There is the cause in the first place and, secondly, the effect produced, the thought, idea or ultimate ranking third in the series.

Moreover, no physical manifestation is produced unless that which is cause or prompter exists previously; but this is thought. And antecedent to the thought itself is the mind in which it dwells. Here again is developed the principle established previously—that the visible and external are effects and ultimates of unseen though real producing causes. But if we carry the consideration further and admit that no mind can be individualised without the previous existence of physical organisation, it will follow that such organisation postulates another antecedent, being elementary existence, the matter of the cosmos; and hence arises in its turn the greater and inevitable postulate of a self-existent, unchangeable and sternal Principle—the absolute of things unseen, the Fountain, the Sun, the Great Illuminator, the Positive Mind. Therefore, from whatsoever direction our start is made, we are brought to the touchstone of truth in all things, above or below— that the things which are seen are temporal but the things which are unseen are eternal. And as the mind—but not that which is without it—generates thought or ideas by coming in contact with external exciting causes—of the local and temporal order—in this natural body of our humanity, so is there the Great Mind which in certain states or modes, not local and temporal, comes in contact after another manner with the mind of man and generates impressions therein, thoughts and ideas, whereby the spiritual world flows through our inward being. And those who know this state by personal experience can do no otherwise thence-forward than prove the visible by the invisible, for there is that within them which is a link between the outward and inward.

[1] See The Principles of Nature, Part I, being collated extracts.
[2] The limitations of thought are recognised, however, on several occasions by Davis. He says, for example, that deeper than thought is the fountain; that in spirit each is like all and all are like unto each; but in thought each is individualised and removed from the other. By means of the inner spirit and the life therein, there is notwithstanding a meeting and melting together of thoughts possible, as between personalities. It is said also that the thoughts of reflective men are from two very different sources: one is spiritual, or from the fountain of principles; the other is sensuous, or from the battleground of sensations; and while these are shared by us in common with the brute creation, we are not unerring therein, as the animals themselves are, the reason alleged being that we are constructed for unlimited development. More than half of humanity is dependent for its thoughts on the senses and is therefore in an unrisen state, cherishing no higher hopes or faith. But when a man thinks from the ideas or essential principles of which his higher consciousness is compounded, his thoughts are identified with the impersonal, sublime and eternal. He discerns truth as an absolute, not a relative principle.—The Great Harmonia, Vol. V, pp. 25-27.

Chapter Two - Seven Mental States

[1]

In a natural classification of human mental conditions, marking the progress of intelligence from the moment of birth to that of the mind's introduction into the world of spirits, there may be distinguished seven states as follows: (1) The Rudimental State, (2) The Psychological State, (3) The Sympathetic State, (4) The Transition State, (5) The Somnambulistic State, (6) The Clairvoyant State, and (7) The Spiritual State.

The Rudimental State.—We have seen already that man in his natural condition is superior to all other forms and personalities in the subordinate kingdoms of Nature. He is the splendid representation of all perfections and energies of the grosser worlds of life. Another essential point is the duality of man—that is to say his twofold organisation. The duality of his physical constitution can be perceived by all observers. The positive and negative principles express themselves faithfully in the outer form and functions of his different members, from the duality of hands and feet to the two lobes of the brain. All external effects being outbirths of internal principles, the duality of man's physical constitution is referable to a spiritual constitution, analogous to the outer form in every particular. His physical body is a demonstration of his spiritual body, and the duality of the one extends to the other, but in a more perfect manner. Within both is that invisible spirit which is the real man, in virtue of which he is the connecting link between earth and heaven. [2] While every soul contains the same elements, is capable of analogous manifestations, and is not therefore gifted intrinsically above another, so that what is possible and natural to one is natural and possible to all, an infinite variety results from different combinations of the same faculties, from education and from the dissimilar circumstances by which parents are surrounded. [3] An unbalanced mental organisation develops corresponding results. One combination of circumstances will brutalise and another spiritualise the human character. Apart from education a life may be replete with crude and unwholesome deeds; and, destitute of organic harmony, it may generate a whole congregation of inconsistencies and deplorable angularities. Such is man in his ordinary or rudimental state.

The Psychological State.—This condition stands next in succession to the rudimental and can be attained in either of two ways—natural or artificial, which is to say, spontaneous or superinduced. Spontaneous psychology is identical with natural mental power, but superinduced psychology means mental power prematurely developed by the direct action of individuals or circumstances. The relationships established by these positive and negative principles give rise to all psychological phenomena. Every man is psychologically influenced by something. Certain minds are constitutionally positive to one set of circumstances and negative to another. But all manifestations of positive and negative principles, when considered psychologically, occur according to the law of equilibrium. Any influence which disturbs the equilibrium of man's spiritual or mental principle is capable of psychologising the individual, so long as the voluntary powers are unable to assert their supremacy. Anything which disturbs permanently the equilibrium of mind carries the soul into captivity. Many are constantly psychologised by some passion or propensity. The mind also is frequently taken into psychological captivity by the physical organism. When disease has obtained a preponderance of power in the system the mind is disturbed by deranged psychological impressions conducted to the sensorium. So also the mental fear of disease renders the body susceptible to invasion by the dreaded enemy. On the other hand, the same psychological principles which can cause disease, when wrongly exercised, are perfectly adequate, when employed rightly, to cure or prevent it. There is also that aspect of psychology which is manifested in wars, panics, popular insanities and sympathetic contagions. A word, a look, a gesture from some master spirit may psychologise a great assembly, and what is possible in the physical and mental world is equally possible in that of morals. We are all endowed naturally with this psychological power, but in different degrees, and to exercise it is a prerogative of our being.

The Sympathetic State.—The philosophy of sympathy is the tracing out of universal relationships to their source, and the seat of the universal law is Deity. All the external phenomena of psychological principles are reproduced in the sympathetic state, with the addition of higher manifestations, and the philosophy of this influence is visible and applicable everywhere. Now, the synonym of the word sympathy is magnetism. [4] Everything has its own magnetic atmosphere, its own medium of sympathetic relationship. Man particularly and pre-eminently possesses this sphere of mind, so to speak, constantly surrounding his body. It is negative or positive, attractive or repulsive, gross or refined, and of lesser or greater magnitude in proportion to his general refinement and development of mind. When there is a full and uninterrupted exercise of all organs and powers of the body; when there is harmony between all vital functions; the body is properly and thoroughly magnetised. The equilibrium of the positive and negative forces is not disturbed; the organisation is in perfect accord with itself; and the individual is neither physically nor mentally under any description of subjugation or captivity. Setting aside the peculiar phenomena belonging to induced magnetic conditions, the sympathetic medium interlinks all organic beings, and examples of sympathetic impressions may be gathered from experiences of all nations in every age of the world. The source of these impressions may be the action of mind upon mind, emanations from material objects operating upon impressible dispositions, or influence of spirits who have departed from the material body. Many visions and strong impressions were received in the sympathetic condition by Jewish seers, and instances of prophetic dreaming—in accordance with the laws of psychological sympathy—are otherwise numerous; for the mind which is in sympathy with a certain current of events may intuitively perceive or feel some particular occurrence which will result from their progress.

The Transition State.—Intermediate between the sympathetic state and the opening of the interior or spiritual senses lies one which may be called transitional. It is characterised by neither absolute sympathy nor absolute perception, but by an interblending of one condition with the other, to the confusion of both. There is constant fluctuation between two extremes. The mind indicates a distinct vision at one moment and utters at another the impressions of its own memory, or will lose its individuality in sympathy with minds or circumstances which surround it. It is not clairvoyant, neither is it occupying a position from which the soul can discern the broad territories of the Spirit Land. The state is one of fluctuation, of passing from extreme sympathy with surrounding things to communion with inward elements and prepossessions of one's own mind, which are magnified to an extent almost beyond belief. Such operations of the soul are interesting to study and analyse, but they have been the cause of much misunderstanding. Moses, Isaiah, Paul, Mohammed, Zoroaster, Swedenborg were all more or less in a transition state of mind, which is intermediate between mental slavery and liberty. More correctly, it is a state in which the soul is strongly sympathetic with hereditary impressions, educational convictions and prevailing forms of belief, while it exhibits also a kind of consistency and independence of thought, in proportion to the preponderance of orderly faculties in the mental structure. [5]

The Somnambulic State.—It may be laid down as a principle of mental science that the sympathetic, psychological, transitional and somnambulistic moods are variations of the mind in its rudimental condition, on the principle that the lowest degree of everything in Nature contains the highest in a latent or undeveloped state. As regards the present subject, we must keep our minds upon the twofold nature of man, remembering that besides the material or visible organs of sense he is endowed with corresponding internal senses, of which the nervous system is the magnetic flexus or the wires that connect the interior being with the objective world. The nervous system may be considered a kind of bridge upon which the exact images of outward objects and influences travel into the sensorium. Should the external senses be confused and deadened, the internal organs of sensibility become—under certain circumstances—intensified in their capabilities and perform alone the functions common to those of the external body. The vital principle, which pervades normally the external portions of the organism, is now transferred to its interior departments, conducting impressions of the most delicate character to the mind. These impressions are very distinct and delightful, because the attention and sensibilities of the mind are no longer distracted by the intrusion of impressions from the outer world. This state is somnambulism. It may be considered as an incipient manifestation of the spiritual faculties and the first demonstration of the independence of the soul. It may be produced naturally or superinduced by manipulations; but, however obtained, the results are the same invariably, though often different in degree. While some persons in this condition exhibit little perception or powers of accomplishment, others manifest much more than their usual clearness of intellect and energy of muscle. But in nearly all cases the same individual, when awake and when in somnambulism, appears like two entirely different personalities. Although the same in character and a state which can be developed easily into one of high mental illumination, somnambulism is not clairvoyance, except in a rudimentary sense. [6] While the somnambulist can move about in light or darkness with confidence and security, avoiding all objects in his path, the clairvoyant, on a higher plane of perception, can extend his vision far into the life of things, can survey the interior of the earth, the human body and the soul. On the other hand, the somnambulist may obtain no impressions or knowledge from the Spirit Land. He can, however, perform things of which he is incapable in his ordinary condition and expose himself fearlessly to dangers from which he would shrink otherwise. He reads, writes, sings, plays, thinks, reasons, not only as if he had the use of his corporeal senses but as if the acuteness of his natural faculties were increased through emancipation from organic thraldom. It should be fostered therefore with religious reverence; it refers to our deepest vitality and casts light upon our future destiny. It does not rely on any solitary and partial claim to consideration. Its roots run far beneath and throughout the general ground of humanity, and it invests the Temple of Nature with new significance.

The Clairvoyant State.—Clairvoyance is the complete development of somnambulism, an expansion of the same state. [7] It is one of high mental exaltation, though here also there may be a considerable degree of accuracy without the subject perceiving anything which pertains to the world of spirits. It is, however, an interior state, wherein it is easy to discover the hidden beauties and dynamics of creation. Whether naturally or artificially induced, the clairvoyant obtains a clearer knowledge of his own mental and bodily condition; he can diagnose diseases and prescribe effectual remedies. He possesses all powers of somnambulists in a much higher degree of intensification and availability. While the ordinary sleep-walker has only a portion of his mind under his own control, the clairvoyant is in possession of all his voluntary powers, except those appertaining to muscular motion merely—to which, however, there are certain rare exceptions.

The Spiritual State.—Mental illumination is that which brings the soul into close proximity with Interior Life, a life which holds communion with the sanctified. It is a high reality, an expansion of the mind's energies, a subjugation of material to spiritual, of body to soul. This superior condition is the flower of clairvoyance, and because of its infrequent occurrence it might be termed a century plant, which blooms once in a hundred years. [8] It is the fruit of a large and beautiful tree, the root of which is the rudimental state; the body is human magnetism; the branches are somnambulism; and the buds clairvoyance, in all its developments. The Spiritual State grows upon the summit of this tree as naturally as the peach succeeds the blossom. Its causes are confined mainly within the constitution of the mind. The individual must have an organic and hereditary proclivity thereto; the temperament must be firm, high-toned and well balanced. Vital and mental irritability are incompatible with this condition, and no turbulent disposition can attain it. The soul must be calm as the morning and full of integrity; the passions must be soft and tranquil as an evening zephyr, while harmony must preside over the sensibilities.

The Spiritual State is rare, because the circumstances indispensable to its development are as infrequent as they are little comprehended. It signifies an opening of the interior understanding and an exercise of interior perceptions. In this condition the spirit not only sees but comprehends. The love and wisdom principles have an harmonious interaction. The mind sees, hears, reasons, understands; and the whole interior man is concordantly exalted. Social and intellectual elements are, however, subordinated to the religious faculties, though the illumination of all elements is equal. When a human mind is truly in the Spiritual State—which corresponds to death on the outer and harmonious mental development on the inner—the spiritual world will pour its love and wisdom into the perceptions of the illuminated soul. The spiritual world does not come to us: we go thereto. When mind attains that certain degree in development which is in harmony with the laws, desires, love and wisdom of the Spirit Land, its inhabitants are ready to introduce the heavenly light and heat of their own souls into the prepared soul on earth, though such soul may not be so high or good as the source of influx. The pre-requisite is harmony, understood as the condition rather than the degree thereof.

When a mind is substantially in the Spiritual State, the upper portions of the head are beautifully illuminated. The superior divisions of the social and intellectual faculties glow with a mellow light centred in the moral faculties and extending upward about four feet. The upper portion of this light is generally some twenty inches in diameter and variegated as the rainbow—indicating the different kinds of love and wisdom excited by the illumination. This light is derived wholly from the interior elements of the soul. When the body is demagnetised or rendered comparatively insensible by a transfer of positive power from external to internal surfaces, the life of the body flows up into the mind, and the soul's elements experience a corresponding elevation. Into the bosom of this light flow the breathings of love circles or wisdom circles—as the law of use may prescribe at the time. Most profound thoughts and contemplations may be introduced into the mind, accompanied—though not always—with the gift of expression in language.

But a mind in the Spiritual State is not entirely dependent on the Spirit Land for great thoughts and revelations. Possessing somnambulistic and clairvoyant powers, while understanding that which is perceived, it can penetrate the constitution of Nature, the deep things of science and philosophy, the beings of this earth and those of distant stars, incarnate and disincarnate humanity. Independently of direct influx from the spiritual world, the mind in this state has a wide field open before it, while under development from the Spirit Land it can be "caught up into the third heaven," to meditate on the stupendous arcana of spiritual habitations. At the same time it does not leave the body utterly until after death, though the physical frame may present all outward appearances of such desertion, and the subject himself is frequently deceived on this point. It should be remembered further that in some peculiarly organised minds spiritual impressions may be enjoyed apart from spiritual perceptions, and vice versa—as in cases of good clairvoyants. Lastly, the Spiritual State is a religious condition. All true prophets and seers of olden times entered therein.

[1] See The Great Harmonia, Vol. Ill, p. 46, and thence throughout the volume, being the consideration of the states at large, herein extracted and summarised as to their essence.
[2] It follows that man is tripartite—a body within a body and a soul interior of both. This point should be noted in view of certain distinctions which will have to be made subsequently.
[3] It is even said that there are souls which appear in spirit—meaning as they are beheld occasionally in the state of psychic vision—like the lean kine of Pharaoh, poor and half-starved. They are really and substantially small, contracted, parsimonious, exciting simultaneously our pity and contempt. In such a nature there is a radical deficiency of substance. It gives off no vitalising emanations. The alleged equality of souls is resident therefore in the qualities of the germinal essence but not in that quantity of spiritual principles whereby is built up the temple of mental being. All men begin with the same

principles of human existence—motion, life, sensation, intelligence—or love, knowledge and wisdom—but the proportion varies in different types of men. The standard of measurement, like the substance to be measured, is, however, altogether spiritual, and there is nothing to show that deficiency of spirituality is determinable by any physical standard. A large or small structure and standard is no indication of a great or diminutive mind. Nor is it entirely a question of temperament, education or situation. It is inherent and essential.—The Great Harmonia, Vol. IV, pp. 49-51.

[4] In so far as this is an acceptable diagnosis, the sympathetic state must be in close root-relation with that other and, ex hypothesi, higher state which is classed subsequently as somnambulistic. There are, however, two kinds of sympathy, and in the present case it is needful to distinguish them one from another. There is that of which Davis is treating, which is of sense and the physical side, or magnetic, being attractive according to the literal meaning of the word. It connects with our instinctive use of the term atmosphere, to describe something which encompasses certain people and which seems otherwise to escape definition. But there is also intellectual sympathy, and the word magnetic does not apply thereto without a change in its meaning. There is no question that the word sympathy in both these aspects corresponds to something very real in personal characteristic, and it is described adequately in the text above.

[5] It must be said that the diagnosis in this instance seems purely arbitrary or fantastic. Alternatively, the use of the term transitional is singularly misapplied, and we have to remember that Davis, not only when he dictated the Principles of Nature but at the period of The Great Harmonia, was an untutored young man, who had little substantial help from books or schooling. If his transitional state is intermediate between that of sympathy and that of somnambulism, it is no less uncritical and no less nihil ad rem to describe the one as bondage than the other as liberation. To be in sympathy is not to be enslaved and to walk in one's sleep—in the literal sense of the word somnambulism—is a maniacal definition of liberty. The one is a normal condition of every human being, while the other is a pathological state, or alternatively is artificial and induced. Throughout the latter part of his classification the word values and diagnoses of Davis are in a state of chaos. He is really trying to describe the history of a mind in its passage from preconceived opinion to a life of free thought, distinguished by elementary inward experience.

[6] Compare The Great Harmonia, Vol. Ill, p. 241, where it is said that somnambulism is clairvoyance undeveloped. The suggestion that simple somnambulism can be either rudimentary or developed clairvoyance may appear strange to the informed reader, but several denominations adopted in this section are instances of inexact phraseology, characteristic of an imperfectly trained mind, which may yet have great lights.

[7] See ante, p. 75 and the annotation thereon.

[8] Care is recommended to the reader in the consideration of this section, on which, one would think, Davis himself had expended more than his usual care. On the part of the present editor it has been summarised after patient research. In the first place, it should be realised that a state, however denominated, which demands hereditary predisposition for its attainment is not spiritual in the sense that has attached to that word through all the Christian ages, not to speak of earlier epochs. It is really described quite correctly as the flower of clairvoyance, by which we are enabled to see that it is spiritual in the sense of spiritualism, or mediumistic—in conventional parlance. When it is said therefore at the inception that the life under examination is one which holds com-

munion with the sanctified, this is to be understood as of that kind which is postulated by Davis as appertaining to the disembodied humanities who communicate with persons on earth—according to the inferences following from his personal experience and according to the records of mediumship. The distinctions in this brief analysis are not to be understood as established for an ulterior purpose. The spiritual state of the Poughkeepsie seer is not the spiritual state of St. Thomas a Kempis, St. John of the Cross, Tauler, Eckehart and Ruysbroeck. Here is above all a memoir in summary form of conditions to which Davis believed that he had attained personally. The issue having been cleared to this extent for the service of readers who might be otherwise in a state of incertitude, it may be left thereat.

Chapter Three - Mind as A Motive and Moral Power

[1]

Man is the masterpiece of creation, lord of the kingdoms of life and activity, an epitome of all forms and structures, a microcosm of all Nature in its broadest sense. [2] He is the focal concentration and sublimated condensation of all powers and principles in the organism of the objective world. It is therefore true that, in his physical and mental constitution, he is the source of great motive power and supremacy. Standing upon the topmost round of the visible creation, a connecting link between the material and spiritual, mind is the master of all below and a prophecy of much that is above. He is destined to put under his feet all enemies—understood as barriers to human progress and happiness. Science is replete with evidence of the superiority of human mind over the gross materials of Nature. Man is governor, director and lord of all subordinate creations, because he is the most perfect combination of all essences in lower departments and kingdoms. He has the power to ascend higher and higher in the scale of knowledge, for he possesses the concentrated qualities and properties of motion, life, sensation and intelligence. When mental cultivation and intellectual philosophy become universal, it will be discovered that there is a very intimate and sympathetic connection between the sciences of mind and its moral altitudes. Man's external and internal conditions are so inseparably connected that by improving the one he improves also the other, and that knowledge which gives him almost unlimited control over the elements of Nature will yet inform him concerning his more interior and moral powers, thus leading him directly to true theology and religion.

When mind is exercised upon superior planes of thought, all material forms are invested with deep and sacred meaning. He who feels within himself the workings of an immortal spirit can in some measure comprehend the kindred intelligence and love emanating from the material forms which people the world of effects. The ideal begets the actual; the principles of mind incarnate themselves in physical structures. But before it can display creative and disposing powers in higher regions of thought [3] the mind must have a broad substratum of scientific knowledge, as a basis of more exalted structures. Hence the mission of mind as a motive power should be comprehended before considering its mission as a moral power. When viewed in the light of Harmonial Philosophy, all true moral growth and wisdom [4] are higher departments of a Divine Temple, resting upon the granite basis of science and extending its turrets into tranquil realms of celestial life. Physical science leads to intellectual and the latter to moral science. Chemical analysis has led to mental analysis, and thence we derive a philosophy of the qualities and powers of man's immortal soul. By this are we directed to universal love and benevolence toward every member of the human family. So also a philosophy of matter supports a philosophy of mind, as a house stands upon its foundation; and a true philosophy of mind enlarges the sympathies and expands the understandings of those who control the undeveloped and unfortunately situated classes. Hereof is the mind's mission as a moral power, and beyond are all its developments as a vast panorama of spiritual realities. There are moments when every soul realises its own attributes and perceives something of that innate force, beauty and grandeur which lie hidden and undeveloped within. No mortal boundaries can limit the sublime flight of mind. It ascends high in the firmaments, contemplates the causes, laws and operations of the universe, displaying everywhere that transcendent power which renders man a little lower than the angels. The principle of reason is its greatest and highest endowment. This is the indwelling light and this the power of understanding by which man reads in the everlasting volume of Nature. Nature is the universal exponent of God, and reason is the exponent of Nature. Nature and reason constitute the only true standard of judgment upon all subjects.

[1] *The Great Harmonia, Vol. Ill, p. 13 et seq.*
[2] *Compare The Principles of Nature, p. 593:—Man considered materially—meaning as lord and master of the planet on which he dwells—is the wisdom, head and king of all animated forms, the perfection of matter. So also ibid., p. 596: The lower forms are developed and perfected in man, for in him are (a) the spiritual, (b) the perfect spiritual, and (c) the celestial forms of the particles of matter. An explanation is given (p. 595) of the term celestial forms, being those parts or atoms which contain perfected in themselves every species of form in the subordinate kingdoms and which become receptacles of spiritual life.*
[3] *There are three departments of human thought, according to Penetralia, p. 9, or, more correctly, there are three worlds open to the investigations of thought, being (a) the indefinite world, intermediately situated between finite and infinite; (b) the finite world, being that of human sciences; and (c) the infinite, to which we feel that we are instinctively and eternally related. Man himself is the indefinite world, and hence "all our knowledge is ourselves to know," albeit—as we are at present located—there is a limit set to research in this direction.*
[4] *It is explained elsewhere in the volume from which this text is drawn that the human mind; when seen interiorly—that is to say, when it is contemplated in a clairvoyant state—presents (1) a fountain of life, (2) a fountain of principles, and (3) a casket of facts. The first is the department of love, the second of wisdom, the third of knowledge—these qualities having express constitutional affinities for life, principles*

and facts. Love is the parental essence of the two other qualities—or elements, as Davis terms them, speaking of course metaphysically and not chemically. The whole nature of man, physical and mental, is not only based upon but is likewise manufactured through the department of love. Phrenologically it occupies all the back portions of the head and is the largest of the mental organs. The department of knowledge occupies the front portions of the brain and that of wisdom the upper portions. Wisdom is the source of principles, knowledge the treasury of facts, love the fountain of all consciousness and motive power.—The Great Harmonia, Vol. IV, pp. 29-34.

Chapter Four - Liberty and Necessity

[1]

The question of free will lies at the root of social re-organisation, and it has been affirmed and defended by the profoundest and most spiritually illuminated minds that the human will is free and unrestrained. I propose, however, to prove that man is a being of necessity, a depending and necessary part of the universal whole. He enjoys a twofold relation—physical and spiritual—to the universe. One is the connection which subsists between his body and external Nature; the other is the conjunction between mind and internal Nature—purity, truth, justice, or, in a word, Deity. Were the mind intrinsically free—untrammelled by any physical object, element or circumstance—the individual would be qualified to select his own anatomy, cerebral structure, temperament and organic powers; but as it must be conceded that no being is at liberty to supervise the formation of his own body, so—at least in this respect—man is a creature of necessity. [2] There is a kind of liberty involved by human individuality, and in this abstract sense everything enjoys a species of independence. No single thing is, however, isolated from all else, for Nature is an inseparable whole, with its parts essential to and depending one upon another. Notwithstanding the dissimilarity and apparent mutual independence of male and female, they depend one upon another and also upon the elements and means of nourishment which surround them in Nature. So also, in proportion to a man's constitutional powers and qualifications, but not beyond them, is he capable of thinking or acting, and he can only be expected to fill the measure of his capacity. [3]

And now as regards the will in its superior relations to purity, truth, justice and Deity, it is held that man is situated intermediately between good and evil, [4] that he has the power to reject the one or the other, and can thus determine his own eternal character, destiny and situation in the world beyond the grave. We have seen elsewhere that he is the highest organisation in the stupendous system of Nature, that he lives, moves and has being in God's Universal Spirit. [5] Attractions, desires and impulses are born within him; those which proceed from his immediate progenitors are temporal, but those which he derives from his Heavenly Father are eternal. He is not therefore situated between good and evil; he stands on the summit of creation, a little lower than the angels, requiring simply a constitutional harmony and a spiritual development to understand and enjoy their continued association. He is not merely a recipient; he is filled with life, motion, sensation, intelligence; he is God manifested in the flesh; he is a son of the Most Glorious and High. As regards his power of choosing between good and evil, he cannot select associations without knowledge of their character and influence, to obtain which he is subject to surrounding suggestions, both material and spiritual. Reasonable action or selection depends invariably upon prior experience and understanding, and consequently the human mind, in order to choose intelligently between good and evil, must first ascertain by actual experience, or by interior perception, what good and evil are. I am led therefore to conclude that man has no absolute freedom of will, [6] because it is not possible to be a free moral agent without having ability to distinguish between the seeming and the actual, the false and true. Materially and spiritually, man possesses universal affinities which he did not create and can neither control nor destroy; he is compelled to act as he is acted upon and to manifest character according to his constitutional capacity and social situation.

There exists, however, a species of freedom or independence in human thoughts and actions; but it is altogether comparative. [7] A start in life is made from the same point, estate or social class, but very different paths are trodden and distinct terminations reached. One person is in possession of a weak and combative mind, which leads on to murder; another is vain, ambitious and secretive, which things end in robbery; a third has some or all of these qualities, but accompanied by prodigal benevolence, as a result of which, under certain circumstances, he may sink so low in the scale as to become a beggar; while the fourth, without better external advantages, has a superior organisation and more harmoniously developed faculties. He is industrious and above the temptations to which the others have yielded; yet he may be thrown out of employment and at last may die of starvation. Now, the enlightened mind will perceive that these distinct paths and ends were of absolute, unconditioned necessity. Society was the first cause of the disasters, while parents were the second, for they imparted the dissimilarity of organisations which caused dissimilar fates.

It is a legitimate conclusion herefrom that an individual is accountable only according to his capacity. Man is both an actor and a circumstance, a cause and an effect. He should be treated not as a being having will and power to do that which he desires, when and where he pleases; but he should be born, educated, situated, rewarded, punished as a tree capable of yielding good fruit only when it is properly organised and conditioned in a good soil. The doctrine of the free will or agency of the soul is contradicted by everything in Nature and Man. [8] Every thought, motive and deed arises from interior laws and combinations of physical and mental economy which are inevitable and unchangeable. The comparative freedom which man seemingly inherits is that of motion within the circle described by his capacity and degree of development. Beyond this he has no more liberty than is enjoyed by a goldfish in a globe of water. [9] But he is a part of Nature and is designed to move as harmoniously in the great whole as the heart in the body; and this conception of his moral state is an unfailing source of consolation and happiness. It removes all doubt as to the ultimate issue of this life; it satisfies the soul that "the Lord God Omnipotent reigneth"; it makes Deity the Sovereign Ruler of human and angelic hosts; and it points to the reconstruction of society, to new methods of educating and punishing—or reforming rather—the human race. It develops the religion of distributive justice, the spirit of compassion, law of love and morality of universal benevolence. [10]

[1] See The Great Harmonia, Vol. II, p. 211 et seq., digested and collated.

[2] Compare The Principles of Nature, Part II, original edition, p. 463. Considering the inseparable connection which is sustained between the universe and Deity, it is impossible to conceive of independent volition. Did such a thing exist, the universe would be disunited, and the Divine Mind would be incapable of communicating life to its various recesses and labyrinths. The chain of cause and effect; the bond of unity, harmony and reciprocity would be broken; and the universe would be no longer an organised system, but an incomprehensible ocean of chaos and confusion.

[3] See The Principles of Nature, p. 629: Many have assigned to the soul a faculty of absolute free will—a power to act or not to act in any specified manner, uninfluenced by interior or external things. Such an opinion is of course rejected.

[4] Compare the corresponding condemnation of those who have given to the soul innate faculties perpetually disposed to wickedness and abomination, delighting to indulge in every species of evil and licentiousness, and seeking its own emolument by a sacrifice of all moral principles. . . . The soul has no such inherent propensities, no desire to injure or dissemble.—Ibid., pp. 629, 630.

[5] He is an offspring of the incessant and successive developments of those mighty attributes which together constitute the Cause of all things,

[6] As neither theology nor philosophy, in the orthodox schools on the one hand or on the other in authorised schools of teaching, has postulated absolute liberty on the part of man, it will be observed that Davis grants here that which is necessary to the responsibility of human being. If some of his statements read on the surface otherwise they must be taken in the light of the qualification made above. It will be seen furthermore that the Harmonial Philosophy is essentially a philosophy of freedom and that no loose terminology should be utilised to place its author in the category of fatalists.

[7] This is expressed elsewhere as follows: It is certainly evident that there is a species of independence possessed by every particle of matter; but it consists only in the fact that forms have an individual being. In this sense the term independence can be applied to all things. But speaking in reference to the whole system of creation . . ., all things are parts of one stupendous whole, and hence is demonstrated the unity and dependence of all things.—Ibid,., p. 636.

[8] The conviction of the soul's independence arises from insufficient development of the faculty of wisdom, from misdirection of all the faculties, and especially from the prevailing superficial modes by which people are educated.—Ibid., p. 634.

[9] The contrary belief is said to arise from confusing the actions of individual faculties, without perceiving the relations which they sustain to external things, to the forms which they inhabit, or to one another. . . . It has been held by some metaphysicians, especially Plato and Locke, that the free will of man is proved by his superiority over all other forms in Nature, he alone being prompted to act, yet at liberty to refuse. But this

hypothesis has neglected to analyse the soul's individual faculties and their specific modes of action.—Ibid., p. 636.

[10] There is another argument on liberty and necessity, which may be summarised briefly thus: (1) Man believes himself conscious of power to move according to a desire of the will; (2) this power appears to be born of and governed by itself; (3) it seems therefore to be self-existent; (4) but the supposed consciousness is deceptive, because no one can perceive the relation between each portion of the soul; and (5) hence all conceptions respecting the inward self are intangible and unsatisfactory.—Ibid., p. 633. It seems obvious that the argument cannot be pressed on either side of the consideration under view.

Chapter Five - What Is Truth?

[1]

Truth is the source of all eternal realities, the origin of all that is high, divine, infinite. Absolute truth is immutable—the same yesterday, today and forever. He who teaches a doctrine that is absolutely true proclaims an everlasting substantialism which rests upon the authority of God. But he who proclaims something that is destined to become obsolete speaks of things merely and not of the principle which holds them together in harmony. When Newton discovered the law of gravitation and proclaimed it to the world he did not set forth a private and peculiar thing but an absolute, immutable truth founded upon an Eternal God. The question—What is truth ?—is the beginning, middle and end of all inquiry. As the term is understood here, it might seem that an angel's mind could not furnish the answer, yet a simple and imperishable definition appears ready to our hand. So far as the world is concerned, the question is answered everywhere according to individual convictions. [2] We must therefore—on our part— disrobe our minds of all preconceived opinions and remembering that while we may consult testimony to get at historical matters, perception for things external and reflection for logical subjects, we must interrogate intuition if we would be enlightened upon religious or moral concerns. Intuition is the deepest source of truth, an innate power by which it is felt—in a word, it is the genius of the soul. Let us realise in the first place that truth is always simple, while error is always complicated. [3] The one is easy as the growth of flowers, but the other is dark and mysterious. Moreover, truth is not susceptible of limitation. That which was true yesterday cannot be merely probable today and only possible tomorrow. It is God-made, and the man who gives it an expression vocalises the celestial life-song of Deity. If this be correct, then people have erred greatly in the use of language. We call it, for example, a truth that yesterday was cold, but the statement may refer only to certain localities. It would be far more correct to designate all occasional or local occurrences as facts and to make use of the word truth only in respect of that which is of broad, unchangeable and universal application. In other words, let us assign to truth a position far above individual minds and circumstances, that it may be superior to everything but God. If we adopt this view we shall rise superior to all forms of sectarianism and pursue the golden pathway which leads the pilgrim eternally upward to the City of the Living God.

And now as regards the promised simple definition, let it be affirmed that truth is the universal relationship of things as they are, while error is the interpretation of things as they are not. [4] As things are, so God has unfolded them. He is Author of the relationship between them, and He is therefore the truth. Of this universal relationship it matters not how much or little I know. If I comprehend the first principle which binds a piece of iron-ore together, I know something of truth, and no human authority can make it more true, though a wiser man may lead me to further truth in the same or in another and higher department of creation. Now the question arises as to how we may know when we have the truth. The answer is to listen like a child to the subdued whisperings of that soul which God has given us. No man can enter the kingdom of truth and happiness unless he be simple of mind, by which I mean an honest, guileless, uncalculating, truth-loving state—a state which in the past and present conditions of human society is about as frequently developed as a Christ is born.

By willing strongly to see and feel truth—irrespective of creeds, men, books, or systems—you are certain to attain it, at least in such a measure as you can employ to any advantage. [5] If you seek what is wonderful or mysterious, you do not seek truth. There are myriads of mysteries, but this is due solely to our ignorance of their nature and relationship. The great standard is that facts are things, while truths are principles. [6] Things exist and their right relation one to another is based upon and is the truth. From such relation the music of harmony issues perpetually. Discord issues from error, because the relation is wrong. See well to this doctrine in all departments of existence, and remember that now is the time to think, feel and do right. By putting off till tomorrow you defraud yourself of immediate happiness and do a similar injury to the neighbour. Let your understandings expand and thus obtain reasons for the inward hope. Remember always that marvels confound and stultify the intellect, while principles [7] are certain to dignify the whole nature of man.

[1] See The Great Harmonia,Vol. Ill, pp. 363-374, extracted and collated.
[2] See on this subject Penetralia, original edition, p. 296, where a species, of relative truth is recognised, being the measure of personal understanding. It is put forward as an answer to the question which stands at the head of this section, but it belongs obviously to another aspect of the subject and is not a definition at all but the delineation of a point of view. The answer is this: Your deepest and highest conviction—that is your truth; my deepest and highest conviction—that is mine. You cannot therefore follow me altogether, nor I you; but each may revolve in his own orbit, to the other's benefit.
[3] According to one of the several definitions offered by Davis, truth is an inherent quality of the spiritual constitution, whereby the possessor is empowered to feel legitimately and to think accurately. Inherent love of truth is an immortal love which— blended with an acquired power of attracting truth from without—transforms a soul into the image and likeness of the gods.—The Great Harmonia, Vol. V, p. 14. Compare Ibid., Vol. IV, p. 19: Truth, according to a philosophical statement, is the absolute coincidence between object and subject, a concordance between things and ideas. Whence-

soever Davis derived this remark, it is at best a confusing definition, because such coincidence between subject and object would be much more than a concordance between the thing and the idea concerning it.

[4] It is obvious that the essence of truth escapes when it is identified with relation. An alternative definition is as follows: Truth is that Divine and Eternal Principle which fills, bounds, connects and equals all; the cause and effect of infinite harmony; everywhere cohesive and consistent at all times, as in the material so also in the spiritual realms of existence.—Penetralia, p. 52.

[5] There is an excellent distinction as follows: The cold, systematic discernment of truth is purely brain-work and intellectual; but the warm love of it is spiritual, intuitional and heart-begotten.—The Great Harmonia, Vol. V, p. 17.

[6] But truth is also affirmed to be an absolute, not a relative principle.—Ibid., p. 27.

[7] Truth is that principle in the presence of which Nature, reason and intuition harmonise, agree and rejoice together, as loving angels of God.—Ibid., p. 32.

Chapter Six - A Spiritual Consideration of Physical Man

[1]

We have seen that outer forms correspond to interior conditions, and that which obtains throughout the cosmic world is true in a pre-eminent sense of man. [2] Let it be remembered also that wisdom is the grand faculty of the human soul and should govern all that is below—whether faculties or affections. Wisdom is the lord of creation, and not only is love itself directed thereby but all its emotions are modified. Love has intercourse with the outer world through the medium of sensation and thus receives a continual influx from the elements of all material things. Thereby also love pours forth its springs of affection for external objects. So do the inner and outer communicate one with another, and over this intercourse that which should reign is wisdom. Will is likewise under the same potential direction. Whenever the faculty of will is instigated by love to perform an external act, wisdom perceives the suggestion, divines its use and directs the will to its accomplishment. When the faculty of wisdom is undeveloped and love actuates alone, the manifestations of will are impulsive and often injurious to the well-being of man. We discern in this manner the importance of (a) elevation of mind, (b) instruction concerning its inward nature, and (c) its relation to the world.

The cause of disunity in actions, feelings and affections is not innate depravity but misdirection of faculties. The baser passions of the soul and every species of licentiousness are referable to the ignorance and imbecility of minds unguided by wisdom and apart from spiritual unfoldment. Let us desist therefore from proclaiming metaphysical hypotheses derogatory to the innate divinity of the human soul; let us rise to the plane of interior and natural thought; and let all external activities correspond to the unrestricted sanctions of wisdom. It is through lack of such government that men have adhered so long to the imaginative beliefs of their love-part, instead of the spontaneous teachings of judgment. Hereditary opinions of every kind are simply early impressions made upon the former faculty. But men who discard all hereditary affection [3] for thought are those in whom is developed the highest faculty of the soul, and this is wisdom. Thence they receive and thereby impart instruction; and whatsoever is prompted within them by the love-nature is made perfect in order and form.

The physical senses of humanity have their correspondences on the inward side. That which we call feeling, in the restricted sense of the term, and which is literally touch, has a close relation to the faculty of love. Hearing—or the sense of external sound—is correlated with the joint action of love and will, but with the latter especially, for thereby this sense is rendered a delicate medium of communication between the inner and outer worlds. The power of seeing is related to the faculty of wisdom, and hence is subject to the will. Seeing is always an act of will, approved or permitted by wisdom—for a person may or may not employ his organ of vision to behold material things. It is otherwise with hearing, for will has no power to prevent the influx of sound-vibrations. Neither will nor love has control over the sense of touch, which is a connecting link between human faculties and the instincts of animal creation. The two other senses, namely, taste and smell, are modes of the sense of touch and are subject neither to the judgment nor the will. Unlike vision, they have no power to resist external invasions.

The connection thus established between outward faculties and ruling qualities within shows that man's external form corresponds to and represents his interior being, or the form and structure of the soul. Be it remembered that forms are created and determined only by their essence—a truth which applies to man and the whole universe. To behold the soul or spirit of man observe, therefore, his material mode of being. Remember also that the real man is internal and only animates the material form, [4] (a) to perfect its constitution, (b) to preserve its identity, and (c) to establish an inseparable connection between the material and spiritual world. [5] All material things created by man are the forms of his thoughts, and these are offspring of the soul. Were he differently insphered and taught, he would not be so far removed as now from the spiritual world. But he becomes individualised in this sphere and preserves his form henceforward. He exists in the other world in a perfect human form, for the Second Sphere is unfolded from the first and is the perfect form of this, its parent and creator.

[1] See The Principles of Nature, Part II, pp. 631-641, extracted and compared.
[2] This fundamental idea of the Harmonial as indeed of Hermetic Philosophy is illustrated after another manner, as follows: Minds absorb vitality and substances generally from the atmosphere which is generated and exhaled by all the spiritual spheres. Hence there is a spiritual atmosphere within that which is material. The soul feeds upon the one and the body upon the other, until—by a refining process—they blend together, and the spirit thereby is made to increase in substance. Human souls will accumulate spiritual substance in strict harmony with their individual aspirations. Those who are on the quest of love will grow spiritually wealthy therein, and so of knowledge and wisdom. Just in proportion as these departments of mind open to the celestial atmosphere,

within the common air, so will love, knowledge and wisdom increase the substance of the soul.—The Great Harmonia, Vol. IV, pp. 54, 55.

[3] It has to be remembered that this statement is not unlikely to convey the very opposite of the author's intention, unless it is read in the light of his other intimations on love, wisdom and will, but especially on wisdom and love. So also the essence of life is likely to escape in the life of thought alone, nor is thought itself of necessity the way of wisdom. There are many images therein from which we may cry to be delivered, and often cry vainly if we are once lost therein. This also is the world of multiplicity and not the world of union. It is right, however, to add that the Harmonial Philosophy of Davis sought no world of union, for this is the world of the mystic and not of the Summer Land.

[4] It is said that the centre of the soul—meaning its place of physical situation—is near the centre of the brain. There is a small nucleus in which is concentrated the vital power of all that constitutes a man. In the lifeless brain this place is not larger than a buck-shot: in the living brain it is as large as a frost-grape.—Penetralia, p. 196. From this centre it radiates over the whole body.

[5] As to the independence of these worlds and especially of soul from body, Davis dwells elsewhere on the fact that electricity is not created by the zinc and copper plates, but is simply developed and accumulated; and he argues that this is the case also with man's spiritual principle. The brain is indispensable to the individualisation of the living elements of life into a healthy and harmonious mind, but not to the prior existence of those elements nor to the continuation of the individual mind after the physical structure has subserved its purpose.—The Great Harmonia, Vol. Ill, p. 69.

Chapter Seven - The Soul in Man

[1]

It is necessary to classify the parts of the soul in order to conceive the relation which they sustain to each other and their correspondence with end, cause and effect. The end or ultimate design is always the cause, which cause institutes an effect, and both these are engaged in accomplishing the end. The soul is composed of three distinct parts, being love, will and wisdom. [2] Love is the first or rudimental element of the soul. It is that liquid, mingling, delicate, inexpressible element felt in the depth of every human spirit, because it is the germinal essence. Will is a living force which serves as the connecting medium between love and wisdom, and is subject to the influence and suggestions of each. It is an innate consciousness of energy. Wisdom is the perfection of love, the sealing element of the human soul and the establishment of the soul's perfect constitution. Wisdom flows from love, is directed by experience, modified by will and rendered perfect by knowledge. Wisdom is the thinking principle, the faculty which explores the fields of terrestrial and celestial existence. It analyses, calculates and commands obedience from all subordinate possessions of will and love.

Love being the first element or essence of the soul is imperfect and unguided. [3] On the one hand, it is parent of impulse, fantasy, eccentricity and inflated conceptions; on the other, of tenderness, kindness, affection, attachment, all pure and unsophisticated sentiments springing from inward deeps and expressed in language, in music, in painting. It conceives all loveliness, gentleness, sweetness in their various modes of manifestation. It is exhibited especially in conjugal attachments, out of which there arises that love for mankind generally which begets families and associations. It has yearnings for the invisible and sublime, finding outward expression in ideal conceptions clothed in words, infusing chastity, refinement and amiability into all other affections. Love has also an attraction for self, sometimes expressed by unrighteous plans for self-emolument, by deception and destruction of life, by all those unsanctified and corrupt inventions which—through misdirection of such love—prevail throughout the human brotherhood. But love involves also unbounded benevolence, finding expression in mighty movements for the amelioration of mankind and the ultimate establishment of distributive justice and universal righteousness. It has furthermore an affection for what is just, expressed by conscientious relations between man and man, and by reciprocity. This is the love of the moral, righteous and holy. It conceives all Divine Perfection, aspires toward the Divine Mind and those exalted sentiments which are the highest attributes of man. Love also gives birth to hope, clothed in contemplation and expectancy of things desired by the other affections of its nature.

From the faculty of love—as basis of the soul—flows that of will, which becomes the mediatorial instrument of the human mind, employed to encompass those ends that love desires. Herein are made plain the three moving principles engaged in the attainment of ends. Love conceives that which is congenial to its affections; it prompts the will to act, in order to accomplish the end; and the will is therefore love's means. Will is a living force which evolves thoughts suggested by the workings of love and expresses them in manifest forms, in movements of the body and in all external actions. [4] As it does not institute any movement of itself but works only as excited and prompted, love is the primary course of external action and will is the effect produced.

The third faculty of the soul is evolved from will and love. It is highest and most perfect, joining and pervading the others, so that the three form a perfect whole. This faculty is wisdom. The office of wisdom is to hear the suggestions of love and will, and to modify them according to reason, form, order and harmony. Love without will would be eccentric, impulsive, disorderly, and when so modified it is held within a definite sphere. But love and will would both be eccentric and ungoverned among material things were it not for the presence of wisdom, which presides over and directs both. [5] Wisdom is contained in love, as germ of the soul, is developed in its body, which is will, and perfected in its own flower. It is the crowning faculty of the soul, the most perfect of all its attributes. It gives order and form to all things in the outer world, and the further its sphere of action is extended, the more will the world display beauty and harmony. The more it is restricted in its actions and the less its dictates are heeded, the more will Nature and man's artificial creations become disorganised and useless, instead of displaying peace, beauty and reciprocity.

The Great Divine Mind is love in its essence—light and life of the universe. The universe is the body of love and its perfect form. But wisdom is the highest attribute and the great ultimate of eternal design. Here then are the three parts of the universal system: The Divine Mind or Love, and this is the Soul; the universe, which is form, means, mediator and body; the Spirit, which is the order, wisdom and grand design of the entire system. [6] The end primarily designed was individualisation of the human spirit, for the attainment of which cause and effect were brought into requisition. This truth is demonstrated in every department of the terrestrial sphere, but is particularly exemplified in the nature and developments of the human soul, which are in exact correspondence with the great system of the universe. Everything is perpetually displaying—in its inward and outward movements—end, cause and effect. Light and life are love; order and form are wisdom. Hence it is highly necessary that mind should comprehend the great truth that nothing exists in the outer world except as produced and developed by an interior essence, of which the exterior is the perfect representative. Among the various arts and sciences may be found demonstrations of this truth and its importance. Every form invented by man represents that inward thought which is cause of its creation. So also every form corresponds to the inward suggestion of love, is created by the living effort of will, modified and perfected by the direction of wisdom. [7]

[1] See The Principles of Nature, pp. 622 et seq. We shall see in the next section that what is here called the soul in man was subsequently termed spirit by Davis, the soul part being identified with the psychical body.

[2] It is obvious that these are faculties or qualities rather than parts or elements. Davis mentions elsewhere that the faculties thought to compose the various portions of the soul—but, more correctly, the moral make up—have been minutely classified under general divisions of propensities, sentiments and intellectual faculties. The first of these are represented as relating to self and to things in the outer world; the second as giving rise to moral conceptions and the sense of justice; and the third as comprising the powers of reason, analysis and investigation.—Principles of Nature, p. 629.

[3] Compare innumerable counter-statements throughout the collected writings, and e.g.—Love is the germ-principle and essence of life. . . . Wherever you behold life, there is love. . . . Life issues from a Deific fountain—meaning, in all its simplicity, that God is love.—See The Great Harmonia, Vol. IV, pp. 31-33. It follows from this hypothesis that the essence of the soul is a Divine essence.

[4] It is testified otherwhere that pure will exercised for a pure purpose can overcome all forms of diabolism, diseases, vices and every manner of bad thought. On the other hand, an evil will is the highest expression of that which is called the devil—it being understood that the last term is, for Davis, merely a figure of speech. Those who would know the plenary bliss of angels should allow their will to do that only which is prompted by their highest affections and approved by their highest reason.—Views of our Heavenly Home, p. 28.

[5] Wisdom is an effect of the full and harmonious development of all the affinities, affections and attractions which constitute the soul and adorn its fair proportions.

Knowledge is acquired and superficial, but wisdom is unfolded and intuitional.—The Great Harmonia, Vol. I, p. 216.

[6] It is difficult to understand how this classification presented itself to the author's mind or how it can be put into logical sequence by the reader. It is ridiculous to distinguish the plan contained within the Divine Mind as a spirit calling for consideration separately from the Mind itself. It is obvious that there are and can be only (a) the intelligence which designs, and (b) the design produced, which in the case at issue is the universe. This is not a means or a mediator, for it is the sum total of manifestation, and there is no third thing to which it can mediate.

[7] Wisdom, intuition and reason are said, in another work, to be words of the same import, and the statement is an instance of a tendency on the part of Davis to make synonyms by force.—The Great Harmonia, Vol. IV, p. 37. Note also that wisdom is called the spiritual sanctuary, the mountain of the Lord, the true saviour of man.—Ibid. It is above clairvoyance, because it is self-illuminated.—Ibid., p. 46.

Chapter Eight - The Spiritual Body

[1]

How do the people commonly called spirits appear to an observer? Are they always dressed and in what style? If they eat, what is their food? How do they perform their various functions and do they bear children? These are recurring questions. In the progression of Nature from the lowest living substance to the complex organisation of man everything follows the principle of evolution. The lowest is radical and the highest may be termed fruition, because it is perfect unfoldment. In the germ or protoplasm, as it is called by Huxley, are deposited the properties and potencies necessary for the development of each particular organism. The visible process is that of progressive development, and this principle is immortal. It is the mode of action throughout eternal spheres, and it gives true explanations concerning the body of the spirit and its appearance in the Summer Land.

Physiologists know that there are organs in man's body—like certain caecal appendages to the intestines—which do not perform any important offices. They are remnants of a lower stage through which mankind has passed; and a time will come when—by operations of evolutionary law—such parts of the human form will cease to be. In the Summer Land certain organs which are now vital are no longer needed and do not appear within the spiritual body. There are no fluids requiring kidneys, no broken-down blood demanding pulmonary air cavities, no physical digestion involving stomach, liver and intestines, [2] no propagation involving external organs of generation. [3] Male and female, however, the spiritual body appears—preserving all the symmetry and intrinsic excellence of our most perfect human form. It is sometimes clothed and sometimes not, according to customs of society or peculiarities of latitude. But the ultimates of all organs are preserved and perform spiritual functions corresponding to the natural body. With regard to food, we must realise the difference between a mortal body and the body incorruptible. [4] Throughout the ages of eternity, all human or angel

76

feeding and all breathing among elements of eternal beauty and youth are accomplished by the mediation of what in the physical body we term erroneously nerves and cellular tissues. Youth and health are eternal because there is a perpetual exchange of these elements, causing and maintaining everlasting equilibrium between the body and the spirit. Sickness, old age, death can never be known where there exists this perfect and just interchange.

Under the protection of her heavenly guardians, the Seeress of Prevost was a remarkable example of cellular and nerve feeding on this plane, but we may recall instances in our own day and country of young women who have lived for weeks and even months without eating anything substantial and sometimes without drinking. But because the patient partook of spiritual meat, which only angels know, the physical body did not waste rapidly away, though its functions were sometimes suspended, and the physiological wonder grew greater, day by day, among men.

The physical body is designed to gather the imponderables and make and prepare an imperishable body for the spirit. [5] The physical organisation contains all substances, forms and dynamics of matter, while the soul—or body of the spirit [6]—contains all essences, laws and forces of mind. The body contains the primates and the soul the ultimates of matter. They represent therefore the two sides of universal Nature. At the death of a man all that is not human in his body will return into the ocean of life; but the human or spiritual organisation, with its interior essence, will be claimed by and drawn to the spiritual sphere of existence, where it will be appointed an abode in the "house not made with hands." The soul is a super-corporeal organism, out of which inwrought essences and integral forces may enter into admirable and harmonious uses. It is the recipient of an inexhaustible fountain, springing up into everlasting life—the outer garment and permanent form surrounding the eternal spirit. The body does not make and concentrate the essence of which the spirit is composed, but—it is desirable to repeat—gives permanent form to the soul, or spiritual body, which encases the immortal image. The soul-structure which covers the spirit is the masterpiece of the physical organisation, even as the palpable and ponderable body is the masterpiece of organic matter. Nature reaches her end in the perfection of the psychical structure, and because it is not possible for any organisation to be better or higher than the human, this structure does not pass away. The things which pass are things which give place to others, but this is in the highest place and its substitute is not found. Furthermore, the elements which compose it are not elements of decomposition. The spirit within is incapable of organisation. [7] It has not been created and cannot be destroyed; and as the aromal body through which that imperishable and impersonal combination of principles expresses itself is made and perfected by this physical body which man now wears, he is every day and moment refining material for that body which he will wear eternally in the worlds beyond. All this wonderful preparation is accomplished by the water he drinks, the food he eats, the air he breathes, the thoughts he thinks and the works and deeds that he performs. [8] The cloth manufacturer procures appropriate materials with which to fashion his fabric, and the manufacturer of the psychical body procures the proper substances with which to build up the psychical constitution. Thus the body of the spirit is material and yet is unlike visible matter, being the last degree of material refinement.

To sum up, the term soul is used to express that fine, impalpable, almost immaterial body [9] which clothes the spirit from the moment of death to all eternity. The soul in this life is composed of all the magnetisms, electricities, forces and vital principles which—in more general terms—are called life, motion, sensation and instinct. The term spirit is used to signify the centre-most principle of man's existence, the divine energy, or life of the soul of Nature. In yet other language, soul is the life of the outer body and spirit is the life of the soul. After physical death the soul or life of the natural body becomes the form or body of the eternal spirit. Hence in the Second Sphere the spirit is surrounded by the physical imperfections of the soul. But the soul is ultimately purified by this spirit, which is king. [10] The soul is chemically related to the body by means of vital electricity, [11] and the spirit is chemically related to the soul by means of vital magnetism. Vital electricity belongs to the element of motion in the soul, and vital magnetism is an emanation of the soul, comparable to the aroma from the life of a rose. If a human being lives out the full measure of life then the vital electricity imperceptibly loosens its hold and dissolves the relation so gradually that the spirit is not even conscious of death until after the change is all over, like the birth of an infant into this world. [12] If, however, the change is forced and premature, the spirit is compelled to realise the fact and also something of the unnatural shock which occasioned death. In such cases there is often a temporary suspension of all sensation, a sleep which may continue for days in the other world. In such cases, moreover, the soul-body calls for further preparation before it can become the vehicle of the spirit. Hours and sometimes days are consumed in perfecting the work of this final organisation. While the beautiful process continues the spirit does not feel anything in the sensuous order, but is all intuition, memory, meditation, love. Its personality is not self-conscious [13] until the new senses in the new body are completed, opened and adapted to the use of the spirit. When, however, the death is natural—that is to say, is the result of old age—the spirit is immediately clothed with its new body, and there is neither sleep nor suspension of identity. But it should be understood that violent deaths signify only the confusion of a moment, and there is hence no reason to fear, e.g., destruction at the cannon's mouth. We should fear rather the moral disadvantages accruing from a struggle in which the inspiration of universal freedom is not at once the mainspring and the end in view.

[1] See Views of our Heavenly Home, pp. 179-184.
[2] This is specifically contradicted in other places and in terms which make any reconciliation impossible between the two statements. See pp. 134, 168, 200, 201 of the present work.
[3] Later on Davis had occasion to answer a correspondent who called his attention to the fact that this statement was in contradiction to the testimony of Swedenborg. Davis affirmed (1) that the perfect human form is an exact representative of the formative

principles which reside eternally in the spirit, and (2) that sex is one of those principles. He said also that during the subordinate stages of evolution these inherent principles clothe themselves in appropriate external organs with legitimate external functions. But when the individual rises into higher kingdoms of life, spiritual progress dominates the material, temporary parts, derived from our animal predecessors, and thus at last the most perfect form is reached as a spiritual ultimation.—Views of our Heavenly Home, p. 232. It seems to follow from these remarks that Davis reverses his former view, but he is meaning to maintain it. He misses the point also when he asks his correspondent whether the latter supposes that a man's teeth in the next world are made of lime. The question is not what they are made of but whether a spiritual body possesses teeth, and why a spiritual body should be devoid of sexual organs and yet have those which are dental. The difficulty of Davis is of course the difficulty of his subject. If we follow analogy by assuming that the spiritual body corresponds to the natural, being an object extended in space and having a spiritual trunk and extremities, that analogy calls on us to go further in the logic of its own position, and we are compelled to suppose something corresponding, e.g. to bowels, with functions belonging to these. But if we renounce the analogy we must have recourse to the purely metaphysical form of the soul, with all that follows in theology.

[4] The food of earth is, however, a matter of importance, because—as we shall see—it builds up the spiritual as well as the physical body. The consequences of tobacco and alcoholic habits are mentioned elsewhere in this connection, and it is affirmed that the spirit body is permeated therewith. The case of a paper-maker is supposed who assumes it to matter nothing what is put into the composition before his article is manufactured. The comment of Davis is that an artist cannot put any admixture of colours on his canvas, because a good picture requires good colours, and it is the same with the food of man. He is making a spiritual body from all he eats, drinks and even breathes.—Morning Lectures, pp. 326, 327. The illustrations offered have of course no ground of comparison with the lesson which it is sought to enforce.

[5] See The Great Harmonia, Vol. V, pp. 376, 377, 378, 382, etc.

[6] This distinction calls to be noted carefully as it constitutes an important difference between the psychology of The Principles of Nature and The Great Harmonia. The earlier work in no place recognises the soul as a psychic body enclosing an essence called spirit. On the contrary, not only does it use soul and spirit as interchangeable terms denoting the immortal essence, but points out specifically that it does. Subsequently there is no question that Davis reconsidered the classification as the result of dipping into one or other of the old theosophies. It is of course largely a question of words, because—as will be seen in an earlier part of the present work—Davis recognised from the beginning the existence of a spiritual body, which he now elects to term soul, confusing his previous terminology and most express distinctions.

[7] This also is entirely at issue with the speculations of The Principles of Nature. See in particular this chapter of the present work. It is at issue, moreover, with that sentence which follows next in the text above, for a spirit which is defined as a combination of principles is obviously a spirit organised. I have dealt sparingly with inconsistencies of this kind, though they abound everywhere. The reader will have understood long since that Davis not only began his intellectual and psychical life as a person imperfectly educated but he remained always a loose and inconsistent thinker, having an exceedingly ready flow of words, the strict sense of which he grasped in part only. His titles to con-

sideration are entirely of the psychic order, and he is to be judged by these, not as a thinker or philosopher and—as there is no need to say—not as a qualified writer on any matter of science, even the simplest.

[8] Had Davis been acquainted with the Eastern hypothesis of the thought body, he would have given a fuller consideration to the last two points. He would have seen that on his own showing the second and interior vesture of the soul is a body of desire, and that if its specific qualities are determined by the life on earth it is not by our food or drink but by all that which goes to make up our character—aspirations, tendencies, habits, thoughts, words and acts. I should add that the latter conception as a mere hypothetical possibility came into the mind of Davis, but he affirms categorically that man's spirit is clothed with a substantial form, having nothing to do with the ideas of which the life of the spirit is composed.—The Great Harmonia, Vol. V, p. 410.

[9] See Answers to Ever-Recurring Questions from the People, p. 20.

[10] Ibid., p. 49.

[11] Ibid., pp. 51-54.

[12] This psychic doctrine is in remarkable analogy with that of Eliphas Levi concerning the astral body—as developed in Le Dogme et Rituel de la Haute Magie. The point is interesting because the work of the French magus appeared in Paris about the same time that the Answers to Ever-Recurring Questions was published in America, so that one could not have drawn from the other.

[13] The meaning is that the reflex act of self-realisation does not take place, but the metaphysical position of the text will not bear examination.

Chapter Nine – The Spirit of Man

[1]

The First Cause of all things is spirit, and it is this also which is the ultimate in man. [2] Matter and motion establish the existence of a First Cause, while the truth that man is a spirit is proved not only by the law of progression and association but by the science of correspondences, in the light of which all sciences should be understood. It is by correspondential investigation that we are led to the universal relation between truths. The universal motion in Nature involves progression, and the whole evolution of the cosmos deposes thereto. So also the universal association in animate and inanimate things bears witness to a corresponding law in the unseen and the future. The truths which are seen are evidence of unseen truths. In the process of natural development every substance enters into the composition of vegetable and animal forms and is individualised in man. By such individualisation it becomes the future and corresponding principle, spirit—representing, in a second condition, the instrument of its individualisation. Matter contains the properties to produce man as a progressive ultimate, and motion contains the properties to produce life and sensation. These together, and perfectly organised, develop the principle of spirit, [3] not as a result of organisation but of a combination of all elements and properties of which the organisation is composed, the latter serving merely as an instrument. The principle of spirit existed eternally, emanating from the Fountain of Intelligence; but it could not be individualised and made manifest without a vessel like unto man. To analyse the principle itself would demand self-comprehension, which is beyond our scope, so long as research depends on material organisation. [4] In a more exalted sphere we shall be in a position to understand the composite existence of this world below. Did the human embryo possess intelligence it would require as much argument to prove its coming existence on the plane of earth as we demand now to convince us of future identity and existence in the spirit. The embryo would not attain perfect physical being, wanting the proper vehicles for development, and it is the same also with the spirit. The perfect development of the child within the body of its mother is the first epoch of physical existence, and in correspondence therewith is the first of spiritual life. From childhood to youth, from youth to manhood and thence to old age are other epochs through which passes our bodily life, and characteristic of these are successive stages of knowledge and experience, involving an accumulation of intellectual properties belonging to each individual. All these correspond to spiritual progression. As the former are developed in the visible form, so unfolds invisibly the principle of spiritual life. As the human embryo contains an essential principle which produces the perfect organisation of man, so is there a corresponding essence which produces spirit as its result.

The end—as already indicated—is that spirit should be individualised, to establish communion and sympathy between the Creator and the thing created. The spirit progresses to the Source from whence it came and so only is fitted for new spheres of eternal existence. The Cause of all things must produce ultimates corresponding with its own nature. If the First Cause be perfect so must be the end also. If the First Essence be progressive in its nature so must be also the ultimate. If the Primal Fountain be Supreme Intelligence it must produce intelligence as a result. If the Beginning be divinely pure so must the end be also. If the First be eternal, so also must be the final end. If the Intelligent Organiser of universal Nature contain within Himself all perfection of beauty and intelligence, beyond the comprehension of finite beings, must not that ultimate which is the spirit of man be in necessary harmony therewith, in specific essences and qualities? As offspring of the Great Father, must it not be pure and divine? If these things be so, then spirit, individualised through the instrumentality of Nature and Man, shall become like the Primitive Essence from which it derives, bearing the impress and containing the properties of its Source. It is from that which the First was and will again be that which the First is.

Matter and spirit have been regarded heretofore as distinct and independent substances, [5] but instead of this total disconnection the object of the foregoing remarks is to prove by acknowledged laws and principles of matter the mode which Nature follows in the development of intelligence, the perfection of which is spirit. It is further to trace the operations of life, movement and sensation from the Great Positive Mind through all intermediate things up to man, to show that in him the eternal principle of Spiritual Nature becomes individualised, the First working through physical Nature as a second to produce spirit as a third and grand result.

The germ of the immortal nature is spiritual, [6] and is detached from the deific ocean of spirit when the human foetus is within twelve weeks of birth. Every stage below or prior to that crisis represents the great animal department. The universal, divine, procreative force first organises the body by means of the governing or fashioning principle within the maternal nature. The grand use of the body is in gathering nervous forces and vital currents, moulding them into its own image and likeness. The ultimate result is the soul, philosophically speaking. It is an organised silver lining to the outer form, and serves—after death—as a beautiful body for the clothing of the golden spirit, which is still more interior and incapable of organisation. [7] The human soul cannot be organised perfectly without the two physical brains, and the impersonal spirit of the Infinite cannot be embodied unless the soul pre-exists, serving both as a magnet and matrix. [8] It follows that there is a period in the foetal formation and development when the spirit enters upon its individual existence. It is at or very near the close of the seventh month that the immortal part lifts up the unborn infant's mortality far above the animal kingdom.

The law of human birth has three stages as follows: (1) Deposition of the positive germ or masculine form of spiritual essences—as they exist in Nature below man; (2) Reaction of the negative spiritual forces on the feminine side, thus completing the circle in the formation of the spiritual body and precipitating the physical body by the operation of natural birth; (3) Deposition and unfoldment of the spirit-germ from this dual vitalic oneness. In other words, the positive side of the spiritual organisation, with its physical vesture, acts on the negative side of the spiritual organisation, with its physical vesture, thus depositing and unfolding the spirit-germ in the soul-substance, and the negative side, reacting, unfolds the organised individual spirit, [9] which is indestructible both in essence and form. As there is a point where minerals cease to be minerals [10] and become vegetable, and another crisis when the vegetable merges into the animal, so is there a critical juncture in the foetal development of the human brain when that receptacle is capable of attracting and detaching a portion of the Omnipresent Principle of God and of concentrating it in the germ state to unfold the immortal personality.

Material or so-called imponderable elements, [11] when perfectly attenuated and etherealised, become exquisitely volatile and forthwith begin to rise out of all visible substances. These elements form that part of man's mentality [12] which is termed very truly the spiritual body, or dress of the most interior and absolutely perfect essence—the spirit itself. The innermost of man is therefore a self-intelligent [13] and intercoherent emanation of eternal elements or ideas [14] from the universal ocean of Divine Love and Divine Wisdom. The first is feminine, the second is masculine, [15] and the two form in man—as they do everywhere—a perfect union. This unity is indissoluble and perfect—like the ingredients of which it is composed. In the progress of time therefore man himself may become perfect, "even as our Father Who is in heaven"—that is, he may become spiritual, free [16] and consciously true to the innermost and uppermost [17] of his being; no longer physical, in the sense of material abandonment, nor devoted, as some are, to the gratification of those avaricious wants which take their rise and multiply in the nerve-soul, between the bodily organisation and the central spirit-essence. It should be understood that temperament is phenomenal [18] and of those etherealised elements which enter into and elaborate the spirit's body, being the nerve-soul just mentioned. The physical body is elaborated, individualised and sustained by the intermediate spiritual organisation. [19] Each works for and upon the other, until the innermost is perfectly individualised and separated from the universal ocean of Divine Essences. [20] Then the nerve-soul takes the reins of government, controls heart and brain, the blood and nervo-muscular systems, retaining this distinction and mastery for years or centuries, or until the divine spirit-essence is permitted to ascend the throne and rule over the kingdom of heaven which is within us. But amidst these terms and philosophical discriminations let it be remembered always that man's spirit per se is an unparticled, indivisible, [21] self-attractive, inter-magnetic, perfect, unprogressive [22] essence, a treasury of ideas, [23] a lake separated from the universal ocean [24] of inter-intelligent principles. Be it also kept vividly in mind— as a rule of faith and practice all through this world—that although men differ widely and antagonise extensively in the realm of phenomena, there is in the deepest of each a fraternal or like essence, by virtue of which all strangers will one day become friends, all enemies eventual lovers, all slaves the peers of masters, all wanderers inmates of one home-world, "beyond the clouds and beyond the tomb."

[1] See The Principles of Nature, pp. 72, 74, 76, 79, 93 et seq., extracted and collated.
[2] It is not a simple indivisible essence, being derived from the ultimate ethers of all elements combined. It is therefore a combined essence, yet at the same time is indivisible in the sense of self-sustaining attractiveness. Moreover, no external essence can decompose it, for the marriage between its essences is harmonious and everlasting.—The Great Harmonia, Vol. V, p. 63. There is of course no relation between indivisibility as such and attractiveness. It is possible, however, that Davis refers here in his confused and confusing manner not to the interior and absolutely perfect essence, the spirit itself, but to the vesture or spiritual body thereof.—See Ibid., p. 74.
[3] The spiritual principle is defined elsewhere as a term employed in Harmonial Philosophy to designate that affectional and intelligent dynamical influence by which the human organisation is animated and governed.—Penetralia, p. 78. Both statements contradict the findings of the previous section.
[4] It is said, however, that the spiritual principle is compounded of infinitely refined essences, and that it cherishes more or less powerful affinities for the several imponderable elements from which it has derived in part its substance and individuality. It is an organised and indestructible substance, clothed by a transitory medium, which is in fact sensation. Ibid. The reference in this place is to the spiritual body, but sensation is also a term applied in the Harmonial Philosophy to an elementary principle of the immortal mind, being that presumably of which the spiritual body is the vehicle in the life to come. It does not appear that Davis gives any alternative or fuller explanation as to his use of the word.

[5] *A certain confusion arises, here and elsewhere, by an indeterminate use of the word substance. It might appear that in the present place, Davis seeks to affirm that there is only one noumenon behind phenomena, whether manifesting as matter or mind, as against those who say that there is a noumenal or substantial distinction between them. In other places he speaks of matter as if it were identical with substance, which philosophically is that concealed behind the material veils. Again it is looseness of phrasing, for his intention is really the reverse. He says otherwise—in illustration of this—that mind, essentially different from matter, is eternal; and so also is matter— essentially distinct from mind. In speaking of spirit as substance he explains his meaning to be that spirit is the absence of nonentity; that matter, after reaching its highest point of unparticled attenuation (sic), becomes a magnetism, of which the spirit takes hold, and the two are married together. The magnetism in question is called celestial, but material in the next sentence. The proof that spirit is a substance appears to be that it can move weight. The theological notion of spirit is mentioned in derisive terms, but substance is not per se an explanatory word, nor is the recurring use of that unfortunate word eternal, sometimes in an absolute and sometimes in an impermanent sense, otherwise than exceedingly confusing. Two absolute eternals, like two infinites exclude one another, and to postulate either stultifies the mind.*

[6] *See The Great Harmonia, Vol. V, pp. 386, 388.*

[7] *See the previous chapter of the present work.*

[8] *See the annotation later in this chapter. The previous section affirms that the soul or psychical body is manufactured gradually through the body of this world, and it does not therefore pre-exist. But if pre-existence is necessary the spirit does not enter humanity—at least fully—till after death. It is to be noted that an earlier volume of The Great Harmonia identifies soul and spirit not less expressly than The Principles of Nature. The alternative view seems to have been presented suddenly to the mind of Davis and also to have left him suddenly, for it scarcely recurs subsequently till the tripartite nature of man is discussed in several places of Answers to Ever-Recurring Questions.*

[9] *It will be observed that at this point Davis recurs to that which he has at first affirmed and then denied expressly, namely, the organic nature of spirit.*

[10] *This is an old doctrine of occult philosophy and is quoted in aphoristic form by Madame Blavatsky in Isis Unveiled.*

[11] *This and what follows to the end of the present section is drawn from The Great Harmonia, Vol. V, p. 74 et seq.*

[12] *See the annotation on p. 106 of this work. A spiritual body can be regarded as a part of our mentality only on the principle that it is a vesture which the mind makes, a thought-body, recognised—as already mentioned—by Eastern philosophy.*

[13] *We have to remember that the Divine Self-Intelligent Being is, by the Davis hypothesis, as according to greater theosophies, an ineffable and simple unity. As such it is incapable of division, of being split up indefinitely and of having its parts detached. If therefore man is self-intelligent—which in any real sense is denied elsewhere by Davis—his generation is of another order than that which appears above.*

[14] *The possible order is indicated unawares by this use of the word ideas. That which becomes incarnate in man, according to some higher theology—with which kabalistic theosophy agrees—is an eternally pre-existing prototype or idea in the mind of God, conceived in His own likeness and therefore self-conscious being.*

[15] This is the root-thesis of all Christian Mysticism—that the soul is feminine—whatever the sex may be of the physical body—and that it may become united with the Christ-spirit, conceived as masculine.

[16] The categorical definition of this possibility may be taken to check the attempted reduction by Davis of human liberty in The Principles of Nature, already noted.

[17] This is that apex of the soul recognised by Jan van Ruysbroeck and other mystics.

[18] This passage offers a curious commentary on the postulated immortality of the psychic vesture. Mutability is the characteristic of phenomena and permanence of that which is noumenal. Eastern Mysticism recognises successive vestures and final liberation from all.

[19] See the annotations on pp. 113 and 127.

[20] Compare the affirmation just previously made that man is self-intelligent, as if ab origine symboli, by virtue of something belonging essentially to him. It has been said also that he emanates or comes forth in a state of intercoherence, which—if it means anything—is a synonym for individuality.

[21] That which is "unparticled" or indivisible can add nothing to itself, and cannot therefore take on further individuality.

[22] That which is incapable of progression cannot grow in self-knowledge.

[23] That which is simple and indivisible cannot be a treasury of ideas: it can only embrace all things in a single notion, and this is what St. Thomas Aquinas postulated of the Divine Mind.

[24] If an ocean is universal no lake can be separated therefrom, and if such ocean—see ante—is one of Divine Essence, no finite essence can be separated therefrom to form the spirit of man. In that which is universal no room is found for anything but itself.

Book Four - Death and The After-Life

Chapter One - Immortality and The Life to Come

[1]

The uncultivated intuition of the human mind has inspired all races of men with a desire for the soul's endless existence and with an undefined belief therein. The decay of this instinctive faith, as reason begins to be exercised upon all themes of thought, is really a favourable prognostication, for it signifies that the clouds and dark forebodings which superstition has thrown over the speculations of the human mind concerning probable realities and possessions of the other world are to be consumed by the sunlight of a free and healthy philosophy of Nature's revelations, of the mysteries which pertain to the moral government of God and the treasures of the spiritual universe.

No substance, physical or intellectual, possesses the power of self-investigation or comprehension. [2] We can trace analogically grosser substances up to the formation of ourselves; thereafter we arrive at mind, intelligence, spirit; but though this is the principle which has enabled us to explore all below it, we find that it is vague and indefinite for us. There is hence (a) too much belief respecting this principle and its composition, or (b) too much disbelief—each being a natural consequence of a principle attempting to investigate itself. Having no means to arrive at a distinct knowledge of the essence of intelligence, [3] we must seek otherwise for proofs of continued identity after death, and to show why we are immortal. There is a belief of ignorance, a belief of desire, a belief of the understanding. The first is unsupported by adequate reasons and is derived from hereditary inclinations or doctrinal education. The second is instinctive or intuitive and arises from a central craving of the human mind. It is considered as a living prophecy of its eternal destiny, but it is grounded on no universal principles and has no substantial basis, save an inference derived from aspirations. The third is rooted upon unequivocal knowledge. It follows from the recognition and understanding of those immutable principles which flow from the Divine Cause into the universe. The influence of the first is to generate scepticism, and of the second to cause anxiety owing to the insufficiency of internal desires in respect of warrant. But the influence of the third is to promote happiness, because the believer can give a reason for the faith and hope within him and because he has a divine guarantee in the fact of individual existence.

The whole foundation is in the absolute indestructibility of matter, or of that universal substance which gives us tangible individuality and constitutes the outer physical organisation of the Great Positive Mind. Matter is eternal; it is in all things and is all things; there is nothing that is not matter or substance. Upon the universality and indestructibility of matter rests the reality of eternal life. We must interrogate Nature to ascertain how matter can constitute an individual and by what means that individual is rendered immortal. [4] She bids us consider the principles of association, progression and development, which laws indicate a perpetual tendency of all forms and substances toward unity, perfection and organisation. We see that mineral substances generate vivifying fluids—electricity, magnetism, etc.—and lose themselves in vegetable organisations. By a similar action the vegetable loses itself in the animal organisation, which emerges into that of man, who—as we have seen—never loses his identity in subordinate forms. We behold in this manner unmistakable evidence of association, progression and development of all matter toward a state of unity and individualisation—from the mineral up to man. All forms inferior and subordinate to man are but parts of him, whose brain receives the essence of that Divine Spirit which resides in and is extracted from all elements and substances, but especially those which administer to the nourishment of the body, to the gratification of its desires and senses. It concentrates, refines and elaborates this all-animating essence and dispenses it to the dependent system, according to the three modes of the essence—motion, life and sensation. It provides this essence with indestructible organisation and enables the interior organisation to manifest intelligence, both as to itself and external things. [5]

The physical organism of man is designed to elaborate the individuality of mind. The use of Nature is to individualise man and of man to individualise spirit. The spirit can preserve its identity apart from the body, because every organisation is absolutely different, and this fact precludes the possibility of absorption, amalgamation and disorganisation. The difference in the arrangement of inherent elements establishes the individual in this life and through all eternity. Were spirits constituted alike they would gravitate to one centre, but being constitutionally dissimilar they can neither be merged in one another nor lose themselves—as some have been led to suppose—in the Universal Spirit or Great Positive Mind.

There are three evidences that the soul will preserve its identity after the change called death: (1) It is designed that Nature should develop the body; (2) it is designed that the body should develop the mind; (3) it is designed that the mind should develop itself differently from other minds and should have life for ever. These are no hypothetical reasons, but testimonies and demonstrations drawn from Nature's own instructions. [6] As regards recollection of the past and reunion hereafter with those whom we have loved on earth, we have only to reflect on the connection which subsists between the first and second spheres of human existence. The relation is as intimate as that between youth and maturity, love and wisdom, perception and memory. The experience, character and progress of an individual in this life are recorded upon and—to a modified extent—will be manifested by that individual in the life to come, and the friend or companion who has impressed us with affection here will be remembered hereafter.

The passage from this sphere into the next is no more a change to the individual than a journey from America to England, excepting the almost complete emancipation—consequent upon the change—from rudimental misdirection and earthly imperfections. To the enlarged understanding there is no death—only the most important and delightful change in the mode of personal existence. And as we are immortal, while the memories of this life remain with us until displaced by others more spiritual, let us resolve henceforward to manifest a well-ordered life and a godly conversation.

[1] See The Great Harmonia, Vol. II, pp. 233 et seq.

[2] Compare The Principles of Nature, p. 630, where it is affirmed that the germ cannot understand its own qualities, but the perfect development can, because it is a higher and unfolded state of the qualities, and is therefore enabled to comprehend all that lies below its exalted state of being. Hence the human mind can comprehend that which is inferior to itself but not that which is above, nor yet its own nature and essence. The limitation is, however, in respect of our normal state; for Davis claimed that when he entered a higher sphere of thought and observation the soul ceased for him to be an indefinite and ambiguous consciousness, or—in other words—that in some form and some degree he was able to investigate and understand himself and others.

[3] It is really an old position of scholastic philosophy and was discussed fully by St. Thomas Aquinas, of whom Davis may never have heard and whom he could certainly not have read, knowing neither classical Latin nor that of the schools. According to St. Thomas, man realises himself in virtue of a reflective act, and so only, i.e., by becoming his own object or casting back upon himself. Self-consciousness is therefore attained by a reflective process, or—so to speak—at second hand, not immediately or by a direct act. This constituted for theology the eternal distinction between man and God, Who knows Himself directly and immediately. It would of course have denied that there was any psychic or interior state by which the human mind could pass into the condition of Divine self-knowledge.

[4] It is said otherwise that man's spiritual entity, unlike that of any inferior being, is the product of an indissoluble matrimonial alliance between all atoms of matter and all principles of mind. It is the ultimate form of all forces, the fruit of the universal tree, retaining the image and inheriting the immortality of its divine progenitors.— Penetralia, pp. 76, 77. The statement that matter is all things is obviously contradicted in other writings of Davis, but he was always apt to speak as the mood of the moment moved him.

[5] Notwithstanding certain distinctions already noted, the terms Soul, Spirit and Mind are—for the most part—used interchangeably by Davis to characterise the one animated and animating principle in man. See The Principles of Nature, p. 593. He states also specifically that Essence, Spirit, Soul and Interior Being are used by him as so many synonyms, signifying the form which animates the body, which body is an outward expression thereof.—Ibid., p. 641. This use of the term form is noteworthy, because it is that of Latin theology, for which—and especially for St. Thomas—the soul was the form of the body. See Dom Anscar Vonier, O.S.B.: The Human Soul and its Relation with other Spirits, pp. 81 et seq. It may be mentioned further that Davis, in yet another place, draws attention to the fact that he regards soul, spirit and mind as synonyms for our mental structure. See The Great Harmonia, Vol. IV, p. 29.

[6] There are others and indeed many in the collected writings of Davis: one of them is presented as follows: From the first fiat that was sent forth throughout the universe one law and order reigns, manifested in conception, progression and perfection. These mark all the work, and all point with the irresistible force of demonstration to the soul's immortality. The human species, as last and highest type on earth, as that which investigates all beneath and around it, as that which has consciousness of the future, endeavours to raise the veil between physical and spiritual existence; and analogy—reasoning from what we know—points directly not only to the probability but certainty and necessity of a future existence—in short and finally to the Summer Land. All organic forms below man not only produce their like but the substances of their material forms mingle with other compounds to evolve new types superior to themselves. But the human type has no superior development and is destined therefore to unfold further in other and higher spheres, presenting not only an image and likeness of Nature and God but a consciousness of identity and individual self-hood.—Morning Lectures, pp. 65-67.

Chapter Two - Evidences of Immortality

[1]

Men have made little progress in knowledge of life and immortality, though looking through the history of Egypt, Greece, Rome and all Anglo-Saxon annals we may discover a slow increase in the number of evidences. Spiritualism was known to the most ancient races, to the Indians of East and West. While whole races have rested solely on external sources of knowledge concerning immortality, as soon as intellect gains predominance, and conscience is liberated from the thraldom of prejudice, the externally convinced mind begins to reconsider these evidences—for the most part with scepticism as a first result. If it be asked how much positive intellectual evidence we have on the question of immortality we shall be surprised at the small amount. [2] What appears to be positive and conclusive turns out inferential and uncertain. Natural religion suggests that there is an adequate supply for all the needs of man and infers herefrom that as the soul demands immortality it will not be deprived thereof. But there is the sceptic's question whether this demand is innate and natural or acquired and artificial. Clairvoyance itself is at best but an inferential evidence because it is not a matter of universal human experience. As much may be said respecting spiritual manifestations: they are local, special and mostly private, albeit those who have received such evidence can affirm that immortality is proved. Now, it is possible for every man and woman, after coming under spirit culture, to feel through all their being the sublime truth that the perfected human soul can never be extinguished, but the evidences which are worth anything are not outside. Man's immortality, to be of any practical service, must be felt in his religious nature, not merely understood by his intellectual faculties. True evidences come through the two inward sources of wisdom—intuition and reflection. Those who dare to be truthful to inward sources of knowledge will feel positive evidences of immortality, and by such the manifestations of Spiritualism will not be sought as evidences but as illustrations only. The manifestations—as to their variety—will gradually retire from the world, but now—as then—we must look within for that principle which causes all effects in the external. When you find an internal conviction of immortality which no sophistry can invalidate you have found a treasure: secure this, then add the illustrations.

The other world is as natural, astronomically considered, as the globe which we now inhabit. The Spirit Land has laws, days, nights, stars, suns, firmaments. In that world are treasured up, not the artificial facts of earthly society but all elementary facts of mankind. Begin with the stones at your feet, and see them ascend through all gradations of refinement, till they become a physical part of the vast second sphere. The finest particles of all things not absorbed by this world go to form a spiritual globe. [3] The existence of such a world is not less demonstrable than any proposition in astronomical science. It requires only an intellectual ascension, step by step, through the material evidences that lead thereto. Mind can be brought to see that there is a spiritual world as readily as that earth revolves—a fact of which men have no ocular demonstration. There are also facts in Nature which astronomy explains by laws of planetary revolution, and you accept this explanation because it covers those facts adequately. So also there are facts in human experience which cannot be solved on any hypothesis save that which affirms the existence of spiritual globes. The phenomena of human consciousness, the spiritual experiences of all races can be explained only on principles which lead inferentially, yet positively, to the existence of such worlds.

The interior clairvoyant senses can gaze upon higher worlds and reveal others within that sphere where we now dwell. These senses address man's inward sources of knowledge, speaking to his intuition and reason. As microscopic and telescopic worlds are hidden from the penetration of corporeal sense, so are concealed the magnificences of the spiritual universe, the kindling skies and indescribable beauties of eternal spheres. But all these worlds are visible to the interior senses. Men and things, planets and angels, future states and vital laws of the Father God—all appear in that consistent order and with that philosophical precision which distinguish truth from the chaos of mythic theology. To the interior senses the changes of Mother Nature are indications of the ceaseless operations of principles which are themselves unchanging—steps from lower to higher, from matter to spirit. A birth, a fleeting existence, a death—these are manifestations of the beautiful laws of progression and development. When the fair foliage with which summer adorns forests, when flowers which garnish earth are changed by the breath of rude autumnal winds, when rose and violet shed their leaves, the philosophical heart is not saddened. These things mean that a brief period of rest has arrived, preparatory to the resurrection of kindred elements, when Mother Nature's domain will be decked again with foliage and beautiful garlands. [4]

The true philosopher sees a form of internal truth—which is full of unfailing consolation—in every outward process and every object. The sun disappears behind the western hills and a dark curtain is drawn over the earth; but darkness reveals stars. Robed in garments of essential light, these royal orbs are visible only when the sun is unseen. The clouds indeed may conceal the distant spheres ever and again, a gloom may settle upon our minds and dreamy slumber may succeed it; yet—ere we are awake—the sun has risen in the East, tingeing the distant clouds with auroral splendour, converting weeping dews into rays of golden light, bathing mountains and valleys, gardens and fields of Mother Nature, with fresher and lovelier radiance.

It is no part of the Harmonial Philosophy to depend solely on outward evidence—perception and testimony; on the contrary, its students are referred to the fixed principles of universal Nature. Now, the physical organisation of man is designed by the system of Nature to manufacture the form and structure of the spiritual principle—or, in other words, man's spirit is a product of his organisation. [5] Man's body is the fruition of all organic Nature, and the spirit body is formed by the outer body. The physical body is the focal concentration of all substances; the spirit is the organic combination of all forces. The representation of every particle of matter is ultimately made by man. The body of the spirit is a result brought out by the physical organisation. I do not mean that the spirit is created but that its structure is formed by means of the external body. Mind itself is not a creation or ultimation of matter, but mental organisation is a result of material refinement. The use of a physical bone is to make a spiritual bone, of the physical muscle to make a spiritual muscle [6] —not the essence but the form. The use of the cerebrum is to make a spiritual front brain out of the cerebellum or spiritual back brain. Inside the visible spine is the spiritual spine invisible. The physical ear is animated by a spiritual ear. In a word, the whole outward body is a representation of that which is imperishable. Mind, essentially different from matter, is eternal, and so also is matter, essentially distinct from mind. [7] These principles, as male and female, live in unchangeable wedlock: one is what I term Father God, the other is Mother Nature. Matter, on reaching its highest point of unparticled attenuation, becomes a celestial magnetism. The spiritual essence takes hold of this material magnetism; the two are married, and a succession of elaborations commences until the whole spiritual structure is completed.

Spirit is substance and, although not unlike matter, it obeys a law higher than gravitation. Every person's experience is a complete demonstration that spirit is a substance, because in each of us it moves the body from place to place. It can even move without thinking, because the hidden spirit-principle is composed of all vital forces. Man's spirit demonstrates its own substantiality by means of its own normal manifestations. Although the spirit of man has substance and weight, has elasticity, divisibility [8] and the several ultimate qualifications and properties of matter; yet—as just indicated—it obeys laws which are superior to ordinary gravitation and the known physical forces. The proof is that man's being is duplex. He has two eyes, two brains, two hands, two feet, two sides to the lungs; the human heart is double, and so is each part of the system. The double visible structures come from dual invisible principles, and these are male and female. They operate reciprocally and regulate all action, all animation. One contracts, the other expands. These principles together form a unit, imparting one action to the twofold system. Water has weight and in consequence runs downhill; but in man's body water runs uphill. The heart is constantly sending blood to the brain. The visible heart performs this function because there is a corresponding spiritual heart within it. The spirit, unlike inanimate bodies, operates upon a positive and negative principle, by virtue of which the spirit holds up the body and the body holds up the spirit. [9] If the spirit's organism is substance, then— as substance—it weighs something. When it escapes the material body, the spiritual body does not weigh more than the sixteenth of a pound, but it continues to absorb the elements of the invisible air until it becomes comparatively weighty, acquiring not only a power of gravitation but also a power to overcome it. [10]

[1] See the work entitled Penetralia, containing Harmonial Answers.
[2] The question of conditional immortality is touched upon in one place; we hear of the "quadruped brain" of some in human form, and that it knows nothing about immortality. In this connection it is said that some eat and sleep for ever, and further that, not having the innate desire, such persons lose nothing by ultimate extinction. Above this class no human being is destitute of the rudiments of immortality. Only a small percentage of primeval races seem to have had personal immortality; but the reference appears to be to certain hypothetical sub-human beings between the beast and man.— The Great Harmonia, Vol. V, pp. 386, 387, 395. Another testimony affirms that some few of every race are not born on the human side of organisation and will not be immortal unless they are cultivated on the spiritual side of their nature.—The Present Age and Inner Life, p. 410.
[3] Around us float the burning orbs of our beautiful solar system. First appears the maternal and paternal Sun; next the infant Mercury; then the graceful Venus; next the dutiful earth; Mars rolls gloriously beyond; the family of Asteroids skirts his mighty pathway; but larger and grander than all their brothers are rainbow-tinted Jupiter and golden-browed Saturn. Nor are these all, for Herschel in the great distance compasses his vast empire of space; Neptune trembles on the threshold of infinity; while farther still other worlds sweep through immensity in their tireless paths. This stupendous system of planetary bodies is perpetually elaborating and giving harmonial proportions to another and higher system, which is spiritual.—The Great Harmonia, Vol. V, pp. 410, 411. As regards the term spiritual, Davis explains that it is used to represent a finer state of material elements—e.g. water is finer and more spiritual than stone.—Ibid.
[4] There is a prolonged debate on the law of immortality at the close of The Great Harmonia, the for and against being given from several points of view. According to one of them, nothing is more susceptible of unequivocal demonstration than the extreme antiquity and universality of belief in immortality, and the question is whether a faith so venerable can be an error. It is of course familiar ground, and so is the counterview presented by Davis.—Op. cit., Vol. V, p. 295.
[5] Compare The Great Harmonia, Vol. V, p. 75, already quoted: The physical body is elaborated and individualised and sustained by the intermediate spiritual organisation. Obviously, this is an allusion to the spiritual body, of which the opposite is affirmed otherwise in the text above and also on p. 115 of the present work. The statement that spirit is a product of organisation is not less categorically reversed elsewhere.
[6] And therefore of a physical organ of generation to make one that is spiritual, which, however—as we have seen—forms no part of the body spiritual of man.
[7] Compare Ch. 1, Bk 1.

[8] The reader will do well to compare this remark with the more categorical counter-statement earlier in the present work. The question is not worth debating intrinsically, but the contradiction serves a purpose by illustrating the flux of opinion or perhaps more correctly of mental sentiment in the mind of Davis.

[9] In at least one place Davis dwells upon an inward realisation of immortality, which is said to flow through our spiritual consciousness like a stream of prophecy. It is an intuitive faith, which transcends mere reason, science and philosophy.—The Great Harmonia, Vol. V, p. 295.

[10] Arguments in favour of immortality are naturally recurring characteristics of Davis in most of his writings, and having regard to the possibility of things in the present digest it is perhaps fortunate that they overlap one another when they do not reproduce each other. It should be understood that I am speaking here of arguments apart from revelations, by which his visions are signified. As a general conclusion to his debates, it may be mentioned that—according to Davis—the soul's immortality is to be counted among the highest truths developed by the Harmonial Philosophy, whereas the Christian world can furnish no invulnerable argument that the human spirit will survive the ordeal of physical dissolution. Harmonial Philosophy brings evidences of man's eternal individuality out of the very rocks and mountains of Nature, out of the laws, forces and characterisations of vegetables and animals, rendering the problems of the future as certain of solution as the results of mathematical calculation.—The Present Age and the Inner Life, pp. 53, 54.

Chapter Three - The Philosophy of Death

[1]

"There is," according to Paul, "a natural body, and there is a spiritual body," speaking in both cases of things that now are. But if there is a spiritual body there is something inside that body. It is designed to hold something called spirit. Man is a triple organisation, (1) His external body is a casing, composed of the aggregate refinements of gross substances. (2) There is an intermediate organisation composed of finer substances, the ultimation of those coarser elements which make up the corporeal body. This intermediate is the spiritual body of Paul. (3) Within this spiritual body is the immortal image, the spirit, the super-essential portion of man's nature, composed of "impersonal principles," flowing from the Deific Centre of this glorious universe. Now a body is a substance, [2] and substance implies the associate properties of weight and force. Such a body must exist somewhere and occupy space, and if it occupy space then all our proposed revelations concerning a Summer Land in the bosom of space lie within the field of probability. Finally, that which is in space must follow the laws of space, including time. Spiritual doctrine teaches that the inmost man is a spirit which flows through our nerve-sensations; which contracts and expands muscles; which causes blood to circulate through the frame; which thinks and reasons, feels better, nobler, purer than forms, forces and things about it; [3] which teaches intellect and heart to recognise something higher than the fleeting circumstances where-unto it is harnessed. It is the invisible presence of the Divine in the visible human. It is the only and all-sufficient incarnation. Degradations and depravities never reach that which lives within the spiritual body. Discords and evils are arrested at the surface: they never get far enough inward to kill the proprietor.

Thoughts associated with the process of dying [4] and with the state of death are dark, doubtful and disconsoling to some minds, while death seems to others a welcome state, productive of peace, blessing, elevation. In a degree it is terrifying to all, whether brave or timid, wise or foolish, old or young. Here now is the philosophy of the great subject. [5] So soon as the human organisation is perfected in form and development, so soon as that period has arrived when spirit exercises its full control over the body, a process of transformation begins. The change is imperceptible, yet progressive and incessant. The body is not in course of dying for a few hours only, but for many years, during which time the faculties and powers of the inner being gradually release their proprietorship over the form, and the soul aspires toward the superior spheres.

When the form is yet in its childhood there are manifested all the angular, eccentric and irregular traits of character, inclination and movement. When childhood advances to youth eccentricity gives way to uniformity, and a circular mode is displayed in form characteristics. When youth attains manhood the perfect circular and spiral make their appearance and are displayed in the characteristics and inclinations of that stage of development. It is at this period that the process of dying or of transformation commences. The spirit is continually expanding its faculties and putting them forth as feelers into higher spheres. The tendencies of the spirit are no longer downward but upward, and this indeed to an extent beyond the power of language to express or of intellect to comprehend. As manhood progresses to old age the body becomes gradually incapable of performing the office required by the spirit, and all faculties seem buried beneath effete materials. One after another they withdraw from the material form. The body, finally, is almost disconnected from the spirit. It becomes a dweller in the rudimental sphere, while the spirit is in the world of spirit, the inner life.

Paul says that there is a terrestrial and celestial, that we are sown in corruption, sown in dishonour, but raised in glory—a familiar word which means brightness. At last the chemistry of actual death approaches and begins its work. [6] All things that make up our corporeal existence bid good-bye to each other. The pulseless hand is extended no longer; the once beaming eyes do not open; the ear vibrates no longer to appeals or loving accents. All is closed for ever. But a blessed, roseate atmosphere fills the heavenly spaces, from the death-room onward to summer realms beyond the stars. [7] About all this I will tell you what I have seen, who have stood by the side of many death-beds. A description of manifestations in one case will, however, suffice for the whole.

A human being lies on the bed of death, and is indeed actually dying. It is to be a rapid death. The physical body grows negative and cold, in proportion as the elements of the spiritual body become warm and positive. The feet become cold first. The clairvoyant sees right over the head what may be called a magnetic halo—an ethereal emanation, golden in appearance and throbbing as though conscious. Now the body is cold up to the knees and elbows. The legs are then cold to the hips and the arms to the shoulders. The emanation is more expanded, though it has not risen higher in the room. The death-coldness steals over the breast and around on either side. The emanation has attained a position nearer the ceiling. The person has ceased to breathe, the pulse is still. The emanation is elongated and fashioned in the outline of the human form. It is connected beneath with the brain. The head of the person throbs internally—a slow, deep throb, not painful, but like the beat of the sea. The thinking faculties are rational, while nearly every part of the person is dead. The golden emanation is connected with the brain by a very fine life-thread. On the body of the emanation there appears something white and shining, like a human head; next comes a faint outline of the face divine; the fair neck and beautiful shoulders manifest, and then in rapid succession all parts of the new body down to the feet—a bright shining image, somewhat smaller than the physical but a perfect prototype in all except disfigurements. The fine life-thread continues attached to the old brain. The next thing is the withdrawal of this electrical principle. When the thread snaps the spiritual body is free and is prepared to accompany its guardians to the Summer Land. [8] Yes, there is a spiritual body: it is sown in dishonour and raised in brightness.

The newly arisen spiritual body moves off toward a thread of magnetic light which has penetrated the room. It touches the spiritual body near the head. It is a chain of love-light sent from above as a guiding power. The spiritual being is asleep, like a new-born happy babe; the eyes are closed and there seems no consciousness of existence. The sleep is long in many cases but not in all. The love-thread draws the body to the outside door, or some other means of egress, which someone has been impressed to open. The spiritual body is removed silently from the house. The thread of celestial attraction gathers about and draws it obliquely through forty-five miles of air. It is surrounded by a beautiful assemblage of guardian friends. They throw their loving arms about the sleeping one and speed to the world of light.

It is to be concluded therefore [9] that we have every reason to rest and be happy with regard to life and death, for the laws of Nature are unchangeable and complete in their operations. If we understand these laws and obey them here on earth, it is positively certain that our passage from this sphere and our entrance into the spirit-country will be as a sleep and an awakening—an emergence into a more congenial and harmonious world. So is there nothing to fear, and so is there much to love in a purely natural or non-accidental death. Let us lament no longer because of the mere departure of an individual from our earth. Though cold and cheerless to material senses, to interior vision and the ascending spirit, the change is bathed in auroral splendour. Let tranquillity reign in the chambers of the dying, for when a body dies on earth a soul is born in heaven. There is nothing lost by putting off mortality and leaving things evanescent for immortal beauties in the Spirit Land.

The voices from that Land may seem like revelations of fancy; but the time is dawning when many shall hear and comprehend the mighty truths their tones impart. Thereafter, at the hour of death and in the chamber of the departed, there will be sweet and solemn music in place of weeping, a quiet and holy passover.

[1] See the work entitled Death and the After-Life, Section I.

[2] It is to be observed that this is a popular use of the term substance, at once loose and incorrect, as the etymology of the word shows. Philosophically, substance is that which stands behind or underlies the manifest appearance of things, and to say that it is ponderable is to confuse all the issues.

[3] Compare The Great Harmonia, Vol. I, pp. 135, 136: The human soul possesses varied passions, impulses, desires, attractions, intellectual endowments—all of which render it capable of harmonious and endless expansion. But these attributes lay it open also to inexpressible misery. If its chords are touched unkindly the instrument cannot but respond to the same tones, and then the vibrations of the spirit bear fearfully on the body.

[4] See The Principles of Nature, pp. 643 et seq.

[5] It is expressed in an axiom as follows: The philosophy of death is the philosophy of change. It is not, however, change in the constitution or personality of the individual, but of situation only—meaning that whereas it abode formerly in an earthly body, it inhabits henceforward a spiritual organisation, in virtue of which it becomes fitted for higher associations.—The Great Harmonia, Vol. I, p. 157.

[6] The body should not be deposited in the earth until after decomposition has positively commenced. Sometimes the umbilical life-cord is not severed, but is drawn out into the finest possible medium of sympathetic connection between the body and the spirit.—Ibid., p. 168.

[7] It is laid down, in another place, as a law of Nature that every true and spontaneous change is attended with improvement in the condition and constitution of the thing which is changed. So is man's death to the outer world a change of importance, both as to place and state. Death is a birth into a new and more perfect existence. ... It is a triumphal arch, through which the spirit passes into a more magnificent country. There is nothing more painful or repulsive in the natural process of dying—being that which is not brought about by disease or accident—than there is in passing into pleasant and dreamless slumber.—The Great Harmonia, Vol. I, pp. 159, 163.

[8] Davis—as we have seen—was the witness of more than one transition, and the following alternative case will serve to illustrate the fact that as no two deaths are exactly alike on the physical and visible side, so all exhibit characteristic variations in the departure of the soul, as this is beheld in the psychic state. So soon as the spirit was disengaged altogether from the physical body, the spirit began to breathe the most interior or spiritual portions of the surrounding terrestrial atmosphere—at first with difficulty, then with ease and delight. ... I saw that she was in possession of exterior and physical proportions identical with those which characterised her earthly organisation, but improved and beautified. She had a heart, stomach, liver, lungs, etc., as her natural body had, previous to its death. The improvements in her spiritual organism were not so thorough as to destroy or transcend her personality, nor did they materially alter her earthly characteristics. I saw her conform and accustom herself to the new and elevating sensations which belong to the inner life. I remarked her philosophic tranquillity throughout the entire process and her non-participation in the unrestrained lamentation for her departure by the different members of her family. The period required to accomplish the entire change was not far from two hours and a half; but there is no

rule as to time in this respect. When accustomed to the new elements by which she was encompassed, she descended from an elevated position above the body, passed out of the bedroom door—all doors being open because it was a summer month—then through an adjoining room, and so into the open air. She walked in the atmosphere as easily, and in the same manner, as we tread upon the earth. On emerging from the house she was joined by two friendly spirits, and after recognising tenderly and communing one with another the three began to ascend obliquely through the ethereal envelope of our globe. I continued to gaze until distance shut them from my view. There was a great contrast when—on returning to my normal condition—I beheld only the lifeless deserted organism, instead of that beautiful unfolded spirit.—The Great Harmonia, Vol. I, pp. 169-172. It will be seen that this personality was possessed of those viscera which are denied elsewhere to the psychic body.
[9] Ibid., pp. 189 et seq.

Chapter Four - The Seven Spheres of The Spirit
[1]

The structure of the universe and all its living beauties, together with the Divine Essence that gives it life and animation, presents an indestructible basis of hope and faith, and a corresponding foundation of human action. It is as a mirror in which are reflected all corresponding beauties yet uncreated, but proved to be in embryo by the universal teachings of natural law. The whole is as one body, and God the Soul and Father of all living and unliving things. Everything is perfect in its way and state of being; everything is necessary; everything is pure, even celestial and divine; everything teaches harmony and reciprocity by an unfailing manifestation of the same. Everything is of, in, through and unto the Divine Mind; all things are parts of Him, as of one whole—even Nature, Man and Heaven. [2] The earths, or the First Sphere, constitute the germ; the Second Sphere is the roots; the Third, the body; the Fourth, the branches; the Fifth, the buds; the Sixth, the blossoms; and the Seventh Sphere is Beauty, blooming with an immortal fragrance. Here is the Tree of Righteousness, wherein is nothing wrong. It is the Tree of Goodness, because nothing is evil. It is the Tree of Immortal Life, because there is no death. It is the Tree of Divine Perfection, because nothing is imperfect. It is the Tree of Truth, because there is no falsehood in the Divine Creations. It is the Tree of Eternal Causation, because there is nothing which was not previously in another form. It is the Tree of Love and Wisdom, because there is no confusion or disunity; all things are working together for good, which is the elevation of all that is low and undeveloped to a high degree of refinement, from which a universe yet unborn will be ushered into being.

The First Sphere is that of the natural world, the habitable earths of the planets, the circle of manifested things. The Second or Spiritual Sphere contains all the beauties of the first, combined and perfected. [3] Every earth is therefore an index and introduction to the beauty and grandeur existing in the Second Sphere. From the natural is the spiritual unfolded, or made manifest. The surface of the

Second Sphere presents regular undulations and great fertile plains. Therein reigns the most perfect order: it is a place of gardens, typical of purity, unity and celestial love. All flowers and leaves are as so many voices proclaiming the beauty of interior perfection and the Infinite Source from which they sprang. Clear and placid rivers flow through these gardens, and therein also are exemplified the ceaseless flowings of love and wisdom, the light and life of all created things. There are also groves of the most charming and enchanting character, and it is impossible to behold these and not be impressed with new and beautiful thoughts.

In the Second Sphere there are three distinct societies of men and women, each occupying a position determined by their degree of cultivation, sympathy one for another and power of approaching each other's sphere of knowledge and attainment. The first is in love, the second is in will and the third is in wisdom. These societies are composed of families, groups and associations; but all are as one brotherhood. Their numbers transcend computation. Most of the inhabitants of Mercury, Venus, the Earth and Mars are dwelling in the first society of the Second Sphere: those of the other planets occupy higher positions in the plane of thought and wisdom. A holy quietness pervades the whole spirit-world, and there is happiness of the most inexpressible character—ecstasies, exultations, glorifications, ascending continually. Such is the Second Sphere of human existence. The relation between it and the earths may be perceived by the similitude of external manifestations—these differing only in degrees of purity and development. It is proper and advantageous that the human race should know and appreciate these truths, that they may be induced to press onward and upward in the ascending scale of progress toward the Great Fount of Love and Happiness.

Inasmuch as on the various earths there are born several millions of spirits in one second of time, from which fact there must follow of necessity as many deaths, so an equal number are being introduced at every second into the Spiritual Sphere. In like manner there is an equal rate of transition from the Second Sphere [4] into the Third, which is the Celestial Sphere. But the darkness incident thereunto is light, and the death is life inconceivable—a transition contemplated with delight that surpasses all human speech. In this Sphere also there are three distinct societies, corresponding to perfected love, perfected wisdom and celestial purity. The first society is composed of those whose last stage of being was in the third society of the Sphere below. They have love, will and wisdom combined to a degree of perfection that surpasses earthly thought. Those of the second are still more advanced and so perfectly conjoined with one another that it requires a high degree of discernment to make a distinction between them. Those of the third society are so exceedingly pure that subordinate spirits are repelled with an innate consciousness of non-association. They are guardian angels to those below them. To one another they impart knowledge and express love, as the sun imparts life and beauty to forms on earth. But the nature of this sphere is entirely above the comprehension of the human race here and now, and what has been said concerning it is but a particle compared with all that is and shall remain untold.

In the Fourth or Supernatural Sphere the inhabitants are of the most exquisite purity and loveliness, and with one united voice—not of speech but of action—they proclaim glory, honour, immortality, eternal life. As they proceed toward the City of the Living God, they illuminate the vestibule of truth and the archway leading thereto. They penetrate all below them with holy influences of wisdom and simple love. They call on all to come away and ascend with them to the Fount of Purity on high. In this Sphere are also three societies and three distinct degrees of love, will and wisdom—each association being unfolded from that immediately below. Viewed from this exalted realm, the dwellers in the Third Sphere appear as beings undeveloped. The first society is almost infinite in numbers, and from them flows spontaneously an element of love that is clearer than clearest water, brighter than brightest crystal. Its reflection clothes the higher societies with a garment of whiteness, pure as the jewels that adorn the crown of the King of kings and Lord of lords. From the second society flows a constant stream of passive and active will, subject at all times to life-giving promptings of love and receiving the high approbations of wisdom. This is constantly ascending and descending. It is also like a great receptacle in which are deposited the choicest thoughts and memories of the angels and spirits of this exalted Sphere. Again it is like a treasury, the contents of which are open to the lower angels, who extract beautiful thoughts from its depths and meditate thereupon. The atmosphere of this Spirit Home is clothed with resplendent brightness, such as reflects the goodness of all things and the use to which they are applied. It is a mirror in which are represented the living beauties of heaven and earth. Such is the loveliness, goodness and wisdom of the Divine Mind that nothing is made in vain, but everything is as a living thought, representative of perfect wisdom. In the Supernatural Sphere this truth is especially manifested.

Inasmuch as life is universal, death cannot mar the constitution of things. By virtue hereof the dwellers in the Fourth Sphere—like those of others—remain for a moment in silence and awake as beings of the Fifth or Superspiritual Sphere. The spirits here are so lovely and attractive that it requires an effort to prevent being—as it were—absorbed into and becoming part of them. As in the Third and Fourth Spheres, the first society is a child of that which is highest in the Sphere below. Love appears as the perfection of wisdom, which wisdom is greater than all the combined love and wisdom described heretofore. As the Spheres approach the Divine Mind they become more simple, more unassuming and pure. So also the nearer that they draw to the Fount of Purity the more transparent they become, and the more do their inhabitants appear to exist—as it were—without external and artificial habiliments. There is an exhalation from each society which forms a halo of glory, surpassing all brightness of the material sun, or any brilliance that illuminates the material universe. Each spirit seems so pure—and the thoughts of all are so celestial—that it is almost impossible to resist the attraction thus presented. There is such a commingling of thoughts and such an affection manifested one for another as seems beyond all captivations imaginable. Every mind is like an opening flower, and every thought is like the fragrance thereof. Their wisdom is as the fountains of heaven which flow to all that thirst, which heal all that are wounded and cleanse all that are not purified. This wisdom is in every thought and movement, in every expression of will and love. But the Fifth Sphere is allied so closely to the Spiritual Sun that it is incomprehensible to dwellers on earth.

By the same manner of transition which obtains below, the spirits of the Fifth ascend to the Sixth Sphere or Supercelestial Habitation. [5] It is the great ultimate of beauty, the crown of loveliness and purity, all goodness and all refinement. Here are the fields of Paradise, and here is erected the House of Many Mansions. Its exterior beauty, grandeur and magnificence show that it was not made by hands but is eternal in the heavens. It is that asylum where all are taken in, loved, breathed upon and made perfect. Every created spirit is invited to this home by the progressive law of the Father. In the Supercelestial Sphere are all beauties of earth and heaven combined, developed and perfected. It is thus removed from human comprehension. Here spirits and angels rejoice with exceeding joy and thanksgiving, but by action and not by speech, by wisdom, not by love. Still love is the all-animating and life-giving element.

The Seventh Sphere is the Infinite Vortex of love and wisdom and the Great Spiritual Sun of the Divine Mind which illuminates the spiritual worlds. Of the body and constitution of the material sun the Univercoelum was brought into being; from the constitution of the Spiritual Sun all the heavens were created; and by it they are sustained, purified and illuminated. [6] Every spontaneous breath of light and love is as a smile of the all-pervading Father and Creator. Thus the spiritual spheres are allied to the Spiritual Sun and the natural spheres to that sun which is material. [7] The spiritual is as a soul and yet a garment to the natural, while the two are joined together as one creation. The Spiritual Sun is an inexhaustible vortex of life and light, which are love, and of order and form, which are wisdom: everything is breathed into being thereby. The great centre is the habitation and throne of the Divine Mind—that Central Positive Power of the universe.

The diagram which illustrates the text will furnish a concrete notion of the Seven Spheres. [8] Let the reader imagine that he is looking on the plane of an immense globe divided through the centre, like an apple cut into halves. The dark margin is the ocean of unorganised matter, in a state of fire-mist or elemental nebulas, between which and the first or outermost circle of suns and planets there are innumerable incipient bodies called comets. The sun and planets of our own system are one group in the first circle—at the right hand and near the bottom of the diagram. In the centre of all is the Seat of Intelligence, the Fountain of Love and Wisdom. The Divine Sun which encircles this sensorium gives off emanations of life and light which energise the whole system of the universe. It attracts spirit and repels matter, according to that law by which rare and dense substances are governed. Experiencing the Divine Attraction in harmony with this law, human spirits leave earth at death and go to the Second Sphere. After many centuries they have progressed sufficiently to ascend into the Third Sphere. But the Central Attraction continues to draw lovingly and tenderly until the spirits of all men reach the Sixth Sphere, which is the closest possible approach to the Spiritual Sun of the Univercoelum.

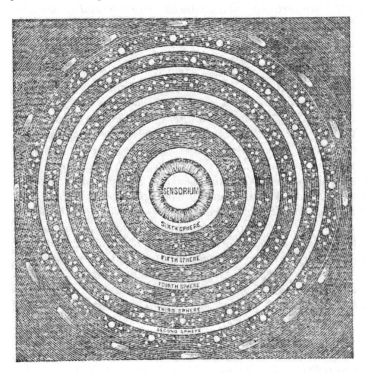

The Seven Spheres of the Spirit are the Tree whose foundation rests in the depths of time and whose top extends to the heights of eternity. It puts forth branches throughout the length and breadth of the universe, casting a refreshing shade over those labyrinths of space whose limits no thought can define. The root or germ of this Tree is in the First Sphere, which comprehends all earths and their inhabitants. Knowing this, let every one strive diligently to cultivate the germ and make its unfoldings perfect; to give its properties and essences a truthful direction; to put forth love, energy and wisdom for the realisation of that which is most desirable, being the development of those principles found in the nature of man and prompting him to profitable action. The keynote of all is unity, and unity is happiness. In view of these things the truth and importance are manifested of that saying, according to which "the things which are seen are temporal; but the things which are not seen are eternal." So also the things that are visible are terrestrial, while the things that are invisible are heavenly. While these truths present themselves in bold relief, the human mind should put forth efforts to comprehend their meaning and importance. It will be discovered in so doing that the mind must be refined and perfected. When this is accomplished the social world will be elevated to honour, goodness and universal peace.

[1] See The Principles of Nature, pp. 647 et seq. collated and digested.

[2] This is the language of pantheism, but is to be regarded as an emotional expression of the moment, for we have seen otherwise that so far as Davis was able to think clearly upon a subject of this kind he was certainly not a pantheist. So also he had no intention to affirm that vice is pure and celestial, and when he suggests in the text above that nothing is unclean we know that he is suffering for the moment from confusion over the value of words.

[3] It is otherwise affirmed that all natural worlds are a system of systems by which supermaterial globes and systems, called the Spirit World, are unfolded and prepared for our future habitations. Every physical planet is designed and commissioned to contribute a portion of the universal Spirit Land, so that after death the spirit of man may have a natural and holy home. The subtle intimacy which subsists now between the body and its living soul is not more perfect or real than that between the natural world and the spirit world during every instant of time. The analogy is as reliable and accurate as science. This physical body, chronologically speaking, is the spermatic foundation of the spiritual body, and even so is the natural world the germ-repository and foundation of the spiritual world. Lessons acquired from the one will teach the beauty and truthfulness of the other. While the spiritual world is material in one sense, it is higher in its constituents and in its order of formation. Elementally it does not differ from those primates which compose rock, tree, animal or human body. The difference is similar to that between a rose and its liquefied fragrance. The best imponderable elements of this world gravitate to what we call the spiritual sphere and help to form its substance.—The Great Harmonia, Vol. V, pp. 411, 412. It is to be noted, however, that this is explicated a little earlier in the same volume, where it is said that the material globes do not create the essences and volatile elements out of which the spiritual world is composed; but the system of planets in space imparts its forces, determines its positions, defines its geographical forms, substantialises and stratifies it, so to speak, and in the end makes the spiritual world an organic, objective reality.—Ibid., p. 409.

[4] Before leaving the subject of the Second Sphere, or primary Summer Land, it is well to take note of an alternative description, not that it is important in itself, but because it serves to illustrate the figurative nature of at least certain visions which came to Davis. According to this account, the Second Sphere is said to be divided into two grand hemispheres, one of which is Love and the other Wisdom. They are connected by an isthmus or strait called Will, and the three—taken together—are steps in a ladder of angelic progression. The territories appear different, as regards geographical features and inhabitants. Taken as a whole, the people in the love-sphere are not so harmonious as those in the sphere of wisdom, while as regards that of will, it is not particularly inhabited by either people, being a kind of bridge leading from one hemisphere to another. Those in the region of love have more affinity with their birthplace, including troublesome attachments to persons or things left behind. On the contrary, those who are in wisdom look the other way—not that they are dead as regards affection for those who remain on earth on another planet, but rather that they know how to love, in what proportion and to what beneficent purpose.—The Present Age and the Inner Life, pp. 417, 418.

[5] The Summer Land within the second and third spheres resembles the inhabited planets—meaning those of the solar system—in this particular: they are constituted, heated, lighted, beautified, diversified and clothed upon with perfections adequate for the presence and sustenance of mankind upon their external surfaces only. But the

fourth, fifth and sixth spiritual spheres are peopled within and without.—Views of our Heavenly Home, pp. 121, 122.

[6] A Spiritual Central Sun, according to a later revelation, shines in the heaven of each of the five Summer Lands through which the spirit of man progresses after his life on earth. Each is a focus of the accumulated love, will and wisdom of the particular sphere of being. It shines, like Swedenborg's Lord of Heaven, and the more interior is the habited zone so is the Spiritual Sun more brilliant and beautiful in the firmament. It is the Lord Whose love and wisdom flow into and nourish the individual wisdom and love of each dweller below and within its influence. A luminiferous ether floods infinite space: it is within and without all things. It is the fire of suns, the purifying presence in all mineral structures, the links in the life of plants, the power which circulates the blood in animals, the bridge by which man material is joined to man spiritual. Among the planets it is an astral emanation, among the suns a solar emanation; over each Summer Land it is the absolute Lord of Heaven; in each human heart it is inseparable from affection; and in every head it is allied to intelligence. Until a better term is given, we will name this omnipresent luminiferous ether the Spirit of God. Neither heat nor cold, neither temporal changes nor decomposition of universes can disturb the spiritual bodies which are under the law of this solar influence and astral ether; and the spirit itself is obedient only to those principles of progression which are will-emanations of the Great Positive Mind.—Views of our Heavenly Home, pp. 118-121.

[7] The reference is apparently to the centremost of those vital suns which, ex hypothesi, gave birth to the visible suns, as stated on p. 18.

[8] This paragraph is taken from The Magic Staff, pp. 339-341, after which the text above recurs to its original source.

Chapter Five - Demonstration of The Summer Land

[1]

The subject of research is embodied in the following affirmation: There is an inhabitable zone, or a circular belt of refined and stratified matter in the heavens, here denominated the Summer Land. [2]

As to the possibility, it is not going beyond the sphere of facts, verified by telescopic observation, to suppose the organisation of such a zone in the heavens. Its probability as a material reality will dawn first upon that mind which understands the causative principles within the belt-building manifestations of cosmical matter. Astronomers testify to the existence of immense zones of matter and that these zones not only continue unbroken for countless ages but revolve like the planets, each on its own centre or mathematical axis. This scientific testimony lays a foundation for confidence in the existence of an inner universe of exceeding beauty and glory. Although at present neither intellectually nor telescopically seen, it seems to me that the honest mind cannot but give due weight to facts and principles of a more interior nature, of which planetary formations and revolutions are merely the physical manifestations. It becomes the true philosopher to turn from the phenomenal realm and from visible facts to an examination of causes and principles behind them, and thereafter to ponder well the far-reaching and fruitful lessons which they impart. All that we know depends on the connection of things one with another, and it is only by contemplating creation as a whole that we can attain true conceptions of its parts.

There are two most important discoveries in science: (1) The persistence and indestructibility of force, and (2) the interpolarity and universal convertibility of force. The first is termed the conservation and the second the correlation of force, teaching the divine lesson that all forces as well as all forms in the universe are immortal brothers and sisters. From these splendid discoveries we obtain a Stellar Key to the Summer Land. Force is as substantial and real as matter itself: nay, more, the materialism of matter melts away in the spiritualism of intelligent principles. Our next step is into the realm whence forces emanate—into the sacred presence of Intelligence, Will, Spirit. These are convertible into electrical, chemical, magnetic, and finally into mechanical force, for spirit is substance and everything is rooted therein. According to modern science, heat, light, electricity, magnetism are different modes of motion—that is to say expressions of force. It should be led in this manner to discover that the universe is essentially dual and that manifestations of energy are modes of an eternal substance which is negatively Matter and positively Mind—themselves forms or conditions of one central Reality. Our philosophy is therefore that the universe is a twofold unity, or two eternal manifestations of two substances which at heart are one, but twain in the realms of cause and effect. In the absence of better words we term these Matter and Mind—inter- changeable, convertible, essentially identical, eternally harmonious, wedded by the polarities of positive and negative forces.

The link or bond which unites the positive side or Mind to the negative side or Matter is found in essence [3]; but in finer analysis it is more correct to term Mind and Matter Spirit, having two forms of manifestation. Matter is thus relieved from the idea of grossness, while mind is reclaimed from its long exile in the solitudes of unapproachable immateriality. There will be established in this manner a harmony of relationship between exterior and interior universes; the polarity of all forms and forces in Nature; the descent of Spirit to earth and the ascent of earth to Spirit; the eternity and unity of both hemispheres of the Univerccelum. To ascertain the certainty of that zone called the Summer Land we must follow Nature's pathway from causes to effects. Here is her unalterable code—that visible forms are effects which flow from corresponding invisible causes. A man's body is the effect of an interior vivifying, organising, sustaining, spiritual individuality. [4] It elaborated his brain, heart, senses, all parts of his physical temple, though each is modified more or less by parental and circumstantial influences, both before and after birth. Applying this principle to the organisation of the stellar universe, what endowed matter with the universal tendency to form globes, roll out into immense zones, stratify as revolving belts, and move in circular paths through immensity? There is but one answer. The spiritual universe is composed of globes, zones and belts which move harmoniously in circles of causation through vaster and more interior heavens. Men look through telescopes and discern the outermost garments of hidden spheres of light. There is just as much certainty that the Summer Land exists as that our mind exists. [5] The eternal law of cause and effect is that on which both depend. Man's body is the demonstration of an interior, antecedent, corresponding, formative individuality; and the solar system is the demonstration of an interior, antecedent, corresponding, formative spiritual universe.

The earth's distance from the Spiritual Sphere alters according to its position in the annual journey round the sun. [6] Sometimes the space is only about fifty millions of miles across. At others—when earth is near the opposite end of the ellipse—it is nearly four times more distant. The tide of the celestial river sometimes flows fast as light and in certain localities faster, yet the shortest time occupied is one hour and twenty-five minutes in a bodily journey from earth to the nearest shore. To more remote localities the distance is sometimes nearly two hundred millions of miles. Now, it is a fact that we rarely obtain direct intelligence from persons who lived in the most ancient ages of human history, while even many modern philosophers, since their death, have given no evidence of continued existence. The inconceivable intervening distance is one of the favourite journeys taken by some of the brightest minds which have lived on earth. It is accomplished both by land and stream, and also by atmospheric excursions. Remember, however, the estimated distance between the Pleiades and our solar system, the five hundred years occupied in the travelling of light between that cluster and our human eyes. What then is the length of time required by missionaries and teachers to make a single journey through some distant mansions of the Father's infinite temple?

If it be asked whether a spirit requires space in which to exist and time to make its transit from place to place, the answer is yes, and absolutely. The inconceivable rapidity of thought itself involves time, and this has been measured correctly; but a spirit is not a thought: it is a personal, bodily, substantial existence. [7] Like every other body, space is indispensable to its presence and time is required for its movement. This being so, and as eternity is an impossible conception unless it is divided into times, while infinity can be approached only through separation into spaces, the eternal progression of man means and can mean only an endless succession of periods through which his mind makes pilgrimages. [8] It retains identity by remembering the essences of past experiences, apart from their details. In this manner it keeps the universe new for ever, its own spiritual appetites healthy and its aspirations eternally youthful. The human mind has aphelions and perihelions like the sun. It travels to the extreme of its orbit in one great sphere, retraces its steps to the centre, and then starts—planet-like—on another journey through the boundless fields of an unfathomable Univercoelum.

It follows that no human mind can comprehend what there is to see, meet, feel, hear and know even in the next or Second Sphere, beyond which—so far as is yet known—no person born on earth has ever advanced. But the love, will and wisdom of the Summer Land are in sympathetic correspondence with the Great Positive Centre of the infinite whole. There is the focus of essential principles at which all may seek information, when prepared inwardly. It is a focus of mental progression and spiritual truth which must be sought by love and absorbed by wisdom. To this Spiritual Sun I go for information, and by contact with it—while in the superior condition—I receive impressions.

The discovery of relationship between the material and spiritual universe, founded on immutable laws, cannot but astonish the boldest poetic imagination and excite the opposition of those who rely for "positive knowledge" upon the testimony of their five senses. [9] The discovery of gravitation was not a thousandth part as important as the disclosure of an inhabited belt of solid spiritualised matter in the heavens, adapted to the new bodies of those who withdraw from this planet through the process called death. The revelation of the shining belt has arrived by degrees, coming through hazy glimmerings of intuition from remotest ages, contemplated by analogical reasoners, demonstrated to spiritualists by messages distinct and positive, telling of a home in the solemn abysses of space, and seen by clairvoyants, who have described the thronging hosts which people that substantial sphere in the bosom of the heavens. The relationship and sympathy between the orbs of immensity, between this world and that of risen humanity, are recognised by intuition and reason. Looking far into the ages past, I find conceptions of realities pertaining to a higher sphere of human existence. The intuition of past generations, like the reason of those now living, offers no conflicting testimony on the possibility of an inhabitable sphere in space, now called the Summer Land. Scientific astronomy has expanded men's minds with respect to the magnitudes and splendours of the universe. But it is my impression that the resolution of nebulae into millions of suns is but a glance within the vestibule of the Eternal Temple. The measureless systems which roll in their harmonial circles shine upon landscapes more beautiful and into eyes more divine than ours.

[1] See A Stellar Key to the Summer Land, pp. 18 et seq., extracted and collated.
[2] It is to be noted that in his first work, as summarised in the previous section, Davis gives account of the external beauties appertaining to the Second Sphere in so far as he had investigated or reflected concerning them at that time. He had not then conceived the characteristic denomination of Summer Land, and it is to be noted that he has nothing to say on the return of departed spirits to this earth—for manifestation or otherwise. The explanation is that his long series of discourses in the magnetic state anteceded the Rochester knockings which sounded the advent of modern spiritualism. He describes the Spiritual Sphere as containing all beauties of the natural combined and perfected. Thus every earth is an index of grandeurs in the unseen world, because the spiritual is unfolded from the natural. The surface of the Second Sphere is said—as we have seen—to present gentle undulations and very extensive plains, clothed with great fertility. The figurative nature of his vision is indicated when he describes these plains as gardens of purity, unity and celestial love. Their diversified paths lead from prospect to prospect, all of which display Divine Love and Wisdom. Flowers and leaves are like voices proclaiming interior perfection and the Infinite Source from which they spring. Rivers of clear and placid waters flow through the gardens and are representations of creation and life. There are also enchanting groves which naturally suggest new and beau-

tiful thoughts.—*The Principles of Nature*, pp. 653-655. The object of repeating these indications is to suggest the parabolic nature of all the visions.

[3] This link is mentioned in *The Principles of Nature*, p. 599, as a mediatorial form connecting the soul and the body, and it is said also that a trinity of such kind exists in every substance, whether mineral, vegetable or animal. This mediatorial form in man does not, however, seem to be the psychic body which Davis at a much later period began suddenly to call the soul and made it intermediate between the individualised spirit and the body of flesh.

[4] Compare many previous counter-statements, according to which individuality is the end rather than the beginning. See also p. 127.

[5] The question as to what is the Summer Land is asked and answered in *Beyond the Valley*, p. 255, as follows: It is the heaven where springtime and harvest-abundance are perpetual. It encircles and outshines an immensity of inhabited worlds, each of which is a spiritual vestibule to the Temple "not made with hands." Compare *The Magic Staff*, p. 339, which terms the Second Sphere a compendium of pre-existent universes.

[6] The plane of the orbit of the Summer Land is said to be apparently at an angle of 20 with that of the sun. The reference is presumably to the First Summer Land, which is affirmed to revolve near the grand orbit of the Milky Way.—*A Stellar Key to the Summer Land*, p. 159. As regards the location of the higher spheres, they lie within one another, but Davis speaks always of spirits ascending in their progress through spiritual worlds, which suggests that the First Summer Land is centre-most, though it does not probably represent his meaning.

[7] It is said with equal plainness that the spiritual world is as substantial to the spirit-body as the earth upon which we walk is to the natural body.—*The Great Harmonia*, Vol. V, p. 410. This is reiterated elsewhere, though the repetitions of Davis by no means make for unity in conception. See *The Present Age and the Inner Life*, p. 413, where—in opposition to other statements and to one of those very bad diagrams which occasionally illustrate his text—it is affirmed that the substantial world of the Summer Land is a sphere, having latitudes, longitudes, poles, revolutions, atmospheres, with all the phenomena which appertain to the present world, but one degree superior—in point of beauty, refinement and every other respect—to the best planet in our solar system.

[8] As explained in a former note, the infinite and eternal are not subject to division or separation.

[9] See *A Stellar Key to the Summer Land*, pp. 5 et seq.

Chapter Six - Celestial Rivers in Space

[1]

From each of the earths in our system great electrical and magnetic rivers flow out and in, like a ceaseless tide.[2] On their soft, golden bosom all death-emancipated men, women and children float into their celestial home. By the same means they and all other voyagers may and do return again and again. The flowing and ebbing of these elemental Gulf Streams correspond in a general way to the forward and backward movements of the blood from its governmental centre—the heart—to the outermost of the human body. As the crimson fluid of the heart pulsates throughout the arteries and veins of the human body, so the magnetic and electric streams of the upper regions start from geo-centres and helio-centres, flowing through the heavenly fields. The directions of these streams are as various as the radial lines from a globe. These living currents promote the refinement and assimilation of atoms among the organs—that is to say, globes—of the infinite body of God. They form and flow forth between all the solar centres and inhabited globes of space, whence they stream onward and inward into the next great sphere of human existence, which we call the Summer Land.

The earth on which we live is a revolving electrical machine, an immense magnetic battery. With a swiftness beyond imagination the earth's electricity streams in great ribbons and winds itself upon its own natural spool at the North, where it is transformed into a more refined motive force—an *etherium* or celestial magnetism. This is positive and warm to the negative and cold volumes of electricity. Its warm stream, rising high in air and flowing above the South Pole, pulsates onward and upward, outward and inward, until it breaks like a note of immortal melody on the shores of the Summer Land. There are also electrical rivers setting toward earth and the various planets in our system from different regions of the Spirit Land. They convey constant pulsations to the life of mankind from the Great Central Sun of Intelligence in the Second Sphere. Yet it is an error to suppose that all personal communication between the populations of earth and the higher spheres is possible only through the aerial rivers. There is no space in the fields of infinitude which cannot be crossed by beings endowed with will. The celestial streams can be forded and the very rivers of Paradise made subservient to the eternal unrest of mind. But the orderly method of travelling between the earths and the interior universe is by means of the rivers described. They are the recognised celestial highways connecting spheres and, globes.

[1] See Views of our Heavenly Home, pp. 76 et seq.
[2] *The theory concerning celestial rivers is put somewhat differently in one of the earlier works and should be taken in connection with the text as it stands above: As there is a vital circulation in the human body so there is a circulation of living forces between the spiritual world and the several planets. The South Pole of the earth sends forth a magnetic stream, and the tide passes through the orbits of Venus and Mercury, very near the surface of the sun, whence it surges silently but swiftly on till it reaches the Spirit Land. From another section of the Spirit Land there starts a lighter fluid, which is also a tidal river, toward the North Pole of earth, and this is unchangeably electrical. It is a positive stream which flows from us to the spiritual world and a negative one from the latter to our own planet. I have observed very often the spirits of our human friends, when at death they pass out of the corporeal body, ascend to a height of some seven miles, where they meet with the celestial river and are transported thereby to their Spirit Home. As there are thus streams of communication between our globe and this bourne of souls, so are there others which connect the latter with every world belonging to our planetary system.—The Great Harmonia, Vol. V, pp. 414., 416.*

Chapter Seven - Constitution and Location of The Summer Land

[1]

The order of the universe is as perfect as its varieties are innumerable. The principles engaged in forming worlds are incessantly decomposing them. In no other way can perpetual youth be bestowed upon the finer bodies in space. Atoms sufficiently refined to ascend above the mineral compound enter into forms of vegetable life. Vegetation delegates its finest atoms to build up the animal kingdom. The most refined animal atoms enter into and support human bodies. The most refined particles of human bodies which are not required to construct and support "the garment of immortality" ascend to form the solids, fluids and ethers of that effulgent zone to which all human beings are hastening. [2] There is thus established and maintained an eternal youth in the spiritual universe. The spiritual spheres have been termed recently Summer Lands and—counting man's earthly existence as the first world of spirit life—there are in all six spheres in the ascending flight toward Deity, Which fills the Seventh Sphere. The Central Positive Power repels the physical and attracts the spiritual concurrently. The circulation of matter is therefore outward from the centre, while spirit travels toward the centre from without. These two reciprocal currents flow incessantly. Inconceivable oceans of world-building materials expand from the Fountain at the centre, while innumerable multitudes of individualised spiritual and angelical men, women and children—from all human-bearing planets in space—are marching inward toward the positive attractive Centre and approaching nearer and nearer the eternal sun-sphere of the Father and Mother. [3]

The formation of the different Summer Lands can be seen in those principles which evolved the suns and stars of the firmament. It is the teaching of science that world-constructing forces are latent in the mass and that the formation of a dewdrop is not less wonderful than that of an inhabitable world. So also the formation of spiritualised material belts is as natural and rational as that of the primordial rings out of which all planets, satellites and lesser bodies were developed subsequently.

But a question arises whether the spiritual zones will not be themselves broken up and distributed through space by counter attractions. I answer here that they cannot be drawn asunder by any superior external force, for they are constituted of ultimate particles, having only remote affinities for the constituents of other bodies in space. Another question is why the Summer Land is not round like a globe rather than a vast zone or stratified belt. I answer that according to astronomical science the primary figure was spheroidal. The oval is consequently the first form of matter—its genesis and also its exodus. So also in music the eighth and the first note are essentially the same. The last sound is a perfect reiteration or reproduction of the first and becomes the basis of another and higher scale, onward and upward progressively. This harmonial law of continuous reproduction will answer the question concerning the zone shape of the Summer Land. According to this law, a broad, effulgent, rotating belt or zone is the first form of world-building in the stellar universe. So also it is the highest and final form which matter is capable of assuming in its most exalted condition of ethereal and essential refinement. Lastly, the physical universe is itself spheroidal in shape, composed of a progressive series of successively ascending circles of suns and planets, and it is nothing but the material garment, the organised body of that interior spiritual universe which was not "made with hands" but is "eternal in the heavens." [4]

As regards the location of the Second Sphere, [5] it is girdled by the First Sphere, or—more categorically—by the Milky Way, just as its rings girdle the planet Saturn. The analogy is perfect. In appearance it is like a beautiful morning. The surface is diversified endlessly with valleys, rivers, hills, mountains and innumerable parks, the trees and shrubbery of which resemble, however, nothing on earth. They are more like the vegetation of Saturn. An incalculable variety of flowers lends a peculiar prismatic charm to the far-extending territories, and the divinely soft ether surpasses all conception. To be there is to be in the presence of holiness, where every tree speaks to the heart and every flower pronounces a benediction. [6] Were the size of our earth multiplied seven million times it would give the extent of a single park in the Second Sphere. The latter, once more, is a magnificent belt, bespangled with countless jewels, and it is part of the Divine Vesture of Him Whose praise is celebrated best in the eloquence of sacred silence.

[1] See A Stellar Key to the Summer Land, pp. 64 et seq. collected and collated.
[2] This is stated by Davis to be the result of most careful examinations of the physical structure of the Summer Land, its fertile soils, lovely groves, vines and flowers. But it is added that the world-rearing principles are attracted from human emanations in all the planets.—Op. cit., p. 115.
[3] There is no question that this presents a better synopsis of the subject than we have seen presented otherwise respecting the formation of so-called Spiritual Spheres by means of emanations from the various planets. It is the latter, however, which appeals more especially to Davis, who recurs to it on several occasions, and notably in The Present Age and the Inner Life, where he affirms, presumably on his own authority, that eight hundred million tons of invisible emanations are given off by the earth annually, not to speak of other planets belonging to the solar system. As he is not able to suggest what becomes of them otherwise, he assumes that they go to form the Summer Land of his visions, a material basis for which was necessary to his system.—Op. cit., pp. 413, 414. The scientific aspect of this notion, with its seeming suspension of the law of gravitation, is naturally not worth discussing.
[4] If it were possible—in the case of a writer who not only admits that all his records are the result of impressions received but regards this method as the only way of truth and illumination—to interpret statements according to the values of their literal meaning, it would follow here-from that the spiritual universe, being eternal in the heavens, anteceded the manifest universe, which is a product of time as to present form and mode, whether or not its elements may have pre-existed. It would follow also that the

spiritual spheres are not composed of emanations from planets or suns now existing, which involves the grotesque idea that they are expanding continually owing to accretions from without. There is no need to accentuate this point, and it is stated only to show once more, but now after a different manner, that A. J. Davis as a seer who saw visions of another world and of the life beyond therein is to be distinguished from A. J. Davis who owing to impressions of another order—and to his reflections thereupon—attempted to unfold a system of the universe. The findings of his seership will be of permanent interest to those who believe that such experience is a general possibility, which in his case may have become actual.

[5] See The Present Age and the Inner Life, pp. 416, 417.

[6] Another intimation that the visions of Davis are to be read as parables or symbolical moralities.

Chapter Eight - Centres in The Summer Land

[1]

The unerring history of each person is written in the Summer Land. A man who lives for himself loses himself. If he wishes to gain the world he as certainly loses it. The immoralities of his purposes defeat him at every step, from cradle to coffin. But consolation is at hand. Death is a chemical screen through which individuals are passed to their true stations in the Summer Land. The spirit, the encasing soul, the life-centres, characteristics and motives pass through the death-strainer; but there are left with the physical body many of those hereditary predispositions and abnormal conditions which gave rise to discordant passions and false appetites. Their effects, however, pass through and remain with the individual long after he has attained his centre in the Summer Land. Individualities are not therefore destroyed by death. Nothing is changed save the dense physical form.

In the temperament and characteristics of the individual are laid the foundations of the different centres in the mansions of the Father's House. If the person starts from earth interiorly cleansed he will arrive at the next sphere in a purified condition; but if he leaves here with earthly and fleshly influences on the soul he will arrive at a corresponding centre with the accumulated effects of these still permeating the inner life and its affections. Thus radical differences in men and women cause different societies beyond, some of them embodying the consequences of immoral motives and degraded purposes by which people have been actuated and made miserable in this world. This is a momentous truth. The Summer Land is a natural state, growing out of causes and effects as logically as today grew out of yesterday. [2] It is made up of persons not only from all parts of this inhabitable globe but of far distant planets constituted like our own earth. All carry upon their faces, as well as in the secret chambers of their affections, the results of life on that globe which produced them. He who has been governed by high and beautiful motives instinctively seeks association with those who have been similarly actuated. He who has been led by low and demoralising motives seeks his like beyond. A man can elect his friends and gravitate to his own congenial Spirit Centre, until the redemptive evangel of regeneration—through repentance and progression—reaches his affections, and pure purposes are born within him. Progression from imperfection is a spiritual transaction, and societies in the unseen spheres are natural exponents of the interior realities of societies on different planets.

One of them is called Altolissa. Persons have returned from it and testified that while dwellers on earth they were influenced mainly by the idea of gaining money, position and power. These characteristics remain, and personality in the Summer Land will take on that for which it has affinity. It will absorb from each society such influences as are in accordance with its magnetic powers and will exclude all others, from whatever source. But going through death has cleansed personalities largely of causes, leaving results treasured up in the affections, and there is benefit to this extent, rather than injury or degradation, by contact with unseen populations of like mind and character. The societies are necessarily on a higher plane than those to which they correspond on earth. But the plane is so slightly removed that it requires little inward change to feel at home.

It has been ascertained by conversations with those who have returned from the Summer Land that persons of demoralising motives in this life have the greatest density on their arrival. In Altolissa—where many go who have lived wholly under the influence of selfishness—the population seems about as comfortable as general society on earth. Jews believe still in the doctrine of their fathers—Abraham, Isaac and Jacob; Roman Catholics hold the views which they cherished before death; and similarly with other persuasions. Progressively and imperceptibly, this sphere will become better and more harmonious. Men will differ less and less upon fundamental principles, but endless varieties of convictions and affinities will prevail over details, and thus are the foundations laid for countless societies in the Summer Land. Death is largely a cleansing process and is the hope of the world, while the law of progress is such that even the active effects which accompany the individual cannot be perpetuated—as evils and discords—throughout eternity. A positive power reigns in the centre of the universe, and by the slow operation of its laws all personalities are purified from their imperfections. Only Eternal Good can exist eternally.

But here and now is the place to get under full sail for a happier harbour. [3] Each person can start on the right track before death. Today is better than tomorrow. All should begin at once to insure their entrance into superior societies. It is important to get a passport to harmonious centres in the Summer Land. Now is therefore the time for each to take his stand upon the solid rock of Truth and of those principles which will abide because they are eternal.

[1] See Morning Lectures, pp. 266-287.
[2] In this connection Davis had occasion to complain that certain misdirected minds persisted in regarding his Harmonial Philosophy as teaching a uniform and all-glorious heaven for every person indiscriminately, and he found it necessary therefore to affirm, or rather to repeat, that the unrighteousness of our present rudimental existence con-

tinues in the subordinate societies of" the Second Sphere.—See The Present Age and Inner Life, pp. 334, 335. It is quite certain that this opinion is written all over his recollections of the life beyond, and the root of it is expressed clearly in the text above. At the same time there are many loose and incautious statements which give colour to an opposite view, and Davis evidently regarded the transition signified by death as carrying with it an unquestionable improvement of every state and case.

[3] In this connection it is well to remember that, according to Davis, whatever thought enters the human mind on earth becomes a resident in the memory and is brought forth freshly in the world to come. If it is a good thought it will interest and instruct there. But as there are thoughts of another order it is proper for us to do and think only that which we would most earnestly desire to remember, and to refrain from things that are inimical to the superior delights of the mind.—A Stellar Key, pp. 190, 191. It is another way of saying that the ascent of the ladder of perfection here and now will bring us to the perfect life hereafter.

Chapter Nine - Winter Land and Summer Land

[1]

This earth is a Land of Winter, of storms and sorrows, but the Second Sphere is a Summer Land of repose and infinite blossoming. Provision is made for the complete gratification of the diversities of spiritual desires, so that all races and all states of mind will be at home in our Father's House which is eternal in the heavens. Let us think of the physical aspect of the Summer Land. Many persons have understood me to say that it is a globe, but it is really a solid belt of land extending above the earth, two-thirds of the distance from the sun and some seventy millions of miles wide, or immeasurably larger than the sun's path around Alcyone in the deep of immensity. Suppose this belt to be open at the sides, filled with worlds, crowned with stars and suns, while overhead and around is a firmament like the heaven about our earth. You behold therefore that which is seen here, but unfolded further and more perfectly—plans of an infinite temple which are here fragmentary only.

The Summer Land is in harmony with that circle of planets called the Milky Way. [2] It is a zone or girdle of real, substantial matter. When liberated at death we do not move on toward the sun but embark on a sidewise voyage directly above the southern quarter of our planet. We gain the shore of a land just like this earth, were the latter a stratified belt of the finest possible particles. Proportions and adaptations are the same. So far as the surrounding immensity is concerned, the Summer Land is bounded on all sides by aerial seas. Imagine yourself standing on one of its shining shores and contemplating with your spiritual eyes, now first opened. Looking toward the Earth, Sun, Mercury and Venus you would see an illimitable ocean of stars and golden suns, and you would realise a holy atmosphere on all sides, while from your feet would stretch an ocean without shore and void of all relations. If, however, your spiritual eyes had the light of far-penetrating clairvoyance you would perceive that the aerial ocean ripples off and divides into beautiful rivers flowing to the planets—to Mars, Jupiter, Saturn, even this Earth—and yet others to distant systems throughout the firmament. These rivers of the heavenly spaces are musical to the ear that can hear them flowing between the constellations.

Very many persons depart every day from our own Land of Winter for the Summer Land. When they are led through the celestial gardens and down by the shining shores, when they hear the lapping of musical waves as they ripple in from remote planets, bringing upon their undulating bosoms new persons who have left their gross bodies, it is as though you were to see beautiful spirits coming suddenly over the water by the seaside. I have frequently called your attention to the naturalness of the Summer Land. Its reality is among the philosophical discoveries of the present outfolding century. You should know that its inhabitants live in harmonious accord with each other, because of the omniscient system which is adapted to the infinite varieties of human character and consequent diversities of destiny. When you arrive there you will not be a stranger, for you will have cultivated some prescience of the House constructed of different and many Mansions. Certain minds go into "the superior state" in natural slumber. The spirit rises up and attains a finer mode of thought and feeling. The life of the spirit is natural. You travel in the sleep-state as though you were awake and in open day. This arises from a projection of your consciousness into the open world about you. The scenes of the Second Sphere are reflected upon the human mind whenever it is accessible and impressible. This is accomplished either by our own clairvoyant powers or by our invisible guardians and their artistic pencillings upon our faculties. [3]

I would now like to tell you about Elgario, the plant of sorrow. In the Summer Land there are melancholy characters, who seem disposed to dwell upon the hard times experienced on earth. They are downcast and sad for a while, but this celestial plant is their sweet medicine and perfect antidote. The sad ones are led to it; they begin to inhale its fragrance, to chew it a little every day; and they learn that this flower is for the healing of God's heart-stricken children. They carry its petals and are influenced; they make bouquets of it and these relieve them of their earth-born sorrows. Thus beautiful births take place out of confirmed despondency. A mother, for example, has been overworked to feed and clothe her children. She has at last died from excessive bodily fatigue and weariness of heart. She is borne away on the silvery river to the Summer Land; but she is still weary. This beautiful plant is brought to her, and it lifts her gradually into a superior state. She realises somewhat of heavenly comfort. She looks about and sees old acquaintances and loved friends. She finds them in the Father's House, where there are many Mansions. If it were not so, the seers would have told you.

[1] See Morning Lectures, pp. 349-376.
[2] It is said elsewhere that within the vast cloud of material globes which compose the Milky Way is a silver lining, an aurelian circle, and it is the Soul's Immortal Home. It is revolving within this visible realm of resplendent suns and planets, and it is comparable to our spiritual body, which is a silver lining within a cloud-environment, being the outer visible form. This interior celestial circle or spiritual world is what we call the Second

Sphere. Within it is the third, next the fourth, then the fifth and sixth. The seventh is the Deific Vortex, a Great Positive Power, Perfect and Divine. Between each two of these Spiritual Spheres there is a system of suns and planets corresponding to the Milky Way.—The Great Harmonia, Vol. V, p. 414.

[3] It will be understood here that by the term invisible guardians we are to understand visitors from the Summer Land, and it may be recalled that, according to Davis, no spirit from our earth has as yet progressed beyond the Second Sphere, though there is sometimes a direct transition from Jupiter and Saturn to the Third Sphere or Higher Summer Land. This being so, a question arose as to mediumistic communications alleged to come from more exalted regions. Davis has explained them by saying that each of the two spheres mentioned above is divided into six societies, or six races of spirits, in different stages of moral culture, and that each of these is subdivided over and over again. Spirits communicating from any of these are said to confound societies and spheres together, the excuse given for which is that words are arbitrary signs of thought. The last point appears unconvincing, and the explanation as a whole did not appeal to the body general of spiritualists, but especially of mediums. Possibly they observed that, the affirmed barrier of communication notwithstanding, Davis had personally visited all the spheres and had paused only on the threshold of the seventh, and that which was possible to him they would scarcely regard as beyond themselves. The alternative descriptions here cited is from The Present Age and the Inner Life, pp. 417-419.

Chapter Ten - Language in The Summer Land

[1]

The languages called dead have certain roots which push themselves up through the memory-soils of the mind and bear fruit after death. Those who have passed on continue for a long time to speak the tongue of their earth-life. [2] Most people think that after death "all is different with the individual." There was never a greater mistake. There are no essential changes in the plan of ultimates. The final type of organisation is the spiritual interior of man and woman. Both reason and intuition sustain the doctrine of no essential change after death. If man's body falls, in sympathy with the chemistry and gravitation of the physical world, the spiritual man does not fall with it. Only the external casing is peeled off, while the personal-inmost goes onward—unchanged and individualised—to the Summer Land. In order to realise that the other world is truly a "home in the heavens" we must grasp the naturalness of the after-life. Earthlings will not be orphans or strangers there. I must know and recognise my acquaintances—and they must recognise and know me—or immortality is nothing. Now, the after-existence opens before us as a continuation of individual progression; in another mansion, another story of the same house "eternal in the heavens." The heavens are not remote. The Summer Land is neither more nor less in the heavens than is this earth on which we at present reside. The mind of man is stationed over his visceral organs, but it maintains a constant communication with all parts of his body. In like manner, the Second Sphere is so situated with reference to this earth that we float under the constant inspection of its population. The earth is analogous to an organ in the physiology of the sidereal system, and the celestial brain, which is the Summer Land, crowns all the system, just as the mind of man covers and crowns the different organs within the trunk.

Perfected earthly languages, carried to their ultimates, become the language of the other sphere [3]; but education still sways mind and thought. The second language used in the higher world is the Language of Music. Truths and beauties of science, high and glorious lessons in celestial principles are communicated by means of symphonies, melodies, songs, hymns, anthems and chants. This wondrous music fills the whole heaven and awakens echoes among distant planets. When the stars are summoned to enter the orchestra and make the magnificent chorus full, then earth itself seems to vibrate responsively to that grand harmonious beat which converts the universe into a harp of infinite perfection. The third language used in the higher world is what we call here the Language of the Heart—more properly the Language of Emanation. [4] Every private affection throws out an atmosphere. Whatever your predominating love may be it emits an atmosphere which winds itself about your person. When the temperament is fine, sensitive, susceptible, the odour and influence will correspond. In the Summer Land this Language of the Heart is carried to an inconceivable degree of perfection, and is the only medium of communication in the higher spheres. It is the language of absolute contact, of personal love-atmospheres—by which is meant that two persons meeting face to face meet also heart to heart, and are friends for ever. On earth it is but hands or eyes or lips that touch and speak; there it is the sweet and perfect meeting of soul with soul. Souls inhale and understand each other. There sweeps through the heart the satisfaction of perfect appreciation of the wisdom of brother, sister or companion. Your secret history is told wordlessly and is for ever known. The details of your earth-life are understood, with all their bearings on your character. The steps are also comprehended that have brought you to your present position in the upper existence. Such confirmation constitutes the happiness which diversifies and exalts the inhabitants of the spheres.

This interior, unspeakable language is sometimes called the Language of Communion—which poets try in vain to reach, which music nearly approaches, with its unsearchable attributes. When your love is warmest and deepest you catch the rudiments of this celestial conversation—so exalting to all who dwell under its blessings in the Summer Land. Let it be affirmed once more that words are not the most eloquent expressions of the soul. There is no joy so intense as that which sparkles in the eye and crimsons the cheek, yet refuses the aid of the voice. There is also "no grief like that which does not speak." There is a mental electricity more mysterious far than the subtle fluid that thrills through material substances. Pleasant indeed is the solitude which is broken only by this silent speech. [5] The speech of spirits drops upon the internal tympanum like music from over the sea. [6] The words are distinct as bugle notes, but they affect the mind as childhood's kisses do the lips, leaving a sweet presence and benefaction behind them. Words of wisdom spoken by angel lips exceed the melody of all earthly music. If you can fancy the voice of silvery streams flowing over cascades of golden sunbeams, or the throbbing of deathless joys through roseate chambers of the pure heart, you may conceive somewhat of spirit voices, as heard by such as have ears to hear. [7]

We know not how radiantly beam the countenances of those who converse wholly in the language of the soul. It is the most expressive and least demonstrative. The griefs and cares of the heart, its fairest flowers and saddest experiences, tremble together in the crystal chalice of pure speech. The voice of a spirit is like the spirit of truth, most eloquent when manifested in deeds, for thus do highest intelligences communicate their thoughts to those beneath them.

The universal speech of spirits is an elemental outburst of the internal, a langauge of thought and feeling, taking the form of that language with which the guest is most familiar. For example, on entering the Land of Spirit the native Portuguese will imagine that those with whom he converses speak only his own language. The modus loquendi must be universal in the other sphere. It takes the form of any tongue and so establishes immediate fellowship, whatever the nationalities on earth. Finally, inasmuch as spirits are transparent in respect of their thoughts and affections, they can never say one thing and mean another. [8]

[1] See Morning Lectures, pp. 377-404.

[2] Compare, however, Beyond the Valley, p. 255. The question is: How do spirits converse? It is answered by saying: Vocal discourse is an invention of intellect. Speech is spiritual only when it flows from the inmost emotions. For these feelings there are no possible sounds, and there is no written language.

[3] This is presumably on the ground that language is, in the Davis terminology, an element of spirit, an idea and a principle which is as boundless as Nature's empire.—The Great Harmonia, Vol. V, p. 69.

[4] It is said in another place that the inhabitants of the Second Sphere—and it would seem that the statement applies generally and not to a particular department or state—do not converse vocally but immerse their thoughts in one another by radiating them upon the countenance. Thought enters the spirit by a process of breathing, or is— more correctly—introduced by influx, according to the desires of those conversing. They perceive thought by and through the eyes, inasmuch as the latter—like the general countenance—are an index to the quality and interior of the workings.—See A Stellar Key to the Summer Land, pp. 189, 190. It is added that they appear also to hear each other converse, but it is owing to a previous knowledge of sound, by which words are distinguished and their meaning apprehended. The hypothesis is, however, that intercommunication is not vocal, from which it follows that there are no sounds, and Davis is probably failing to express his real meaning. The kind of language intimated is apparently that of man at the beginning of his physical evolution, for which see ante, pp. 63-65.

[5] It should be mentioned that according to an incidental testimony of Davis, he was in the habit of communicating personally with spirits after (1) an inward way, in which soul spoke to soul; and (2) after the normal mode of physical speech, when he was answered in the same manner.—See The Present Age and the Inner Life, p. 125.

[6] See Answers to Ever-Recurring Questions from the People, pp. 72, 73.

[7] The reference is to intercommunication between disembodied spirits and those on earth. Later on it is the communing of disembodied spirits one with another.
[8] Op. cit. y p. 75.

Chapter Eleven - Travelling and Society in The Summer Land

[1]

Having a power which is higher than organic force, the human will can overcome material gravity, and thus the spirit-body may rise and float with the speed of light upon ethereal rivers of space. A voyage on the celestial seas may be accomplished quicker than a telegraph-operator could record the fact for the daily press. By this power of the spirit's will, in harmony with invariable celestial tides, man will be enabled after death to travel from the Summer Land to different departments of the heavens with more ease and infinitely more pleasure than you can now travel to foreign places on this globe.

The Summer Land, more especially those portions in connection with the inhabitants of earth, appears to my interior eyes like a neighbouring planet. It is the next room in the house not made with hands; but there is an infinite number of other rooms. Characteristics and peculiarities of the lower sections may not prevail in higher divisions of the sphere. In that which lies next to us the law of social attraction is as operative as in this world. It is not easy to tell why, but the dwellers are gregarious and remain very near each other. In more refined sections the people are influenced by other interests. Gregariousness becomes distasteful to those who seek the finer attractions of the Summer Land. New and larger affections render former selfish relations almost antipathies. [2]

The next sphere of human existence is only another department in the great educational system of eternity. There mankind has opportunities to outgrow the errors and follies of this life, and thus myriads become prepared for yet another ascension. If a man leaves this world in good spiritual circumstances he may proceed at once to a better brotherhood and be engaged in higher duties, in obedience to higher sympathies and attractions. Those who pass in darkness of spirit, who have brought upon themselves discord and misery, leave earth without these finer attractions, and they become subjects for the philanthropic treatment of others who have souls for higher sympathies. Individual affinities and antipathies come from the action of the temperaments of different spirits in the vicinity of each other. When you pray therefore, let it be for the highest manifestation of the Kingdom of Heaven, for a social condition above the plane of ungovernable attractions and repulsions, for blessings above the sphere of antipathies and unwise sympathies. Mankind has yet to learn the difference between passional inclination and that spiritual love which attracts and ennobles its object. The former is "of the earth, earthy" and is not found in the celestial brotherhoods. The wisest do not encourage indiscriminate inclination; they rise into the celestial atmosphere of pure, immortal affection; and thus the wisest person in the Summer Land is the most loving. Divinity, in its central life, is love. Fraternal love is at the bottom of the heavenly companionship. The best brotherhoods in the Summer Land work diligently among inferior associations to bring about heavenly peace and concord. [3] When the inferior societies are harmonised, the earth will be more harmonised also. In addition to these missions there are others to those who are constantly coming from earth and from the planets in space. When we arrive, each in our turn, we shall find persons perfectly acquainted with all that we have ever done. Angels' eyes are clairvoyant. However faithless, however worthless, you cannot get away from them, neither can you escape from yourself. Carry this memory with you through life. It is not the gospel of fear but the doctrine of truth, which puts a check on the play of ungoverned appetites. In the Summer Land, as seen by clairvoyance, [4] I discover three distinct associations of men and women, each occupying a position determined by the degree of cultivation, sympathy one for another and power of approaching each other's sphere of knowledge and attainment. Each society is encompassed by a peculiar sphere or atmosphere, being an exhalation from the specific quality of their interior characters. Every spirit has a peculiar sphere and also a general one in which it can exist with pleasure. [5] Spirits know and associate with each other according to the quality of the sphere exhaled from their interiors, and according to the relative degrees of brightness encompassing their forms. They have affection for one another in proportion to the similarity in the degrees of love and purity to which they have attained. Thus are the three states or societies established.

In the first society is an immense number of infants and uncultivated spirits, as these have proceeded from earth. The atmosphere which encompasses and protects them is gloomy and rather uncongenial, because it is an emanation from uncultivated intellects. Viewed comparatively with that existing on earth, there is yet an exceeding purity among them. They are in the plane of natural thought, that is, they are just emerging from the instructions and impressions of earth into the wisdom of the higher societies. In the second group or society are those who have become highly instructed in the principles and truths of the Divine Mind. All who die on earth with minds unfolded properly are congregated herein, because here they can associate agreeably. They are enveloped with an atmosphere of resplendent brilliancy, which indicates purity and elevation. It appears like the interfusion of many colours unknown on earth, so perfectly conjoined and blended in such harmony that the whole aroma is itself a representation of purity and refinement. It is a sphere emanating from the whole body of the society, indicating the wisdom of the spirits composing it. Their wisdom consists in a knowledge of truths and principles [6] concerning material and rudimental things, while the inconceivable variety of colours surrounding them arises from dissimilar stages of advancement. Yet all are in the same grade of wisdom and thus form one society, which is just emerging from a superior knowledge of visible effects presented on earth to a perception of their interior causes, essences and modes of manifestation. But they are not in possession of superior wisdom concerning the uses for which causes and effects were instituted. The third society is clothed with an aerial garment which is a perfect representation of the character and perfection of their interiors. I behold it in all colours and in a variety of reflections proceeding from the subordinate societies. These render their spiritual emanations so very beautiful that language is inadequate to describe it. This third society is on the plane of effects, and those composing it have a perception of all ultimate design, of the universal adaptation of things to each other. Their minds are exceedingly luminous, laying open the externals of things and perceiving the character of the interior. Their vision extends to every recess of their own habitation and their knowledge comprehends all subordinate material existence. Their wisdom is light, love, brilliancy, even ecstasy—to a degree that transcends description. They behold the vast landscapes of the Spirit Home and are not only in a state of emergence from causes to effects but from their own sphere to the third world of human existence.

Notwithstanding the dissimilitude between the three societies there is perfect unity among them and dependence one upon another. There is a continual aspiring affection from the infant intellect to the high wisdom of the third society. There is a unity of action which causes all to live for one another, like a brotherhood. Each group is well situated in reference to the specific state which each is compelled to sustain. The conditions are perfect in proportion to the degree of wisdom and refinement. The lowest appears inferior in comparison with that which is above, but to man on earth it would represent a high state of perfection. The lowest contains and involves the highest, while the latter comprehends and pervades the whole. Thus it is that all preserve an order in their lives and situations, and one is continually unfolding the possessions of another. Thus all go onward to a still higher sphere of spiritual and intellectual elevation.

Swedenborg says truly that in the Spirit World the different associations, nationalities and religious sects continue. Philosophers of the atheistical school make their notions a matter of association, so that the children of parents who think as they do, [7] and persons in other brotherhoods, have large gatherings, where they enjoy festivities and conversation. Human nature here is human nature there. Archilarium is the name of an open pavilion where these teachers gather multitudes together.

A brotherhood of affiliated souls is seen upon the west of a beautiful mountain called Starnos. Hereon is another pavilion of exceeding beauty, like a building made of trees, flowering shrubs and countless vines, full of indescribable colours. Flowing by the side of this pavilion is a river called Apotravella. The congregation sings to its tides, and there are times when the vast, many-arched temple throbs like a harp, responsive to the musical revelations of that celestial stream. The temple-chief is a Turk who is still a follower of Mahomet. He often sees and adores the gifted man who represented Mecca. Other dwellers in this region believe that further portions of the Summer Land will yet take great interest in the prophet of God. The chief has a young bright wife, and together they constitute the host and hostess of that vast pavilion. The doctrine of polygamy is not practised in this brotherhood. [8]

The race of Gnostics is almost extinct, but a few are gathered together in the valley of Ori, where Ephelitus, the oldest among them, holds his levees. He was a scholar and propagandist in that early sect. He draws about him those who wish to hear of scenes and toils in Rome seventeen centuries ago.

La Samosata is the name of a convent or monastery, and there are persons who believe still that the Roman Catholic faith is God's exclusive religion. It is a place shut in by mountains that fill the distance, like Alps upon Alps. Could the earthly astronomer gaze thereon he would seem to be contemplating new star-fields, of beauty and magnitude beyond his ability to transmit in language or trace on maps. La Samosata is so vast that it might contain all Roman Catholics who have entered into the spirit-world during many past centuries. It sends down inspirations and benedictions to fellow-believers on earth.

Zellabingen is a vast German association, composed wholly of persons who had not acquired the power of song before death, yet possessed an ardent love for music. Their present association actualises what was here ideal. Some of them are centuries old and yet younger than any grown person on earth, for every change in the cycle of their lives is to them the beginning of a new age. Lindenstern and Moraneski are Russian and Austrian associations. The former seems to be immersed almost wholly in matters of history, with reference to races of planets. They have lost much of their attachment to their native globe, and they are almost Teutonic in their studious methods. They are peculiarly truthful, unselfish and disinterested. On the other hand, the Austrian assembly is concerned almost entirely with the formation of the best governments for the peoples of earth, though they do not seek to exert political influence over kings and emperors. On the north of Mount Starnos is a beautiful Spanish association called Acadelaco or Eco del Eco, as nearly as I can remember. Miantovesta is an Italian brotherhood distinguished by some of the loveliest women that have ever lived on earth. From time to time the members journey to the Zellabingen Society; their sweet singers take part in the anthems of its groups, the voices blending like drops of dew in the air. Remembering this magnificent melody, I think sometimes that the early Christians may have derived from it their conception that the kingdom of Heaven is devoted to works of music and prayer.

Monazolappa is the only exclusively African realm that I have seen in the Spirit World, and it is there I learned that a large percentage of the progeny of earth's early inhabitants never attained immortality but went out of sight into the laboratories of matter. [9] Oahulat is the name of a brotherhood of Sandwich Islanders. Wallavesta and Passnata are regions of peaceful Indian tribes. The hatchet is really buried and the pipe of peace is smoked. The old dreams of sachems and wigwams, great forests and shining lakes for bathing and fishing are more than realised in the Summer Land.

There are still other things to speak of, the vast white flowers Archibulum and Aurealia—the general name for a class of pulsating lilies. The first is constituted so as to give an image of children grouped in its centre. Many admiring spirits seem to think that they see therein a beautiful representation of the Son of Mary and Joseph when he said: "Suffer little children to come unto Me." It is one of the most marvellous floral developments in the Garden of God. It is contemplated by Rachel and other beautiful Jewesses of the old Hebrew Scriptures. The Aurealia are graceful golden plants growing by the peaceful homes of pure souls, where they vibrate in the soft zephyrs of the immortal sphere.

Do not forget, in conclusion, that I am speaking of scenes in the Summer Land, the next door neighbour to all that circle of planets of which the earth is a member. What would you say if you should hear somewhat concerning the third sphere, of the one beyond that, or of another and still higher?

[1] See A Stellar Key to the Summer Land, being extracts from pp. 163—183, so far as this subject is concerned.

[2] It is said that spirits in the Summer Land approach each other according to the relative degrees of brilliancy which surround and encompass their forms. Thus association is determined and made perfect by the law of congeniality and affinity, or affection. There is affection one for another in proportion to similarity in the degrees of love and purity to which they have attained.—Op. Cit., pp. 185, 1 86.

[3] It is said elsewhere that at the end of certain festivals in the Summer Land the audience divides into sub-societies for the accomplishment of certain missions. Some of them accept missions to other brotherhoods, not yet harmonised, in other and more distant parts. Some visit our earth and rescue unhappy persons about to destroy themselves. Many are thus saved, and where the misfortune cannot be prevented, friendly spirits are at hand to soothe the sad one's darkened passage to another sphere.—A Stellar Key, pp. 180, 181.

[4] Ibid., pp. 175 et seq.

[5] We are assured in another place that every principle wears appropriate garments, and that the life within the blood—like sensation within the nerves—puts on an armour of many-coloured atmospheres, compounded of particles derived from the constitution within—even as grass grows out of the soil, or hair upon the head. The atmosphere thus formed about a person may be pleasing or repulsive. It is this which makes it possible for the bloodhound to track the slave, the dog to find his master, the sensitive to show when a particular person is near his house, and for two people to think the same thought at the same moment. Real individuality and spiritual status can be ascertained by the aura which—nolens volens—surrounds everyone, precedes and follows him everywhere—under all circumstances—and reveals him not less completely than words can impart an idea to the mind.—Views of our Heavenly Home, pp. 40, 41.

[6] It seems to be said of the Second Sphere generally that everything therein is created and manifested only by and through the exercise and direction of wisdom. Hence there is perfect order, while inexpressible happiness flows from the exquisite harmony and unity of action. Everything is appreciated as a blessing conferred by the light and life of Divine Love and by the form of Divine Wisdom.—A Stellar Key, p. 191. But it will be observed that here, as sometimes in other places, Davis is applying to the whole, that which is characteristic of some of its parts only. He gives ample evidence otherwise—and some of it is quoted here—that there are regions of sorrow, darkness and deception beyond the grave—the places of suicides, places of the gross and carnal minds set free in this state from earth, not to speak of the fabled dominion of Diakka.

[7] This should not be understood as suggesting that children are produced in the Summer Land as the fruit of any psychic or spiritual relation of the marital kind which

subsists therein, for the marrying and giving in marriage, if indeed any, is of another order. It is a union of heart and mind.

[8] It is difficult to understand the motive of this statement, for, according to Davis, all dwellers in the Summer Land are like the Image in Shelley's Witch of Atlas, that is to say, sexless beings, having no organs of generation, so that monogamy and polygamy— as these are understood here—are alike impossible. On the other hand, a subtle and intimate union of heart and mind is postulated generally of all the higher spheres, the dwellers in which are thereby united as closely as lies within the measures of union, according to its understanding by Davis. It is worth while to mention this because the idea of two souls predestined for each other from the beginning is favoured by Davis, but he is not at all clear as to the nature of the bond between them, and does not indicate how it can be distinguished from the general bond of each society, order, or hierarchy. The truth is that he has not understood the old legend on which he has drawn and has placed the male and female aspects of wedded psychic love in separate psychic vestures or bodies, which opposes the spirit of the legend.

[9] This is repeated elsewhere, as already seen, and not as information received but as the considered opinion of Davis concerning some of the links between man and the animals which preceded the human epoch on this earth. On the question whether all human souls are necessarily immortal he struck occasionally a rather uncertain note, but ultimately took the affirmative side, even in cases where there is no vestige of desire or intuition on the subject. So far as I can recall, the question of the survival of animals is never discussed in his books, and though his Summer Land is this world thinly spiritualised, it is never relieved by the presence of out kith and kin in the lower scales of animated being.

Chapter Twelve - The Diakka and Their Earthly Victims

[1]

Seen from Starnos, or from the right shoulder of the beautiful mountain east of the Seven Lakes of Cylosimar, [2] lies a wonderful and mysterious portion of the Summer Land. It appears like an immeasurable wilderness covering the whole sphere to the South-West and throwing a shadow far up into the dome of the rosy-blue heavens. It is so attractive that great self-government is necessary to save one from hastening to enter a country which has for millions of ages excited the admiration and curiosity of the imperfect inhabitants of all worlds. The observer is amazed with the apparently boundless magnitude of this celestial wilderness and by its wonderful aerial crown, so bright and prismatic as to make immediate surroundings black. It impresses the beholder that hills and dales and forests beneath must be splendid with diamonds and golden riches, too perfect for earthly eyes. All external appearances of this Wilderness of the Diakka convey suggestions of a mysterious and occult character. It is a Garden of Eden and yet also a place where the morally deficient and unclean enter upon a strange probationary life. [3]

A Diakka means a person with an occult temperament and propensities, springing from overcharged self-consciousness. Intellectually he may be a Bacon, a Byron, a Shakespeare; but, being morally deficient, he is without active feelings of justice, philanthropy or affection. He knows nothing of what men call gratitude; the motives of hate and love are the same for him; self is the end of his being, and he thinks that all personal life will be absorbed ultimately in the all-consuming self-love of God. Though unbalanced, he is not, however, an evil person. He takes delight in personating opposite characters, often amusing himself with jugglery and tricky witticisms, secretly tormenting mediums, causing them to exaggerate in speech and falsify by acts. Nevertheless good physicians of love and ministers of truth labour among the Diakka, so that each and all are delivered ultimately. When you go into their wonderful wilderness you find yourself in a garden of beauty. The Divine Love and Wisdom are there, shining in splendour from the sad-leaved trees and emanating from feathery and downy grasses that carpet the beautiful land. The trees resemble in their foliage our pine and fir; but they cast a wonderful golden shade throughout the entire realm. Yet the light of the upper sky shines through all, even far down into the foundations of the land. Thus, although there is an amazing solemnity, a tearful sadness and melancholy murmur, magnetically subduing the egotistic extravagances of the inhabitants, yet travellers from other countries enter the society of the Diakka and enjoy their life and scenery.

The intellectually gifted, witty and tricky Diakka are not restrained from visits to earth, because personal education through experience is part of the scheme of developing personal responsibility. By permission of superior minds they play important parts in assaults upon bad governments, pernicious customs, evil social conditions, and frequently upon religious errors and superstitions. But for these spiritual freebooters little progress would be made. In the concerns of spiritualism they delight in flattering mediums and making magnificent promises to fortune-seekers who interrogate such persons for private gain. Some of their amazing promises are accompanied with most satisfactory evidences of spiritual intercourse. They puzzle spiritual philosophers by a mixture of alarming doubts about immortality. No more romantic farce than the boon of being reincarnated was ever played upon human imagination by the sportive Diakka. They take a gipsy-like pleasure in travelling from place to place, from circle to circle, from medium to medium, passing themselves off under assumed great names. They are perfect in all sleight-of-hand performances, from their extensive knowledge and control of the subtlest elements and laws of exterior chemistry. In circles for materialisation they play fantastic tricks for the entertainment of the credulous, though it is not to be inferred that the creations of art are all false to the originals. The Diakka are masters of the Black Art, and most of their materialisations gather up chemically and represent literally the face, form, expression and even the style of clothing by which a personated entity was commonly known and recognised before death.

The Diakka themselves were once human beings. They are derived from every tribe and nation under the sun. They have died, as we shall die, and now they return to molest men and women, like "chickens coming home to roost." They are begotten of humanity, and they come back to reciprocate with their producing causes. [4] Men's bad and brutal passions reappear in their children, who shower back from the Wilderness of the Diakka the effects of such tendencies upon susceptible persons, the innocent and the guilty suffering alike. What timid investigators of spiritualism are shocked at—the false and disgusting among mediums—might arouse, with more justice, their attention to those cardinal immoralities in society which generate what they abhor.

[1] See the work under this title passim.
[2] See next chapter.
[3] There seems evidence for concluding that the revelations of Davis concerning Diakka were received with less confidence by Spiritualists than most of his other visions, and it has even been suggested that they were his way of explaining and minimising the counter-revelations of Thomas Lake Harris. On the other hand, some occultists have regarded the account as affording a glimpse of sub-mundane life, such as that attributed to elemental. Of these, however, Davis knew nothing, and had no room for them in his system. The Diakka are disembodied human beings, and when he speaks of angels they are merely advanced souls who had once lived on earth, or in one of the planets. As regards the doctrine of demons, this is considered at length only on a single occasion; but it is in an exceedingly confused manner and does not call for reproduction in the text of the present work. The remarks are embodied in a criticism of certain mediumistic phenomena which occurred about 1853, and suggested pandemonium to the witness who put it on record, being a certain Dr. J. A. Gridley. From the standpoint of Davis, all devils in the universe are living in the symbols of the mind, on the middle ground between our material and spiritual organisations. What are called evil spirits originate in the conflict of our nervous system, when one state of mentality is indulged at the expense of blessings which may be conferred by the other. If we dwell too much in the spiritual sphere it will draw us out of harmony with the laws of the outside world, and if the material sphere is suffered to becloud our spiritual and supersensuous nature the same operation will occur in a reverse sense. In either extreme, the mind is beset with imaginary devils, evil spirits and hells. We are not therefore to believe in evil spirits upon evidence personally received. It is to be recognised that if we are in bondage to the external we become mediums for the fantastic impressions of existence, derivations from the old notions of good and evil deities, as taught, e.g., by Zoroaster. Good communications depend upon good states of mind. To have true impressions we must live true lives.—The Present Age and Inner Life, pp. 320-370. The criticism is not convincing, but it establishes the point that, for Davis, there were neither angels nor demons except in the sense of progressed or unprogressed humanities. He claims further to believe that spirits work occasionally upon unfortunate persons by means of symbolical representations or dramas for the sake of securing reformation.—Ibid., p. 370.
[4] In The Genesis and Ethics of Conjugal Love it is said otherwise that the Diakka occasionally meddle with the affairs of individuals through correspondingly inclined mediums, who are largely responsible for the intercourse.

Chapter Thirteen - Scenes in The Summer Land

[1]

Beyond the Diakka Reservation—where congregate the bright-witted, the striving, the sceptical, the darkness-loving, the sunset haunted beyond the colour line where its sombre luxuriance ceases and the reign of light begins, there is a vast continent of what may be called Religiousness. We stand almost beneath the path in which our sun rolls towards the Pleiades. Far away fields of mossy green and gold; mansion-like chapels, immense cathedrals, decorated with shadowy vines; bright, billowy trees, white paths between; solemn music filling the soul with unutterable sacredness; processions of thoughtful men and women, of singing and worshipping children; long lines of people who were once halt and sick, maimed and blind, deaf and dumb—all impress you as beings of a new world created in the heavens for those who are wholly devoted to the love and worship of God.

The chapels and temples are dwelling-places of grave and dignified popes, cardinals, bishops, priests, founders of secret orders and saints from every kingdom and principality that ever existed since the foundation of human history. Here you behold the immemorial awe and holiness of what is called very ancient in religion. Sacred clouds of past ages hang over the gates of each half-hidden sanctuary. The slumbers of ten thousand centuries seem packed away in these structures. There is an oppressive pleasure in contemplating such solemn antiquities. The effect is instructive and ennobling. The feeling suggested is one of annihilation in God, delightful loss of personal existence in the Ocean-Spirit of the Infinite, or again it is of the many mansions in the Supernal Home. These great societies of religiousness exert very wonderful influences over the human family, whether on earth, in the nearest approachable planets, or in the Summer Land. They send forth upon the golden and purple seas of human life a fulness of religious warning and aspiration, an influence that moves millions—as if it were a breath from the very mouth of God. Their great empire stretches from North-East to South- West, pervading a country almost as large as the entire dry land of earth, and their history is coeval with that of the human race. Their mission is for the unification of mankind in "one faith and one baptism," while the progress which they make from age to age attests their earnestness and success.

They believed while on earth and believe still that whatsoever they did not then or do not now possess is beyond knowledge and attainment. In its true form and greatest abundance theirs is the spirit of love, beauty, wisdom, worship: of such is their view. What better can they do as ambassadors of everlasting truth than reach out hands full of salvation to mankind? There is, however, another great section scattered over a country as large as Asia. Herein are representatives of every imaginable sect. Plains and valleys, groves and fountains, rivers of living water exceed all expression in holy beauty. The sects are fraternising over a common purpose—the great work of saving mankind from endless desolation and of promoting the desirable state of universal purification through grace and the second birth. Doubtless a perception of this impressed Swedenborg to affirm that, in all the heavens, the "word" was read according to its spiritual sense and in the ancient language of correspondences. In this region there is profound veneration for "Bible truth." That which they understand as religion is the chief concern of immortals who, not being enlightened upon great interior principles, but finding that they have time still to "make their election sure," are incessantly at work upon each other and as missionaries to all accessible earths in their universe.

Beholding all this splendour in the House of Many Mansions and realising how intellectually contracted, yet spiritually honest and faithful, sectarians naturally are, even after death, you will acquire a foretaste of fields open for usefulness to the lover of mental freedom and eternal truth. But if you think that a time will ever come when every mind shall comprehend simultaneously the whole truth and be all as one, then you have little knowledge of human nature, the inflexible laws of progression and that harmonious system of government which flows from the Father God and Mother Nature.

Brighter than brightest crystals is the scene embracing the Seven Lakes of Cylosimar. Beautiful emanations surround some, while others seem to inhale the fragrance and to absorb very light of heaven. I would remain here and contemplate for ever, for here I could adore and worship. Hither, amid the glories and superabounding goodness of Divinity, I would attract all whom I love tenderly. Looking eastward is a hill-belted country, where dwell after death the inhabitants of planets like Venus, Mercury and several satellites. The people are steeped in sunbeams. Over the sparkling fields and upon the sky they look dreamily. An indescribable beauty, a delightful fragrance fills the atmosphere; but the population is materialistic, heavy-minded and half developed: they are insensible to all this loveliness. Here also come many from all countries of earth, especially from Africa and the South Sea Islands. [2] They float along like inanimate bodies, carried helplessly by the sovereign law of that attraction which determines destination. But the Paternal Divinity never forsakes such dependent children. In every sequestered nook a man or woman—embodying a matchless union of parent, friend and guardian—stands with outstretched hands, ready to receive all guests and begin the unfolding works upon the new-comers. Hither come half-developed children—born imbecile, deaf mutes and so forth—little chaotic minds, embryonic hearts. They float into the hospitalia of this heavenly world.

Surpassingly delightful is the scene to the southward—a great harmonious temple of wisdom, the empire of celestial love and supreme mental illumination. [3] Into the sacred circles of its most noble brotherhood come the wisdom and love of higher and more interior spiritual universes. Seekers for true wisdom find here a perfect repose of soul. By the divine impulse of attraction are drawn into a single group such minds as Humboldt, Herschel, Columbus, Galileo, Newton, Franklin. This empire of wise souls renders glorious the very sky above it. Angel ambassadors, empowered by this society, speed to earth for the overthrow of hypocrisy and fraud, and to awaken a consciousness of those punishments which follow "deeds done in the body." Under the administrative jurisdiction of this brotherhood, even the meddle-some Diakka are constrained to perform many beneficial missions among the needy of mankind. The country devoted to the brotherhood covers as much space as France and Italy, but its glories cannot be portrayed in words. Nezzar is the great river flowing nearly East and West. On its northern borders dwell the most gifted men and women known in human history, while on the southern congregate all those interaffiliated inhabitants who were once born upon Mars, Jupiter and Saturn. There is also a glorious stream of living water called Lustrade, having four beautiful tributaries: Gedor, meaning a mountain city; Palestro, or a country of the East; Esus, signifying the goddess; Alnamon, which is unrestricted communion. From this wise brotherhood the earth's inhabitants have received benefits and blessings since their earliest beginnings.

Much further East is the mountain-encircled valley called Ara-Elm-Haroun. Haroun is the original of Aaron, and the word with its prefixes signifies Valley of the Stranger. Here come angels of tenderness for ministration to constantly arriving suicides and also to many who have been insane. Tranquillity broods over the Vale of Haroun. The mountains yield only music, floods of pure light, love and happiness. A rich summer gladness thrills through all the landscape; but the suicides would hide themselves and the insane do not rest in the beautiful land beyond the tomb. Only the full-grown human life is happy after death. The others hasten back to earth because their work was not finished, their life had not known the fulness of that terrestrial experience which lay in their natural path.

.   .   .   .

Supercelestial associations—which shine like spiritual suns in the firmament—are modelled, for the most part, upon the plan and principles of the perfect human body—not alone on the form but its internal vital organs, with all their ties of connection, circulations and essential processes. Heart and brain have their true stations; "all are members of one body." Here we behold what gave Swedenborg his impression that the entire universe was one "grand man." The Divine Image is a likeness of the perfect human form, for this is the final form into which matter and spirit blossom. When this climax is attained there begins the operation of progressive law in essences, properties, powers, forces, attributes and combinations. Through all degrees of individual and communal life, onward and inward, with endless ebbings and flowings, from outer to inmost sphere, and back again from the inmost through another reconstruction of the universe, for ever and ever the law prevails. In these supercelestial societies, which are in exact and typical correspondence with the population and geographical appearance of higher and more interior spheres, I observe yet other principles of organisation, association and government. In lesser communities are organisations based upon the shape and functions of a five-foliate leaf, while the law of crystallisation is manifested in yet others. Elsewhere are systems of social life and education founded upon the principles of flowing water, beginning with the fountain and ending with the ocean which washes protecting shores, thence passing through rhythmically graded groups until a climax is reached in liberty—that crowning reward of the children of our Heavenly Parents. The principles and structure of the stellar universe are adopted by numbers of other associations as the truest plan of systematising and harmoniously uniting human interests. Some associations are composed of highest natures, which have "the law written upon their hearts," requiring no ordinances, nor so much as a thought concerning their common interests or methods and ends of life.

The principle of use is the universal principle which prevails in the Summer Land. There is consequently the plainest evidence of design everywhere, a primal love in all affections, an intelligent thought and purpose in every organisation and movement. This principle distinguishes our Heavenly Home from human experience on earth. Happiness and prosperity are secured to each member of society, on payment of the inflexible price, from which no true angel appeals— that he or she contribute faithful service to the prosperity and happiness of others. When may we look for the advent of such a kingdom of heaven on earth? It is the reign of universal justice through universal love. Let this thought, desire, aspiration alone fill the mind when reciting the Lord's Prayer. Otherwise the prayer is vain and the lip- service returns to those who utter it like "sounding brass."

.   .   .   .

The flashing rivers of light flow out of the darkness of distance with pulses of undying music, among the flower-covered lands in our Heavenly Home. [4] Through the boundless dome move suns rolling for ever, and move revolving planets. Dazzling comets sweep by, enveloped in splendour, like flaming angels of God. There is fragrance of innumerable flowers. Subdued by shadows of overhanging trees, a crystal light spreads from the bosom of rivers. The landscape is broad and grand on every side. There are mountains filled with splendour, homes of many Brotherhoods. Beautiful birds—bright representations of affections—pour music through the summer air, making sweet-breathed roses tremulous, sending musical throbbings through fragrant hearts of lilies. Mountains and streams glow with warmth of overflowing love, and laughing rivers shine with Divine Wisdom. Amidst fruit-laden trees and heavenly groves are dwellings for children of God. There is a vast congregation of persons—artistic, literary, scientific—bound together by deep and grateful recollections. Mental freedom, moral culture, free discussion characterise this august organisation. There is an inner group among them who report tidings received from a more interior universe. A beautiful and accomplished goddess is the presiding divinity.

Centuries ago most of them lived on earth—in Greece, Rome, Germany, England, Scotland, France, Italy. It is a very ancient association, yet how youthful the wisest appear. But there are also recent arrivals—clergymen, editors, artists, writers, lawyers, statesmen—who, strangely, seem older than those who lived in the days of Pythagoras. They are still of the earth, earthy, and some display inferiority by manifesting importance in the presence of superiors. Most of them take outside rank in this celestial university. The heavenly host aid all visitors, all who have come newly, and with equal grace help mankind universally.

Children play among the blooming groves in the rosy background. Their tender imaginations are nurtured in this natural home of poets. There are associations of mothers watching over and waiting for their unascended children. These lean their faces with touching affection against the laughing little beauties and seem to listen for remembered tones. The rich significance of woman's soul is poured like elemental wine into every child's bosom. There is above all an angel mother whose very presence is benediction, whose face is radiant with divine illumination. Mother of the gods, I behold your holy families along the slopes of the musical mountains. Where you are there are no lost little ones, no orphans, none who are homeless.

.   .   .   .

Self-luminous, independent of stellar and solar light is the Summer Land. [5] Its streams, rivers, fountains glitter with their own immortal radiance. Its mountains and undulating landscapes are ever green, beautiful with diamond effulgence, more "delectable" than any pilgrim dreams, while the firmament glows with suns and planets, clusters within clusters, constellations within universes, far beyond mind's conception. High thoughts visit us from the heavenly Alps. A thousand stainless societies are visible in the Summer Land, whose inmost life is in rhythmical movement with the concerted harmonies of more celestial and supercelestial universes. The effulgence of these holy centres exceeds the brightness of a thousand suns. Streams of perfection spread from these living fountains. O perfect life. Let us measure our existence by the even step of this progressive army. Domestic enjoyments, based upon true conjugal unions and interwoven with fondest affection of children and kindred, abide therein. Natures on earth uncompanioned, lonely hearts longing for unchangeable love, here find their own. Fields of splendour, [6] many mansions in the Heavenly Home, celestial warmth, harmonious light and beauty, "beyond the clouds and beyond the tomb," when our time shall come, we shall glide forth upon the magnetic river, and—accompanied by faithful guardians—shall find our own place in the Temple of Father God and Mother Nature.

.   .   .   .

When I had an opportunity, for the first time, to contemplate a celestial garden, it was unlike anything that I had seen in this world. It seemed to be a far-extending avenue of flowers and beautiful trees, with persons innumerable walking leisurely, lovingly, arm in arm, and thousands of beautiful children at play through the devious labyrinths. I heard the songs of birds which resemble those of this planet, under the equator, but some excluded all rays except the yellow or in other cases the blue. They were so transparent that I could see their whole physical interior. There is nothing so expressive of pure, immense, heavenly love as the blue bird, while the yellow represents that mellower affection which comes from wisdom. The songs of these birds echoed from a place where minds meet occasionally for deliberations, as in a Brotherhood. There were numberless varieties of flowers differing from those on earth, saving one which resembled the violet. There were also curious vines growing over lofty trees and bearing countless throbbing flowers in place of leaves. Each corolla pulsated like a harp, and every flower seemed conscious that it was part of a divine life and plan.

There is an island which takes its name from the purposes to which it is devoted and is called Akropanamede. [7] There is a beautiful cluster of springs which they name the Porilla, and each of them gives off sweet musical sounds—

full of unutterable significance. The harmonious notes blend with those of streamlets, and these lose themselves in a river flowing by the flowery paths of the Hospitalia. This name is given to one of the temples where persons who have suffered on earth from particular engrossing infatuations are taken to be cured. The teacher-physicians appointed on that island are called Apozea. There are many on the Isle of Akro- panamede. Rosalia is another island and a region of great splendour, where persons dwell who have never lived on earth. Some are of Mercury and Venus. Batellos is near Rosalia and is so termed because certain educated Greeks sought its retirement soon after their arrival in the Spirit World, as a suitable place to celebrate the advent on earth of Plato's Doctrine of the Deity. Poleski is situated in another part and is frequently visited by former inhabitants of this earth who are still searching for ancient wisdom. It is in close relation with Alium, where certain ancients repaired for the foundation of a Brotherhood composed of persons born long prior to the origin of the Old Testament. Finally, there is Lonalia, an island inhabited by young people who died as orphans on earth. Here they are introduced to those who are their parents in spirit but of whom they were not necessarily born physiologically here below.

There is a temple of affectionate thought and practical wisdom called Concilium, and there the voices of women are heard frequently. They meet to acquire information on what it is best to accomplish upon the Earth, Mars, Jupiter or Saturn, the planetary populations of which all need to be visited frequently. In this beautiful temple are gathered the wisdom, intuition, hope, love, poetry and music of multitudes among the sweetest, truest, most earnest women that have lived here below. Elsewhere I have seen a vast congregation of those who were distinguished for their philanthropy in this life. Some of them have charge of soldiers who perish on the field of battle. These are introduced by degrees to a new and different life. Persons of both sexes who are engaged in labours like this are distinguished by particular vestures, with which no silken gauze or gossamer fabric can bear comparison.

. . . .

The feasting sometimes visible in the Summer Land is a great joy to behold. [8] That great Spiritual Reformer, our Brother, said: "Consider the lilies of the field, how they grow; they toil not, neither do they spin; and yet I say unto you, that even Solomon, in all his glory, was not arrayed like one of these." The beautiful truth contained in this passage was exemplified in my first vision of a great feast in the world of spirit. What is called manna in the Old Testament is there a literal manifestation, dropping like snow from the bosom of the heavenly realm and becoming like the purest honey distilled from the depths of the upper air. The beautiful substances made from this manna are in all possible forms, each possessing a flavour and odour of its own. Out of the one substance all forms and varieties of food are made—an art in chemistry which men will discover in this world one of these golden days. When we get where aerial emanations are granted for food and know how to gather up the spiritual particles that float in the invisible ether, then we shall live the life of the lilies.

[1] See Views of our Heavenly Home, pp. 184 et seq., being selections in respect of the subject to the end of p. 215. It may be noted that in Answers to Ever-Recurring Questions from the People Davis explains that there is a philosophical reason for the expression Summer Land. He says that the difference between this and the adjoining sphere is as wide and marked as between the seasons of winter and summer. The world of earth at its best contains only the rudiments of the next world. Here sickness and death terminate the career of men; there they can experience neither. Here the minutes of life are counted as by grains of iron and sand, but there time is measured by ripples of love and wisdom. Here evil renders existence comparable to a stormy winter; there is music of perpetual summer. But the realities of the higher life will shine at length into that which is below; the kingdom of Heaven will come, and blend the two worlds so perfectly that every part of earth will be supremely blessed and beautiful. Until the dawn of that holy day it is natural and truthful to think and speak of the Spirit World as the Summer Land.—Op. cit., p. 59. The two expressions are therefore synonymous, but Davis forgets that in the pages immediately preceding he has created a distinction between the Spirit World and the Summer Land. The former is the universe of inner life, out of which the spirit of man never passes. He feels, thinks, decides, acts as a resident therein, and death only removes the cloud of matter from before his spiritual senses. The Summer Land is a localised sphere within the Spirit World,—Ibid., pp. 57, 58.

[2] In this connection it may be mentioned that, according to Davis, the physiological colour of races does not continue in the Second Sphere, but their peculiarities do. The complexions of disembodied spirits are in accordance with the state and degree of their moral development, so that a bad white man is likely to appear with a blacker face than a simple-hearted and well-conducted negro.—Ibid., p. 65.

[3] The allegorical nature of many of these visions, as regards at least their mise-en-scene, will probably strike the reader, and seeing that there are many temples as well as many mansions in the psychic house of Davis, it will serve a purpose to compare the sanctuary mentioned above with a purely figurative temple in which Davis says that he was accustomed to hold commune with other devout brethren. It is described as of modest structure and wide dimensions, having been erected by a Master-Builder on an unchangeable foundation. It is all beautiful within and bears on all its parts the seal of wisdom. It stands upon a spiral-like eminence, commanding an unlimited view—in a word, the living panorama of creation. It is built upon three terraces, which are the mineral, vegetable and animal kingdoms. Over the arched entrance of the temple is inscribed the word Perception, and about a mirror in the spacious vestibule there is graven the word Memory. The interior is a place of pictures, being archetypal ideas of things manifested but imperfectly through external forms. A light flows in through windows which are called Senses; but a more mellow and resplendent radiance descends through the dome, representing the faculty of wisdom, and it is a medium for the influx of Truth from the Spirit World—that the sanctuary may be fully illuminated and its members filled with joy. Beneath the dome, in the middle place of the temple, is an altar, which is that of Justice, full of divine beauty; and the name of the preacher who stands thereat is Reason—the commissioned advocate of good and right. Before him—resting on the altar—is a sacred volume, or universal compend of Art, Science, Philosophy, Theology, and of the architectural principles upon which the church is built. It embraces the history of causes and creation, the genealogy and experience of nations, and it contains the likeness of its Eternal Author. The language is that of the forms and sym-

bols of original thought; its sentences cannot be transposed; and its consecutiveness prohibits the possibility of human interpolation or change. To an attentive congregation composed of twelve spirits—which are Desires—the preacher expounds the teachings of the Holy Book—being that of Nature—the Author of which has erected the temple also, and Pie it is Who inspires the preacher's words. The central and most prominent member is a Desire for Unity—a great and good layman who bows in prayerful silence and eagerly receives all suggestions that breathe of harmony. The principle that Justice and Truth generate happiness, which is the native religion of the soul, is a sufficient text from which to preach the continual sermon of a righteous life, in unity with the neighbour, the cosmos and the Father.—See The Great Harmonia, Vol. II, pp. 65-67. It will be understood by everyone that the temple here delineated is the personality of Davis the seer, but while it is consistent as an emblematic picture, it will be seen later on that he—as an intuitional philosopher—was not invariably satisfied with the findings and declamations of Reason, which is installed thus as sole celebrant.

[4] For this narrative see Views of our Heavenly Home, pp. 152-155.

[5] See Views of our Heavenly Home, pp. 194, 208.

[6] Views of our Heavenly Home, pp. 215, 216.

[7] Further particulars concerning this island are given in Views of our Heavenly Home, pp. 150 et seq. It is said to be shaped like a pear, and its inhabitants are known as the Brotherhood of Plana de Alphos, who are engaged in works of benevolence and art. The temple is called Aggameda. It is a vast building, but then the island itself is 2500 times the size of Europe.

[8] Davis speaks also of a celestial festival, held—according to his vision—in 1851. The melody of its music filled the whole heaven and the spiritual landscapes throbbed. Subsequently he learned that no musical instruments existed in that part of the Summer Land, but he ascertained that its inhabitants have such perfect acquaintance with the powers and sounds of the voice that they can produce thereby all possible varieties and shades of instrumental music.—A Stellar Key, pp. 179, 180.

Chapter Fourteen - Ultimates In the Summer Land

[1]

By the term Summer Land is meant a sphere of perpetual youth where the effects of moral imperfections continue, where the consequences of bodily and mental infirmities are visible in those who are hampered by such infirmities when they go to that land from earth. [2] Ultimates in the Summer Land, as distinguished from primates and proximates, may be stated plainly and briefly. Search the scriptures of Nature—the handiwork of the firmament—for in them you will find the holy truths of eternal life. To understand the apocalyptic glories of the universe study the Genesis of this God-inspired volume. The Genesis and Exodus of the book are the Primates and Proximates. The Ultimates you cannot see in this world, except logically—as the outcome of philosophical principles. An intelligent mind, to make intellectual progress, must think as Nature prompts him—from primates on and up, through endlessly successive complications, to ultimates. Whoso questions Nature aright reads truly those scriptures which teach of God and eternity. As spiritualists, as searchers for eternal life, let us contemplate Nature in man and woman, Nature in God and therefore God in Nature. Man goes to the Second Sphere with the ultimates of all his parts and functions. The ultimates of every race in the Summer Land establish a community of their own. When this world is unfolded into an all-embracing state of civilisation it will represent the highest source of joy in the Summer Land. Extremes and ultimates meet in the sphere to which we go at death. Here they meet only on the surface, there from the interior. The Negro will never fully understand the Caucasian in this world, because the Caucasian will never fully understand the Negro. The two opposite races meet in the Summer Land. Does not the Bible say that "the least shall be greatest in the Kingdom of Heaven"? There are Christians who believe sincerely that the person who is here the most thoroughly "poor in spirit" will be richest and greatest there. You will find that there is a deep meaning in this sentence. Those who superficially exalt themselves are naturally abased, because the next step they take from a false exaltation is certain to land them in a lower position.

In the Summer Land the Negro and Caucasian will represent two great opposite races. Men do not take their complexions with them—the primates, fictions or falsehoods—but consequences, ultimates, realities—these they do take. Ultimates are developed after death, and what here corresponds to Negros, Caucasians, Indians, Mongolians, Malays are there visible and distinguishable by many radical characteristics. In the Father's House there are "many mansions," because there are essentially different modifications of the human family. Each wants a comfortable, happy place in the Second Sphere. In the Summer Land there are localities for all divisions of the race. There are always wings to great palaces. The Caucasian world moves through one wing, and the African world is free to move through an opposite wing of the infinite palace. Nature is just as powerful and beautiful and eternal as God. God and Nature work together. The male and the female go on through all eternity. [3] Intermediates also continue long. The principles that are at work making tiny shells on the seashore are eternal principles. They are working as faithfully in the higher spheres as within and upon the earth. They round out globes and make roads throughout the universe. All progress in science points toward an approaching discovery of the Summer Land. It may seem to you that this spiritual world is afar—a vast and remote existence, into which astronomers have not peered. But it is my belief that astronomers, with their physical instruments, will on one of these future days recognise the Summer Land. It is not remote. We move every moment in its presence. [4] Our earthly planet rolls in its orbit under the observation of inhabitants of the Spirit World. Astronomically speaking, the earth is on one side of that vast galaxy of suns and planets termed the milky way, and directly across this great physical belt of stars we find the sublime repose of the Summer Land—receptacle of immortal inhabitants who ascend from different planets belonging to our solar system. All these planets have celestial streams leading toward the heavenly shores. There is a point at which they blend, widen and expand into a mighty river, and thus become a flowing element of perfect beauty in the Land of Spirits. It seems to give out music from all its variegated margins and vast congregations are visible on its shores, learning its harmonious sounds. Along the banks appear to be grasses, having silken fibres reflecting the rainbow colours of the diamond, or giving off a purple brilliancy mellowed softly down into an atmospheric immensity of its own.

The Spirit World is thus brought into our experience; the very life of it is seen and realised. Its existence is not more mysterious than the formation of a man's body out of the invisible life of his nerves. I believe fully that the existence and actualities of the next sphere will become a part of science and that its philosophy will be as plain as the existence of such planets as Mars, Jupiter and Saturn.

The Spirit Land is revealed to our intellectual perception according to the natural laws of progress and development. [5] It is harmonised with the oracles of intuition, so that poetry and prophecy begin to assume a new significance. Paul who "died daily," Paul who was often "in the spirit" glided past the subordinate sphere and was "caught up into the third heaven," seeing things not possible for man to utter. [6] The Harmonial Philosophy unfolds the magnificent order of the spiritual worlds with the same precision that it treats of the physical kingdoms of Nature. If it be asked what is the ulterior object, and what does the Harmonial Philosophy propose to accomplish for man?—the answer is, To unfold the Kingdom of Heaven on earth, to apply the laws of planets to individuals—in a word, to establish in human society the same harmonious relations that are found to obtain in the cosmos. It is therefore wholly of humanity, as it is also wholly religious. It sees the Divine Love crowned by Divine Wisdom.

[1] See Morning Lectures, pp. 421 et seq.
[2] It is obvious that Davis begins here in the opposite sense of his meaning, as a place where physical, mental and moral imperfections are shown forth in their consequences does not answer to any rational conception of a land of perpetual youth. He is meaning to indicate that the results of our life on earth—good, bad and indifferent—are carried with us into the next sphere. It is a modified doctrine of Eastern Karma, though it does not operate by way of reincarnation.
[3] This statement is important for the Davis view concerning the world to come and for the ultimates of which he is treating. In true spiritual union the male and female dissolve one into another, and if the union be permanent then it is possible to say concerning it that which is affirmed in one of the uncanonical dicta ascribed to Christ, when speaking of the Kingdom of Heaven—namely, that the male is with the female, neither male nor female. The alternative given above is the doctrine of separation in respect of the two halves which are designed to be one soul.
[4] It is said for this reason that when a man dies to the external world he becomes alive very soon to the world that is within. Without leaving the chamber of death he may be able to take immediate note of things to be seen and heard in the realm of spirits. That which was previously on the inward side of persons and objects generally is now on the outward side. But he can see also what occurs in the room where he has died. He is in the omnipresent world of spirits.—Views of our Heavenly Home, pp. 92, 93.
[5] See The Present Age and the Inner Life, pp. 55, 56.
[6] St. Paul does not speak of things that are impossible but of things unlawful to utter.

Book Five - Religion and Theology

Chapter One - History and Philosophy of Evil

[1]

As the five phases of babyhood, childhood, youth, manhood and maturity are marked steps in the journey of individual life, so are the five historic doctrines of the cause and cure of evil remarkable in the progressive development of the life of mankind. They may be denominated the ante-human, the inter-human, the super-human, the spiritual and the harmonial. In the individual and the race, implicit and immeasurable faith characterise the flower of infancy. The thinking principle, the human mind is folded lovingly within the heart. The earliest theology or doctrine of God was monotheistic, but that God was concealed and incomprehensible. He accomplished in the hiddenness every good and evil thing. One was the smile of His mouth, the other the frown of His brow. With one hand He recompensed the righteous, with the other He punished the guilty. Hence in this theory God has no compeers upon whom to impose the origin and cause of evil. [2] Why the unfathomable Deity sent into the world disease, misery and death was no question to be entertained by man. According to the ante-human theory evil came from God, and the cure consisted in sacrifice, to placate the imaginary wrath which lived and worked in secret behind the stars.

We come now to the second development, corresponding to the childhood of the race and called here the inter-human theory, characterised by a doctrine of fatalism. It held that all evil is a necessity of human existence and that man was the helpless subject of fortuitous circumstances. To the question who made necessity the philosophers of this period answered—The Fates, personified forces regarded as intelligent and sacred. The doctrine of many gods replaced monotheism. As time went on, in the plenitude of mythological developments, every known human state and circumstance had assigned to it a particular superintending deity. The suggested cure of evil was happiness, bodily ease, mental tranquillity, sensuous delight.

But the aggregate life of mankind graduated from childhood into the flush and surge of youth and so felt the sublime emotion of self-containing power. At this particular juncture originated the doctrine that man is a free moral agent. A proud feeling of individual responsibility supplanted slavish subservience to outer circumstances. Herein was originated the superhuman theory of evil, and with it a return to the doctrine of one God, one Maker of laws; but man—on whom they are imposed—can disobey, and can take the cost and consequences. It was fabled that evil and misery began with a war of the angels waged in the very presence of God, long ages prior to the advent of man upon this globe. As regards our own race, every individual is wilfully wicked and personally responsible. But the Eternal Bosom was boundless in the quality of mercy and longed to exercise this saving attribute if man would but allow Him. Thus was inaugurated a system of superhuman medicine to cure evils of superhuman origin. It was an ecclesiastical hypothesis altogether, a scheme of arbitrary benefits and penalties revealed in an arbitrary manner by an arbitrary God, to accomplish the arbitrary ends of Divine Government. [3]

The soul of the race in its manhood realises something of its mundane business and celestial destiny. The spiritual theory of evil—which belongs to this state— regards the fact of established intercommunication between the seen and the unseen worlds as a panacea for human misery. It affirms that our good and evil affections attract corresponding qualities and influences from the Spirit Land. Wilfully wicked affections, with those imposed and inherited prior to the possibility of willing, obtain their pabulum from spiritual fountains. Voluntary drunkards and voluptuaries become mediums for the gratification of unsatiated appetites which survive the ordeal of death. Hereditary viciousness is believed by many to be confirmed and stimulated by wicked spirits, while spirits of goodness, purity and truth exert all their power to inspire man's better nature, to rescue also and to elevate. To this theory the remedies are attached logically, as follows: (1) Belief in personal immortality, (2) sitting in circles for demonstrations, (3) becoming mediums for communications, (4) prayer for silent communications, (5) personal goodness based upon willing affection for moral and religious truth, (6) spiritual education of the young, (7) abstinence from all constructive reforms, except for religious development, (8) allowing personal evils and national injustices to have their perfect work, (9) belief in the continual supervision of a personal God, (10) belief in special providences on the part of God and of His angels, (11) waiting for celestial powers to inaugurate—in some sudden, supernatural, universal manner—the long prayed for kingdom of heaven on earth.

But we arrive finally at the Harmonial Theory, corresponding to the maturity of the race. Its watch-words are Association, Progression, Development; its principles are Love, Wisdom, Liberty, Justice, Happiness. To that Truth which is eternal, backward as well as forward, it has recourse reverently to search out the origin of evil. [4] But it finds that absolute goodness is the only element about the Holy Centre and that no earthly intelligence can separate the Eternal Mind from the Laws of Nature. These universal Laws flow through all gradations of being, with that immutable strength and precision which characterise the Central Fountain of Mind. They are the vital principles by which the Divine Mind is organised and regulated for ever. They are summed up concisely within and written legibly without on the human constitution. They ultimate into grades of countless variety, while in each of them the varieties of life and diversities of organisation are innumerable. This truth underlies the Harmonial Philosophy of Evil— a Word of God heard in the garden of the universe. These differences necessitate parallel dissimilarities of quality, position and office in the empire of animation. We discover that elemental wars and physical changes in earth, water and air are indispensable to human progress. So also, in the human race, social inequalities and national conflicts are essential and necessitated by the divine laws of Association, Progression and Development. The intrinsic usefulness of evil is plain as the sun at noon, though the soul of more limited vision will be fired with holy indignation at words like these. Let it grasp intelligently the discrete spheres and graduated planes unfolded by the divine laws, or setting aside an intellectual perception of all this unity let the soul picture the stupendous truth, and it will be on fire with another zeal. In the lower world of ignorant strife whatever is, is wrong, while on the Harmonial Mountain whatever is, is right—or is in process of becoming better. Those who stand thereon can behold with what beautiful certainty "ever the right comes uppermost and ever is justice done."

There are two hostile forces [5]: (1) The wilful and ignorant; (2) the selfish and educated. Among their various aspects are peace versus war, liberty versus slavery, truth versus error, virtue versus vice. Between these pairs of opposites there is light on the origin of evil, thus: Sin is the child of evil, evil is the child of error, error is the child of ignorance, ignorance is the first condition of an immortal being whose whole existence is regulated by Association, Progression and Development. On this sequence may be superposed another, as follows. The existence of individual beings necessitates positions in space; positions in space necessitate various conditions, and these involve corresponding circumstances; but circumstances mould the individual to their image and likeness, either good or evil. Evil is the temporal subversion or misdirection of absolute and omnipresent good, and good became inverted by man's ignorance and error. Ignorance is the predecessor of knowledge, and man began therein because he is designed for endless progress. Evil is the dust and incident of our pilgrimage through the wilderness of experience. Ignorance is a negative or passive fulcrum upon which the intellectual lever of spiritual progress acts with an almighty and universal sweep. Individual accountability is not destroyed by this doctrine. Justice, liberty, purity, love, wisdom, truth, progress, happiness are laws which no man can violate; but he has power to comply or not with those varied temporal conditions by means of which these principles carry forward the stupendous business of the Univercoelum. Man's willing faculties give him unlimited mastery over relations and conditions, but against the fixed laws of the physical and spiritual universe he can do absolutely nothing. He has no physical or mental power either to create or destroy, but to modify and change only. Herein consequently is found his individual and associative accountability.

In the limpid light of this philosophy the long-perplexing problem of free agency is solved. Man is seen to be at once a subject and a power, an integral child of eternal dependence, but at the same time master of his individual vineyard. As such he is able to impair or prevent his own happiness, as also to deprive others of their temporal rights and local liberties. From this standpoint we can perceive the origin of the doctrine of praise and blame, with the evolution therefrom of so many vindictive codes, so many tyrannical institutions and depraving plans of punishment. We can understand why one who obeys the fixed laws is beloved as a saint, while he who transgresses them is hated and con-

138

demned as a sinner. Lastly, we can see why it is that implacably hostile forces disturb the world's progress and why transient antagonisms seem to postpone the realisation of universal peace.

Let us now define our position on the whole subject in summary form. We repudiate the theory that evil was originally premeditated and sent among men by the Divine Mystery, and yet there is a truth within it which no mind can reject. We repudiate the theory that evil is a hopeless fatality of the physical universe, and yet there is a truth herein which all should accept. We repudiate the theory that man is capable of violating God's otherwise immutable laws, and yet in this doctrine we admit an approximation to reality. We repudiate the theory that man's affections rule his thoughts and attract corresponding controlling influences from the Spirit Land; yet we do not close our eyes to the solemn validity of its fundamental law. Finally, we accept the harmonial theory of evil—that man is designed for a career of endless progression, to which all evils and sufferings are incidental, temporal and educational, working out, when not abused, "a far more exceeding and eternal weight of glory." [6]

[1] See the volume under this title passim.

[2] There is an alternative presentation of the subject in The Principles of Nature, according to which the primitive peoples believed that certain winds which came from above not only breathed among them a malignant element but inspired them with evil thoughts. This was the first conception as to the origin of evil, an opinion prevailing for many ages.

The cause of these winds—when causes began to be investigated—was held to be an unseen, undefinable, evil spirit or deity which either had the atmosphere for its habitation or was itself that medium. Being antagonistic to humanity, he destroyed their social love and instilled a spirit of envy, hatred and deception. At a later period, the cause and source of evil was transferred from the atmosphere to the sun itself, which was regarded as the countenance of an angry and unholy being who poisoned the air, and this poison entered into those who breathed it. Still later, certain Eastern tribes conceived of a spirit existing between them and the Good Deity, thus establishing a barrier to their communications with the Divine. It continued to prevail up to the time of Zoroaster, who established a faith in two antagonistic, eternal Beings, presiding over good and evil, and having distinct natures corresponding to these principles.—Op. cit., pp. 378, 379, 411. See pp. 219 et seq. of this digest.

[3] The counter-opinion of Davis as to the origin of evil does not deal with the problem. He finds no intrinsic corruption in the soul of man because that soul comes from the Infinite Fountain of goodness and love. So-called evil and sin are therefore external, not from the soul in its essences but from that which he terms superficial sources. As to these, he says that the primary sources of evil are hereditary organisation, a statement which obviously explains nothing and justifies nothing in the great economy of things. Man is just what his organisation compels him to be.—See The Present Age and Inner Life, pp. 333, 334.

[4] It being recognised that there is no absolute evil, considered as a principle, it follows that apparent evil is merely the misapplication of good laws. By the powerful impulsions of our passional forces we may bring good natural laws and pure substances into false relations and thus develop pain, disease, discords, dissatisfactions, dissolution and

death.—*The Great Harmonia, Vol. IV, p. 59.* Two things are certain in this connection: (1) That few people are nowadays concerned with affirming a principle of evil in the sense of the old Persian religion, and (2) that no one disposes of the fact which we term evil by explaining that it signifies misapplication. The sins which cry to heaven for vengeance do not cry less loudly when they are labelled with another denomination.

[5] The whole subject is treated differently in another place, where Davis begins by saying that the Laws of Nature are not creations or institutions, but emanations and things inherent. They do not tell us what God thinks or wills, but rather how He lives, how He must inevitably and immutably act. It is argued herefrom that if a single law belonging to the constitution of God could be infringed upon, violated or suspended, the Divine Being Himself would be threatened, as well as the universe, with disorganisation and chaos. To speak therefore of man violating this or that law—though Davis confesses that he has used such language frequently—tends to impart wrong conceptions of God, as also of our human powers. Thence he proceeds to consider whether sin is a transgression of the law and affirms that such a proposition is both fallacious and pernicious, recurring at this point to his previous debate respecting the immutability of law. He then goes on to say that there is no evil in the world, but there are conditions to be changed. So also there are no essential falsehoods, for all these are relative, and it is a question of degrees and conditions. Truths and falsehoods are but changes rung upon certain absolute entities, being objects, impressions and reflections. Error falls under the denomination of variations from the central line of coincidence between object and subject, and is only a negational condition of truth. There is one law of exaggeration and another of diminution, and these—considered by themselves—are no less essentially perfect than the law of harmony between objective and subjective realities. In telling what is termed a falsehood man substitutes either the law of diminution or else that of exaggeration for the middle law of harmony between things and ideas.—*See The Great Harmonia, Vol. IV, pp. 15-22.*

[6] There must be added to this the doctrine of a thesis which—in one or another aspect—is presented more than once by Davis. It affirms that the mental and physical constitution of man is harmonious, perfect and divine in its nature—meaning probably, essential or original nature. The reason is that it represents that Great Cause from which it originated. The deceptions, dissimulations and other evils in the world—and in ourselves also, presumably—do not flow from the interior of man's nature, but are a consequence of his unholy, imperfect and vitiated situation. The interior, which is of divine origin, cannot be made evil nor contaminated.—*The Principles of Nature, p. 410.* Finally, *The Approaching Crisis* has a very long section on the "true origin of evil," which unfortunately loses itself among criticisms of Christian theology and the story of the fall of man, so that it scarcely touches on the real issues of its subject. It disposes of diseases, wars, and other cruelties by affirming that they are consequences of progressive development in Nature. It affirms that evil is an arbitrary term applied to inequalities and misdirections when these have been outgrown and that as regards positive evil it does not exist, (a) because there is more harmony than discord, (b) more heat than cold, (c) more light than darkness, while (d) nothing is absolutely devoid of goodness. It is obvious that the problem is evaded in a consideration of this kind.

Chapter Two - The Cure of Evil

[1]

The abuse of evil consists chiefly in being conquered by it, permitting discord to become positive and master. The true use of evil consists in journeying over it to whatever is best. Evil is not a principle but the temporary subversion of individual rights, the inversion of private faculties, traceable to the protracted night of human ignorance and thence perpetuated through after ages by the power of selfishness. Reformers have no mythological devil to wrestle with, no wicked self-existent principle. We stand erect, prepared to overcome evil with good, to harmonise and straighten the misdirected works of ignorance and selfishness, to fulfil the local conditions of fixed laws, to build up the temple of individual harmony and to heal the nations thereby.

We must probe the depths of human misdirection; the deep seas of existence must yield up their contents. Superficial reform is unworthy the full-souled philanthropist. Look truly into the fountains of human evil and suffering and you will discover their three sources in (1) imperfect organisation, (2) defective education, (3) immoral situation. The primary misdirection comes about through hereditary transmission of passions and disease. Herein our hope for humanity—never so large as now—is the march of mind in fields of physical science, the control of generative conditions, and improvement of the type of procreation. The next fertile fountain of misdirection is education, and hereon are fixed the national hatreds of the earth. Each nation has a stereo-typed pattern of what is right and wrong, a peculiar conscience or standard of judgment which is branded upon its youth, and thus our soul comes to esteem as sacred that which another is taught to regard as secular. It comes about even that the conscientiousness of the one is identical with rascality in the other. [2] The third misdirection, being that of situation, consists usually of inherited inclinations, educational bias, individual interests, friendships, pride of relatives, the world's keen- eyed supervision, and the private ambition to be commended and successful. The control of situation over character may be illustrated in a variety of ways, but it can be said in a single sentence that the law of self-interest is subverting and twisting many of the noblest attributes of human disposition, and that under the despotic sway of custom the individual, though perhaps well organised and educated for a straightforward and noble existence, is rendered weak in principle and hypocritical in conduct by means of his circumstances.

We come now to the question of cure, and the Harmonial Philosophy would institute three practical methods: (1) A school of prevention, (2) a system of palliation, and (3) a work of reformation. We require a school of prevention to teach that the true Saviour is within each human body. His name is Wisdom and his manifestation is Harmony. To prevent the development of evil from deranged conditions, Society must give to its children—the fathers and mothers of the future— an education in the sphere of physical laws and spiritual principles. Immortal ideas and fixed principles should be grafted in the young mind as the only foundation of scientific and moral improvement. Upon no other ground can we expect a generation of noble men and worthy women, who—by harmonial marriages—will bestow upon the world the unfading glory of good offspring. There are, however, hydra-headed evils which no school of prevention can reach, and hence the necessity of doing some negative good by a system of palliation, including charities, methods of wholesome restraint and philanthropic institutions. As regards reformation, the Harmonial School proposes constructive work, based upon the eternal principles of association, progression and development, to prevent evil, vice and misery. We hold this possible only through the divine energy of immortal ideas, awakened by means of polytechnic institutions and impartial periodicals under the control of cultured and harmonious minds. My faith is unbounded in humanity's power to help itself, when purified by experience and exalted by unfolded reason. But the world is replete with lofty impulses which defeat themselves because they are apart from wisdom, and with local rivalries which crucify the helpless and innocent, apart from evil intention. My spiritual rest is perfect upon the bosom of Father God's immutable laws, and I hold that the world would receive more universal good from twelve healthy and energetic minds—in pure love with each other through harmonious perception of those Divine Laws—than from all the millions who have no such redemptive faith as a basis of action, A few minds animated as one man with the universal sweep of ideas could revolutionise the globe. Progressive wisdom in a few minds may harmonise the nations. To insure a speedier prevention of evils and a reformation of the masses, to accelerate emancipation from the ills that distract and deform society, let the wisest and noblest men and women adopt the fixed laws of association, progression and development. By this is not meant that man's faith in fixed laws is essential to the works that he may achieve. He may know and believe nothing, but even in miserable darkness he still floats forward upon life-currents of the universe toward the far-off era of ultimate redemption. [3] He might have hastened the birth of harmony in his soul, have diminished the woe of others and multiplied the recipients of happiness: yet he floats onward. But let the children of earth be educated in the glory and grandeur of the eternal principles of God; let them be stimulated systematically to examine the divine revelations of Nature; let their spiritual hearts be encouraged to beat responsive to angel breathings and holy harmonies of creation; let them be taught to rise above social discords, the oppressive antagonisms of sense; and then behold with what speed will spread everywhere the Harmonial Religion of Universal Justice.

[1] See History and Philosophy of Evil.
[2] With this and the general context we may compare The Great Harmonia, Vol. IV, p. 23, according to which (1) War is not evil, except to a man of peace; (2) polygamy is as natural at one stage of development as oranges are natural in the South; (3) the attribution of evil to this and that plane of society is characteristic of an undeveloped mind, yet it is a profanation and indeed a sort of atheism. The proper point of view regarding the whole problem—and the only way to its solution—is to look for that time when all discords will be overruled by good, and when war, slavery and those unfavourable aspects of life which we desire to be taken out of the way will somehow come into line

with the universal interests of humanity. Our part meanwhile is not to go forth with a plan to conquer error and thereby to stimulate combative habits in our fellow-men, but to do rather the positive good work by constructing harmonial temples of thought and welcoming the world hospitably into our happy homes,—See also Ibid., p. 25.

[3] This has to be checked by that somewhat exotic opinion which has been the subject of previous annotations, being the existence of a Divine Spirit in man, of which his soul part or psychic body is the vesture. There is affirmed concerning it that our inmost nature or essence is not corrupted but pure and also immaculate, tending—like the fragrance of flowers— toward heaven. See The Present Age and Inner Life, p. 334. It is a reflection of old Gnostic doctrine and enters, more or less, into most pantheistic philosophy. Davis did not fully understand the materials with which he was dealing, nor perhaps realise that they were out of joint with his whole system; but he could have scarcely missed the fact that he had stated what was virtually the opposite, and sometimes even categorically.

Chapter Three - Birth of Mythological Theology
[1]

There was never a word uttered or a sound formed which could convey the least conception of that All-Pervading Essence, that Great Spiritual Principle and Omnipotent Mind which dwells within the Vortex whence suns, systems and universes extend through immeasurable space, the expressed thought emanating from Infinite Purity and Perfection. Concerning the many conceptions which sprang from the youthful misguided intellects first-born among human species much might be related, but I will speak only in general terms as to the origin of mythological theology. When men had lost their primitive habit of radiated expression in the manner already related and had become socially miserable as a result, it proved that they were not advanced sufficiently in intellectual discernment to discover the actual cause; but one who was superior to the rest proclaimed a pretended discovery and was regarded consequently as an inspired chieftain. He announced that the winds or breathings which came from above sent forth a malignant element. Here was the first notion as regards the origin of evil, and it remained a prevailing opinion for many ages, during which time the human species was distributed gradually over the globe. In distant settlements of the original family certain more advanced intellects began to search a little further, and especially into the cause accountable for these hostile breaths. Being unacquainted with the disturbances occurring constantly in the equilibrium of the atmosphere, they referred the said breathings to an unseen, undefinable evil spirit supposed to brood over the whole region or world in which they dwelt. The atmosphere itself was held to constitute this spirit. It was an advance of one step in the theology which prevailed among them.

But envy, war and deception grew with the years, and subsequent generations did not suffer the cause of evil to remain here. They abandoned the impression of their forefathers as to a cause resident in the atmosphere, adopting a belief that the sun itself was the face of an angry, unholy being who disseminated evil and caused the atmosphere to instill it into their minds. The author of the scheme was adored as the inspired son of previous generations, and people even began to fear the presence of this philosopher. They trembled at the images which he shadowed forth in hieroglyphical characters. They fell before and worshipped him, with all expressions of veneration which belonged subsequently to the ceremonies of idolatry. They erected a large and massive edifice, with apartments constructed according to his will, and raised him to the highest seat in this temple. He became prophet, emperor and god for all nations and tribes within the circle of his influence. He had discovered their chief enemy, their fiery deus, their angry and consuming antagonist, who would—as he instructed them—destroy the world on which they lived—as also their own bodies and spirits, in that invisible atmosphere by which the globe was encircled. This would transpire assuredly, if not hindered by his own almost omnipotent presence. There is an old maxim which appealed to his hearers not less appropriately than it does to dwellers on earth at the present epoch, and it was uttered in contemplation of a similar condition, when it said: The priests bear rule, and the people love to have it so.

Temples multiplied and corresponded, both in their interior and external construction, to the consuming vengeance of the luminary which they abhorred so much. Around these temples were placed brazen images of frightful monsters. The minor edifices were under subordinate officers, chosen of the potentate to convey his mandates to the weak and ignorant under his rule. Here were the beginnings of hieroglyphical language, in which cities embodied at once history, school and creed. Everything was constructed to represent some outward object or some conception of the mind. Thus it was with the original inhabitants of Central America and the Pompeii of the far past. At length their governor, [2] finding it possible to conceive the resting-place of their sun-god, began to improve on the long-established opinion by proclaiming that the sun represented a fountain of fire in the realms below that huge animal on the back of which dwelt all the human race. Following from this notion, it was held in succeeding ages that after the spirit of darkness had passed away, the sun arose and throughout the hours of day represented that great fountain from which it sprang and into the depths of which all must descend inevitably who did not obey the mandates of their ruler. Such was the message formulated by the sun's presence, and when it sank at the day's end this was to renew its powers in the fiery abyss, that it might have the strength again to diffuse among men the heat, the spirit, the breath which would carry the same tidings. After this manner were the wind, the atmosphere and then the light and warmth of the day-star charged with producing that which resulted solely from disunion in social interests and hence in the feelings, affections and intention of the first dwellers on earth. But as intelligence advanced it became necessary to remove the source of evil from the sun itself to inconceivable nether realms, where it was thought impossible for the chimerical invention to be discovered and exposed.

So far concerning mythological theology as it developed in the distant settlements [3]; but it will be remembered that the primitive family dwelt in Asia and originated the misconceptions under notice regarding the origin of evil. These were improved upon ultimately by a more enlightened mind, who referred his source of knowledge to a good spirit dwelling in one of those breaths to which all evil had been previously attributed. He spoke of the great waters which covered the face of all things, or rather existed alone, of the spirit who slept therein, of the desire conceived in his heart to have living worshippers, of his consequent awakening, of his breathing forth another spirit which moved the waters, of the great cosmic egg therein, of its expansion as a result of the motion, and how the world came forth therefrom. But there was also a spirit of evil which dwelt in the winds or breaths and sought to establish separation between the spirit of man and the creative spirit. It was from the wrath of this being that the new teacher offered to preserve his believers, who were further required to make appeasing sacrifices. By so doing they would live for ever in the presence of the spirit of good, the oldest of the sacred triad. [4]

The Eastern tribes received and cherished the doctrines of this new leader until the time of their separation, when one of them migrated to China, a second to Japan [5] and a third to Egypt. [6] It was, however, among the aboriginals of America that human thought first took a proper, truthful and natural direction on these subjects. [7] They dwelt in a beautiful garden, where all things above and about them created comparisons with the doctrine received from their forefathers. They came to see that the winds or breaths were not—as they had been taught—evil and were led to suppose that they proceeded from a Good Spirit, who desired to fan their heated brows after their toils and travels. This manifestation of goodness unfolded tender dispositions, and the people dwelt in love with one another. They worshipped the sun which made the earth fertile and the moon which gave them light when the greater luminary had passed away to its rest. They were conscious of a Spirit Land of transcendent beauty, where they would behold the Good Spirit, where they would be subject to death no longer and would do no injury. It was the spontaneous teaching of Nature and the corresponding prompting of the principle within that brought them to this knowledge. Disunity was not in their midst; wickedness was therefore unknown; and their thoughts were unpremeditated, true, even celestial. On the other hand, Central America, like Southern Europe, descended from those who had removed—as we have seen—the origin of evil to an abyss below, of which the sun was a messenger. They had advanced beyond other nations in all arts and sciences, and their theology—like their language—was proportionately developed. It was after the Deluge, however, that there rose a chieftain among them who established the traditions of three generations before him, and among other things that his people—regarded as the sole survivors of this catastrophe—had been saved from destruction by a previous ruler, the latter having entered into a covenant with the spirit of wrath who had created the gulf of fire, and in virtue of that understanding he and his tribe were left to people the earth, while those who were wicked descended into the burning realm below.

Hereof is mythological theology in its origin and early developments.

[1] The Principles of Nature, pp. 377-382, 396-399. As this is a purely psychical revelation, it is reduced here within the strict limits of its subject, The original contains char-

acteristic declamations of Davis on the mischief of the official theologies, but their result is only to cloud the issue.

[2] The reference is apparently to one of a long line of hierarchic rulers and not to the promulgator of the alleged original doctrine.

[3] The account also alludes apparently to early colonisation of Europe.

[4] The account of this development of doctrine reflects Hindu theology at a very far distance, and indeed the original text—which at this point is distressingly confused and confusing—calls the great spirit of the waters Parama or Brahma, and the spirit which moved the waters Narasayana or Vishnu. No name is given to the evil spirit.

[5] This allocation is speculative, for the original speaks of China as if it were not part of Asia and says that the second tribe went to the East of Asia.

[6] All this appears to have taken place before the general deluge.

[7] The reference is to the Indians of Northern America, and the predilection shown in the narrative is at once interesting and curious. It is not to be accounted for by a sort of patriotic feeling towards the aboriginal inhabitants of the land to which Davis belonged. The typical American spirit of his period is not prominent in his writings, and though he may well have come in contact with several of the Indian tribes then surviving, or at least some of their members, and may have been impressed favourably under reasonable reserves, we have no record on the subject. It is not to be accounted for by the fact that he knew their traditions better than those of the old world: there is nothing to show that he was acquainted with any, except in a most cursory sense; and it is only because of their simplicity that he was spared from making out of them the impossible and deranging medley which otherwise distinguishes the text above. It is not, as I think, to be accounted for by the fact that Davis was abnormally psychic and peculiarly open as such to impressions from the past of his geographical environment. To understand it we have rather to regard the religious entourage amidst which he wrote and thought, and against which he was in violent rebellion. We have to regard New England non-conformity, the kind of moral and theological principles bequeathed by pilgrim-fathers, Salem witch-hunters and persecutors of Quakers. We have to regard the doctrinal and intellectual status of the American Episcopal Church and that which Latin Catholicism must have looked through all these glasses, as it was unknown at first hand to Davis. In respect of all and several we have to consider their eschatological position, and we shall then begin to see what it was that appealed to Davis, in and about the year 1845, when he remembered the traditions and beliefs of North American Indians. The "happy hunting-grounds," or Spirit Land—as he says, "analogous to the one on which they dwelt, in all its productions, so that they might hunt, adore the good spirits, and love one another"—were the archetype of his own Summer Land; and of all the celestial spheres superposed thereon this was the archetype in turn—not one whit less geomorphic because they were more rarefied. And when a few years later the Rochester knockings threw open a thousand doors to the phenomena and philosophy of modern spiritualism, its eschatological precursors were still "the placid waters," the "meandering streams," the "gardens of beauty and delight"—in a word, the paradise of Iroquois, Mohicans, et hoc genus omne. Perhaps there is no section in all the works of Davis which is so hopeless, judged by all standards, as that on mythological theology, but it deserves a place in this digest on account of the field of thought opened up by this one reference to the happy land of Indians.

Chapter Four - The Garden of Eden

[1]

The Garden of Eden corresponds literally to the ideas of peace and beauty. Those streams of water which are described as flowing through the Garden were rivers, the courses of which have since been changed by volcanic action within the earth. They correspond to notions of fertility. Adam and Eve answer to two distinct nations which became associated ultimately, forming a single nation in the interior of Asia. The Tree of Knowledge corresponds to the undeveloped embryo of perfection and intelligence. The terms good and evil are used to express the proper fruits thereof—evil being the gross, imperfect, undeveloped, and good being the same things raised into a perfect state. That serpent which is represented as being more subtile than any other beast of the field, corresponds to the secret, imperceptible progress of an unfavourable mental development. Eating of the fruit of the Tree of Knowledge represents an experience of the fruits of the good, which at once begets a knowledge of evil. Thus it is that experience begets knowledge, and had the inhabitants of earth not seen the very lowest degrees of evil and wretchedness, succeeding nations would not have known and appreciated that which stands in contradistinction to these.

After this manner the associated nations, as above mentioned, entered into a knowledge of good and evil, which knowledge corresponds to having their eyes opened. Becoming thus aware of their evil dispositions, they endeavoured to conceal them by making external garments, the aprons answering to fearful secretiveness and a dread of having corrupted characteristics openly manifested. [2] This again corresponds to depravity, and in this sense the people conversed deceitfully with each other. Having lost their original high grade of purity and innocence, as the consequence of an evil and vitiating situation, they continued to sink further. There came, however, a period when out of these associated peoples there sprang two new nations, designated as Cain and Abel in the primitive history. The former were distinguished for external show and highmindedness, while the latter were meek and unsophisticated, with principles corresponding to the innocence of sheep. All that war and devastation which arose after many ages—or after they had become great peoples—signify the predominance of ignorance and folly over peace and goodness. The Land of Nod answers to barrenness, while the multiplicity of the nation which sojourned in that portion of the earth corresponds to the prevalence of universal artificiality over all that is naturally pure and righteous.

We discover in this manner that the conceptions of Adam and Eve, the Garden of Eden, the Fall of Man and original sin are more or less mythological and parabolical. [3] They were traditional among Eastern peoples, and so continued for several ages, without any particular modification, but were ultimately introduced, in an exceedingly altered form, into the writings of primitive history. [4] The Jewish knowledge concerning the Fall was due to Persian manuscripts, translated into Hebrew during the captivity at Babylon. [5] The tradition became venerated in Israel as the symbolical representation of something substantially true. The conception of an evil spirit or devil may be traced in like manner to the magi of Persia, who deified the principle of evil, but even so late as the first Christian writers the terms devil and Satan were not used to signify any definite and established principle of being, but rather an influx or impersonal spirit of wickedness—a notion precisely similar to the primitive belief of mankind. It was all that which interfered with peace and tranquillity of mind. So also the terms Sheol, Hades and Gehenna, which are rendered by us in the summary designation of hell, were employed metaphorically in the sacred writings of the Jews to signify a local burning abyss, but subsequently a condition of darkness, death and the grave. In no case do the terms used in the Bible describe a fount of evil and sin. Symbolically, hell connotes all things that are opposed to the light of investigation. There is, finally, the doctrine of a general resurrection and judgment. Without dwelling upon beliefs which prevailed hereon among various sects of Jews and Persians, for long centuries prior to the time of Christ, it will be sufficient for the present purpose to point out, in respect of both notions, that in the New Testament these also are used in a symbolical manner—as, for example, by Christ Himself—to represent states of mind, in order that hearers, with the Eastern world generally, might understand the teachings presented. Neither general resurrection nor judgment is taught in any page of the Bible.

[1] See The Principles of Nature, pp. 335 et seq.
[2] The allusion is to some speculations on the origin of vocal speech as a means for the concealment of thought and emotion.—See ante, pp. 63 et seq.
[3] See The Principles of Nature, Part II, p. 551.
[4] Ibid., pp. 549-551.
[5] This is mere romancing. Davis says elsewhere that, looking at the subject rightly, Adam fell upstairs—whatever this pleasantry may be held to mean. Alternatively he "fell onward," or out of his butterfly existence into manly health and laborious progression. It is a poor interpretation of a great symbolical mythos, and so is also what follows, where it is said that Adam was born from the skies; that he inherited an incalculable fortune, without having earned a penny of it; that it was therefore unappreciated, like other superficial riches; and that his advantages took wings and fled, dropping him in one of the open fields which were longing for a man.—Morning Lectures, pp. 7, 8.

Chapter Five - The Deluge

[1]

By those who depend upon superficial history for their knowledge, the Deluge is believed to have been a universal submersion, which is, however, a physical impossibility, because the atmospheric envelope could not sustain aqueous vapour in sufficient quantity to cover the whole earth after condensation. Moreover, geological evidence is against such an occurrence. The moral evidence is equally strong, for it is unreasonable to suppose that Nature put forth her efforts to produce the highest type of physical organisation in man, as part of her unchanging obedience to the Great Positive Mind, only for the race to be swept out of existence.[2] It is unnecessary to explain here the primary physical causes engaged in producing the catastrophe which actually took place. It was by loss of equilibrium between interior and exterior forces that molten currents at the centre of the earth became agitated in an inconceivable manner, and the natural relieving vents were inadequate to restore the disturbed order.[3] Hence the voice of the earthquake thundered through the bowels of the earth, which trembled even to its centre. Fire, smoke, mist and rain encompassed the whole globe. The tribes existing on the land intermediate between what are now called the eastern and western hemispheres were nearly all destroyed, and those that survived in the end fell to the ground stupefied. About three days elapsed before equilibrium was restored, at the end of which time the northern portions of the earth being elevated, while others were depressed, the waters rushed from the former regions, and the seas, lakes, gulfs and rivers became established as at this day.

As regards the survival of human beings, certain tribes which had separated from others located in and about the valley of Shinar, having migrated to China and Japan, remained unharmed. When quiet was restored to Nature, they sent to ascertain how it had fared with their elder brethren in the valley of Shinar, but as these were not to be discovered, and as they knew of no other nation existing upon the earth, they concluded that they were themselves the only survivors of the great catastrophe. Their chief proceeded to instruct them that the others had perished through not offering sacrifices to satisfy the demands of Brahma, to fidelity in which observances they must refer their own escape. He taught his people to make a brazen image, representing the god of the sun. The head of this idol was like that of a unicorn and the body analogous to a fish. Annual sacrifices were offered hereto in commemoration of their survival. From this time they became worshippers of the sun, moon, stars and milky way, which they regarded as abodes of spirits, each being the god of its respective sphere or planet. Their ruler and prophet was designated Fohi by later generations, and modern writers have identified him with the Noah of the primitive history. The account of the deluge and that which followed thereon was preserved in the mythology of this tribe, the father of that family which was spared by Brahma being named Xisuthrus, also regarded as identical with Noah in the Jewish account. The sects known as Buddhists and Jains preserved the same traditional account, which passed over ultimately to Greek history and theology in the story of Deucalion. This was the last evolution of tradition concerning the Deluge, as recorded and explained by the chief and leader of that isolated Eastern tribe to which reference has been made.

[1] See The Principles of Nature, pp. 391-395, condensed and arranged.
[2] The main point of the traditional story in all its forms and under all variations is obviously that the human race was not swept out of existence, but reduced to a single family.
[3] Davis discusses the occurrence of various floods, both after and before the appearance of man on this planet. He says, for example, that at the end of the so-called cretaceous or early in the tertiary period, there were violent winds and seas accompanied by

heavy rains, caused by the ascension of vapour into the atmosphere. The bodies of water thrown into agitation produced similar commotions in the uncondensed beds of the sea and acted also upon the low surfaces of land, which became generally overflowed.—Op. cit., p. 280. He speaks also of several geological transformations and volcanic catastrophes—subsequent to man's appearance—which altered the features of the earth in many portions, changing the courses of rivers and the positions of seas. Ibid., p. 344. Again, the Pacific is described as suddenly overflowing land which was before a great valley and causing an abrupt division between Europe and Asia.—Ibid., p. 347.

Chapter Six - The Spirit of Prophecy

[1]

The mode of Oriental prophecy was to interpret signs as indications of future occurrences, but such signs were seldom in correspondence with the things signified and had therefore no prophetic character, even if the event foretold came subsequently to pass. [2] To prophesy an event truly a person must be in communion with the original design of the Creator and with the laws by which it is fulfilled. It is impossible to foretell any occurrence absolutely by indications of external event or circumstance, for the former occurs as a result of immutable law, while the latter is contingent and fleeting. By immutable law I mean that universal tendency of all things which cannot be frustrated or changed. We become acquainted therewith by analysing external, physical manifestations and discovering their interior cause and governing principle. By acquaintance with the interior and moving principles of Nature we enter into communion with the Divine Mind and its universal designs—being those effects and developments which are manifested throughout Nature.

These distinctions are necessary to establish a division between real and unreal prophecy, for there are prophecies preserved in the records of primitive history which are true, righteous and divine. Their authors were instructed concerning the interior workings and tendencies of Nature, and they proclaimed things to come upon the unalterable relations subsisting between cause and effect. Their inward faculties were expanded, and they were able to recognise the hidden operations of Divine Law. That which they foretold should be regarded as substantial evidence of an enlightened judgment and lofty spirituality. When they affirmed that "an end shall be made of sin and transgression, and everlasting righteousness shall be brought in," they were inspired by the grand truth of a universal resurrection from immorality and unnatural social conditions. So also the mind which foresaw that "death would be destroyed, and he that hath power over death, which is the evil" was prompted by a high and true conviction, to which Nature bears evidence everywhere. It conceived furthermore that this mortal corruption which mars the happiness and peace of society would be exchanged for genuine principles of Nature, and that mankind would thus be rendered incorruptible. It saw finally that a time would come when those vitiating influences which poison the mental and social world should be removed and that humanity would be clothed with happiness and immortality.

Now these things have been proclaimed by all the pure and inspired prophets since first disunity began, and they affirm the final restitution of all intelligent beings to primitive innocence and universal harmony. It was seen plainly that when such things came to pass there would be no more sorrow nor pain, for the old corrupted order would be at length over and all would be renewed, which renovation would constitute "a new heaven and a new earth, wherein would dwell righteousness." Evil would be banished ultimately and "the sun of righteousness would rise with healing in his wings." Such minds associated with the interior of all things, and if they spoke not of higher spheres, the reason was that as yet the world was insufficiently enlightened to receive the truth concerning them. They foresaw also that a Great Exemplifier of moral and spiritual qualities would appear ultimately, and would manifest so high a degree of purity, gentleness and loving-kindness that he would become unto the world a type of social harmony and spiritual perfection. Such prophecies show that these authors knew the principles of Nature and the design ever manifested therein. They were fitting receptacles for the influx of true wisdom, and their forecasts are capable of demonstration, being based upon unerring laws which ultimate in the effects predicted.

David the king uttered many truthful prophecies concerning the prosperity of Zion and the advent of a great Reformer, who would combine all physical and spiritual perfections in the present rudimental sphere. He alludes more definitely to the birth, preaching and spiritual kingdom of Christ than any previous writer in the Old Testament. [3] His distinct and obvious testimonies could not have had reference to any king who arose subsequently in Israel. He states also that the kingdom of Jesus would comprehend the heathen, that they would come into His possession and that He would inherit the uttermost parts of the earth, under a reign of peace and righteousness. So also Isaiah could and did prophesy that which was fulfilled only when the Messiah came to establish purity and social unity. He spoke concerning the Mountain of the House of the Lord and the magnificence which will characterise the great Temple of Mankind after goodness and virtue shall have become developed fully. He saw that the germ of righteousness was deposited in Nature and in man, that this would unfold its qualities as a tree of life ascending through celestial spheres. He saw that One would come who would "judge among many nations" for the moral resurrection of the world. He saw that this would cause all nations to "beat their swords into ploughshares, and their spears into pruning-hooks," so that "nation would not again rise up against nation, and that they would learn war no more." He saw that the time would arrive when neither Jerusalem, nor any other city nor Temple wherein sectarian teachings are promulgated, would be the sanctuary of the true worshipper, but that such sanctuary would be the expanded earth and unfolded heavens. He saw—in a word—the ultimate triumph of those principles which Christ would inculcate, that this great moral Reformer would see "the travail of his soul"—being the development of his social and spiritual government—"and

151

would be satisfied"; and lastly that a time would come when unto these Divine Principles "every knee should bow, and every tongue confess that in them they had righteousness and strength." The prophet Jeremiah has only one allusion to the great Moral Reformer, His social and spiritual kingdom. It is brief but sufficiently definite to demonstrate his seership and his power of spiritual perception. [4] Ezekiel utters many indefinite yet truthful sayings concerning the Zion of the Lord and the Tree of Righteousness, the seed of which would be planted by Jesus. The book of Zechariah contains prophetical allusions concerning the birth of Jesus and His spiritual government. He is represented as a branch of that great tree, the body of which is composed of all mankind. It was destined to bloom with the immortal fragrance of interior purity and of true gentleness without. In place of a branch, Malachi testifies concerning a Sun of Righteousness, who would be king over all nations and would liberate the enslaved people from suffering and wretchedness.

It should be added that all these prophetical allusions to the birth and teachings of Christ were general and not particular or circumstantial, the latter—as also specific information concerning times and seasons to come—being beyond the reach of prophetic powers.

[1] *See The Principles of Nature, pp. 421 et seq., selected and arranged.*
[2] *In the work from which this section is derived, Davis discourses also concerning omens, oracles and the interpretation of dreams. Readers of signs and of things communicated in sleep were believed—he says—to be in communication with celestial beings. They were not impostors but were deceived on their own part as to the extent of their knowledge and the reliability of their imaginative impressions. Many prophets rose up among the Persians, Chinese, Chaldeans and Egyptians, who recorded their pretended communications with deities. They practised also artificial methods of inducing sleep and dream in susceptible subjects, but the visions obtained in this manner were unreal and unprofitable. Dreams, visions and prophecies became indeed the agents and causes of an immense amount of deception. The urim and thummim—which were in use among the Egyptians, according to Davis—were a modified medium of obtaining knowledge of the future and of sustaining those whose lives and talents were spent in the occupation of prophecy. He does not allude to its purpose among the Hebrews. From these and other extended observations which it would serve little purpose to reproduce, even in the most summary form, Davis proceeds to establish—apparently on the ground of his own psychic investigations—a hypothesis that all prophecies contained in the primitive history—which appears to signify the chief books of the Old Testament—were drawn from innumerable manuscripts of ancient seers. The sacred writings of each nation during the era of oracles were exceedingly large, and after the age of prophecy selections were made from their materials, and thus each nation framed its own records. The Jews copied extensively from all, preserving those only which were in consonance with their theological system. In connection with this dubious proposition, Davis hazards the frantic suggestion that the original manuscripts in possession of the Jews were in the Greek language.—Op. cit., pp. 414-421.*
[3] *Davis refers especially to Psalm ii. 7-9. where he regards David as impersonating the Son who was to be born.*

Chapter Seven - The Doctrine of Redemption

[1]

The beautiful and sublime truths imparted by the Harmonial Dispensation will be promulgated hereafter by lips more touched with the Promethean fire, more blessed with powers of inspired eloquence. My mission is to utter in plain language new lessons of spiritual progress and to enforce old lessons in more practical and soul-exalting form. The Hebrew notions concerning a Redeemer to come originated—as we have seen—in a genuine spiritual perception. It was the germ of a perfect truth that in the great future mankind would realise that it was full of imperfections and weakness, that it needed a saving power, a redemptive personage, an uplifting energy, a purifying principle. What was first a mere speculation became established as a positive fact. In the spiritual history of the world the great law-giver Moses lives as an interior reality, related for ever to the spiritual history of our race. So is Jesus a spiritual fact. Whether both are historical personalities is of little moment. The essentials of all things are saved by the fundamental principles of Harmonial Philosophy, the beauty and catholicity of which is seen by its free and fearless sounding of all deeps in human history, as a consequence of which it accepts the vital reality in all religious creeds, for there abides in all a sovereign and eternal truth. The root of these principles is in reason, which always implies harmony. It. is much more than a mere power to think and talk logically, more than the power of grasping external facts: it discerns also essential principles by which alone the significance of facts can be comprehended. It begins at the heart of things, with fundamental Nature, and thence proceeds outwardly, for every man of reason and every woman of intuition knows that God is in the deepest heart, an inexhaustible fountain of love as well as of wisdom, expanding through all that illimitable structure which is called the physical universe.

Now, God's method of living in the universe is the method of reason in mankind. Rooted in intuition, starting up with the lightning flash of thought and often with an inexpressible conviction of what is and is not true—such is reason, a perfect grouping of all the elements and attributes which make up human mind. We know that mind has an internal desire for knowledge, while in virtue of reason therein it seeks consistent knowledge and utility arising therefrom. What is it in man that is thus athirst for knowing? It is that harmony of all faculties and attributes in the human soul which we call wisdom. The Author of this harmony is also the Author of wisdom. It is reached by the axis of the human mind coming to a parallel in the plane of its orbit—so to speak—with reference to the harmony of Deity. The unity of man's spirit with the Divine Spirit is felt instantly when the fulness of wisdom is attained. This is the new birth—the attunement of our inner nature to the harmony of eternal principles. Wisdom penetrates through the physical to those profound depths wherein God abides. Wisdom begins where science comes to a pause. The world's true redeemer is wisdom, because it passes through the vesture to that which is essential, to the spirit through the body, to the life within the law, the science within the substance. It recognises as a central principle the balance of things, the equilibrium of forces, the adaptation of substances to one another throughout the whole system. This central law is justice and the highest expression of Infinite Mind. Man is an image thereof, alike without and within, from hands and feet to the duality of the physical brain, from the brain to the inward qualities and the balance between reason and love. So also Deity and Nature are counterparts, the wisdom and love which produce that loving justice which is the best practical definition of the world's true Redeemer, and of which wisdom is the apprehending and applying faculty.

[1] See Morning Lectures, pp. 28 et seq.

Chapter Eight - The Spirit of Antichrist
[1]

The genuine Christian is one who goes about doing good and does good while remaining at home, but not evil anywhere. The Christ is a saving spirit and the antithesis as such of evil and destruction. Whatsoever partakes of and imparts the saving principle illustrates the true Christ. Person or principle, he or it is Christian. Whatsoever, on the other hand, militates against the advancement of truth, whatsoever opposes the growth of science and the light of reason or intuition—that is an antagonist of the good principle, that is an enemy of mankind and that also is an antichrist. The Word of God is composed of love, justice, truth, wisdom and liberty. So also, and whether in or out of religion, principles are infallible and imperishable words of God. The Christ-principle is one of perfect justice and reciprocity, of doing to others as you would have others do to you, of unbounded sympathy, saving charity, practical benevolence, inspired by a warm love of truth and crowned by reverence for that which is truly supreme. To cherish a worshipful love for God and Nature is to be at once Christian and religious in the largest spiritual sense. The antithesis of all this is easily formulated. To live unjustly, to produce discord and enmities, to misinterpret truth, to deal falsely, hypocritically and with duplicity, to act maliciously and selfishly, to harbour passions, prejudices and appetites is to be necessarily and diametrically opposite to the redeeming principles, and hereof is Antichrist.

But sectarianism does not judge by the standard here laid down, for each and every sect holds everything anti-christian which does not concur fully with its adopted creed. So do they denounce one another and so combine to condemn the findings of science. So also they have arisen as one man and one power to affirm that spiritualism is Antichrist. It is not that spiritualists are worse persons than their neighbours but that the future looms before it as something larger, grander, more permanent than the present. The opposite of sectarianism, its spirit is one of love to mankind, of liberty, sympathy, unity. It teaches that all may become brothers and sisters, that all are on their way toward the infinite, from a countless variety of paths which lead to one Positive Mind, to one encircling sphere of immortal glory and happiness, to larger and grander experience in individual progress. It holds that crime and punishment are in proportion one to another, that one is balanced by the other. It proves the other world to be as much a part of this existence as the human brain is part of the spinal marrow. It opens the human brain as the sun opens the petals of the flower; and as Minerva sprang from the brain of Jupiter, so the human spirit comes forth and rises into that existence which is a continuation of this. It brings a great knowledge of the future, for the old materialistic school of infidelity has no chance with spiritualism. Men who had no knowledge of the future and no faith in man have now a scientific assurance and a beautiful hope. Its truths come as an illuminating religion, expanding the human heart, opening the rational powers and enabling the mind to see that there is no break in the laws of progress. It is this which sects and churches call antichristian, but were it so then human intuition has no power whereby to distinguish truth from error.

Against all such false testimonies, we know that the era of spiritual harmony is here and now approaching and will be part of our common inheritance. It is coming in virtue of principles implanted in human nature. Let us therefore, on our part, be just and natural in our spiritual growth, that we may be firm as the everlasting hills. God is the central magnet of the universe; the spiritual world is a continuation of that which is natural; there is no surprise in store for us when we shall ascend to the higher life; it will be comparable to a stream of water flowing for thirsty souls and a feast of food for the hungry.

Herein is that spiritual truth which gives help to all and, further, extracts it from all. Instead of finding an antagonist in popular science or philosophy, or an enemy in any reforms, spiritualism recognises in each and all but old acquaintances, even true friends and relatives. The modern spiritualist stands erect between social and religious extremes, a central influence, a medium for the expression of progressive principles, a friend to all who would grow in wisdom and harmony.

[1] Morning Lectures, pp. 139 et seq.

Chapter Nine - Heaven and Hell

[1]

Swedenborg's interior eyes penetrated the profoundest secrets of heavenly beatitudes, contrasted with the dismal wretchedness of the infernal state. He imparts the true philosophy of opposite mental and spiritual conditions. [2] Men have suffered more from imaginary ills than from actual causes of sorrow. In Christendom the most solemn subject is the eternal fate of a large part of the human family. There is evil and there are consequently doers of evil; there is vice and hence there are vicious characters; there is sin and this means that there are sinners; crime involves criminals. For all these heaven is too good a place, and so arises that condign realm of the wicked which is called hell. It is most important to escape this eternal penitentiary, most natural to desire the safety of children and relatives; hence obedience to fundamental rules of salvation, the practice of religion and morals.

Every thinking mind believes that everlasting happiness is the just destiny of those who are called virtuous, pure and truly righteous. On the other side of the subject the Bible says that "the wicked shall go away into everlasting punishment," and here is the contrast to that state of the just made perfect, of whom it is said that they shall "enter into eternal life." The despair of thousands arises out of this contrast. And yet, as spiritual philosophers, we must contemplate the fact that there are evils, sin, wickedness; and, as philanthropists, we cannot repress feelings of sympathy and solicitude concerning the sorrowful condition of a large portion of the human race.

The personal existence of each human being unfolds a world of perplexing problems. When did this human fact begin? No mind can comprehend fully the when and where of such origin. In man's physical body we find vestiges of all states through which he was evolved physically. We find also in his mental equipment, and more obviously in his propensities and appetites, distinct traces of the mentalities and vital potentialities which have served as his progenitors. He is the immediate result of the marriage between a man and woman, but who can calculate the forces which, acting in and through father and mother, culminated in his individual life.

The foundation of hell in man is his mind, affections, passions and wilful propensities to generate discords. So too is man's heaven founded upon his mind, his love of truth, purity, justice, peace and universal good will. [3] But it is not true that man is individually the creator of his own misery or happiness, for "no man liveth to himself," alone among causes and effects as their lord and master. He is part of a stupendous whole and must move with the whole. The hell of any individual is the accumulated discord of causes and effects in society, within him and without. He is part of an irresistible social machine, a part of positive political life, part of an endless river of being which ebbs and flows in every good as well as in every evil channel. It is thus as a part and medium, not as a creator and not as an original force, that man experiences so much of hell as reaches into his consciousness, and also enjoys alternatively what little of heaven may succeed in pressing itself between the meshes of the discords into his waiting heart. [4]

If therefore we permit reason to carry us intelligently into higher realms, into the vast spiritual spheres beyond the tomb, we shall behold this truth—that the individual is—to some extent—in hell or heaven according to his actual condition and surroundings. His faculties of will and rationality are important but they are not causes, not the projecting creators, of his companions and scenery in the Summer Land. Man's rationality and will-power, I repeat, are inseparable agents in unfolding and fixing the condition and experiences of his present and future. [5] The perpetuity of hell on the left and of heaven on the right do not depend on the individual. Whatever is true in these terms depends on the system of the Divine Mind, which is "harmony not understood."

156

[1] See Beyond the Valley, pp. 264-268, condensed.

[2] This must not be understood as an unqualified endorsement of the doctrine in Swedenborg's celebrated work, entitled Heaven and Hell. On the surface it is obviously an expression of concurrence with the spirit of that work, but even here the general views of Davis concerning the after-life offer a correction at large to this utterance of the moment.

[3] This is, roughly speaking, the doctrine of Swedenborg in a somewhat crude reflection rather than in a summary form. Davis says expressly that the Swedish seer endowed the human soul with freedom and rationality, but that these attributions will not bear the light of science and fact. If Davis, however, is speaking of the soul as a vesture of Divine Spirit, according to his later view, then the seed of postulated freedom and reasonableness is obviously not in the vesture; but if he is speaking of the spirit itself, an individualised Divine Essence apart from rationality and freedom is not a thinkable proposition.

[4] Davis is seeking to express the view that man is largely made what he is by circumstance and inherited tendency. We shall find, however, later on that man is affirmed to be master of his circumstances, while the doctrine of progress which Davis propounds everywhere shows—ipso facto—that he can overcome disqualifying tendencies. Moreover, the notion of a Divine Nature in man which is above sin and discord renders all these considerations the essence of fantasy. It is just, however, to add that this notion was brought in unwarily by Davis, that it has no place in his system and is indeed thereby excluded.

[5] It should be understood that liberty and reason are only denied to the soul as part of a declamation against Swedenborgian and other Christian eschatology. Man free and accountable gave colour to the conventional idea of rewards and punishments, and Davis did not see that there was another way of escape, in the liberty of the divine subject.

Chapter Ten - The End of The World

[1]

Geology teaches among her first lessons the rise, growth, perfection and disappearance of various classes of vegetation. There is similar testimony respecting the primitive life of the warm seas and through the whole animal kingdom. At the present day certain types of birds, beasts and fishes are becoming slowly extinct. Time is a fine-comb, and the hand that grasps it is called progress. All ferocious and venomous animals, all poisonous insects and plants, everything that comes out of filth and shocks our civilisation, are destined—like these earlier classes and genera—to pass out of existence, and their extinction—to these as to those—will be the end of the world. The conclusion cannot be escaped that the human race is preordained to pass through the same experience. The theological or intuitive dream concerning an end of the world is therefore based upon fact and is not a mere figure of speech. It is the upshot of a principle as well as a conception of its open manifestation. Races and nations rise up; they reach the maximum of material prosperity and then slide down a rough declivity toward the sunset of their history. To such dying nations again it is the end of the world. The physical globe will follow this same law after its mission is accomplished, though now it is still in its youth, while humanity has but reached its thirteenth year in true civilisation.

Much will have happened when another hundred thousand years shall have passed away. The notes of music which come through spiritual communications, from lofty summits of inspiration, enable us to catch glimpses—however imperfect—of that good time when earth shall blossom as the rose. When men shall have grown spiritually larger and finer in body they will have fewer and fewer children. The early races propagated rapidly, and this is still the case in lower strata of society; but rising higher in the scale the married are less productive, and in thought ascending further and further up the mental range it is credible that a time may come when those who are fathers and mothers will see their offspring as angels, "neither marrying nor giving in marriage," having risen above the mission of propagation and become ready for that wondrous apotheosis which shall close the long pageant of human history. Thereafter our planet itself, by slow disintegration, will distribute its atoms to innumerable solar bodies ready to seize such chemical opportunities. So will it cease and its population will look down from the Summer Land upon the close of the sublime drama.

Once more, the cerebellum will one of these days cease to have any function with reference to reproduction. The finest, most poetic and spiritual mind gathers nearly all its propagating powers into the front brain and top faculties. Such persons have few children. Men who are yet full of the world's blood still believe that many children, better propagated, would be great blessings to the future. Only friends of progress dare to speak the whole truth on this subject. To our eyes the heavens are open, and our souls are filled with inspirations of the coming time, knowing that the better will dominate what is merely good, that the best will dominate the better, and that out of earth's dark places the white lilies of peace shall spring with an immortal beauty.

[1] *See Morning Lectures, p. 67 et seq., extracted and collated.*

Book Six - Revelations of Harmonial Life

Chapter One - The Law of Correspondence

[1]

The human mind begins by taking a literal view of everything—whether spiritual or material. Its first apprehensions are confined strictly to the apparent, but wisdom, rising on wings of ideality, penetrates to that which lives within, and so judges "not from appearances, but with a righteous judgment," or from the core to the outward, not from the mere husk. So does it render a true verdict concerning that which is interior, spiritual, eternal. As in everything else that it encounters on the way of progressive thought and experience, the mind's first step in theology is to take a literal view of ancient spiritual writings. But intuition expands, and the second step is to take a figurative view—as, for example, of Bible language. Minds in this state apprehend that old prophets and new apostles indifferently have spoken in metaphors, writing emblematically, with a great wealth of figurative expressions. In this manner the Bible students throw off the material and literal conception, seeking pictorial, figurative interpretations, correspondences, contrasts and analogies. Swedenborg, being a scientific and philosophical thinker, started systematically to raise interpretation of metaphor, emblem and symbol to the dignity of a science. He reduced, in his own opinion, all scriptural externalism to an intelligible spiritual account. His principle of transliteration was something more than analogy or comparison: it was what he called the science of correspondence, meaning that the internal of any object—whether person, thought, affection or thing—is ever represented in its external, and vice versa. Thus a lamb will be a lamb only to the outward eye of him who looks over the fence, but to the spiritual mind it will indicate the principle or state of innocence. The following familiar examples are given by De Guay [2]: "The earth in general corresponds to man; its different productions, which serve for the nourishment of men, correspond to different kinds of goods and truths— solid aliments to various kinds of goods and liquid to kinds of truths. A house corresponds to the will and understanding, which constitute the human mind. . . . Garments correspond to truths or falsehoods, according to their substance, colour and form. . . . Animals correspond to affections: those which are useful and gentle to good affections, those which are hurtful and bad to evil affections; gentle and beautiful birds to intellectual truths, those which are ferocious and ugly to falsehoods; fishes to the scientifics which derive their origin from sensual things; reptiles to corporeal and sensual pleasures; noxious insects to falsities which proceed from the senses. Trees and shrubs correspond to different kinds of knowledge, herbs and grass to various scientific truths. Gold corresponds to celestial good, silver to spiritual truth, iron to natural truth, stones to sensual and precious stones to spiritual truths."

So does Swedenborg go through the mystic sphere of psycho-scientific research and succeeds in reducing the whole Bible—or at least so much of it as, according to his superior illumination, was written correspondentially —to a consistent system of interior interpretation. It must be evident to all that the Swedish seer struck ever and anon the core of Divine Fruit on the Biblical trees. [3] At almost every second step his foot was planted on the basis of everlasting truth. Had he always struck solid ground, the world would have found in him an infallible teacher; but he touched spiritual truth just unfrequently enough to show that he was liable to err, which notwithstanding I do not hesitate to say that the science of correspondence is the closest approach to a great discovery in the substantial sense of spiritual communications recorded in the Old and New Testaments.

But there have been and are persons who have conceived that inasmuch as there was a spiritual sense in the literal word so is a celestial concealed within the spiritual. Others may be expected to discover one that is heavenly above that which is celestial and yet others to unfold a deific sense. The reasoning is sophistical, and all such fanaticism is foreign to a healthy mind. For the rest, the internal and external of all things are married together and correspond literally to each other, and that which is true inwardly is true also without. [4] Hence no religious truth can be incompatible with scientific or philosophic discovery in a corresponding department. So also there can be no antagonism between natural and revealed religion. The changeless God Who "built the palace of the sky," and communicates through various mediators with men, can speak no inconsistent word. In their proper understanding, word and deed harmonise universally. The world's internal conviction, the intuition of all peoples, correspond hereto, and the principal is of universal application. That which is true in the domain of science is true in the social realm, in politics, governments, the internal history of particular races, and true equally—intimately, delicately, eternally—in every component part of our mental existence.

[1] See Morning Lectures: Twenty Discourses delivered before the Friends of Progress in the City of New York, 1865. Discourse entitled The End of the World, pp. 52 et seq.
[2] Letters to a Man of the World, No, xii.
[3] The doctrine of correspondences did not, however, originate with Swedenborg, who was a learned man of his period and was—almost indubitably—acquainted with the Latin literature of kabalism. There is no need to dwell upon this point, which is familiar to students of the subject, but the scriptural exegesis of kabalism—and especially of the Zohar, its chief storehouse—is based wholly on the analogies between things within and without. Davis puts the general thesis quite intelligibly elsewhere: The reality of all external things exists in an invisible condition, and forms are a constant manifestation of their inward reality.—The Principles of Nature, Part I, p. 92.
[4] It is affirmed that, owing to the universal law of correspondence between parts and the whole, the organisation of man stands forth as a complete history of the race, and

that it repeats—section by section—the entire plan and destiny of the wide-spread sys-
tem of the universe. So also man's body, from base to summit, is a recital at once of its
physical growth and of its psychological progression. There is a perfect correspondence
between certain parts of the body and certain parts of the head, between systems of
visceral organs and groups of mental structures, between nerves in body and brain. By
careful observation of signs and symptoms above or within the phrenological parts the
physician can determine what organs or nerves are affected in the dependent organ-
ism; and thus, as the body is an epitome of physical growth, of psychological progress
and experience, so is the head an epitome of every organ, system, quality and principle
comprised in the body.—The Great Harmonia, Vol. V, p. 42.

Chapter Two - Moral Law

[1]

Throughout the vast ocean of organic life all known laws and forces, whether in celestial spheres or on our own globe, are acknowledged to perform their office— unless incidentally obstructed—with perfect justice and equity. Moreover, as the material constituents of all things are combined in man, he can exemplify this principle, and thus a true conception of corresponding justice may be obtained. The laws that govern organic and mental constitution operate— according to their nature—with steady and undisturbed action. But if any of these laws are hampered by incidental or intentional impediment or violation there are natural results involved. If the demands of physiological law are not properly obeyed a corresponding result of necessity follows the violation. So also violation or disregard of the mental law carries with it no less certain consequences. As regards both, their interruption, like their fulfilment, bears witness to their essential harmony, for good or evil is produced accordingly as they are transgressed or obeyed. [2] The truth is that all movements produce their appropriate results, which are pure and happy when any law is fulfilled in all its requirements and demands, but the reverse in the contrary case. It follows that the law or principle of goodness is in operation constantly, between which and its infraction—or between harmony and disunion—may be discerned the unbroken reign of never-ending justice. Power, wisdom and goodness are combined in the general and specific composition of all things, from the lowest upward to man. They point to that Infinite Source from which they emanate, as also to higher and more perfect attributes than are discerned in manifest things.

All spheres in the immensity of space follow unfailingly the law according to which they were produced originally and are governed always thereby. The strict exactness of those specific forces and motions in each part composing the celestial orbs; the beauty and union displayed in these with respect to each other and to their respective centres, manifest the Divine attributes of meekness, compassion and mercy; and at the same time are a true and correct signal of distributive justice. Individual and isolated observations, apparently disconnected with the universal law of motion, will impress this conclusion yet more deeply on the mind. The evidences revealed in traditional histories of the world, including many investigations of physical sciences and established axioms set forth in contemplation of Nature and Art, carry with them convictions of the attribute under consideration. The natural developments of this earth, from grosser stages up to animal creation, unfold one harmonious chain of progression, while life, sensation, intelligence have followed in their respective orders as legitimate results of inherent laws. Throughout the vegetable kingdom may be observed a constant giving and taking, that one may sustain another for the maintenance of the kingdom as a whole. So also herein is developed the truth of universal reciprocity, kindness and mercy. This harmony, this universal sympathy and charity correspond to the infinite, ineffable compassion in the Great Fountain of all existence. The animals themselves exhibit more lenity and instinctive justice than are often displayed by the misdirected principles of mankind. They show also unqualified attachment. From lower to higher states of animal existence there is one chain of universal sympathy, corresponding to the reciprocity observed in the animal kingdom and to the unperverted morality of man, all of which are in analogy with the law of planetary worlds.

And man, who is the perfection of all and governor of his own being, possesses the combined refinements of justice, mercy and benevolence, shrined in unclouded reason. [3] By this he may comprehend truth, subdue artificial feelings and desires which are unlawful developments of his proper nature. He stands thus the emblem of distributive justice and universal compassion. His highest attainment, his most happy and blessed condition, is to exercise justice without distinction. So therefore, from man to animals, from animals to vegetables, from these to the material sphere which contains all, and thence through the immensity of space, there is the seal of harmony, magnificence, beauty, of justice, mercy, sympathy, eternal benevolence. From the first attribute to the last, from that combination of all which constitutes the grand totality, there is developed and expressed in all things, visible and invisible, this gospel of eternal truth. Power, wisdom, goodness, justice, mercy, truth —the truth which is these—is with them, as they unfold from it and manifest it in their turn—such are the gradual developments of the one absolute principle, and this principle is the Divine Essence.

[1] See The Principles of Nature, Part I. pp. 113-118, extracted.
[2] A consideration of moral law, its transgressions and their consequence, is not without suggestions concerning the old religious problems of moral and spiritual death, which are mentioned once only by Davis. He was of opinion that the idea of moral death has arisen from a superficial view of social disunity and of disunity in thought and action. As shown previously, he maintained that the innate divinity of the spirit of man prohibits the possibility of spiritual wickedness or unrighteousness, thus reproducing unconsciously the thesis of more than one heresy and of at least one non-Christian religious system. The desires of the spirit are said to proceed both from within and without—from the material relation which man sustains to his fellow-man and the universe, and from affections springing up within and controlling the outer. These affections are the elements of the spirit, which desires purity and perfection. It is the principle within that illuminates the external, whenever any divine thought is presented for contempla-

tion. It is this which recognises goodness; it is this which is the element of love; and this is the immortal principle. Its workings and effects are the morals and affections of man. Morality is then a consequence of the unchanging divinity of the spirit and is deathless, like the laws that govern all subordinate organisations. Moral death is therefore a manufactured expression, meaning nothing. Spiritual death is an alternative form of its wording, and is an impossible figure of speech. Man has not retrograded toward the lowest point of imperfection; indeed retrogression is another word without meaning, for everything is unfolding life and beauty, according to the law of progression and eternal development.—The Principles of Nature, pp. 413, 414

[3] So it is said elsewhere that moral laws refer especially to the mind, wherein are the ideas of duty, of right and wrong, of individual responsibility. It is said also that man is always punished in proportion as he infringes upon his sense of right, though the latter may be partially developed or altogether of an educational kind. The moral man suffers from physical transgressions, and the physical man suffers from moral transgressions.—The Great Harmonia, Vol. Ill, pp. 338, 339.

Chapter Three - Perpetuity of Character

[1]

Character is the medium through which the soul expresses itself, or that form by which the whole mind so manifests. It adheres and does not inhere or form a part of man's inmost. It is a mirror, so to speak, by which the soul looks at itself, a lever upon which it acts, a door through which it passes in and out of the temple. Character is not the soul, neither is it an expression of man's inward nature. You are never more mistaken than when you believe that you know a person's spirit by its characteristic manifestations. Inward nature is compelled to express itself through form, but such form may be the creation of an unfortunate parentage or education. There are three degrees of human character: (1) That which is inherited from Father God and Mother Nature; (2) that which we derive from our immediate, earthly father and mother; (3) that which is acquired by our private habits, or from those with whom we are in sympathy and social communication. There is therefore a foundation character which is innately divine and for ever beautiful. It is God-like, because it is an individualised detachment of the Monotheistic Principle. It is pure, immaculate, the same in essence as in conformation. This radical, innermost, imperishable character is seldom manifested in our present rudimental life. The second or progenitary character—which man inherits from man—is almost always visible. These two are beyond our absolute control. [2] The body is inherited like a dwelling-house, and its faculties are the furniture—also inherited with the habitation. It is impossible to change radically a single faculty; it is hard even to make superficial alterations. But there is a third character which comes within the circle of individual responsibility. Varieties of disposition and contrarieties of temperament—in individuals with whom a man lives in contact—go directly toward the formation of superficial character, and this is that character sustained and manifested mainly by mankind.

Man is called to become acquainted with psychological principles of self-development. These will put into his possession the greatest amount of power by which he can control and modify not only his superficial character but the secondary to a considerable extent, or that derived from his progenitors along both lines. When a man knows how he obtained the superficial character through which his spirit is forced to express and misrepresent itself, his knowledge is equivalent to a psychological power by which it can be modified. [3] By increase of knowledge and wisdom there is acquired ability to undermine and eradicate the superficial. Go deep into human nature and you will find a pure and imperishable inheritance, an incorruptible essence and character, a being whose inmost can disclose the celestial structure. The primary character, derived from Father God and Mother Nature, is immortal. The secondary character, imparted by mundane progenitors, is built over the deepest and inmost. This hereditary possession continues through the present world and may for centuries in the next, but it is capable—under self-control—of harmonial modification. The tertiary character, formed and fixed by habit, has a duration determined by the strength of aspiration to outgrow it and by the associations which aspiration attracts about you. Associate with those who are stedfast in their efforts to attain righteousness. The perpetuity of tertiary character is a question of time, not of eternity. You may strive to overcome and may experience defeat; each defeat is Nature's affirmation that nothing absolute can be done without co-operation. It is necessary not only to have assistance of friends in this world but the spiritualising aid of neighbours in the Spirit Land. It is a great consolation to know that all evil and sin which we condemn in human nature adhere only to those strata of character which are of temporal duration.

A man may take himself apart and thus attain the power of self-rectification, may remove acquired peculiarities which militate against the expression of inner- most characteristics. The Architect's Divine Idea is alone immortal, not the house which He builds, nor the paint with which artisans embellish it. The imperfections of acquired and parentally inherited character ultimately pass away. Nature will do her work, and you will experience at last a complete realisation of her original Idea. It follows that Nature's ideas of a man may be realised in this life; but, unless they be duly overcome, inherited and acquired characters will survive death and accompany you when you enter the chambers of the Eternal Mansion. You will not lose individuality there; you will be known as you were known by father and mother, such recognition being by the principle of universal sympathy. Neither death—with all its mysterious chemical energies—nor the grave—though it weeps on all sides for months and years together—can cleanse the spirit of certain characteristics which adhere to it, as a consequence of rudimental existence and organic developments. The saving scheme is to elicit that which is integral—the natural image or harmonial character beneath all that is inherited or acquired. But as a general principle natural characteristics are carried into the Spirit Home. The true Irishman does not lose his national or individual peculiarities. The different races preserve a momentum and, for many periods, continue to run the race of a national progression. [4] Ultimately, however, by a closer approximation of tendencies and interchange of sympathies, over-arched and beautified by system, divergent races converge and assimilate, acquired and parental characteristics are dropped, till there shines forth alone the innate and beautiful, the celestial and divine character, derived from Father God and Mother Nature.

Most persons exhibit first that character which they have derived from their immediate progenitors, and then that acquired during childhood and adolescence. But there are few whose inter and super structures of character are transparent and plastic enough to reveal the form of the Divine Image. There is now and then a temperamental conformation which affords an opportunity for the innermost to express and delineate itself between the interstices of acquired and inherited characters. In such cases we have reason to rejoice exceedingly that human nature, in the midst of discord and imperfection, can so manifest truth and goodness. It teaches us to look within and behold the imperishable. The best idea of our Divine Progenitors is there—the inmost, harmonial and everlasting.

Here therefore begins a grand lesson of individual responsibility, the knowledge that circumstances are not your masters but that you have the power to overcome, and the knowledge that external character which does not declare the spirit is like the burr surrounding the chestnut. A time arrives when the burr falls away and the sweet meat of the nut is visible. Hope for everyone is based upon this fact—that all external and inherited imperfections are ultimately to be mastered and eradicated, so that not a vestige shall remain to interfere with the happiness of immortal mind. This notwithstanding, each individual will differ everlastingly from every other individual. There is no one type proper to all mankind. You will be developed therefore in the likeness of your own interior character, bequeathed antenatally by Father God and Mother Nature.

[1] See Penetralia—s.v., Questions on the Origin and Perpetuity of Character.
[2] It is presumably in this sense that Davis questions the free will of humanity, as we have seen much earlier in the text. He protests loosely and strongly, but sooner or later revises his own statements. He says, for example: I tell you that man is not free. He is not free to choose, except in so far as his faculties are cultured to see and his heart is intuitive to understand; but such culture and such intuition, for the most part, are effects of his inheritance and of his surrounding circumstances.—Beyond the Valley, p. 267. And again: Does not a man's will determine and choose between the evil and the good? Yes; man's will does consciously co-operate with the drift and election of his inclinations. But how did his evil tendencies originate?—Ibid., p. 343.
[3] As this illustrates one aspect of the power of thought over the body, it may be noted that, according to Davis, the ideas of the brain, whether expressed or otherwise, descend into every department of the dependent organism. Thence a "sphere" issues which tinges, favourably or unfavourably, every thing as well as every person with which the individual comes into contact. Thus does each lend his character to the garments on his body, the furniture in his room, the companions about him. If his ideas be false, these things are affected in the sense of falsity. The subtle essences of the thinking principle flow beneath and rise above whatsoever appertains to the individual and to the orbit in which he moves.—The Present Age and the Inner Life, pp. 328, 329

[4] This is a recurring statement of the view taken by Davis, and it is one which follows logically from his fundamental position that the transition from this life to the next involves no radical change in the being who thus goes forward, while the place to which he removes is in direct analogy with that which he has left. At the same time a certain natural progress is involved and this bespeaks improvement. The worst are better off than they were, while the best benefit in proportion as the spiritual world is superior to that which is physical. Compare Beyond the Valley, p. 266: Very close reasoners in theology will admit that man's power to act in this world is limited; but they hold that the power to choose— the election of either good or evil—is an outcome of the individual nationality and will. On the spur of the moment, Davis is denying this argument; but what is the power to overcome circumstance except the power of the will? It should be understood that I am not concerned with adjudicating on the question of free will but simply with establishing the fact that is granted by Davis in this fullest sense, even when he sets forth to deny it. Moreover, his denials are usually the outcome of an overweening anti-theological basis, which carries him away, so that he forgets his own findings elsewhere.

Chapter Four - The Modes of Love

[1]

As affirmed already, the principle of love is that also of life, for the two are identical in essence, though the principle assumes many forms in manifestation. All originate from the Great Central Source of Life in the universe. It is to be said further that they differ from moral affinities or intellectual sympathies, but it is in their manifestations and not at their roots. The principle of love is divisible into six forms or modes, of which self-love is the first and lowest. In its natural and normal state this is the soul's especial guardian. Self is the only court of appeal from things without. Jesus tells you to love your neighbour as yourself, making individual conscientiousness the standard of judgment. Self-love is the pivot on which the spiritual mechanism revolves; it is the foundation of the living entity, the source of all known instincts. The desires of self-protection and self-preservation spring from thence, and it fixes in a certain mysterious manner the eternal continuation of the individual. The next ascending form is conjugal love, which elevates the mind above the plane or sphere of self-efforts and endeavours for the happiness of self. In a natural state of development it urges the soul to seek its counterpart or equivalent, prescribing, compelling and sanctifying in refined natures the marriage relation between the sexes. The soul learns thereby that mere self-existence is but half-existence, self-doing but half-doing. The third form is parental love, having its own demands, its own laws, its own methods of fulfilment. The fourth is fraternal love, the soul's desire of fellowship with its kind and the key of universal association. Its magic word is brotherhood, yearning for friendship, demanding social compacts, leaning toward united interests. Filial love is the fifth form, and it elevates the eyes of the soul toward real or imagined superiors. It seeks the just made perfect, angelic intercourse, and aspires toward the Divine Being. It reveres aged persons, and its natural root is in the child's love for its parents. The sixth form is universal love, being the antithesis of the love of self, though not its antagonist in well-balanced minds. Universal love spreads her wings and transports the soul into boundless realms. It bestows the idea of universal sympathies and dependence one upon another. The desire of liberty springs here-from, and so also does the soul's eagerness for perpetual discoveries and endless progression. Though it abides in every human being, there are few as yet who are aware of its sublime emotions.

All these loves, though pure intrinsically, are capable of a dual misdirection, to be characterised as extremism and invertionism. The extreme action of self-love gives rise to isolated excesses, to avarice, extravagant needs and inordinate desire for personal possessions. In its inversion, on the other hand, self-love leads to carelessness, personal neglect, disregard of life and possessions, indolence and all the inharmonies which are due to an absence of healthy self-interest and preservation. The extreme action of conjugal love leads to excessive sensuality, disregard of individual attachment and true marital relations. Its inverted operation is indicated by coldness and even repugnance to the opposite sex, not to speak of scandalous vices. An extreme action of parental love manifests in passionate fondness for children as such, while its inversion is exhibited in dislike to the young, passing occasionally into various exaggerated grades. Fraternal love in its extremes appears in a variety of aspects, from inordinate love of society, genial company, regardless of quality and shrinking from being ever alone, to the preference of friends above even wife and children. The inverted action may engender hatred or hostility to one's own sex, animosities, feuds, vendettas, and so on without number. The exaggerations of filial love inspire idolatrous sentiments and disproportionate estimations of those who are called great, while its inversion manifests in disrespect for superiors and may lead into scepticism regarding a Supreme Being. In its extremity universal love is hasty, precipitate, impetuous and unable to brook restraint, while its antithesis or inversion begets scorn of the world, cynicism and murderous dislike of humanity. Inverted fraternal love acts only within the narrow limits of acquaintance, but inverted universal love condemns the whole race of man.

These six loves, within their reasonable degrees and under their due directions, are angels of the Kingdom of Heaven within you; in an extreme state they make shipwreck of the soul; inverted they are demons of rancour, pride, hatred, malice and revenge. Regarded at their highest, they are sources and givers of life, spirit, intuition and inspiration.

It remains to be said that love is developed from the blood. This is not its cause or creator, for, on the contrary, it arises out of the ultimate sanguineous essence, [2] as the beautiful and graceful Venus is supposed mythologically to have sprung from the foam of the sea. Blood is possessed of life, and life is identical with love. Sex is the fundamental law of existence—that is to say, the male and female, positive and negative principles. Those who comprehend this law in its fulness hold that key which will unlock all mysteries in the world— including those of science, morals, religion and spirituality. It is the Alpha and Omega of all production and generation. In the Divine Source it is love and wisdom, the ultimates of which, made in their own image and after their likeness, are in the soul of man. Blood-love, remaining within its own measures, is, however, temporary and changeable, as illustrated by the ties of consanguinity, which are always weakened by time. No love is stedfast, save that which has taken up its residence in the cerebral substance, by a progression of blood-love into the love which is spiritual, and is therefore permanent.

That ultimate essence of the blood to which reference has been made is the sacred menstruum of love, the seminal secretion, the seed of life, which flows through the system—alike in woman and man. It is not obtainable from common blood in the circulatory system until this has been vitalised by the operation of spiritual love thereupon. This brightest and holiest of principles in the mental empire acts upon the finest sanguineous atoms in the nervous system and spiritualises them. The ultimate or spermatic essence is thus produced, and can be expended (1) in spiritual activity, yielding fruit in various ideas, or (2) in physical activity, yielding offspring of either sex. Every improper and inordinate expenditure of the love-essence is nothing less than a destruction of so much body and soul.

[1] The Great Harmonia, Vol. IV, p. 73 et seq. selected and codified.
[2] It is to be questioned whether this statement represents the meaning of Davis in any clear manner, nor is that which he proposed to convey certainly ascertainable. Possibly he understood blood as the medium or channel through which life manifests in animals, its correspondent being the sap in plants.

Chapter Five - The Law of Association
[1]

There is a constitutional affection manifested between every particle and compound in being. This is the Law of Association, which is the rudimental principle of Nature established by God Who is love. It creates, develops and perfects man, distributing the race, in common with all created things, to those places of the earth which are congenial with their respective qualities. Every form in the vegetable is distributed according to this law, which is especially and fully developed in the human form. It constitutes men differently, gives them diverse inclinations, passions and properties of soul. But if it thus distinguishes them, the variety is necessary to harmonise and unite the whole. [2] Diversity manifests order of development, is the mode of progress, the source of happiness, the spring of life and energy. Men inherit their various attributes from the womb of Nature, where they have been deposited and impregnated by the love and wisdom of God. Such attributes constitute the affinity which man sustains to Nature and to her provisions. There is no desire of man for the gratification of which she has not provided means, more especially when such desire is governed by that wisdom which should regulate its satisfaction also. This inseparable relation between man, Nature and Divine Principle is established by the Law of Association, and it is Divine Law because it is the love and life of Deity. It distributes impartial blessings to all, and for every action dispenses an adequate reward or punishment.

On this indestructible basis rests the connected law of reciprocal justice and consequent morality and happiness. Every being is entitled by Nature to liberty and happiness. If the desires of any single being are not gratified there is an unjust absorption in some parts of the body general of humanity, which does injury to absorber and absorbed. Those who have superfluous gratifications are as miserable as those whose wants are supplied inadequately. It is an injury for one to have more than he can well employ and unjust to deprive anyone of that which is necessary to his existence, or of any blessing to which he is entitled by Nature. To prevent absorption in any part of the great human body the wisdom of men must recognise the Divine Law of Association, by making all situations and all degrees of human industry correspond to its uniform requirements. Man must become acquainted with his own nature, the God Who made him, and the laws which unite all created things. It is the Law of Association which establishes harmony and forbids injustice to anything. There is another truth—that man has an important duty and an end to fulfil. Hence each must have a distinct position in the great structure of society, which position must be determined by his constitutional qualifications and his ability to discharge obligations. He must gravitate to his peculiar centre, to whatever soil, climate, occupation may be most congenial with his natural dispositions, as these are governed by wisdom.

Each man is an organ of the great human body, but in the present condition of things one is opposed to another, absorbing its strength and happiness, and thus generating every species of evil, pain, wretchedness and disorganisation. But it is proper that each individual, as an organ of the general body, should occupy a position agreeable to the demands of his own nature and that of others. Distributive and impartial justice would thus be generated, promoting health, unity and happiness throughout the frame. To establish harmony in society, every man must be well instructed and properly placed, so that his movements may accord with those of the whole. Society can only be harmonised by enlightened wisdom, under the rule of which discord cannot arise. It will make all industry attractive, every dispensation just, and will determine every position by specific qualifications. It will advance the lower strata of society until every man shall do that for which he is destined and all contention shall merge in the harmony of the whole.

By acquaintance with the law of association and its distributions, and so only, can there be established a true brotherhood on earth, a perfect system of order, analogous to that displayed in the structure of the universe. [3]

Under such a scheme the lowest and most imperfect will occupy the lowest point in society, and a graduated development will characterise the ascending groups, until they rise to the highest point of human perfection. He then who is most perfect in physical and spiritual constitution will occupy the highest position as governor, will pervade the whole by wisdom, directing it righteously according to universal order. Every group in human society will be comparable to a planet; all groups will revolve about a central object, embodying all industries, all

169

knowledge, all human wisdom, and such object will be as a sun of the entire race. Moreover, the various departments of society will represent the solar system in their exchange of purified parts. Persons in the lowest society, who advance and become capable of associating with the second, will be enabled to ascend, and this progressive development will continue through all groups, even to the central power. There will thus be a constant supply from the extremities to the seat of government. Proximity to the centre will be determined by innate capabilities and relation to wisdom. Every individual will feel attraction toward that centre, but his true capacity to approach it will be in proportion to purity in his progress and correspondence with the law of reciprocity, in virtue of which each group will form a congregation of affectionate and inseparable individuals, working for each other's welfare. Mankind, so incorporated, will represent the harmony of the solar system, wherein no disturbance is discoverable, because the central sun is parent and governor, whose prevailing influence maintains an indestructible equilibrium. So will God's kingdom come and His will be done on earth as it is in heaven. The race of man, formerly misdirected, will be brought to the fulness of the stature of a perfect being. The Sun of Righteousness will arise over the horizon of universal industry and shed its genial rays upon fields of peace, plenty and human happiness.

[1] See The Principles of Nature, Part III, pp. 737-741.
[2] Another view of the subject develops some variations of aspect thus: A man cannot sin and suffer alone, neither can he do right and be happy all within himself. Humanity is one vast organisation, and when its heart beats the blood flows to the furthest extremities. One among the members cannot suffer without involving the others. Unity and sympathy of the parts constitute the golden charm which binds the whole together, so that there can be no absolute isolation. The ignorance of parents is preserved in the bodily and phrenological developments of their offspring. These indicate where the progenitors have buried their low and uncultivated thoughts. Society never inflicts punishment upon an individual which is not paid back with compound interest. So also every evil carries within itself the elements of decay—an inherent sickness which renders evil a self-punishing process. Hence individuals and societies are equally the causes and victims of sin.—The Great Harmonia, Vol. III, p. 359.
[3] The analogy here instituted implies that there is a vital correspondence between Divine government in the universe and that exhibited in the constitution of man. Davis classifies the latter as follows: (1) Physical laws, being the basis of intercourse between man and the cosmos of which he is part; (2) organic laws, being those which relate to all physiological or functional forms of matter: they are the bond between man and the rest of animated Nature; (3) moral laws, which obtain in reference to intelligent and spiritual beings, fixing the sentiment of justice in the soul, or of right and wrong. Davis says that they come into action only on this plane, forgetting what he would be the first to acknowledge, that there is a moral government of the universe, seeing that from his own standpoint it is an intelligent scheme of things.—The Great Harmonia, Vol. III, pp. 334, 335.

Chapter Six - Individual and Social Culture

[1]

Individual harmony is essential to family harmony; that of the family is essential to social harmony, social to national, and national to universal harmony among inhabitants of earth. The whole therefore proceeds from perfection in the individual and depends thereon. The individual consequently is moulded into a complete likeness of the whole. Now, there are two distinct classes of human beings, those who are victims of society, born under hostile circumstances and influences of past and present generations, and those who are born superior to circumstances—owing to favourable physical and mental organisations. Unhappy or evil consequences flow from unfortunately organised and situated individuals, while happy and good consequences are the outcome of those who are organised and situated fortunately. Being higher in the scale of development, the latter are receptacles of wisdom and knowledge, which it is their duty to impart to those less happily placed. The origin of social good and evil is here accounted for without reference to any complete or partial depravity of the human or the individual soul. If physical organisation is defective and progenitive dispositions are antagonistic to harmony, it does not follow that the soul itself is innately defective. If vitiating circumstances are overpowering to individual capacities and conditions, and if the person becomes their instrument, it does not follow that he is giving expression to carnal and depraved propensities. Nothing has been more misconceived than have the native capacities and attributes of our indwelling spiritual principle. Nothing trammels its impulses, or clouds the firmament of reason, like the hypothesis that all evil and disunity are developed by the perversity and inborn iniquity of the human heart.

There are three sources of evil: (1) Hereditary misdirection; (2) Educational misdirection [2]; (3) Social misdirection. The disunity prevalent on earth is the result of conditions and circumstances which make affections evil rather than of evil affections. Man is an incarnated divinity; he is not intrinsically evil and cannot love anything intrinsically evil, though he may be bent or misdirected. The cure of evil can only be accomplished by removing these three causes of human misdirection. The indwelling forces of mind are pure and perfect in germ; they produce corresponding consequences in their proper development; but when a defective organisation, situation, or education urges the passion-forces into a state of inversion those evils are developed with which reformers contend. Hereditary defects of organisation cannot be entirely removed, but those defects which grow out of vitiating situations or education may be overcome by natural and spiritual agencies, even as diseases are cured in the physical system. Happiness is the end of all human desire and endeavour, while spiritual culture is the agency by which it may be attained. The counsels are to work in all things for the Kingdom of Heaven on earth, for the attainment of true happiness, for peace with oneself and the world; to be content with the past, thankful for the present, patient for the future and expectant toward all that it promises. To live thus is to live harmoniously; so living, each day will strengthen resolution, till a day will come when it shall be more difficult to go counter thereto than to obey its laws unfolding incessantly within. Live thus, and every morning the spirit will feel new and pure as an infant. Your companions will grow into your likeness, and discord will not enter your midst. Be simple-minded, willing to be taught, willing to forgive. Here lies the secret of harmony, and harmony is the most perfect form, the highest manifestation of wisdom and all her attributes. It is the guardian angel of universal love, who teaches that proper organisation, cultivation and direction of the soul, and her innate elements, which will unfold a just, beautiful and aspiring individual. When the individual is unfolded into harmony with himself he has grown into immediate connection with the spiritual world, into communion with its Maker. Harmony proceeds from God into the universe; the individual unfolds into harmony, and thus the animal becomes human; the human becomes the Divine, God and man unite, completing the chain of sympathy, and develop into one harmonious whole.

It requires little time to learn what is useful and just; and beauty, aspiration, harmony are explained in the fields of universal Nature, as in humanity. An harmonious individual is a revelation of Divine Mind. The science, chemistry and mechanism of creation are represented in the human form; the holy elements and attributes of God are incarnated in the human spirit. To be like heaven, let us aspire to heaven; to be like God, aspire to God. Harmony must begin with the individual, whence it will spread over families, societies and nations. Then the whole will represent the individual; the individual will reflect the whole; and God will be all in all. [3]

[1] See The Great Harmonia, Vol. II, pp. 123 et seq.
[2] The distinctions between false and true education are dealt with in Morning Lectures, on the symbolical theory that the human mind is a soil and is cultivated according to method. The truly educated are those who have come out from within, who have grown up from the condition of a mental quadruped by the development of their immortal faculties and attributes. The mind is liberated by true educational methods, not cramped and incarcerated, as happens too often in the case of a traditional curriculum. Its discipline has freedom for its object. It seeks to unfold and perfect from the properties and essences that are within. The true teachers are science and philosophy, which lead the mind into spheres of infinitude. The spirit is taught of these and becomes, under their auspices, its own instructor. There is a freedom herein, attainable by willpower and as a result of inward growth. Internal growth is the only real growth. We should start from this centre and so shall enter a region of higher convictions, which are gifts of the spirit to each, and all that belongs to bondage shall be put under our feet.—Op. cit., pp. 238-252.
[3] The question as to the mode in which individuality is attained by man is mentioned in one place. It is through a marriage of male and female, of the cerebrum and cerebellum. This marriage makes the soul an immutable unit or oneness, wherefore the soul lives when the body perishes. Again, the perfect marriage between cerebrum and cerebellum settles the question of the soul's individuality.—The Present Age and the Inner Life, pp. 408, 409.

Chapter Seven - Progress and Perfection of Man

[1]

The only hope for the physical and mental amelioration of mankind is based upon a slow but steady intellectual progress, and this must be the result of a steady, patient but firm and decided investigation as to the causes of present evils. The experience of past ages and their errors will serve as a monitor for the future. Misconception of the real principle which actuates man has erected the structure of society on wrong foundations. It seeks isolated rather than the general good, at the peril of the morals and peace of the world at large. But after every allowance for the circumstances and conditions in which he now is, man has not lost irrecoverably his true nature. There are lofty and noble characters who do not hesitate to sacrifice their individual interest for that which they feel is truth. Possessing a high sense of conscientiousness, a deep and solemn veneration, the very elements of moral philanthropy compose their nature and desires, whence they search deeply into the causes of those social efforts which are manifested about us, the disunion and disorganisation which engender vice and misery, with the personal and national wretchedness consequent thereupon. Under their guidance and that which is like unto theirs, the progress of light and knowledge will develop the true relation between man and that Nature to which he belongs, [2] the law which controls both and the principles which govern humanity. The legitimate effect of this new spirit—new and yet old as the world, because it is that of good will—shall diffuse through all ranks and degrees a universal fragrance of affection which will bind the interests, feelings and associations of men in one united mass. So is the course onward. Truth is a high mountain, but man will ascend the heights. All that is of an opposite nature will be subdued by the love of truth. The world will be cleansed and renovated, and then our race will stand forth in the brightness and beauty of its nature. One universal good, one constituting principle, one spring of thought and action, one grand and lofty aspiration—the love and quest of perfection. All will compose but one body therein, and the organs thereof will reciprocally assist and promote the good of each other. There will be no absorbents, no excrescences, no superfluous or imperfect parts, as there will be no wretchedness, individual or general, and no distress. Then will the race be perfect, even as its prototype, the man Adam; and the Earth will be one garden, the true Eden of existence, with humanity as one nation standing erect therein, free from spot or blemish. Then shall that great Tree, concealed so long from mental view but the roots whereof are eternal, assume its true form and spread its branches over the nations of the world. All interests beneath it will be one interest, all morals one glory of light and righteousness. It is the true Tree of knowledge, and its fruits will be the beatitude of mankind. This will be the true millennium, when the united voices of the world will unite in the grand chorus: "Peace on earth, good will to men."

These prophetic thoughts are based upon the principle that as truth is positive and eternal it must subdue error, which is only temporal and artificial, and as knowledge is truth in its realisation [3] it must overcome its opposites, being ignorance, superstition, vice and misery. The one is the root of those laws which control the universe, while the others belong to crushed and perverted understanding. The hand of truth and wisdom is omnipotent and must prevail. [4]

[1] See The Principles of Nature, pp. 13-16.
[2] It is explained that Nature—as understood by Davis—is not the earth merely, nor yet the empire of elements, nor even the outward physical universe, but the "wholeness" of all things and principles, the beginning and the end, the substantial and "centrestantial," matter and also mind.—The Great Harmonia, Vol, V, p. 31.
[3] It is not therefore that knowledge which is spoken of elsewhere as external and only a husbandman of the inner vineyard. It is explained that whatever is interior is feminine, while the masculine is that which is external. All the elements of love, all attributes of wisdom, all instinctive philosophy, with the analogical and harmonious philosophies, are feminine, while the sensuous and inductive methods are masculine and positive in their operations. When, however, the terms knowledge and wisdom are used synonymously by Davis to signify intelligence, then wisdom—because of its positive nature and outward searchings after truth—is called justly a masculine department of mind and the companion of the love-nature.—Ibid., p. 41.
[4] It is affirmed that intuition is the embryo or basis of all intellectual and philosophical principles, and as such embodies and underlies the entire system of Wisdom. Wisdom is perfect faith. It discerns as well as believes in all truth, and is the eternal prophet of truth.—Ibid., TP 45, 53.

Chapter Eight - The Mission of Woman

[1]

As are a country's institutions so are the people, and as the people so are its institutions. Action and reaction are inevitable, and therefore just that influence which man exerts upon the position and character of woman, the latter will exert necessarily upon the world in return. A few enlightened minds know how dependent society is upon the morals and refinement of woman, and they know also that she is and must be that which man and society make her. [2] Female character has a fundamental and vital influence upon the world, building the foundation of peoples, by presiding over the sphere of childhood, the sphere of family and the social sphere. According to surrounding circumstances and the quality of materials which she is compelled to employ will be the elements which woman furnishes, whereupon to erect the mighty superstructure of nations and the world. Through the medium of childhood she moulds the individual; through the family she influences and refines her husband; through the social medium she spiritualises legislation and government.

Female elevation and consequent liberty are inevitable results of social reorganisation and true republican government. Woman is a beautiful combination of immortal affections; but should the sphere of her movements cramp her expansion, dissatisfaction—and perhaps dissipation—will be developed. The internal and spiritual circles are spheres in which she particularly fulfils her mission. The female element should be incorporated completely into the three spheres already mentioned and be allowed its legitimate action therein. It is not possible to prevent her action in these circles, but it is possible to encompass her with deforming environment, to put her in possession of heterogeneous materials, and thus render her work imperfect and unprofitable to the race. She imparts constitution and character to the individual through the medium of childhood, domestic example and social intercourse. But she is only an instrument and dispenser of those influences, conditions and tendencies with which her husband and custom have surrounded both her and her offspring. By way of compensation to her, and for its own interests, the world should supply her with good matrimonial relations, home advantages, ennobling social institutions, to enable her to furnish society with noble minds.

Woman exerts a positive influence upon the constitution and character of individuals until the national sphere is reached, when—compared with male influence —her power is negative. Thereafter the wisdom principle pervades the individual, for the purpose of modifying, harmonising and developing the mind further. Man has properly but two circles of action—in the national and universal spheres, being circles of government and harmony. Woman cannot produce harmony of herself, but she can furnish elements for its elaboration; man cannot produce these elements, but he can discover and enforce the principles of discipline. Thus, childhood, family and social spheres are circles of love, while national and universal spheres are circles of wisdom. Female influence is positive and potent upon individual constitution and character until the point of merging is approached. Thereafter it acts as a balance-wheel to the higher portions of governmental and constitutional arrangements.

As regards the three spheres, that of childhood is a garden, and its cultivation depends almost exclusively upon woman. Herein the love principle is at home. Immortal germs of individual constitution and character are deposited in the soul's rich soil; the tenderest buds of affection spring forth; and the gentle horticulturist watches them day and night. She needs to be informed that true marriage is the most sacred of all relations into which the immortal soul enters, that its consequences endure for ever. Those who receive and act upon this philosophy will impart it to their children, and they will not be found wanting in their culture of the figurative garden.

According to the organisation and education of the female spirit will be the home she presents to her husband and children. The female presence therein is the spirit of the man's life: it is a spirit of love, a revelation of refinement, grace and beauty. She needs to be educated in the duties of life, in the nature and extent of the mission which Deity designed her to perform. She needs to be disabused of the enslaving conviction that merely keeping house and bringing up children are duties involved by the letter of the marriage contract. Her mission is sublime and universal—to people not only the earth but all the spiritual spheres. She needs to learn that harmony may be established in childhood and the home, and from husband and children it will then radiate upon her own soul and on society. So instructed, she will not be found wanting in those spiritualising influ-

175

ences which should permeate every department of the sacred household sphere and cast a halo over the holiness of home.

Woman builds society by building the foundations of childhood and the home, and society is a great edifice of female action and influence. Woman breathes forth an atmosphere which modifies that heavy and oppressive influence which ordinarily circulates among men. She sheds abroad upon the world of mind a warmth of spirit which soothes, enlivens and develops the better nature in the soul of man. Constant association with pure and cultivated woman is one of the most powerful promoters of sympathy, morality and religion. With her dwells something of that sublime influence which angels impart to one another in higher spheres. But she needs to be instructed that her mission extends to the threshold of national government, as a representative of her situation and influence. She should know that she is not some lower ingredient in the constitution of humanity; that her angelic endowments and immortal qualifications were not given to her as toys are to children; that she is not to be insulted by flattery, deceived by false attention, enslaved by heartless promises; that she is man's eternal companion; that upon her depend the harmony of the individual, the family and society; that the destiny of the race is in her hands; that the virtue, refinement and elevation of all are dependent upon her heart and mind, upon her philosophy and upon her actions.

In fine, let this truth be remembered by all, [3] that female elevation and consequent liberty are the natural concomitants and inevitable results of social reorganisation and of a universal republican government.

[1] *See The Great Harmonia, Vol. II, pp. 181 et seq.*
[2] *It is said elsewhere that woman is man's equal, or rather man is woman's equal— but not in the same spheres. There will ever remain a physiological and psychological difference between them—giving, however, no reason for any antagonism of interests, no foundation for the dogma of woman's inferiority or man's supremacy. They are two halves of a globe, designed by their organisation to meet, coalesce, unite life to life and so form a world. Each is adapted to experience that metem-psychosis of life and individuality known as the exchange of soul which occurs in real marriage.—Ibid., Vol. IV, p. 226. The following extracts, taken from the same source, are in general consonance with the text above and with the characteristic views of Davis: The glory of beauty and greatness of soul which are woman's as well as man's have never been truly seen on earth—meaning that even those who can look within see only in part, as through a glass and darkly.—Ibid., p. 225. Woman's constitution in general subjects her to far less danger in conjugal love per se than man is exposed to; and yet, as society is constructed, no one is more afflicted by conjugal misdirection than woman.—Ibid., p. 226. The ignorance and superstition of centuries have exerted a deplorable influence upon her nature.—Ibid., p. 227. In all ages of the world and among all people—heathen as well as Christian—she has been subjugated uniformly by the undisciplined will of man.—Ibid., p. 230. As a social and relative being, she has been elevated poetically to the companionship of angels, but as an individual and fellow-worker with man scarcely a word— until of recent times—has been heard in her favour. As a dependent and relative being, she has been admired, defended, worshipped, yet kept down everywhere by political*

injustice.—Ibid., p. 231. She is consigned everlastingly to the day of small things.—Ibid., p. 241. And yet, did she know herself, woman—as it has been said long ago—wields, an archimedean lever, whose fulcrum is childhood, whose length is all time, whose sweep is eternity.—Ibid., p. 257.

[3] The reference to liberty recalls the fact that Davis, in common with much spiritualism of his period, was accused of promoting doctrines of free love; and as some of his expressions may have given a certain countenance to this accusation, it will be well to set down at this point a single decisive statement on his part, which will do duty for much else that might be quoted at need: There is but one true marriage, namely the marriage of the right man with the right woman for ever.—Events in the Life of a Seer, p. 248. Nevertheless he considered that the enforced prolongation of certain states of marriage was worse than the state of divorce.

Chapter Nine - The Ethics of Conjugal Love

[1]

The principles of matrimonial association are universal and eternal. The law of affinities develops the true relation between one atom as individual and another. [2] The association of particles or spirits, thus drawn to together, is an outward expression of inward marriage. The law of conjugal union is represented first in the structure of the Divine Mind and next in His relations to the universe. The essential elements of Divine Mind are embodied in the form of love and His attributes in the form of wisdom. Love is a female and wisdom a male principle, and these generate in their relation and unity the whole universe of matter and mind. Subsequent manifestations of conjugal union are less grand and perfect but not less unmistakable, throughout all kingdoms of Nature, and as in the Divine Mind so are its ultimate products—the human children of God.

Every individual, in the abstract sense, is an embodiment of love and wisdom. The soul is organised into an image of love and intelligence, into an image of wisdom. So is each human soul constructed upon male and female principles. But every individual, considered in a relative sense, embodies only one of these principles and hence experiences affinity for its apparently dissimilar self. Heart calls to heart. The female is alone without her true companion and the male without the female. The one is seeking the wisdom principle and the other that of love. Soul is on quest of soul, and life looks for life. There is no happiness apart from true conjugal relation.

But conjugal love must be responded to by conjugal love, or else the spirit will be unhappy. The female, being love, possesses within her soul immortal springs of beauty; but if she be associated with a companion whose powers and attributes are insufficiently great and noble, kind and generous, the result is uneasiness and discord. [3] Hereof are the legalised attachments of worldly marriages, which not only distract but arrest the development of beauty and happiness in the enslaved soul. True marriages are natural, inevitable, harmonious, eternal; but no ceremony, no promise, no written agreement can unite that which is separated inwardly or increase the sanction of union in that which is eternally joined. [4] If two are married legally, and if this outer expression of unity has no other cause than fascinations of features, advantages of position or wealth, or accident of circumstance, then is the female living unconsciously with the companion of another spirit, and so also the male—in violation of conjugal law. Both are dissatisfied and unhappy. The best evidence that two individuals are not naturally and eternally married is when dissatisfaction and unhappiness are the consequences of external union, while harmony and contentment are outward signs of true inward union. The laws of God and Nature are superior to human enactments, yet we must submit to human legislation and conform thereto, looking for that time when it shall be at one with Divine Law. [5]

Every individual is born married; every male and female has a true and eternal companion, depending on the spontaneous conjunction of affinities, of principle with principle and spirit with spirit. [6] A true conjunction of souls is the invariable consequence of abiding in the Second Sphere. There is but one true marriage, and it is quite possible that a person who has had several companions on earth may not—even so—have met with the real associate of the spirit's joys and travellings. Let such spirit rest assured that it has a mate somewhere, somewhere an eternal associate. Perhaps the true companion has already gone before, and in such case the spirit on the search for its companion may well feel drawn toward the higher world.

When true union is enjoyed, the love principle, or the female, is the actuating, prompting, life-giving portion of the Eternal Oneness, and the wisdom principle is the governing, guiding and harmonising portion. Thus the twain are one in essence and organisation. There is one home, one purpose, one destiny, even as there is one God and one religion. The true marriage is first natural, then spiritual, then celestial in its progressive growth; and the eternally conjoined have an unfailing evidence of their destiny in the experience of a continually unfolding love one for another—growing stronger and stronger as they pursue life's path and near the Spirit's Home. The human soul is capable of inconceivable expansion; its sensibilities are almost immeasurable. The embodied principles of love and wisdom seek and implore the presence of each other. To every individual, its counterpart—or the one most loved—is purest, greatest, most beautiful of all beings, because there is an inwrought adaptation of desire to desire, impulse to impulse, organisation to organisation, soul to soul. This philosophy of marriage is that which angels know. It is the only true marriage, prophetically or incipiently indicated here on earth, enjoyed in all spheres of seraphic life, and established by that sublime law of association which unites atom to atom, spirit to spirit and God to the universe.

These principles of matrimonial union are self-evident to the spiritually enlightened, and as regards their daily application to the race as it now is, the male should seek the female with most pure and unselfish motives. The principle of internal affinity should alone actuate him in desire for a conjugal companion. [7] There is no security—no probability of happiness—apart from principle. [8] The indwelling consciousness of right in every mind cannot be violated with impunity. So also in the female, purity and permanency of mind, fulness and congeniality of soul should be the foundations of her attachment. She will never then repent the hour of marriage, as too many are compelled to do, having yielded to some external fascination, excitement or illusory advantage and thus secured to themselves a life of sadness and misery. [9]

In general conclusion, righteous marriage [10] —being for the human soul unspeakably superior to the mere incidental corporeal function of propagation, a function which covers, with utter satisfaction, the entire disc of the animal's periodical conjugal attraction—is the holiest relation and one most essential to perfect progression in Nature's pathway. It should therefore be steadily sought and lived for, from early youth to that period when the formation of such a blessed unity of spirit is at once chaste, beautiful, spiritualising, harmonial. It is a blessing to meet one's mate in early years, to form the heart attachment, live consecrated to that ideal, until the consummation of the outer relation, when the law of mutual and similar development will most naturally and spontaneously begin upon the twain its perfect work. The doctrine of the mutuality of spirit-growth, as the means of perpetuating otherwise transient unions, makes all conjugal infelicities quite perilous, if long indulged or permitted to strike deeply those chords which bind heart to heart. The intellectual faculties should be cultivated sufficiently to endow the affections with a clear image of the ideal companion, that one whom the soul's heart yearns to embrace evermore with a deathless love, deriving from the ever-breathing life of Deity. Each individual needs this all-supporting, everwatchful, beauty-giving, nuptial unity. Joy, enthusiasm, inspiration come with true marriage. Like a sweet aroma from a garden of immortal flowers cometh the love of the nuptial partner of our present and future progression. Each unto the other is the whole world—shall I say, God manifested in the flesh? The words of true love are words of God.

[1] See The Great Harmonia, Vol. II, pp. 201-210, extracted and collated.
[2] The attraction involved herein is said to be the love-law of all organisation, and it is the same in the physical as in the spiritual world.—The Great Harmonia, Vol. IV, p. 277. Attraction in mind is identical with attraction in matter, and love is the life of atoms.— Ibid., p. 279. Wherever life is, there is attraction; and wherever attraction is, there is marriage. Attraction is the cause and marriage the effect thereof.—Ibid., p. 280. The love principle is the principle of life, for life and love are identical in essence. The principle assumes innumerable forms of manifestation, all of which spring from the Central Source of Life in the universe.—Ibid., pp. 73, 74. Marriage is the union of the essences of two atoms.—Ibid., p. 280.
[3] It is said that on the inferior planes of the physical and human worlds there are perpetual marriages and divorces—being minor unions which are external and quickly terminated.—Ibid., p. 282.
[4] True marriage is not only the union of essences but it is likewise the interpenetration of the particles composing those essences. This is the only seal or test of real affinity.—Ibid. Marriage is immutable. Matter and mind are eternal, and by marriage they propagate the worlds. So is man's front brain married to his back brain; the two generate all the thoughts of human beings and fix the soul's individuality not less surely.— Ibid., p. 289.

[5] *This notwithstanding, all minor marriages are transient, though they are or may be beneficial to the progressive development of mankind. The scale of marriage is septenary, being (1) Sexual, which—in its isolation from other motives—is brutal, fictitious and inconstant; (2) Circumstantial, or founded on external considerations, and this is the prevailing marriage of the present age; (3) Intellectual, or founded on mental appreciation, and this is at best the science of love, not love itself; (4) Religious, or springing from a sense of duty in obedience to religious theories; (5) Spiritual, or coming from mental fitness, and though not necessarily permanent it may so become; (6) Celestial, being the union of love and wisdom; and (7) Harmonial, being not only a union of love and wisdom but an interblending of two souls.—Ibid., pp. 300-306. The two last are distinguished by a trick of description rather than in their nature.*

[6] *This requires to be checked by a later statement, as follows: Every soul is born married—that is, each has a counterpart. But this counterpart was not foreordained. It is not a fixed law that a certain man shall ultimately wed eternally a certain woman, for the marriage relation is progressive and may pass through several points of discipline before the true counterparts meet to part no more.—Ibid., p. 304. The question of progressiveness does not belong to the subject, because it is allowed that temporary ties may be assumed before true counterparts meet to part no more; but the text above says that every male and female has an eternal companion, and that which is eternal is not only foreordained but actual, a parte ante et a parte post, which the text below denies.*

[7] *By such just, chaste and harmonial marriages alone, it is testified that healthy and well-constituted offspring can be brought into existence.—Penetralia, p. 77.*

[8] *The principle is, according to a later statement, that true marriage does not so much become spiritual as it is essentially of the spirit. It is the most interior and most divine relation possible among humankind. It is essentially and inevitably monogamic, considering woman as a Messiah of love to the man and man as a Messiah of wisdom to the woman. Herein lies the progressive perfectibility of mankind.—The Great Harmonia, Vol. IV, pp. 392, 395, 396.*

[9] *At a much later date Davis issued a little volume called The Genesis and Ethics of Conjugal Love, which is useful as a summary of his opinions, though it contains very little that is new. He affirms (p. 19) that sex is derived from the spirit and that spirit is therefore the only cause of true marriage. So also conjugal love differs in its very nature from every other essential principle (p. 22), for its laws are spiritual and its conditions inmost and absolute. Love in its legitimate exercise is defined (p. 52) as the fulfilment of that conjugal law by which—from Divine Love and Divine Wisdom—woman and man were conceived and confirmed. True marriage—meaning an essential union of two spirits—is as rare as angels' visits (p. 77), but it often happens that blood-marriages are advanced to spiritual unity and happiness, because the lower includes the higher in a germinal or undeveloped state. As regards divorce, it is said (p. 97), somewhat convincingly, that if there be any criminality in the case, it is a greater crime to get wrongly into the marriage state than to be taken legally out of it. A question, however, arises as to what becomes of that law of predestined marriages and the two halves of the soul— incomplete apart from each other—insisted on so strongly and at such length in The Great Harmonia, Vol. IV—what becomes of it if blood-marriages, meaning marriages rooted in mere sense and mere physical desire, can be promoted to the condition of love rooted in the spirit? It is curious that this difficulty—having occurred to Davis—is formulated at some length in The Ethics of Conjugal Love (p. 99), but he only suggests con-*

cerning it that an harmonious union formed on earth may be dissolved in the world to come, meaning that the predestined spouse and bride may meet there, all other earthly bonds notwithstanding. It remains, however, that spiritual unity is spiritual unity and can refer only to that state in which—according to the Davis hypothesis—marriage is indissoluble.

[10] See The Great Harmonia, Vol. IV, pp. 386, 387.

Chapter Ten - Philosophy of Special Providences
[1]

The belief in special providences and consequently in the ability of man to move his Maker by prayer and supplication has been universally entertained by mankind, and there is a consequent certitude that the Deity bestows particular attention upon this earth and its inhabitants. Savage, barbarian and patriarch are impressed equally thereby. But as individual and national experiences accumulate, as the principles of research and civilisation are unfolded, such opinions are systematised and comparatively sublimated. After the crude and petty manifestations recognised by the untutored Indian as manifestations of Supreme Attention, we find more dignified exhibitions of Divine Design and Power recorded by later teachers. Thus they recognise immediate interpositions in the birth and finding of Moses; in the captivity and escape of the tribes under his control; in his miracles, commandments and government; as also in the incarnation of Jesus, his life, miracles, teachings, and in the kind of death which he experienced; in the endowments of apostles, priests and popes; in the supreme authority invested in the Holy Bible.

The origin of the general notion may be traced primarily to ignorance. [2] Those who acknowledge a belief in supernatural manifestations or special providences have defective understanding of the Deity and His works. The same belief has also a secondary origin in desire. Some nations and individuals seek to be regarded as especially important and righteous in the sight of their Creator; and after first deceiving others, for the purpose of obtaining the approbation and emoluments consequent upon such positions, they ultimately deceive themselves. Finally, the belief which we are considering can be traced also to education. There is, however, a faith of the understanding in the local and universal government of God, in the perfection and immutability of the principles of Divine Legislation. These are so admirably arranged as to comprehend the mighty orb, the falling sparrow, the insect's eye and the human soul. Like Nature itself, the laws of Nature were not created by Deity but are the attributes of His Divine Existence and the inevitable developments of His Divine Essence.

They are outer manifestations of His own internal principles and are beyond the possibility of being changed, suspended, transcended or destroyed. The one belief which is capable of satisfying the reasonable demands of the soul is that God is perfect and immutable, that He lives through all things and has made life, harmony and happiness attainable by all. When the human mind conceives that

God is impartial, that He displays His natural and harmonious attributes throughout Nature and in the deepest recesses of the soul, then it will rest and be happy, invincible by the invasions of fallacious education and hereditary prejudice. God is sufficiently minute, local and immediate in His providences to impart life and beauty to everything throughout the ramifications of infinite creation. He possesses within Himself the principles of all life, motion, sensation, intelligence. According to the absoluteness of self-existence, His celestial principles unfold and flow into the smallest atoms and organisations in Nature. From the inexhaustible plenitude of His infinite life He unfolds a vast combination of laws which will go on eternally, elaborating human spirits, and will continue to improve them more and more, in proportion as the circumstances of birth, climate, education and government advance toward intellectual development and individual perfection.

In considering special and universal providences with a belief of the understanding, the highest comfort is based upon the glorious truth that our earth is environed by a spiritual world, as indeed are all earths or planets belonging to our solar system. In truth, there is a great sphere of spiritual existence which girdles our material sphere, while encircling the former is a galaxy of more refined and magnificent spheres which are inhabited by spirits drawn on by the eternal magnet of Supreme Goodness. Thus there is a chain extending from man to Deity, and all that we can desire in the form of dispensation is supplied and handed down to us by and through the spiritual inhabitants of higher spheres, as links in the chain of love. But let it be remembered here that all spirits and angels were once men who lived in physical organisations, as we live now, and died, as we shall die, prior to their departure for the spirit home. All we have relatives there, according to the consanguinities of flesh and according to spiritual affinities. And the spirit world is not far off but very near—around and above us at all times. That which was truly joined here is not separated there. Death does not divide, nor does it remove the loved ones beyond the reach of the spirit's desires or prayers. A vast variety of good suggestions and righteous impulses can flow to us from some of our natural or spiritual kindred who reside in higher spheres. So also when the soul is praying earnestly for knowledge or for light, it is reasonable to believe that the great and good who have lived on earth may draw nigh and perhaps insinuate valuable thoughts into the understanding of the praying spirit. Hence we can say truthfully that Providence imparts special information, not indeed by direct and immediate design but by the operation of those natural and unchangeable laws which govern the universal combinations of mind and matter.

Spiritual intercourse is developed and rendered practicable by the Law of Association or the Law of Affinities. Should particular responses from the spirit world contradict what others have revealed, then the only criterion to judge of their truth or falsehood is the unfailing standard of Nature and Reason. The embracing nearness of the spiritual world and its accessibility furnish the soul with every advantage it should desire through the media of providential dispensations. But if the aspiring Christian heart is dissatisfied with the indirect manner in which its prayers to God are thus answered, be it assured that no human spirit has yet conceived a thought sufficiently magnanimous or sublime to be applied to the Great Father, nor yet even to one of the glorious beings who—once a resident on this or another earth—now treads the beautiful paths and flowering valleys of the Spirit Home.

Think not, however, because God is so inconceivable in His greatness, so elevated above special prayer and special action, that He is far removed from our spirits. In Him we "live, move and have our being"; we are in Him and of Him. [3] As the trunk, branches, twigs, leaves, buds, blossoms and fruit of a tree are unfolded from essences in its germ, so does the Great Germinal Essence of the Universal Tree unfold and develop the minutest branches and blossoms which adorn the stupendous whole. [4]

[1] See the volume under this title passim, in so far as the subject is treated, the references thereto being extracted and collated throughout.

[2] But a sympathetic reader will note throughout this section, and will find it worth his while, that Davis answers himself to the satisfaction of anyone who is in agreement with the findings of his short essays on prayer. There is providence enough in the notions of local and universal government by God. That which is local is special, in comparison with that which is catholic and is therefore general. He is really trying to enforce the very obvious truth that there is no arbitrary intervention and that God does not stultify His own laws. The lifting up of our arms is as an evening sacrifice, but the lifting up of our arms does not cause the sun to stand still, because a personal or national cause happens to be at stake. If there is a chain of spiritual intelligences extending from man to Deity and in uninterrupted communion with man, God operates therein and thereby, so that the providences are endless, while it is certain that manifest laws may be continually interacting and counterchanging with hidden laws, which Davis should be the last to doubt. His argument comes to this only—that the Divine workings are hierarchic and remain always within the hierarchic law. This is therefore really an essay on the proper understanding of special providences, for the benefit of those who believe or hope that at one or other stage of their own or the world's necessity the God comes out of the machine. He does not, and man's need will never be His opportunity in this manner; but the need is met notwithstanding through the medial laws of the worlds, and the tears of humanity are still wiped away, though it is not by a hand stretched down from a Great White Throne.

[3] And so it comes about that the gift of real prayer insures its proper answer and brings the desired change, as something that takes place in ourselves. On the hypothesis of Davis, the lesser prayers, actuated by lesser interests, may be answered in a good time by the lesser providences, being angels and communicating messengers; but unto him who calls for God, and desires Him with undivided heart, the God who is within answers, and this is the God in the universe.

[4] Davis argues elsewhere that the conventional idea of special providences is great-uncle to polytheism, or the doctrine of a multiplicity of deities who take interest in human actions and can arrest the laws of matter for the benefit of friends and destruction of enemies. All the germs of truth in this doctrine are quickened into life by the facts of modern spiritualism. Polytheism is the first and crudest statement of spiritualism. Under the sway of science and philosophy, the extravagances of ancient faith are modified

or displaced by the rational doctrine of angelic ministrations.—Answers to Ever-Recurring Questions, p. 105.

Chapter Eleven - Of True and False Worship

[1]

True worship is an involuntary act of the inmost affections. Will and understanding can determine and regulate the act, but they cannot originate and inspire the feeling, which rises unbidden from the bosom toward the supreme attraction. False worship is not, however, necessarily hypocritical. It is false in the sense of being a result of religious teachings, instead of coming from the affections, and the sentiments of the worshipper have no real part therein. Worship of the Supreme Spirit of the Universe is possible only to those who feel and are therefore attracted powerfully toward the sacred essence of Infinite Love. Any sentiment less profound, any attraction less vital, leads to the worship of a lesser god in an inferior manner. Inasmuch as the masses, including the most enlightened among them, are inspired with no deep spirituality of feeling, they do not rise superior to religious materialism. They do not exemplify in practice that religion—pure and undefiled before God and the Father—which is "to visit the widows and the fatherless in their affliction and to keep oneself unspotted from the world."

False worship in religion is often an attractively artistic, an exquisitely artful, exercise in fashionable churches. The foundation of religion is believed by many to be the "sacred volume." By such minds the real works of God—the universe and its starry skies—are overlooked as of little moment. Empirical rules, for worshipping the Almighty acceptably, are obeyed as scrupulously among us as not more formal or falser rules are followed in India, China, or Japan. In pagan countries—or, more properly, in countries more pagan than ours—religious ceremonials are outwardly more crude, but no one can affirm that worship is less sincere there than in the popular institutions of our country. Sincere and true worship may be outward and objective or inward and subjective, but the act is invariably in accordance with the real moral and intellectual growth of the worshipper. False worship, on the other hand—as affirmed already—is in accordance with the individual's religious instructions, as also with social temptations and governing circumstances.

[1] See The Fountain, with Jets of New Meaning, pp. 162 et seq.

Chapter Twelve - The Influence of Prayer

[1]

True prayer—oral or silent—is of the bosom, not of the brain. [2] It is the legitimate child of emotion, undisturbed by suggestions of the intellect. Hence, as

184

a purely spiritual exercise, springing from the love-gravitation of the finite toward the attraction of the infinite, prayer is likely to include a variety of conflicting elements —fervency, rapture, sense of reverence, fear, confidence, rest, joy; but selfishness also and egotism. Spirit is the source of that emotion which seeks utterance in prayer. Closet prayers are petitions for benefits or expressions of gratitude, praise, submission—too deep for words— whispered to the Infinite from the silence of the sincere spirit.

The earnest and sincere nature is invariably devout and prayerful. Devotion is the allegiance of mind to its objects, labours and enterprises. Such a mind, when apart from intelligence, prays for special favours, nor is that God unchangeable of Whom it conceives. It is thought that prayer "without ceasing" may attract God's attention, overcome His original reluctance to grant favours and induce Him for once to modify or suspend the operation of natural causes and laws. A mind capable of such a conception is happily not capable of perceiving the blasphemy involved, nor does it recognise the equal earnestness of every other devotee attached to conflicting forms of religion in every part of the globe.1 The faithful in different Christian churches, beginning with the head of the papal system and ending with the youngest exhorter at a camp meeting, are praying for antagonistic results. Warriors call upon the God of Battle; peacemakers petition a God of Love. Modes of prayer familiar to the Christian heart count for nothing in those immense regions where Mohammedans have called upon Allah for twelve hundred years, while those of Buddha, Brahma or Mohammed are as nothing in countries which pass under the general term of Christian. Yet all prayer is essentially the same, differing in expression only—as there is difference in the birth, temperament and education of the individual.

A child-state of thought is essential to fervent prayer. Everything wonderful is possible to the ignorant mind. The absolute impartiality of God and the unchangeableness of Nature's laws are inconceivable by partial and inconstant minds. In the beginning man made God in his own image and likeness, and unto that primal masterpiece has man addressed ever since his childlike invocations. There is a theory that the Infinite requires of finite creatures vocal recognition, glorification and entreaty. This has resulted in routine praying, so that the phraseology of prayer—as well as the peculiar emotions summoned to stimulate utterance—have become monotonous and mechanical. As a labour-saving expedient, the more logical and not less sincere heathen have instituted praying-machines, which—it is affirmed—maintain an untarnished reputation for morals and demand nothing by way of salary for religious "services rendered."

An ardent, poetic temperament, stimulating a mind much more developed in the moral than in the intellectual faculties, is most successful in expressing the beauty of holiness by prayer. True prayer is the expression of virgin imagination, warmed and fed by spiritual passion and devout meditation. [4] Religious feeling is the poetic brooding of the spirit. It is cherished most devotionally in youth. Being an intimation of that infinite and eternal life of which the spirit is a part, the feeling grows in the inmost heart and is revealed in the picturesque language of prayer. Analysis of the development and formation of the religious character would reveal elements indispensable to true poetic genius—e.g. apprehensive consciousness of dependence; love of solitude, with its melancholy and brooding; love of the supernatural, with its delicate imaginations and bold appreciations of the Supreme Power; love of ideas, with its conflicting consciousness of ignorance and intuition strangely intermingled; and lastly love of life, with its moods and mysteries, faith and doubt, attempts and failures, reveries, sorrows and despair. More or less active, these elements are found in the sincerely religious character, especially during earlier years of development.

Finite good within yearns toward the Infinite good. The spirit's natural impulse is to enlist in God's service, and prayer is the formal act of enrolment. [5] The ambition to be an officer and not a private in the Lord's army is deemed a holy ambition. The protection of the Almighty is a feeling with which Eternal Love and assistant angels clothe every human heart that pours itself out in prayer. [6] There is doubtless a certain correspondence between man's life and his prayers —not because of his prayers but because of the mental and moral condition out of which they spring. Religious persons believe that every day, like every great labour, should begin and end with prayer, which, under God's blessing, will make the day and the labour prosperous. But all experience proves that obedience to the laws of truth and justice is attended with far greater happiness and prosperity. A man must first desire to do good, and his exertions must correspond with his desires before he can realise much strength and comfort from prayer. The firmest will and the toughest muscles give out eventually in a bad cause, while success is certain to crown the weakest and humblest labourer in the cause of truth, love, justice and peace. Who would attempt to pray for a harvest without having first ploughed and planted the ground? Prayer is a healer of diseases, but only when faith is sufficient to stimulate the will-power, whereby crippled functions are aroused to new life. Prayer feeds the poor, but only when attending angels bring aid from the rich. Labour—righteously and persistently bestowed—is the surest self-answering prayer, and it never lacks the benedictions of God and Nature. The most sincere and uncompromising love of truth, the strongest will, combined with the clearest practical wisdom, burning with fervent religious feeling and exemplified by tireless industry, are certain to win. [7]

To sum up therefore, considered as "the soul's sincere desire," prayer is natural, and its effect is often salutary. The windows of the mind are opened skyward, and influences from higher intelligences may pervade the soul of a suppliant. He is rendered "more receptive of all noble and elevated impressions." But no soul can pray sincerely unless it feels a need or is filled with joy, thanksgiving and adoration. But it is our impression that the Perfect Soul of All is not disposed more kindly than before toward any suppliant. He Who is acknowledged by all to be "without variableness or shadow of turning" is unlikely to change His policy to suit the popular voice. We advocate therefore the efficacy and beauty of that silent aspiration which opens heaven to the individual. We believe that there is a world of wisdom for us to learn and our prayer is that all may make rapid advancement in all good ways. [8]

[1] See The Fountain, etc., pp. 180 et seq.

[2] Prayer is a spontaneous act of filial love, the soul's involuntary yearning for perpetual aid, an intuitive acknowledgment of gratitude for the fact of existence, a desire for additional benefits and continued happiness.—Penetralia, p. 50. It is strictly spontaneous with those who—being children in the sentiment of religion—feel inward demands which only prayer can fully supply and stimulate.—Ibid., pp. 50, 51

[3] It is affirmed that all human history returns a negative answer to the question whether God is influenced by prayer. All experiences termed special providences are open to a different explanation.—Ibid. The answer as well as the question is beside the true subject. The point is not whether prayer can change God but whether it can and does change those who pray in the proper spirit, and to this there is no doubt that Davis would have answered affirmatively—as he does indeed substantively in different places of his writings.

[4] There is an answer as follows to the question whether prayer should be oral: True spirit-prayer ascends noiselessly, as falls the glory of morning-dew. The answer comes—welcome as a shower of rain—when the soul most needs nutrition.—Ibid., p. 51. So Davis sees after all—and could not do otherwise—that some prayers are answered. It depends on the prayer. From a mystical point of view we pray and are heard always; but the whole is an inward working. On the one hand, it is not the calling of material lips and tongue, and the answer is not in the cloud or the fire, nor yet in the thunders of heaven.

[5] The normal effect is twofold: (1) To open and prepare the soul for spiritual influx and illumination; (2) to attract a portion of the angel-world into harmony with our interior necessities.—Ibid., p. 50. From this point of view it is part of the ministry of spirits.

[6] It is said otherwise that true prayer is the result of no intellectual perception of persons, relations, effects or principles. It bursts suddenly forth like a shout of joy, or cry of fear, a word of praise, a note of music, a shriek for help. Hence all scholastic lip-service, like a blessing hurriedly spoken by hungry mouths over a feast of fat things, is an inevitable profanation.—Ibid., p. 52. It is said also that there is no need of prayer when there is no temptation and no discord. The good man's life is a perpetual prayer.—Ibid., p. 51.

[7] One further extract will serve to indicate the general sentiment of Davis on the whole subject. He says that when the hour of real prayer comes over the soul, all formal prayers—like riches—"take unto themselves wings and fly away." Experience intervenes and prescribes its own remedies, its own penalties, and experience is the only divinity school from which the mind can derive unfailing education.—The Present Age and the Inner Life, p. 33. As a man of psychic experience, it is curious that our seer should have missed altogether the psychic power developed by public aspiration in great assemblies, where a certain formality of prayer does not seem less necessary than are known songs and hymns in collective singing. Both are of the magic of crowds, and there are times when they can and do electrify. Which of us can question the power of the National Anthem in the preservation of loyal unity of spirit?

[8] See Answers to Ever-Recurring Questions, pp. 113, 114.

Chapter Thirteen - Of Purity in Purpose

[1]

The spirit of man is constructed on a plan of pure reason and harmony, which lies in the very foundation of the human mind. The spiritual universe is filled with designs. It is owing to this fundamental fact that the question Cui bono? has been ever and still is asked of every new thing started. The first conception that must be reached—before the mind of the spirit is fashioned into the harmonious proportions of pure purpose—is that of inborn use. "That which is born of the flesh is flesh, and that which is born of the spirit is spirit"; but that which is flesh dies, while that which is spirit goes on, is immortal and cannot die. A purpose that is conceived in the spirit, which is brought forth in the beauty of its powers, which goes before the soul like a pillar of guiding light, is certain to consecrate and renew. Pure and high purpose is possible to spirit alone. Ambition is earthly, aspiration spiritual. They are analogous, just as common sense bears a likeness to the superior condition, with its pure and independent clairvoyance. A human mind may be actuated by ambition and may succeed in the road which it indicates; but the success is for earth and its hour. Another mind floats dreamily in celestial rivers of aspiration and may not be successful according to popular standards; yet that soul succeeds in what is permanent and glorious, because its pure purpose brings the inmost spirit into harmony with truth which is eternal. [2] There is no failure for the mind that is moved exclusively by a high purpose in its external relations to mankind.

When a man desires to be of service to the universe, when he yearns to live not for his own sake alone but for the advancement and spiritualisation of millions, he has that saviour within him which will preserve him from harm and defeat through all disasters and besetments. Merchant or mechanic, however low and undignified or however high and commanding his business in life, he who goes to that business with a desire to benefit others is baptised and strengthened by the purity of his intentions. Take therefore that desire to your heart, so beautiful and heavenly in itself; live to make others better; and at the same time you will make yourself more effective in all you do, more gladsome also and still more ready for good deeds. A beautiful warmth will pervade your home, will follow you into street and society; noble beings will associate with you wherever you mingle wisely and lovingly with your fellow-men. Assuredly there is eternal value in pure purposes.

[1] *See Morning Lectures, pp. 188 et seq.*
[2] *There is a high sense in which purity of purpose may be defined as the concurrence of personal intention with the laws of being, in the light of which Davis counsels as follows: For physical happiness obey the physical laws; for organic happiness, obey the organic laws; for moral happiness, obey the moral laws; but let it be remembered that one set of these laws cannot be violated without disturbing the peace of the general economy and the life comprised therein. The moral law is superior to every other. Therein lies the true source of happiness and of the peace which the world can neither*

give nor take away.—The Great Harmonia, Vol. Ill, p. 344. That which is moral is here understood spiritually, as indeed should be all that which pertains to the order of things. In its plenary comprehension the reign of law is the reign of unity.

Chapter Fourteen - Intellect and Intuition

[1]

The intellect, summarised in knowledge, constitutes but one-third of that wondrous organisation called the human mind, and it is also the poorest part of conscious mentality, for which reason perhaps it is the most self-asserting. If from one point of view it is the embodiment of all wisdom, in grasp gigantic and marvellous in its sublimations of argument, from another its conceits are stupendous and its self-importance ranks greatest of all. The roots of intellect start from experience; the trunk, branches and fruit of the knowledge tree constitute memory; but destitute itself of vitality, its possessions are acquired from the realm of things without. Much knowledge in a man's mind—the details of which exist in remembrance only—is like much furniture in his house. It may serve him and promote his selfish interests, or it may oppress and stultify his entire nature. The highest discovery of intellect is fragmentary and fleeting; the hour's fact is rooted in the hour's experience; the rest is a chance that the individual may be profited in virtue of memory and judgment.

Only a higher faculty than intellect in man can discern the limits of his powers in respect of intellect. The voice of the whole nature can alone reveal that which the whole nature yearns to possess. The totality alone can sit in judgment upon the testimony of the parts. In its own right intellect can freely criticise, condemn or justify the instincts; but these have the advantage of being radicals, while intellect is nothing but accumulated trappings of sensuous experience. The instincts rise naturally, like birds of paradise, into the mind's higher imponderable atmosphere, and there they change rapidly from "creeping things" into angel-winged intuitions, with clairvoyant powers and boundless aspirations. From such higher powers the policies and limitations of intellect shrink away, like affrighted fowls beneath the lofty courage of the soaring eagle.

Without the uplifting light and holy, loving eyes of intuition, [2] the intellect is not only limited in power but is proud as limited, jealous as proud, selfish as jealous and demoniac as selfish. [3] The selfishness of conditioned intellect is the original sin. Its possessor thinks only for himself. To compass sea and land, to trample on rights and liberties of others, to triumph over the downfall of compeers, to erect fortunes on the ruins of opponents— these are a few among countless crimes of this part of man's nature. It is the enemy of that beautiful spirituality and unapproachable purity understood as the Divine Guest, until it has been "born again," has entered the superior condition and has received an influx of that holy light which floods the universe with eternal beauty and harmony.

Intellectual light is lamplight, having sensuous observation and external experience for its oil; but the light of wisdom is the light of the sun. By the first we perceive and value things of sense, but the oil of the second is derived from essential, immortal principles of all life, and thereby we perceive and accept the truths of eternity. When intellectual faculties are used exclusively in conjunction with selfish instincts, ordinary affections and interests, the higher powers of the spirit are covered with blinding scepticism concerning invisible things. Dark indeed is our temple when the "lights in the upper chamber" have gone out. At the same time the instincts, as roots of the affections, are derived from the fountain of all life and light. In their primitive state they are the same in animals as in men. By a process of development they become refined and less selfish, when they are known under the name of affections. Having "grown large and public," by a continuation of the developing process, but loving, above all things, whatsoever is good, beautiful and true, having universal love in their hearts and everlasting light in their eyes, they receive the lofty and significant title of intuitions. Here is their full-orbed development, characterising the possession, experience and fruition of the seers of the spirit, and the synonym of such intuition is wisdom.

Wisdom is a supernatural faculty, when viewed by the earth-looking eyes of instinct. Even the affections— properly so called—do not understand its royal nature and heavenly characteristics. They bear the same relation to wisdom that is established by the body of a tree, which is the sustaining column of strength and growth, midway between the roots—or instincts—in the earth beneath and the fruit-boughs—or intuitions—in the heaven above. It is impossible for the instincts to have sympathetic fellowship with the intuitions; [4] and inasmuch as instincts and intellect are natural allies, while affections take side with intuitions, so there is a perpetual struggle going on in man's nature, as between powers of darkness and powers of light. At the same time it is no part of my testimony that intellect per se is the source of all follies and wickedness perpetrated in the world. The protest is solely against the fruits of unrisen intellect, based on selfish instinct and fed by experience derived solely through the senses.

Intuition may be otherwise described as a power by which the soul arrives at the conclusions of pure reason without the process of reasoning. [5] It is the soul's telegraph, transmitting truths from the depths of genius to the summits of wisdom, acquainting the inward man— as by a single flash—with that which he might be long years in acquiring laboriously by external methods of investigation. In the Harmonial Philosophy intuition is regarded as the soul's authority in all religious development. Nature, reason and intuition are accepted thereby as the only media of revelation. They represent the spontaneous development of Nature's own religion. The counsel is therefore to try the method which they offer, for the world needs a Deity, in the sense that antagonistic notions concerning the existence and attributes of such a Being are not only numerous enough but sufficiently unsettled and unsettling to neutralise consistent faith on this important source of all reasonable theology.

It may be added in conclusion that woman is more endowed with intuition than man. She sees often at a glance the legitimate conclusion of an argument, as

190

she discerns the soul of poetry and the character of an idea, while man depends especially on the process of deliberate reasoning. A pure-minded woman, whose faculties are in the beauty of integrity, is the best medium for instinctive perception of truth. Jesus was a woman in all the organic essentials of His spiritual nature. Truth- feeling and truth-loving, he spoke upon the authority of his intuition, offering no argument and breathing forth the emotions of His inward nature. "I and My Father are one," said He, for He knew Himself in harmony with the principles of Nature and hence also with that Hidden Soul of Nature which is God.

[1] *See Arabula, selected extracts. As regards intuition, compare The Great Harmonia, Vol. V, p. 304, according to which intuition is innate or integral. It is the combined wisdom of the constitutional instincts, the source of faith and hope, the prophet of the spiritual world. It is an inward witness testifying to the soul's birthright, which is an eternal possession in the Spirit Land. It is an interior knowledge and assurance, a sixth sense, added by development to the five, and thereby are higher truths discerned.*
[2] *Intuition is defined in another place as pure reason—being that kind which does not inwardly need for its growth the gymnastic exercises of outward perceptive faculties. It is the inwrought wisdom of the eternal spirit, which transcends schools and confounds the doctors in the temple. Acquired information is the kit of tools by which the intuitive and inspired mind demonstrates its constructive truths.—The Great Harmonia, Vol. V, p. 14.*
[3] *The idea of innate justice as a principle of mental constitution is connected with this subject by Davis, and he appears to identify intuition with conscience, as something deeper than all transmitted qualities and bias. This innate wisdom is beneath every man's inherited ideas of right and wrong, and it cannot be reasoned down. After a prolonged silence perhaps, it arises in its own might, and by its internal condemnation makes a strong man feeble. When inspired by its approbation, one man can put ten thousand to flight, for one man with a clear intuition of rectitude on his side is sustained as by the strong arm of omnipotence. It is important therefore to know whether our views of right and wrong arrived with our blood—meaning that they were inherited from our ancestors—or from the fountain of all spirit—the Infinite Source of every good and perfect gift.—Views of our Heavenly Home, p. 62.*
[4] *The true explanation of this, from the author's standpoint, is given elsewhere, when intuition is identified with spirituality.—The Great Harmonia, Vol. V, p. 32. It is said further to be not merely an innate conviction, an instinctive consciousness of truth and the power—as already intimated—of discerning the conclusions of reason without its processes, but also a central dialectician who inspects the substantial principle of truth itself, an infallible logician at the throne of the superior animation, who predetermines the forms in which truth shall address itself to the individual mind.—Ibid. To speak of intuitions in the terms of dialectics and logic is of course the reverse of the writer's meaning; but it is only an unfortunate choice of words, and the meaning contrives to emerge. He has affirmed already that instincts pass into intuitions.*
[5] *For this and what follows see The Present Age and the Inner Life, pp. 46, 47.*

Chapter Fifteen - Of Spiritual Audition

[1]

"Happy are they," said Father a Kempis, "who penetrate into internal things and endeavour to prepare themselves more and more by daily exercises for the attainment of heavenly secrets." Among the treasures of the human mind, which are more numerous than stars, more precious than the constellations combined, is the power of hearing sounds which are unknown in the outer universe—soul-sounds, absolutely inaudible to the physical ear. Apart from personal experience, who can believe that there is a boundless ocean of intelligent sounds beyond all ken of sense? The ears of the spirit are opened seldom in this life. Clairvoyance is a familiar power in comparison. "Their eyes were opened" is an expression which occurs in the most ancient stories of mental illumination. "The scales fell from their eyes," and thereafter a voice was heard. It was vision, however, which preceded and led the other senses, because sight is the handmaid of intellect and the sunlight of the inward man. With the open ears a voice is heard, but with newly unfolded vision understanding becomes enlightened, and love flowing in therewith, the heart and soul hasten to the side of truth and Deity.

The sounds of spirit lips vibrate through an ethereal sea which is as much finer than the common air as is electricity than ordinary water. The waves of these sounds touch the ear of the spirit and beat only thereon—inmost of all sounds, music in the labyrinth of hidden nerves of hearing. But the voices of the external universe exert their influence also upon the listening soul. There is a telephony between stars and suns: these also communicate with one another in a speech unknown to the ordinary man of earth. A most exquisite insight into the laws of audition is indispensable to a true comprehension of wonders heard by the spiritual ear. Distance is seemingly no impediment to the flight of sounds. Neither intercepting currents of winds nor the presence of vast masses of terrestrial matter can prevent the words of the spirit from reaching the prepared listener. But the experience is rare because of the great and constant demands of the body and of that world wherein the body dwells.

The hearing of sounds inaudible to physical ears is a fact which foreshadows the ultimate life to be, although—unlike the power of vision—it is a part of mind—as seen already in the case of bodily audition—which is very slightly under the sway of will or desire. It may be developed suddenly, and the hearer may receive in a few moments an adequate voice of warning or of government for an entire lifetime. Again, the spiritual ear may be opened and as quickly closed and sealed until after death. Or it may be unfolded slightly, enough to admit the speech of remote earthly babblers, the groanings and moanings of sorrowing and imprisoned persons here and there in the world, bringing nothing but confusion, the uncontrollable feelings of wretchedness .and despair. This unhappy form of audition is common enough and a source of exquisite suffering. To overcome such a phase of clairvoyance at its inception there may be recommended a persistent attention to subjects of sight, thought, feeling—especially those of action.

Chapter Sixteen - Of True Inspiration

[1]

In that eminently religious state wherein the soul is elevated or unfolded into the spiritual sphere of human existence, man stands on the apex of the material world and infinity opens its endless variety of scenes before the prepared vision. The mind is capable of realising its connections with the united spheres and of uttering, through inspirations flowing from the two sources, those great principles of truth which belong to both departments. This state is perfectly natural and attainable by every person. It may be enjoyed in the full possession of outer consciousness, apart from the magnetic sleep, [2] and it is then the result of consistent progress to a high state of personal harmony with the principles and attributes of that Divine Spirit which animates the Temple of Nature. Thus exalted, the mind is a medium for no isolated current of inspiration; the illumination is general and expands in all directions. The explanation is that all faculties are equally refined and exalted. The state may therefore be denominated a spiritual resurrection of natural passions and attractions into the moral and intellectual departments of the mind, which are themselves cleaving to a world of more perfect knowledge.

The term inspiration may be defined as significant of vision and prophetic perception, accompanied by a light of understanding, or of the rational principle. [3] True inspiration is based upon psychological principles: it is of various kinds and is graduated as regards quality and quantity. It is the illuminating presence and influence of God in the soul. It is co-essential and co-extensive with the human mind, and yet—in consequence of social inequalities, ecclesiastical materialism and individual imperfection—high inspiration is enjoyed by few of the earth's inhabitants. Pure inspiration is, however, confined to no particular person, age or nation: it is universal as the Spirit of God. There are four general sources of thought or knowledge: (1) The life-springs of the soul, (2) the suggestions of external Nature, (3) the well-springs of humanity, and (4) the inexhaustible fountains of the spiritual universe. Plenary inspiration and infallible knowledge belong to God alone; but God lives in the soul of every animated thing and in the same proportion as His life-essence is immanent therein so is that living object a receptacle of God's truth, an exponent of His goodness, a prophet of His love and an expounder of His inspiration. Where God is, there is illumination. He has not withdrawn His Spirit from Nature, nor His germinating principles from the soul of man. The mind that will may feel, and he who seeks to be inspired may draw from one or all of those sources through which the Infinite communes with the finite. The spiritual worlds are so many scales of music, extending from the remotest orbs to Deity. If man would learn this celestial harmony he must join the heavenly band and strive to swell the symphony by becoming himself a harmonious note in the scale. As certainly as this universe is warmed by love and enlightened by wisdom, as certainly as God is the Resident of the magnificent edifice of material creation, of which the spiritual universe is the dome, so shall every human soul emit that light which the presence and omnipotence of an All-Perfect and Ever-Living God shall impart by the spontaneous breathings of His Omnipotent Spirit.

The human mind is benefited permanently when the reason-principle is illuminated: this constitutes true clairvoyance and the true spiritual condition. Once more it is enjoyed only by that soul whose entire faculties are attuned one to another and all to the constitution of things. Properly considered, the spiritual and inspired state is the complete development and harmony of the individual. [4]

[1] See The Great Harmonia, Vol. Ill, pp. 295 et seq.

[2] This statement is worthy of note as probably indicating the condition in which— from his own standpoint—Davis would have explained the genesis of some among his later works. The Principles of Nature was dictated, according to the claim, in a state of trance magnetically induced, but subsequently he worked by impressions and by voluntary transition into what he terms an interior condition. The impressions were for him inspirations, received—as he says above—amidst full possession of normal consciousness.

[3] It is, however, defined alternatively as a quickening and vivification of the truth-attracting affections natural to man, while revelation is the appropriation and comprehension of the resultant thoughts and ideas by the truth-containing faculties. The human mind is said to be capable frequently of inspiration when not capable of revelation commensurate therewith, for the spirit can and often does feel vaguely the indwelling presence of some great truth for months and even years before the intellect is sufficiently enlarged to individualise and express it. Where there is no intellectual comprehension of an interior truth there is no revelation to that person. Inspiration, without a reasonable understanding of its import, is enthusiasm; but if intellectual comprehension be blended with inspiration, the result is a philosophical or practical revelation to the mind.—The Great Harmonia, Vol, V, p. 16.

[4] It depends on constitutional integrity as an effect of physical and mental equilibrium—which is thorough health—and as the foundation of every known excellence. It is the basis of truth's harmonial temple. Such inward personal righteousness, such balance between forms and forces, unfolds a hungering and thirsting love of truth. At times it is even painful, but it swells the heart like a spiritual rosebud and enlarges the mind's capacity.—Ibid., p. 17.

Chapter Seventeen - The New Birth

[1]

There exists in almost every mind an indefinable conviction that the New Birth is a supernatural effect and that in order to understand what is meant by a new heart, or to have experience of the change implied, we must enter into a state different from the whole system which characterises the unchangeable universe. A miracle would be the development of something in antagonism with established atomic laws and atomic affinities. A change of heart, however, is no supernatural manifestation of God's grace. We believe earnestly in a new birth and a succession of new births, that there are many who need to be born and patched up a good many times, because there are many who seem to have been badly born from the first—"conceived in sin and brought forth in iniquity." [2] But there are other natures born in righteousness. We thank heaven for these beautiful bows of human promise, even though they come without especial intention or merit on the part of their progenitors. We do not accept the doctrine of a supernatural spiritual conception, nor a new miraculous birth. But almost every religious person in Christendom can remember to have experienced something like a change of heart, and if we were intimately acquainted with the religious experience of Mohammedans, Persians, Chinese—who have nothing essentially at war with the spirit of Christianity—we should recognise that it is the same as ours and under the same law of psychological contact with Deity. They also know the new heart, though some of them may have never heard the name of Jesus.

We find a most practical view of this question in the New Testament. Jesus did not pretend that there was anything miraculous in His gospel of the New Birth. No man can enter into the kingdom of harmony unless he be born—first—through physiological harmony, or water, and—second—through the balance of his affections and faculties, or through the spirit of wisdom and justice. All truth is read with new eyes when the spirit is wise. If you be really born again, the world's Bible as well as Nature will be to you as new volumes. The doctrine is plain and beautiful that the new birth is not possible, "except a man be born of water and the spirit." Many of us will know something more substantial about being born again one of these coming days. Mary's Son put water before spirit—born of water, that is, of physical cleanliness, physical harmony, away from disease; and of the spirit, that is, of the balance of powers of heart and faculties of brain—such a one can enter into the Kingdom of Heaven. He said also that the Son of Man should be lifted up—the only begotten of God. What is the only begotten? It is the spirit of truth issuing from this beautiful marriage between water and spirit—the nuptial union between body and soul. The power and spirit of truth rise out, the only begotten, and thus the individual is lifted up. Out of what is he lifted? Out from his personal Satans, his unclean spirits, the pit of his demons—his passions, appetites and inversions. The only begotten is the principle of truth, rising from the secret recesses of superior faculties. A new birth lifts the mind above dependence on externals, for the only begotten in the spirit begins life by drawing upon the Infinite Father for truths and principles. When there is a true marriage between body and soul the offspring is legitimate truth. The truer your marriage the higher and more beautiful are your spiritual children, the great motives and ideas. Whatsoever is good, whatsoever is useful, whatsoever is consistent, whatsoever is beautiful, whatsoever is spiritual, whatsoever is celestial, whatsoever is heavenly and eternal—hereof is the progeny of the spirit. It is the birth of God in the heart, and in all directions it is eternal progression.

Let us therefore go to work with water—I mean, let us cleanse out our affections, erect a high standard and set out for personal harmony.

So soon as we experience a conviction that Divine Love is cherished for us in heaven we are exalted to a high state of selfless joy and praise. When a feeling that heaven has adopted us possesses our affection and imagination, the whole soul is bathed in magnetism of spiritual enthusiasm. In some natures such a change is no less rapid than the influence of magnetism—as this passes normally between operator and subject. But very often such magnetic changes are only a temporary exaltation of religious faculties. We advocate a condign elevation of reason and intuition. [3]

[1] See Free Thoughts concerning Religion, pp. 126 et seq., condensed.

[2] Davis proposes elsewhere to substitute elimination for conversion, a change of terms which would involve one in ideas, did his references to the new birth indicate on his part an understanding of the exact spiritual meaning attaching to this form of words. He approaches it rather nearly in the text above but has forgotten something essential in the substitution here attempted. Presumably he had the very dubious evidence before him of hectic experiences at religious revivals of his period in America. According to his alternative view, to be truly converted is to rise above individual defects, imperfections and evils, which are largely a consequence of heredity. It is to eliminate such misdirections, and this is the mind's highest achievement. Individual errors must be cast out of the character before the mind is capable of true happiness and before it is qualified for the perception and expression of pure and simple truth. All this is excellent within its own measures, and indeed obvious enough; but it is not the change of heart mentioned in the text, for the cogent reason that to purify is not to transmute. So also Davis says truly that every individual has a deep, constant, prayerful work to do for and within himself, and thereafter for and within the whole human family. Such work, however, may be a consequence of the second birth or it may be a preparation of the ground previously, but it is not the second birth itself, which comes about by awakening to a consciousness of the Eternal Presence within us. It is not a supernatural occurrence in the sense that Davis understands this word: indeed it is an entrance into the knowledge of that which is native to heart and soul. A near analogy in symbolism is the changing of water into wine, and of course Hermetic literature teems with correspondences. On the question of elimination see Views of our Heavenly Home, p. 275. See also The Great Harmonia, Vol. IV, p. 98, for a curious alternative substitution. The writer believes that he has discovered another agency of human regeneration in being generated rightly, or beginning the world with a righteous soul and body, and appears about to unfold his views on this subject but is drawn aside into the means of universal salvation, the matter of which is mere repetition of things that he has said frequently.

[3] See Answers to Ever-Recurring Questions, p. 158.

Chapter Eighteen - The Kingdom of Heaven

[1]

Every person has an ideal, the realisation of which would, in such person's opinion, constitute that perfect happiness which is the usual understanding of the Kingdom of Heaven. Now, an ideal comes (1) from the particular organic structure of every mind and (2) from the condition of that spirit which lives within the structure. In other words, the ideal is modified by circumstances, is in their image and their likeness. It is material or spiritual, little or large, in proportion to the construction of mind, and it represents the status of the spirit. In either case it is the first thing to analyse, when in search of individual conceptions of the Kingdom of Heaven, or perfect personal happiness. Such happiness is, I think, always held to consist in an equal development of spiritual parts and physical organs, in the supply of every want without friction and the gratification of every desire without exorbitant expense or excessive industry. The realisation of such an ideal is at present impossible on the face of the earth. The fundamental principles of love and wisdom within us make a perpetual demand upon the universe and upon each individual possessor. Out of their wondrous depths springs that onward drawing ideal which is happiness in attainment, but in frustration the source of unrest, dissatisfaction and that feeling of incompleteness which flashes painfully through self-conscious mind.

It is indisputable that happiness would result from the harmonious interaction of all faculties. [2] This is what all the world is after. The secret consists in removing unnecessary friction in one's own pathway and from that of others. Whoso does this is on the shortest, safest road to the Kingdom of Heaven. The fact that this world cannot bring the complete realisation of any one of our interior ideals and that an ideal only partially fulfilled can never satisfy the spirit causes our nature to demand life after death for the purposes of growth. Man is made upon imperishable principles, each of which is the harmonial voice of God, speaking through all parts of the tree of life, moving its leaves in the winds of circumstance and vibrating them in the currents of terrestrial affairs. Each of these principles is a word from heaven, from God's own central Spirit. The spiritualist is a believer in eternal life. Every voice from heaven proclaims eternal ideality and opportunity for actualisation. It is the upwelling revelation of truth from within that no ideal, however perfectly realised, can satisfy the whole spirit; and the consequent dissatisfaction, unrest and yearning foreshadow the future which is in store to receive and welcome us.

There is no primogeniture in this harmonial doctrine. Every man and woman inherits equal wealth and power from the innermost. The shortest road to the Kingdom of Heaven may be defined otherwise as the mastery of our proper persons. [3] A man can come from the darkest place in this social Egypt and find the Promised Land. He can stand on his own feet, a proprietor of those great truths which no material gold can purchase, and so doing he will be the representative and promise of what is possible in the ultimate of every human life. It is as easy to begin now as at any future time, begin to make the best of what is ours, to shorten the road to human happiness. These sayings are not fictions. I know that a true Harmonial Philosopher—a real, spiritual, living soul— can rise up to higher life in the midst of his present circumstances, whatsoever they are and howsoever they seem, in the friction of the daily round, to combine actively against him. Neither his bodily diseases, his habitual passions, his great wealth, his extreme poverty, nor even his ignorance can utterly deprive him of heaven and the holy angels. He can become the candidate for an eternal voyage, because his spiritual ship is freighted with every means of happiness and progression. [4]

And now as regards what is known in orthodox circles as the expected advent of Christ's kingdom, let it be said that by the words Son of Man we understand Divine Love, and by the terms Heavenly Kingdom we attain a conception of Divine Harmony. We believe that the Son of Man has come in every person who is spiritually born out of envy and hate into Divine Love— being love which is pure and selfless, seeing and seeking only the good and happiness of its object. We believe also that the Heavenly Kingdom comes in every man's soul when he outgrows strife and passion, when he ascends to the high tableland of peace, charity and wisdom. It is the office of every true Reformer, every spiritualist, to hasten the day of such peace and righteousness. [5]

[1] See Morning Lectures, pp. 110 et seq.
[2] So also it is said (a) that spiritual love, wisdom and liberty are the Eternal City; (b) that the narrow way thereto is personal harmony, while the strait gate is pure reason.—The Great Harmonia, Vol. IV, p. 189.
[3] The kingdom itself is described as the reign of universal justice— established through universal love, as the only possible foundation. In reciting the Lord's Prayer, no other thought and aspiration should possess the mind: failing this, the prayer will be mere lip-service, even as sounding brass.—Views of our Heavenly Home, p. 215.
[4] For an interpretation of the divine maxim that the Kingdom of Heaven is within see The Great Harmonia, Vol. III, p. 360. It is neither here nor there; it is not left behind in the perfumed bowers and holy labyrinths of Eden, nor does it lie far off in the future: it is a state of the soul or mind. So also the new birth consists in dying to a low, contracted selfishness. The counsel elsewhere is to seek the fountain of wisdom; so shall we soon attain the Kingdom of Heaven on earth.—Ibid., Vol. V, p. 417.
[5] See Answers to Ever-Recurring Questions, pp. 167, 170.

Chapter Nineteen - The Divine Guest

[1]

God and Nature are one; the earth and human family are one; nothing lives for itself alone. But the Divine Guest dwells only in the consciousness [2] of those who—lovingly and willingly—work and live for the progression and benefit of the whole. While all work for all by immutable laws of Divine Necessity, to make such necessity our choice is the way of blessing. We exist only as successors and heirs of departed myriads who struggled through pain and wretchedness after happiness in this world. But the fleeting excitements and sensuous pleasures of selfish natures bring no true happiness. The godly feeling goes out of the spirit when selfishness grasps the sceptre of passion. Unless you live to benefit others as well as yourself there is no felicity for you, and you can have no positive feeling of God's presence. From one point of view every condition is good; the darkest night is as good as brightest day, death as good ar life and pain as pleasure. Even selfishness is good, for it lives honestly within the five senses, walls in the

198

land, sows and reaps, builds houses, gets married, cultivates the sciences, develops works of art, multiplies the species, prolongs individual life, and—lastly—according to natural law, all that it does for itself it leaves to those who come after; yet they only who live to benefit the world—lovingly and willingly—find true happiness in the bosom of Nature and God.

The gladdening consciousness of God can become a guest of every mind: this and this only is your saviour. It will defend you against the strong temptations of instinctive passion and the subtler, more deceitful perils of atheism and false ambition. This is the Divine Life and the Divine Light within the veil of the Temple. It makes known that which we may look for and find in others. There is a happiness in it which the unrisen intellect is incompetent to grasp or discern. It is the holy and sanctifying presence of use, justice, power, beauty, love, wisdom, truth. Exceedingly beautiful, grand, uplifting, abiding is this consciousness of God. It is altogether clear-seeing, and looking through the externals of life it finds the saving love, the essentially divine, harmonial, everlasting truth in the very inmost soul of things. Let us open our higher faculties and welcome in our hearts a full revelation of the Divine Guest.

The light of this Guest was exalted by Plato above the intellect. Theactetus and Plotinus describe the principle of its interior illumination as "that which sees and is itself the thing which is seen." As revealed to Plotinus, the Divine Guest was "the One that is not absent from anything and yet is separated from all things, so that it is present and yet not present with them. But it is present with those things that are able and are prepared to receive it, so that they become congruous, and—as it were—pass into contact with it, through similitude and a certain inherent power allied to that which is imparted by the One. When therefore the soul is disposed in such a way as she was when she came from the One, then she is able to perceive It, so far as It is naturally capable of being seen. He therefore who has not arrived thither may consider himself as the cause of his disappointment and should endeavour, by separating himself from all things, to be above all. . . . We denominate It the One from necessity in order that we may signify It to each other by a name and may be led to an indivisible conception, being anxious that our soul may be one."

Let us hear the voice of this Divine Guest, overflowing with the quintessence of truth, speaking to us of the Mother and the Father, teaching us to love wisdom and lifting us into its holy presence.

We have seen that man cannot ascend the highest summits whereon he might comprehend the attributes of his own being, that there remains a superior part, an alpine peak of unapproachableness, a private height of consciousness which continues a supreme mystery to its proprietor. [3] It is rendered still more mysterious by the celestial influences which move about it, which touch and fill it with longings after wisdom and knowledge. Doves, descending from unknown arks, alight within its recesses. Telling of far-off things, they awaken daydreams of the lands of immortal beauty, enkindle flames of love and adoration for things and persons in a higher realm. Very few human minds are strangers to these mysterious whisperings in the heights of consciousness; but in the haste and

199

confusion of common life it is not often that anyone enters into the golden silence long enough to interrogate them. The popular method is to gratify celestial inter-positions by attending public worship or by indulgence in pictures, poetry, music and the drama. But there are always a few persons who seek to feed such long-ings by occasional associations with spiritual natures, [4] by consolations through favourite agents of communication with the departed, [5] and— most rarely of all—by the cultivation and calm enjoyment of an inner life.

It follows that there is a power enthroned in man's consciousness, to which the matter of his body and the mind in his possession are alike servants. This power is the pivot on which his universe revolves, and he may be lifted thereby above all ordinary ties and dependencies. He becomes conscious of an existence independent both of Nature and Deity, [6] and is constrained to accept the sub-lime responsibility of an endless individual life. This pivotal power in man is pre-cisely that energy which is called will. [7] Upon the diamond point of this power there turns the entire universe of mind. Will is the sovereign energy which moves the lever, the central force which animates and exercises all the organs, the self-conscious Jupiter, superior to the other deities, who forges and hurls his own thunderbolts through the heaven of the inner universe. Mind and matter alike obey will, for either in its absence would be destitute of life or motion. Will and causation are interchangeable terms, for causation is an exercise of will. Man is conscious therefore of what is called originating. So also through the senses without and from the spirit within he derives his dual consciousness. The perfect wisdom of the Infinite is seen in nothing so completely as in this duality of our nature and in its manifold operations.

[1] See Arabula, passim, beginning collated extracts.
[2] The question of self-knowledge is not discussed at any length in the works of Davis, but we have seen that he denies the possibility of its attainment in any real sense. The following remarks on consciousness are in one of his later writings: The sunshine of consciousness is lightest and most prismatic when the spirit is king and rules benignly over the lower realm of the senses. Such a mind walks with the celestial Parents, for the inner life throbs in unison with the infinite heart. The holy energy of love floods the pri-vate purposes; healing and happiness are in the faithful exercises of the will. But such delights can be experienced for brief moments only, with long and painful intervals be-tween, because of the storms to which consciousness is subject from the universe with-out. An undisturbed interior communion for even sixty minutes might disturb the just and necessary relations between mind and sensuous life. . . . Consciousness is twofold in its constitution and manifold in practical operations; but certain and complete failure would follow an attempt to exist consciously in both worlds at the same time. . . . The sunshine of consciousness is delightful with "the pure in heart." The only door swinging on golden hinges which admits a traveller to the immediate presence of the Divine Fa-ther-Mother is that of interior feeling in free communion with eternal principles. All outer search after the Everlasting Centre fails to satisfy. Facts realised by the senses or even hidden facts of consciousness, are fruitless unless their inner life is experienced.— Views of our Heavenly Home, pp. 19-21. It should be mentioned that the writer sets out to illustrate what is meant by double consciousness, understanding this expression not

in the light of abnormal psychical states—of which there were few ordered records in his day—but as experience possible to the mind in the worlds within and without. The inward state sketched at the beginning recalls some ecstatic experiences on record in the annals of Christian sanctity, the exceeding brevity included.

[3] For this and what follows see the section on "pivotal power" attached as a preliminary to Views of our Heavenly Home, pp. 23 et seq. Compare also pp. 115, 332 of the present work. It is suggested above that the cloud upon the height of consciousness will remain for ever, but this is contradicted elsewhere, and that which will follow its lifting is one of the rewards laid up for the people of God in the world to come.

[4] Meaning those who are like-minded in our present sphere of being.

[5] The records of modern spiritism offer the fullest evidence of a negative kind that no communications from the heights of human consciousness have ever been received through the channels with which it is concerned; and on the basis of its own programme it may be questioned whether they are to be expected.

[6] The reference is to the opinion held by Davis that the spirit of man is never to be absorbed in the Divine Eternal Spirit.

[7] The reader should refer at this point to the section entitled The Soul in Man, where it is explained that will is the medium through which love operates and has no movement of its own, except as excited thereby. There is nothing in this section to suggest that will is the highest factor in the triad described therein, but—on the contrary—wisdom is the moderator and governor alike of will and love. In the face of this ruling it is difficult to understand how one only of the faculties should descend from unexplorable heights of interior being as the "pivotal power" of all.

Chapter Twenty - Finite and Infinite in Man

[1]

Human nature is organised and equipped for progression throughout the ages. Each faculty and quality of its being is replete with an irresistible tendency to unfold in the direction of an endless career. It happens therefore that whilst one attribute of man's nature is slumbering, or between sleeping and waking, another may be making real advancement in its legitimate sphere. Contradictions and painful paradoxes in character are largely referable to these inequalities of development. The proprietor of the temple is at once a king of earth and an angel of heaven; but he himself and his palace were built by constructive forces which antedate his consciousness of being, over which forces he could exercise none of the privileges of self-government. Hence spring the monstrosities as well as angels of humanity. One inherits a noble physical constitution, associated with, an equally noble brain, but another a sickly brain and sicklier body, making intellectual and physical development impossible in this life. A brutal brain is the mother of brutal thoughts and practices. A low, coarse, nervous system is the cause of coarse and low physical sensations. The small brain is a hovel instead of a palace, and therefore a hovel instead of a regal life will be poured therefrom into society.

The animal instincts and characteristics of the lower world are visible at the basis of human nature. The truly human arrives only when the animal is quiet and tame, while the inner angel comes only after instincts and intellect have been transfigured. Human nature has in its organisation two spheres—physical and spiritual. There is consequently a consciousness of the senses and of the world outside the senses, but—in the interior life —a consciousness of God and of the infinitude of eternal spiritualities within God. Instincts and intellect belong to consciousness of the senses, while the affections—and that flower of intuition which is wisdom—belong to the consciousness of God. [2] This superior consciousness is what metaphysicians call religion. It takes hold of principles, because in these alone can the mind achieve absolute development. A principle contains within itself all facts and events which are allied to it in the nature of things. By becoming conscious of a principle, the essence of all that has been, is or may be possible to the operation of that principle comes within the grasp of the spirit.

Man never realises God until he becomes conscious of principles. Justice, love, beauty, truth, power have no existence in the intellect, except as eyes may look at bright objects "through a glass darkly." But to the higher spiritual consciousness these principles are visible and are worshipped as attributes of God. St. Augustine said that "God is nearer, more closely related to us, and therefore more easily known by us, than sensible, corporeal things." In other language, man's consciousness of principles is his consciousness of perfection and infinity. An intelligence without consciousness of these principles is without God in the world; but that person whose interior nature is vitally aware of principles is a veritable angel presence. He who feels not only the warmth of love but also its beauty and eternity is in the self-consciousness of God—or, alternatively, so and so only is God revealed to human nature. This is therefore, and finally, the essence of all life's experience—the capacity of man for spiritual consciousness of eternal principles. It is not only a revelation of man himself to man but of God also to man, with superadded gleams of the infinite progressions and inexhaustible possibilities which are in God.

[1] See Arabula, or the Divine Guest, pp. 364 et seq.
[2] This is presumably the sense in which we are assured elsewhere that we are saved through wisdom and not through knowledge, for mere knowledge does not prevent wrong doing. Intelligent persons "sin against light and understanding," though their knowledge may develop cautiousness, prudence and policy. It is wisdom which is the soul's seer of justice, and the eternal judge between right and wrong. Another argument recurs to the idea that knowledge is external, a product of the faculty of mind by which an argument is comprehended. It is also that wealth of faculties by which we perceive the obvious relationships subsisting between cause and effect. The fact that ignorance, truthfully considered, is the greatest foe of human progress and happiness does not make knowledge—in its abstract consideration—saving. There is in man a principle superior thereto, and this is the faculty of justice. It is justice which is saviour of the mind and soul, for in the plenary development thereof it is not only the sovereign ruler of knowledge but of those affections and attractions which actuate and enliven our en-

tire being. This justice of the mind is synonymous with wisdom.—The Great Harmonia, Vol. IV, pp. 169-175.

Chapter Twenty-One - The Spirit and Its Circumstances

[1]

Man alone is capable of knowing the difference between himself and his circumstances. When his spirit realises itself as a centre around which all circumstances revolve like satellites there is born within him the first assurance of his implanted prerogatives and kingship. This sense of supremacy may come in one of those memorable moments when a man is driven to his highest mental point. There descends a flash of celestial lightning from the spirits' heaven and then is born in an instant a strong divinity within the soul; but it is rarely that an appeal so sublime comes to human nature. Something of it is known, however, in nearly all private lives—it may be in a moment of decision which compels the climacteric determination of all our powers. The strength is declared from the inward fountain, and we realise that there is an infinite difference between ourselves and all that is moving about us—that we are spiritually masters and that every circumstance which proposes to govern us is designed to be subservient.

The world is filled with substances with which spirit is constantly in contact, because spirit is itself substance and is connected through the finer substances with those which are coarser in the visible world. [2] Man's spirit is like a sun, revolving on its own axis and throwing off by its centrifugal power (1) its most delicate substance, that is, the body of the spirit; (2) a coarser substance, that is, the physical organisation; and (3) those still coarser, which are the circumstances round about it in the world. [3] Everyone is either a king in his central kingdom or else a subject. It depends entirely on our constitution, education and state of mind whether we be master or servant. Our position and progress will be determined by our power, not by our force. Force is animal, and its manifestation is followed by exhaustion, but power belongs to the deep ocean of omnipotent life and therefore never subsides. Linked with the Eternal Spirit, it flows through all physical and mechanical laws, through all the organic phenomena of the visible world. The spirit's battles are to be fought through power, not through force, though this is necessary to motion, life and sensation. That power which is at the centre of life, which is destined to gain the mastery, which takes hold upon infinitude, which is twin-born with justice, truth, virtue—all that is pure and noble—is the coming lord of all circumstance. The time arrives when it is born and revealed from within. Life in its early stages has the impulsive ambitions of force, but there is a power within and above, shaping our destiny. Whoso feels this power experiences also a principle, and whoso feels a principle experiences good and truth—that is to say, God. But whoso feels God in the form of Truth and Justice living within his soul is never conquered. [4]

The shortest method to conquer circumstances is to ally ourselves with principles. Circumstances are like concentric circles encompassing the spirit at their centre: (1) physiological circumstances, derived from our parents and conditioned in each of us by methods and habits of life, by all that we do, as indeed by all that we neglect; (2) phrenological circumstances, being those organs which exert upon personal disposition and character a distinct and positive influence; (3) social circumstances, being those of immediate surroundings, which control our actions more than all other influences, but are transitory in their nature, while at the same time acting directly upon character; (4) physical or geographical circumstances, the conditions of the outside world in which we are born and reared: these are most external of all. To conquer that which is disadvantageous in this fourfold sequence we must secure our spirit by an indomitable adherence to some divine principle. In proportion as we are loyal thereto we shall receive inspiration, and thus power is added to that life which is integral and eternal. The divine in ultimates always gains a victory over the earthly and unworthy. Whenever consciousness of a principle is born in the human spirit, from that moment it ceases to be a thing and becomes a power.

Take any divine principle—such as liberty or brotherhood. Learn the beautiful lesson of strict loyalty to your deepest convictions respecting them, become harmonious with them and you will become to the same extent a power. Instead of feeling weary in battling with hostile circumstances you will receive accessions of celestial strength from invisible sources. If you are absolutely loyal to a principle, God and Nature—or immutable Justice and Truth—breathe into your nostrils "the breath of life." Have a truth, and stand by it. Be faithful to your best experiences and highest convictions. Then you can surely and noiselessly overcome evil with good, and thus reach the inmost heart of the Eternal Mind.

[1] See Morning Lectures, pp. 145 et seq.
[2] The human spirit is regarded elsewhere as identical (a) with consciousness and (b) with vitality. As we have seen in the case of the Divine Mind or Spirit, it is an organised substance because it moves organised substance.—See The Principles of Nature, Vol. I, p. 55. The logical position of such a dogma is of course odd, but there was probably implied in the mind of Davis the idea that there must be a bond of relation between things which communicate with each other—e.g. the mover and the moved. The relation between the organic and inorganic, between elements and compounds is sufficient evidence that such bond is not organism.
[3] These remarks may be serviceably compared with previous speculations on the physical body as the manufactory of the spiritual body and on the latter as the vessel of individuality.
[4] It will be seen that indubitably the implicit of these things is freedom, so that we are enabled again, and even more convincingly, to restrict the sense in which Davis has proposed on other occasions, especially in The Principles of Nature, to restrict human freedom. The truth is that he did not measure correctly the full value of his language and said therefore more than he meant. That which he intended was to establish a circle of necessity surrounding man which no one can overstep and which nothing intervenes to suspend. It is this also which he is saying virtually in the text above, and it will

be seen that he even mentions liberty as a divine principle, like brotherhood, though the terminology is loose enough as usual, and should not be interpreted as postulating a principle of brotherhood in God. It is obvious that if man can become master of his circumstances at the price of war with these, and can enjoy the fruits of victory, he is free within the measures of his nature, though he is still within the circle of law. The notion of freedom abides in that of law, in the concurrence of the individual with the mode of universal being.

Chapter Twenty-Two - Prospects of The Spirit
[1]

Experience is the book of life, and he is a good student who knows how to read its doctrines, while he who acts upon them is being educated in the school of God. The creation is just beginning to be unfolded to man. To the ancients this world was the centre of the universe; but now we forget the earth in contemplating the unutterable immensities of infinity. The true scholar can read even from leaves of trees, as the true preacher can see "sermons in stones" and the man of goodness can discern "good in everything." Here is the kind of vision which looks into the soul of all. Man sees better and further into the meanings of truth when his bodily eyes are closed. The bottom of the deep well is invisible; the purest water flows from springs which lie beyond the reach of mortal vision. Every faculty in the mind has eyes looking backward and forward, down and up In animals they are termed instincts, but man, unlike these, adds to his vision the spectacles of experience and learns to probe the events of life.

With undeviating regularity, a beautiful order is maintained in every department of the physical system which environs the external senses of the soul; but may we not also cultivate some acquaintance with the order of the inward world, seeing that the same God governs all? The external departments yield up their secrets to our research, so that we see and know, and why therefore should this Divine Administration remain obscure in the various degrees of the spiritual universe? The reason must be sought in man's short-sightedness and inexperience. We need therefore the power of vision, which is vital, and that acquaintance which is true culture.

The value of a progressive earthly experience can be comprehended only by realising in the plenary sense those definite relations which subsist between this world and the Spirit Land. Here and now is the first sphere of human experience; here the essences and elements of all Nature arrive, for the first time, at that point of organic growth and refinement when they are endowed with a permanent form—that of the human soul. The form of this soul is unalterable, for it is the final product of the powers and essences of the soul of Nature. This world is the manufactory of spirits, and the storehouse is the Spirit Land. Though it may be highly educated here, the human spirit finds the true reading in the world beyond. The Second Sphere of our existence is of more worth and is enjoyed more by contrasting rudimental and sensuous experience therewith. So is sunshine more beautiful after a terrible storm; so is our estimation of the joys of health augmented when compared with the sorrows of disease.

That which the mind does not learn correctly on this earth it must acquire perfectly in the spiritual sphere hereafter. How relieved will be thousands of minds when they have unlearned their earthly notions concerning God and the universe. The degrees of true experience in their earlier and later stages are comparable to the bud and the full-blown rose, or to child and mature man; but they are also distinct phases of homogeneous principles. The law of experience is a law of growth and progress, and progressive experience harmonises man, as pebbles are smoothed and rounded by irresistible tides washing over the shores. To be ushered into life naturally, to have a natural experience, to die naturally, to glide naturally into the spiritual universe—such is the true law of our manifest being, and by applying the teachings of Harmonial Philosophy we may be attuned to this law, which is comparable to that of music. So may the brotherhood of man become a sanctuary of joy. Man's life begins in discord, but harmony is in store for him. Our lives, like our mouths, will discourse sweet music if we profit by experience and so display in our own persons that great principle of harmony by which God is manifested in the world. So may our individual lives go on through successive stages of rudimental being into the measures of a wider mode, until the great of all great prospects opens before us and the life which is ours for ever unites its music with the mighty organ tones of the spiritual spheres, into which we shall be received at length in the life of the world to come.

[1] *See The Present Age and the Inner Life, pp. 392 et seq.*

Chapter Twenty-Three - Final Destiny of The Spirit

[1]

The present structure of the universe will change ultimately, and a new universe will come forth. [2] When all worlds of material organisation shall have performed their respective missions by the individualisation of immortal spirits, when each world shall have disorganised and fallen back into its original vortex of chaos, where will the spirit reside? The answer hereto will be best understood by recurring to the soul's travellings. After individual souls leave this and the other earths they ascend to the Second Sphere, where they undergo an angelic discipline, by which every physical and spiritual deformity is removed. When all spirits shall have progressed to the Second Sphere the earths and planets in the universe will be depopulated. The earths and suns will die, their life being absorbed by the Divine Spirit. He will expand His inmost capacity and attract the glowing elements of His being which permeate the boundless expanse of matter, and all matter which is not organised into spirit will fall into its original condition. But the inhabitants of the Second Sphere will ultimately advance to the

Third, then to the Fourth, then to the Fifth, and last to the Sixth, which is as near the Great Positive Mind as spirits can ever approach. It is in the neighbourhood of the Divine Aroma of Deity, is warmed and beautified by His infinite love, illuminated by His all-embracing wisdom. In this ineffable Sphere, but in different stages of individual progression, all spirits will dwell. They will be held together by attractive emanations of Deity, which will embrace the entire Sphere. The Universal Father will thus gather to Himself all images of His creation; and the House of Many Mansions will be filled by the members of the ingathered family. This may be considered as the Home of the spirit, but still greater missions and blessings will determine the paths in which every conjugal oneness will tread.

When all spirits arrive at the Sixth Sphere, then will the Deity contract His inmost capacity, and the boundless vortex will be convulsed with new motion. God will create a new universe and will manifest different and greater elements and energies therein. New spheres of spiritual existence will thus be opened, as much superior to the present unspeakable glories of the Sixth Sphere as this now is above the Second Sphere. The highest Sphere in the present order of the universe will constitute the Second Sphere in that new order which is to be developed. Thus there will be Four Spheres for spirits and angels to pass through at the consummation of the new unfolding, as there are four now between the Second and Sixth Spheres which we have been considering. There have been developed already more universes in the manner here described than there are atoms in this earth of ours. As the human mind is incapable of computing the millions of centuries required for those souls which inhabit the Second Sphere to progress into the one above it, so it would be worse than useless to hint at those ages which will roll into the past before we begin to approach that change of universal relations about which I have spoken. [3]

It follows that the spirit will have no final home, because rest would be intolerable to an immortal being, but the spirit will progress eternally. It will be always in harmony with surrounding circumstances, and so will dwell always in heaven. It will walk in those shining paths which angels tread. Let us then live justly, truly and purely: by so doing our position will be glorious in those innumerable spheres where the spirit will reside.

[1] See the section entitled "Concerning the Spirit's Destiny" in The Great Harmonia, Vol. II, pp. 243 et seq.

[2] This section contains what may be termed a "harmonial" distinction on the outbreathings and inbreathings of Parabrahma. In place of all things returning to God the hierarchies of intelligence are located unendingly in the Thomist state of Beatific Vision, subject, however, to a "harmonial" saving clause, in virtue of which there is nothing lost or cast out. It is an interesting presentation of the Davis scheme of eternity, but it is only a variation of St. Thomas Aquinas and of the Paradiso conceived by Dante. The philosophical basis of the idea is summarised in another place, where it is said that the most powerful attraction in the universe, namely God, cannot absorb the soul, because the soul does not love God objectively but subjectively—meaning that the soul loves God through the centre of its own individuality and not outside of itself. The self is that eternal standard of consciousness and, moreover, is that portal through which the soul

looks toward all remote prospects. The highest counsel of human duty is to love the neighbour as we love ourselves. Self is the immutable rule, the pivot upon which immortality revolves, as a world turns upon its axis, and without it there is no human existence.—See The Present Age and the Inner Life, p. 411. There is no question that Davis is here attempting to express at least one great aspect of a great mystical truth, namely, that God is within or immanent, as well as transcendent or outside the self and the universe. To love God as a Being without and apart from ourselves is great and high and holy, but it is the love of a Divine Neighbour and as such is objective, whereas, in the better understanding, it is in Him we live and move and have our being, which is not a neighbourly relation but one of ineffable permeation. If we can realise this, the soul is steeped in God, and the mode of realisation is by loving Him as He who is within and not apart from our own subject. This love demands a code, which is the shaping of all our life and being into conformity with the Divine Mode; but, as Davis says also, self remains the standard, for it is we always who love, we who conform and we who realise that God is within.

[3] On the subject of successive universes compare The Magic Staff, p. 341, where the same view is put forward.

Book Seven - Health and Disease

Chapter One - The Philosophy of Health

[1]

If we desire to comprehend that just condition of body and mind which is termed health, we must become acquainted with those causes and laws which develop and sustain that condition. Perfect health is perfect harmony, a state when the immortal spirit circulates equally through every organ and tissue. All departments of Nature give unmistakable and demonstrative evidences that health is the true and normal condition of every living thing. The laws of Nature converge to one only end, being the establishment of perfect harmony, and there is nothing qualified so completely to represent and enjoy that condition as the human constitution, because only harmonious principles, proceeding from an harmonious and Divine Mind, could elaborate an organism so exquisite. Health of body and mind is happiness of mind and body. Again, it is the permeation, penetration and actuation of the spirit in every particle of physical and mental being.

The human organism is a world of motions, a solar system, or otherwise a universe in miniature. As the sun distributes heat, life and beauty to the various planets beneath its influence, so does the brain diffuse life, movement, sensation, power to the various organs, muscles, nerves and membranes. So also does the heart send its vital current through every avenue. Disease or discord is the inevitable consequence when anything disturbs the circulation of the spiritual principle from the brain. Perpetual equilibrium of physical and mental temperature; unfailing reciprocity of life, substance, sensation; faithful discharge of functions natural to the various organs; penetration and interpenetration of the spiritual principle, without exaggeration or diminution: these constitute the immediate causes and conditions of health. [2] But there are others, deeper and more essential, which lie in the invisible bosom of vitality, so we must therefore proceed to examine the nature and influence of that living principle which moves and illuminates the human body. Vitality is a part of Divine Mind associated with and acting specifically upon organised matter. There is demonstrative evidence that the universal principle of life or mind is substance. Matter cannot move without a principle of motion being applied to it; the primary source of life and power is the Divine Mind; therefore every relative or approximate principle of life or mind is a substance. It requires substance to move substance, and the moving principle must be superior to the principle which is moved. We are thus led to conclude that the mind or spiritual force which inhabits and moves the combinations of matter in man's physical economy is a substantial principle. It is organised substance engaged in moving organised substance, and the unrestricted operation of all its principles is indispensable to that condition which is termed health. But just as the spirit acts upon matter, so does Nature act upon the spirit within. The principles of action, development, refinement and reciprocity are the same everywhere, and are unchangeable. Therefore health consists in the unhindered operation of these laws, firstly, between the spirit and the body, secondly, between both these and universal Nature.

Health consists otherwise in a series of events or revolutions, each of which is attended with some important change in the general structure. They result from the operation of reciprocal, positive and negative, or alternate forces, produced by the interior powers of the soul. Beautifully do these hidden powers manifest their action in subordinate portions of the individuality. The blood makes a revolution every three minutes; we breathe periodically, move periodically, think periodically, do all things, experience all things, understand all things according to the universal laws of periodical movements. [3] Like earth itself, man experiences daily and yearly changes, resolved into regular and specific revolutions. Woman has her periodical experiences, perfect and unvarying. The four great events are birth, health, sleep and death.

When an individual is perfectly healthy, the organisation is a splendid representation of spiritual beauties and symmetrical developments. With merely physical perceptions we are charmed by the well-formed, beautiful infant, elastic and joyous youth, splendid and accomplished man in his prime, while even more captivating than these is the aged man, his body unbent, his mind radiant with memories and sparkling with conceptions of the future. But the internally healthy man, beheld with spiritual perceptions, looks like an illuminated world, a typical summary of the life, beauty and harmony of the universe. The brain is surrounded by numberless radiations, like a glowing sun. Greatly to be desired is the attainment of this state, elevated above the depraving effects occasioned by transgression of Nature's immutable laws. Greatly to be desired is the knowledge by which it can be imparted to unborn generations. Greatly to be desired is the ability so to train them that it shall be as difficult for such generations to violate physiological and psychological laws as it is for us to obey these. It is necessary for happiness that the human head should be glorious as the sun, bright with the halo of righteousness; that the entire structure should represent faithfully that undisturbed harmony which pervades the universe. So accustomed should we become to moving, sleeping and thinking right that it should be as hard for us to deviate from the regular path prescribed by Nature as for earth to depart from its orbit. Indeed if we were so constituted and situated as to be perfectly healthy, it would not only be exceedingly difficult to violate the laws of Nature but even to realise that we possess any system which demands our vigilance. However, we touch here upon health raised into a heavenly state, and such it is in its perfection—not a mere physical condition, but the outer manifestation of an inward reality, the right arrangement and the right manifestation of those forces and elements which constitute the immortal soul.

[1] *See The Great Harmonia, Vol. I, pp. 43 et seq.*
[2] *In certain questions and answers prefixed to a later volume, Davis postulates that physical health is the first condition for the attainment of the chief end of man, which is to individualise his spirit and prepare it for the Summer Land (See, however, ante, pp. 113, 115, 117). Such health is said to consist in symmetry of development, energy of will, harmony of function and bodily purity. These results are obtained (1) by inheriting a sound constitution; (2) by obeying the law of temperance in regard to food and drink; (3) by giving free play and equal exercise to the muscular system; (4) by exerting the will-power to keep the passions in subjection; (5) by sleeping, working and living in accordance with the requirements of natural law,—The Harbinger of Health, p. 3.*
[3] *It is said that the physical system is perfectly and mathematically periodical during all the life of health. A particular hour of the evening is the hour for sleep; a particular time in the morning is the waking hour; and so also there are times for food, times when you can work more easily and also better, times when the constitution reminds us that a period should be put to the work. But all goes on automatically, and neither in resting nor working does thought dwell upon the body. Nature is thus full of physiological and psychological antitheses.—The Harbinger of Health, pp. 20, 21.*

Chapter Two - The Philosophy of Disease
[1]

DISEASE is a want of equilibrium in the circulation of the spiritual principle through the physical organisation. In plainer language, disease is discord, and such discord or derangement must exist primarily in those spiritual forces by which the organism is actuated and governed. The spiritual principle is a unit made up of lesser principles—that is to say, of motion, which circulates in the muscles; life, which circulates in the blood; sensation, which circulates in the nerves; and intelligence, which circulates in the brain. Physicians believe in the existence of hundreds of distinct and individual diseases, each of which develops peculiar signs and symptoms, whereby the complaints are detected and treated. But interior perception discovers that all are simply and only symptoms of one disease, caused or created by a constitutional disturbance in the circulation of the spiritual principle. In other words, they are modes by which a general primary discord manifests itself in different constitutions. Disease is not therefore a thing, not a matter to be removed, but simply a condition to be altered. It is a change suffered by one or other of those materials—preexisting already within us—which, given an harmonious state of the body, go toward formation of bone, muscle, nerve and ultimately toward the comparatively immaterial principles of motion, life, sensation and intelligence. Diseased parts or organs are simply evidences that spiritual equilibrium has been constitutionally or generally disturbed.[2] This spiritual disturbance is therefore the disease and not the variable symptoms experienced locally. To restore afflicted matter to its proper position in the animal economy, the original spiritual harmony must be re-established. The spiritual principle must be reached through the same mediums which it employs, as instrumentalities, in operating upon and governing the organism. These mediums are electricity and magnetism. When equilibrium is disturbed, and the result is a negative or cold state, a positive principle must be introduced into the organism. When the positive or heat state is produced, a negative force should be introduced. In either extreme harmonious circulation, healthy temperature and proper atomic motions will be thus restored.

The principles of positive and negative, or male and female, are universal. The human brain is constructed upon the principles of the galvanic or magnetic battery, and its physiological peculiarities are expressed throughout the entire system. The same duality of arrangement, the same galvanic action characteristic of the brain are discoverable therefore in every dependent part of the human organism. Duality is an unvarying manifestation of Nature. The male attracts the female, and vice versa, and while opposites thus draw, so likes repel each other. [3] True oneness is constituted of opposite relations, or a proper adaptation of positive and negative principles. The brain is constructed upon male and female principles: the cerebrum is positive and the cerebellum negative. It is the adaptation of these opposite structures to one another that develops mind and all processes of the body which are subject to the control of mind. It is central harmony of magnetic poles and spiritual powers which causes our various organs to perform their appropriate functions with such exquisite order.

Now, the zinc of a galvanic battery generates a positive and the copper a negative fluid, but this phenomenon can be produced only by introducing sulphuric acid into the vessels in which these metallic plates are situated. The analogy between this and the human brain is perfect, for Nature never contradicts herself. The two hemispheres of the brain correspond to the zinc and copper plates, while the spiritual principle dwelling in the brain and developing motion, life, sensation and intelligence, corresponds to the sulphuric acid which pervades the metallic plates and originates the positive and negative forces in the ordinary battery. All human organs have likewise their positive and negative surfaces. The interior of each organ corresponds to its external structure. Internal surfaces are called mucous membranes and the external serous membranes. The first excretes a semi-fluid or alkali and the second an aqueous fluid or acid: one is positive and the other negative. The mucous membrane generates a negative and the serous a positive force. The secretions and excretions of the system are carried on and the physiological processes perpetuated by these membranes. All this is accomplished by the spiritual principle, [4] operating through the media of magnetism, electricity and the brain. Here we find the origin of vital magnetism and vital electricity—fluids vastly superior in refinement to that mineral magnetism and electricity which emanate from the earth.

The food we eat, the air we breathe, the water we drink contain more or less of the gross kinds of magnetism and electricity; but they are refined and sublimated by entering the batteries of the human body. What was mineral electricity and terrestrial magnetism yesterday may by this process constitute tomorrow a part of our thinking principle. In perfect health the serous and mucous membranes constantly generate positive and negative forces, acids and alkalies. By supplying the spirit and being supplied in turn, these two forces preserve an equilibrium of physical temperature and atomic motion throughout the organisation. But if anything disturbs the circulation of the spiritual principle a corresponding disturbance results among the positive and negative membranes, [5] causing one of the forces to preponderate over the other. If the positive forces are impaired the system passes into a negative state, and alternatively. The first deviation from a healthy condition is therefore accompanied invariably by a change of temperature and consequent motion among the atoms of the body. Action and reaction being natural and inevitable, should the spiritual principle be repelled from the external to the internal membranes, the temperature will be lowered and atomic motions diminished, producing a slight negative state in which alkali and vital electricity preponderate, with sensations of coldness and the concomitants thereof. But should the vital principle be drawn from the inward to the outward membranes and tissues, the temperature will be raised and atomic motions accelerated, producing a slight positive state, in which acids and vital magnetism preponderate, with sensations of fever and cognate symptoms.

The causes which throw the system into preponderating positive or negative states, and develop those local consequences which are called diseases, may be classified under the seven following heads, understood as general and including innumerable particular causes: (1) Hereditary constitutional predisposition, (2) Accidents or injuries, (3) Atmospherical changes, (4) Situation, (5) Occupation, (6) Habits, and (7) Spiritual disturbances. As regards the last, external spiritual causes which, by disturbing the spiritual principle, produce discord, must be distinguished from those primary forces in the organism which themselves suffer disturbance prior to the development of disease. The human soul is endowed with countless springs of immortal activity which render it preeminently capable of endless harmonious expansion. But the same attributes render it capable of experiencing inexpressible misery. It follows that the living principle is surrounded by countless influences which are adequate to the development of spiritual and afterwards of physical afflictions. The point is that it is the man and not his body who is first affected thereby. At times they act individually and at times in a state of concentrated combination, their legitimate consequences being faithfully recorded upon the dependent system and experienced ultimately therein.

It has been said that whatever disturbs the totality of consciousness—being the spiritual principle in the body—invariably throws that consciousness into one of two conditions—either positive or negative, comparable to the sides of a balance suspended by the hand of justice. If the body is born healthy, the scales are balanced perfectly, but, by disobeying repeatedly the principles of harmony, one end of the balance sinks gradually, and thus equilibrium is lost. It may require years for good constitutions so to cripple Nature that the legitimate consequences are felt; but the law works unerringly, and the system is thrown either into an undue positive or an undue negative state. Among evidences of positive disharmony are lung and brain fever, bilious fever, malignant, puerperal, yellow and typhoid fevers, eruptive and cutaneous diseases, rheumatic gout, with all disturbances which arise in the serous membranes and terminate in fevers, inflammations and eruptions. Among evidences of negative disharmony are pulmonary affections, catarrhs, bronchitis, consumption, epilepsy, catalepsy, dropsical diseases, dyspepsia, atrophy, structural diseases, internal cancer, prolapsus, female diseases generally, impotence and sterility, dysentery, epidemical influenzas, internal cramps, convulsions and Asiatic cholera.

Nature is built upon principles [6] of justice and reciprocity, and it is at her tribunal only that perfect justice can be obtained, because Nature is enlivened and governed by a Great Divine Positive Mind, a vitalising and super-celestial Principle, which is perfect, just and eternal. We are blessed inexpressibly by the inexhaustible fountain of the universe: our sphere of health and happiness is eternally progressive. When body and mind remain in their normal sphere of action the individual experiences enjoyment in its purest form, which is actually dwelling in a heavenly state. But when any of the causes cited are permitted to act upon the spiritual forces their legitimate consequences are developed with a form and violence proportioned to the deviation from the sphere of health. Some constitutions, as intimated, can resist disease for years, while others sink into a low state by the action of slight causes in a few days. But although disease is an evil, connoting deforming consequences, some persons seem to be exalted spiritually when thus arrested and subdued in their careless career. The laws of Nature are God's thoughts and cease not to guide, guard and administer justice. Though often admonished and at last chastised for disobeying the laws of life, our afflictions may therefore work out for us a far more exceeding glory. There is almost always a subduing, refining, spiritualising influence which emanates from seeming evils of physical affliction. Under the silent influence of many diseases the material temple falls, as it were, piece by piece to earth, and the indwelling spirit unfolds its delicate proportions, until it is prepared to tread the sunny paths and associate with the radiant inhabitants of a superior country. Disease is a strange process by which to subdue and purify, bringing the soul into conjunction with the eternal, but it is a revolutionising ordeal, and in this sense should be regarded as a blessing and sustained with patience.

[1] *See The Great Harmonia, Vol. I, pp. 99 et seq.*
[2] *The point is put more tersely in The Harbinger of Health, p. 19, where Davis affirms that all diseases are referable to the soul principle in respect of their origin.*
[3] *The same view finds re-expression at considerable length in The Harbinger of Health, in a section under the same title as that of the text above. The variations, however, are for the most part those of terminology and do not call for remark.*
[4] *The distinction between physical and spiritual man seems to stand forth prominently throughout the present section, not to speak of other places. However, it occurred to Davis that so far as disease is concerned it is not true that man has a body to be cured apart from his mind, or a spirit, soul and heart to be cured of sin-diseases separately from his body, for in our present rudimentary state the physical and spiritual organisations are one and inseparable.—Op. cit., pp. 383, 384.*
[5] *It is at this time and under these circumstances that medicines of the kind tolerated by Davis are appropriate and may be administered with beneficial results, for the disturbed principles are then struggling hardest to restore the material parts to their own*

places in the temple. To give medicine or magnetism when the soul-principle is comparatively quiet—or when it is about midway between the two extremes—is unsuited to the requirements alike of body and soul. All effort to restore equilibrium is made by the soul-principle with due regard to the law of periodical changes, and the true treatment for the healing of all diseased parts or organs will be governed by the kind, period and degree of effort which the soul is putting forth in the physical economy. When we suffer most the soul is making its strongest effort in the direction of health, and it is striving less with the disease whenever the disturbance is less realised. The middle state is a sort of temporary health period, and neither medicine nor magnetism should be administered. The subject should seek either complete stillness or at need resume his normal occupation, always shaping everything with reference to the period of struggle.—See The Harbinger of Health, pp. 22-24.

[6] As the term principle is used frequently by Davis and recurs most of all in his discussions on health and disease, it may be mentioned that he regards it as possessing two significations, being (1) an immutable mode of action, as, e.g., a mathematical principle, which means an unchangeable law regulating the science of numbers, or a physiological principle, which is some fixed mode of action natural to organs and functions; (2) an immutable and immortal substance, ethereal, spiritual, beyond the detection of the senses, as, e.g., the soul and spirit of man, or Nature and Nature's God. The one is a mode of being and acting; the other is that which acts.—The Harbinger of Health, pp. 188, 189.

Chapter Three - The Philosophy of Sleep

[1]

The laws of Nature guide and govern alike the least and greatest things. There is a centripetal and centrifugal force which acts upon the wheels of a watch with as much precision as on an orb which rolls through the firmament. There is a law of hydraulics which acts alike upon human blood and the fathomless ocean. So also there is a law which controls pain and pleasure, motion and rest, sleep and wakefulness—a law of action and reaction. In accordance with this universal law the pendulum of a clock if pressed in one direction will swing to the opposite extreme. So also the human body after exertion and wakefulness reacts into a corresponding state of repose, and this is sleep. Motion and rest, action and sleep are therefore causes and counterparts of one another, and are guided by the same laws. In the waking state the spiritual principle is diffused throughout the entire organisation, which is thrown into a high state of activity. The blood flows faster, the nerves are more acute and the brain is more energetic than when the spirit is sleeping. To assert that the spirit sleeps contradicts prevailing opinion, but once it is held to be substance it becomes subject to laws which govern material bodies. On the one hand, spirit or mind demands rest as a compensation for activity, bestowing life and activity, on the other, as a compensation for rest. It is not the lungs, blood, muscles, nerves or brain that are exhausted by exercise, but the corresponding forces of the spiritual principle, actuating these physical structures, that become weary and demand rest. Hence the philosophy of sleep is simple, for sleep is that mode by which the fatigued soul withdraws partially from the physical organism and gathers inwardly for purposes of recuperation. At the same time it remains sufficiently within them to inspire the involuntary systems with constant motion, that they may fulfil their appropriate functions. The place into which it retires is the most interior portions of the viscera and the deepest recesses of the sensorium. The superior brain or cerebrum yields up its powers to the cerebellum and this resigns in turn to the medulla spinalis. During the period of natural rest the cerebellum never sleeps, and in the waking hours the cerebrum is in constant activity, guiding and controlling the organisation.

When spirit is buried in blissful depths of natural sleep, diseased structures are benefited and advanced toward health. [2] There is quietude throughout the living temple. Natural sleep is, however, enjoyed but seldom. The inebriate, the gamester and he who turns night into day know scarcely anything of those charms which surround the rest of temperate and harmonious people. Sleep is fraught to the former with soul-haunting dreams and terrors, but to the latter with living blessings. [3] For them, the spirit as well as the body rebuilds each defective structure, gathering into itself the organic elements and essences exhausted by the hours of action. The spirit refines and transforms material substances into vital forces, but such forces cannot be drawn into the spiritual constitution until voluntary movement has ceased. The spirit, when asleep, moves with the greatest precision through the whole organic domain, but especially the inner chambers of the sensorium and the ganglionic and lymphatic batteries of the visceral system. The anatomical and physiological principles of the mental organism build up and endow the vital structures with new forms; but the principles of chemical, electrical and magnetic action are—or should be—at rest. For this reason an almost empty stomach is most conducive to peaceful and profitable slumber.

There are numerous spiritual phenomena connected with the state of sleep, [4] and hence on retiring at night it is of utmost importance to be not only at peace with oneself but also with the world. The Kingdom of Heaven is within us, and conscience is the divinity which rules therein. To obey its dictates is to do the will of God, and this is to unfold in our own souls that glorious paradise of peace and righteousness in which each thought and desire exhales the serene elements of goodness and truth.

[1] See The Great Harmonia. Vol. I, pp. 149 et seq.
[2] It is an old recommendation to sleep with the head to the North, and Davis affirms that by so doing (a) the magnetic forces are established in the vital system and (b) the vital electricity is directed upon the brain and cerebral nerves. In his opinion the natural consequences are dreamless sleep and health.—See The Harbinger of Health, p. 217. Another counsel is to lie on the right side.—Ibid., p. 216.
[3] It is said otherwise that the amount of sleep which a man requires depends on his temperament. The most active men sleep the least. Those who work fastest sleep fastest. Each must determine the amount needed by each and see that the minimum is ob-

tained. He who steals necessary sleep from the night steals from the Lord, and will be punished by suffering and premature old age.—Ibid., p. 253.

[4] There is hence all the more reason for a counsel given elsewhere—that impassionable and psychic persons are not to regard all their "night-thoughts" as whisperings of departed spirits.—The Harbinger of Health, p. 216.

Chapter Four - The Philosophy of Healing

[1]

Progress is a law of Nature, and to resist its tendencies is to resist the workings of the universe. From the inexhaustible fountain of celestial love and wisdom flow streams of motion, life, sensation and intelligence, constituting oceans of Divine vitality. On the margins of infinite space these oceans scatter the most beautiful orbs, as flowers of unfading hue and eternal fragrance. For every germ that adorns the margins of earthly streams there are millions of orbs on the shores of infinitude, and they are flowers unfolded in the illimitable gardens of space, in accordance with the great laws of progression and development. The earth is one of those flowers which the oceans of celestial love and wisdom have planted, and man is the most beautiful of its developments, the ultimate of creation and germ of seraphs. Through all the habitable worlds, Nature has evolved man in the image of God, possessing all her wealth, completing the chain of life and love extending from spirit to matter, from God to the ends of the universe. But man has frequently and conspicuously deviated from the true path. Being a concentration of everything beneath his exalted position, man possesses universal affinities, and this has caused the human soul to misapply its attractions and attributes. By an extreme gratification of inherited tendencies, it has resisted and violated the developing laws of Nature and the Divine Mind. Man experiences attractions toward everything, because he is made of everything, but following the strongest impulse he rushes into fearful extremes, ignoring that indwelling wisdom which is his guardian angel. It comes about in this manner that there are diseased spirits, and disease has developed physicians. The mission of the true doctor is not to the body, which is a subordinate portion of the individual, but to the spiritual principle. Man is a unit, and it is neither true that he has a body to be cured of diseases apart from his mind, nor a spirit, soul and heart to be cured of sin-diseases apart from his body. [2] The body is an associate of the soul, and it cannot feel, think or act without the spiritual principle. All diseases originate with that portion of the oneness which acts upon matter. So also the true physician places his hand upon moral as well as upon physical diseases; he cures the maladies of future generations by closing the floodgates of individual excesses and manufactures healthy organisations by the improvement of those who are parents of generations to come. The medical and clerical professions are therefore one at the root.

The philosophy of disease teaches us to recognise that distinct causes are engaged in the production of spiritual and physical disturbances. The only true medicines in Nature, operating upon the body through the spiritual principle, are clothing, food, water, air, light, electricity and magnetism. The Spirit of the Universe breathes forth those unchangeable principles of association, development, harmonious purification and refinement which educe the essential elements of life, spirituality and happiness from the grossest forms of visible matter. The Divine Essence is in all things; it is the spirit of plants, animals, men and angels; it is the mainspring of all motion, sensation and intelligence. The principle of advancement and purification not only develops and individualises the human soul but surrounds it with kindred, congenial agents to furnish nourishment and enjoyment. The seven elements or medicines just enumerated are vehicles by which the Divine Essence of Nature penetrates the human soul. Through these medicines Nature heals Nature and Spirit communes with Spirit. Dress is a medium through which air, light, electricity and magnetism flow into the organism. It may seem artificial but is not. Every created form has natural protective habiliments in addition to skin or cuticle; even flowers have their aromal vestures. Experiencing the attractions of this universal principle, man clothes his body, but his selection of materials and mode of wearing do not harmonise with principles of health and happiness, and a wrong use of clothing develops discord in the spirit. [3] Some kinds of cloth conduct electricity rapidly to and from the body; other kinds have corresponding affinities for magnetism, producing different and higher consequences. If the body is dressed in very electric materials it will lose much of the warm and positive element, entailing lassitude, nervousness and negative diseases. If magnetic garments be worn under proper circumstances health will result, though a high state of physical temperature is produced by conducting from the body too much organic electricity. These things being understood, it is right to use various habiliments, whereby to beautify the person and harmonise the soul. Had man been less richly endowed with intellectual attributes he would have been clothed like the animals, but not being himself an animal, the kingdoms below him are under his control and he can select from the great wardrobe of Nature those materials which will best subserve the purposes of personal health, refinement and elevation.

Food is a medium through which the spiritual forces of Nature, or of the Divine Spirit, act upon and support the human constitution.[4] The spirit of food cannot be detected by chemical instruments, because it is the essence of the celestial principle which animates the worlds. Everything conspires to keep alive the flame of divine consciousness in the soul. The food that we eat is saturated with elements of Divinity. The innermost elements of life and nourishment which reside in food can be appropriated and analysed only by the spirit of man. In a future period of man's history it will be selected and prepared for body and spirit in accordance with musical principles. The adaptation of compounds, odours and flavours to the constituents of the organisation will be perfectly natural and harmonious. There are three kinds of food which possess different quantities of positive and negative vitality. There are negative, passive and positive combinations of matter which man selects and appropriates to the needs of his constitution. To ascertain where these combinations exist, and how and where to adapt

218

them to his system are things necessary to his health and happiness. He must learn what to eat in disease and how to preserve harmony throughout his being in health. Contrasted with animal substances, vegetable food is negative and fish is passive. Mutton, beef, veal, venison and so forth contain more spiritual vitality, are positive and in a higher state of refinement and concentration. Fish, being intermediate between vegetables and animals, cannot furnish much valuable nutrition. Vegetables are not so near men as animals and are incapable of imparting that vigour which the human constitution demands. The digestive and purifying processes of physical man are adequate to the appropriation and spiritualisation of animal substances, when compounded properly and taken in such quantities as wisdom sanctions. We must not become sectarians in the physiology or philosophy of food, but should pay attention to the uses of things. Wisdom should decide how, when and where negative, passive and positive nutriments are essential to our bodies. This is a great secret to learn. In certain diseases negative or vegetable food is influential in restoring the organism to a state of health. It is the same with positive or animal substances and with the passive matter of fish. If the system is in a highly positive state, the use of negative foods for a sufficient time will supply the requisite alkali and vital electricity, with an equilibrium of matter, power and temperature as the result. So also negative diseases may be cured by the proper use of positive foods.

Water is a medium for the influx of electricity. It is essential to life and health, imparting vital electricity by its prompt chemical action. When used internally, water enters readily into combination with the blood; externally it is a powerful anodyne, alterative, tonic, diaphoretic and restorative. In its various degrees of temperature it is an agent for the development of happiness in the individual and for the restoration of harmony in the sick.

Air is a medium through which living emanations from the sun of our planetary system have access to the spirit and body of plants, animals and man. There are two kinds of atmosphere surrounding the globe which we inhabit—one of them unfolded from the interior departments of the earth and one proceeding from the orbs and suns of immensity. One is local and affects the visible organisations distributed over the face of the earth; the other is universal and acts upon invisible principles of vitality which animate and actuate the various combinations of matter, including the human economy. The latter may be considered the spirit, of which the atmospherical envelope of our globe is as the physical organisation. The particles composing the air which we breathe are globular, having interstices or openings between them, into which the spiritual atmosphere of the Great Positive Mind flows perpetually. In everything therefore we can feel and see the Divine Principle; all are physical mediums through which the Celestial Spirit—or God—communicates a portion of His essential properties to the soul. The Deity abides in food and water and air, imparting harmonial and spiritual principles through these instrumentalities. Air is a powerful agent in the production of harmony or discord, health or disease. Mind and body are influenced equally by the spiritual and physical envelope of our earth. It is a divine medium, not only suitable for the influx of physical elements, whereby the conjunction is maintained between soul and body, but for the communication of celestial essences to the interior of the unfolding spirit. [5]

Light is a medium designed to refine and exalt our spiritual sensibilities and reveal to them the form, colour, relation and proportions of natural objects. It contains the elements of terrestrial and universal magnetism and electricity. There are, however, two kinds of light—one proceeding from the suns and planets of immensity, the other from heated or decayed substance. The former are endowed with a spiritual principle, deeper in their bosom than the electrical and magnetic elements which reside in light undeveloped. Light in its essence is love, and love is life: it penetrates and thrills through every particle that enters into the composition of the soul. It is the material vehicle of Divine Life. It acts upon our spiritual principle with great quickness and mysterious power. When Nature is bathed in glorious emanations from the source of light and life, the mind cannot but perceive something of the loveliness which characterises that Second Sphere to which we are journeying. But though we are designed to enjoy the light of heaven, we cannot share in that privilege unless we comprehend the many-sided influence of that element which pours forth from the sun to our earth. The natural development of everything is influenced and controlled by light. Wherever heat, light and electricity dwell there are the best health, the greatest happiness and the purest intelligence.

Electricity is a medium of universal relationship, [6] and it dwelt originally in the mighty vortex of uncreated worlds. It is an omnipresent principle in Nature, pervading the vast universe which—like a shoreless ocean— rolls around the Supernal Mind. The Divine Mind employs electricity as a medium of communication to all realms of being: it expresses the pulsations of Divine Soul through all ramifications of Nature. So also the human mind employs electricity as a medium of communication to every part of the organism. Diseases can be prevented and cured by a proper application of electricity—meaning, however, not that fluid which is accumulated by electrical apparatus from surrounding substances and the atmosphere, but that which resides in these. The object in either case is establishment and perpetuation of equilibrium in the electrical mediums and moving forces which permeate and actuate the body; but this can be accomplished only through the instrumentality of the Spiritual Principle. The latter must rise superior to the dependent system, must exert its health-giving, magnetic, harmonising influence upon the various organs, nerves and muscles submitted to its control. Electricity will be a powerful agent in the hands of future generations, especially as a means of harmonising the human soul and rendering its various attributes capable of the highest illumination.

Magnetism is a medium of great power and unspeakable importance, but I refer to that spiritual element which encompasses the Centre of Omnipotence, and connects all mind with matter, rather than to the gross magnetism which flows from the rarefication of terrestrial electricity. Every human soul is surrounded with an atmosphere more or less pure and influential: it is an emanation from the individual comparable to the fragrance exhaled by flowers. [7] The soul can exercise thereby a favourable or unfavourable effect upon contiguous individuals, in proportion as they approximate to reciprocity in their positive and negative relations. The further that two persons are removed from such reciprocity the more they will repel each other, and vice versa. In all ages of the world there have lived those whose physical and spiritual constitutions qualified them to exert a powerful influence on the body and mind of others—even to the working of miracles and curing the lame and palsied. But while the ancients employed the indwelling virtue, or magnetism, they believed that human diseases were caused by wicked spirits or devils.

Hereinafter follow certain maxims by which the diseased mind may be directed to the sphere of health and harmony.

1. Be it remembered ever that the human soul was made for a great and glorious destiny, as the principles of Nature, the voice of intuition, the immortal aspirations of the spiritual principle and the unchanging testimonies of wisdom do all affirm.

2. In view of this destiny, it is wrong to devote the present life, or beginning of existence, to insignificant or inglorious pursuits, and it is unrighteous to acquire habits which may ultimately become our masters.

3. Remember that the strife after material riches begets discord and deception, by which the progress of the soul is retarded.

4. Do not seek after fame, because the desire and effort deform inward beauty, and the soul is neither righteous nor happy in the pursuit of this object.

5. Do not allow your affections to flow in narrow or unclean channels, nor your feelings to exceed and hamper the principle of wisdom.

6. Let kindness possess your whole nature, and be sure that uncharitableness never invades the inward sanctuary.

7. Remember that happiness, being an effect and not an end, should not be the aim of your endeavour.

8. Eternal progression and development are the only objects for which we should pray and labour.

9. Realise that the healthy cannot continue in such condition, nor can the sick be healed, unless the laws of health are comprehended and applied to daily life.

10. Let each individual study himself and become his own physician.

11. The soul can rise superior to every species of discord, and thus subdue disease, by self-magnetisation, or —this failing—by the magnetic or spiritual influence of another, in accordance with the laws of positive and negative action.

12. The power of will can repel, overcome and banish every description of discord and unhappiness; but it is most important that this power be developed practically from birth and directed through channels of wisdom.

13. Bear in mind—ever and in all things—that Nature must be obeyed and not violated or subverted.

14. Realise that wisdom is the world's saviour, the extirpator of all sin and misdirection.

15. Be cheerful, joyful, exceeding glad, though death is knocking at your door.

16. There is nothing to shun, fear or deplore in any department of Nature, or in the Sanctuary of the Divine Mind.

17. Remember that sleeping, eating and drinking are means by which we exist physically.

18. In health, the standard whereby to judge of the quality and quantity of food, water and the amount of sleep to be taken, is the unexaggerated suggestion and simple demand of each several constitution.

19. In disease, the standard should be one of intuition, reason, time, age, situation, occupation and circumstances.

20. Those who employ their intellectual faculties almost exclusively should generally abstain from all salt food and stimulating beverages.

21. Never sleep upon any description of feathers, for they impart no life-giving elements and absorb many of the atmospherical energies which emanate from the human frame.

22. It is better not to exercise the body than to do so in the absence of some object superior to the mere process of walking, for the mind having nothing to accomplish exhausts itself and the body which is its material vehicle.

In conclusion, I have spoken of a saviour whose name is wisdom. It is that wisdom which is co-essential and co-eternal with the Creator of all things, which is incarnated more or less in every correct movement made since the world began, which is the embodiment and image of universal harmony and the ever-blooming flower of the Divine Mind. This wisdom is, in a finite degree, a bright and protecting angel resident in each human soul; and I believe that the power which preserves the world of matter from chaos and confusion will save also the world of mind from evil and from discord. Its exercise will be followed inevitably by identical and corresponding results in all places. The form or body of this wisdom is that which we call harmony, and when it has been realised in universal society there will be established in its fulness that "Kingdom of Heaven and its righteousness" which has been ever prayed for and anticipated by man.

[1] See The Great Harmonia, Vol. I, pp. 213 et seq.
[2] The necessary caution is given in another place that if any one believes he can violate the conditions of health and at the same time recover his original vigour by yielding to the self-restoring mercies of his spiritual constitution, he will meet with complete disappointment. Nature is as loving and as just as God, but neither will guarantee impunity from the effects of violation. There is no specific for any human transgression and hence there is no safety in habitual disobedience. The best medicines are scarcely more than hints to Nature in man. They operate like oil on wheels, but broken wheels cannot be repaired by oil, nor can infirm life-processes be restored by medicine. Every physical as well as moral transgression is visited in due time with just and certain punishment.—The Harbinger of Health, pp. 32, 33.
[3] In addition to the recommendations of this section, Davis had particular views on the use of flannel as a slow conductor both of cold and heat. He seems to have favoured its use, next to the skin in all seasons, while recognising that everything depended on constitution and employment.—Ibid., pp. 202, 203.

[4] For this reason it is said in The Harbinger of Health that food, like medicine, exerts an influence upon the whole constitution. All good medicines are therefore nutritious to the entire system, and all good food is, or may be, medicinal in its influence—as water, for example, which is both nutritious and therapeutical. The best Materia Medica is the best apportioned cupboard of food, and its judicious use is the best medical treatment.—Op. cit., p. 177. As regards the total abolition of animal diet, Davis believed that it was only a question of time, for men will not slay and eat when they become true philosophers and spiritualised poets. At present, however, the world is physiologically adapted for the consumption of animal substances, so that he does not recommend total abstinence from flesh meat. He says characteristically that beefsteak eaten to excess will "swear outright" in human speech and conduct; but, on the other hand, an exclusive fruit and vegetable diet, persevered in for years, will not build factories.—Ibid., p. 176.

[5] Davis had a theory also that as a man inspires the physical atmosphere so does his mind conduct itself in thinking and willing; but this meant only that life in the vitiated atmosphere of a small room affects the health of mind as well as the health of body, which is of course obvious.—Ibid., p. 68.

[6] It is suggested further that electricity may be the origin and cause of life, both animal and vegetable, and that the instantaneous action of thought and feeling is telegraphed thereby throughout the animal frame.

It is obvious that the first point involves the second, but although it is a common thing to speak of electricity as life in loose talk the progress of science since Davis made the suggestion has done nothing to justify it. Our knowledge of electricity and life is confined still to their manifestations. On the question of identity see Op. cit., pp. 211, 212. Compare Ibid., p. 158: Electricity of immensity is the conveyancer—that is, medium for transmission—of all vital action in the universe. In this case it is not life but its vesture.

[7] Magnetism in its broadest sense signifies the principle by which one object is enabled to attract, repel and influence another. The source of this principle is soul. Crystals, various mineral bodies, plants, trees, fish, birds, animals, human beings are all endowed with the magnetic principle, because all are endowed with a soul, which is the mystic life of boundless Nature flowing from the Fountain of the Great First Cause. The word soul must not be confounded with the word spirit; it is used here to signify that harmonious combination of the principles of motion, life and sensation which move, warm and perfect the physical organisation. Each natural body of matter is differently capacitated and hence is differently supplied with soul-principles. The consequence of this difference is a magnetic polarity between one body and another, while the consequence of this universal polarity is the evolution and manifestation of all physical motions and mental phenomena.—Ibid., pp. 89, 90. Therapeutically Davis recommends the judicious use of human magnetism in nearly all cases of disease, and especially the use of one's own magnetic energy on different parts of one's own body. The left side can treat the right side, and vice versa; the vital centres can give the surfaces a thorough magnetic sweating; the hands will do the bidding of the brain; and the brain will act obediently to the commands of well-ordered judgment. It should be borne in mind, however, that to practise magnetism successfully we must have, as de Puysegur says: (1) An active will to do good, (2) a firm faith in our own power, and (3) an active confidence in employing it. Magnetism is a sublime spiritualising agency of energy and health and an all-pervading sympathy which connects us with the absolute condition and sufferings of our fellowmen.—Ibid., pp. 97, 98.

Chapter Five - The Medical Value of Clairvoyance
[1]

The judicious employment of clairvoyance in the diagnostication and treatment of disease is a legitimate use of its power. In the detection of hidden sources of human misery and of conditions that generate physical discords no sight less penetrative than that of a genuine clairvoyant can avail much. This notwithstanding, the careful instructions of scientifically trained judgment are more in harmony with rational sense than the blunderings of undeveloped or non-medical seers, only a few among whom can reveal the causes of disease. The condition of seership is one of great impressibility and is too apt to take on and reflect the fears, surmises or established convictions of the patient. Every sufferer—whether blessed or not with intelligence—will have definite views regarding the nature and probable cause of his complaints and connected misfortunes. The clairvoyant is almost certain to become involved therein and to be misled by contact with the dominant feelings and judgment of such a patient, unless the seer or seeress is in full possession of the faculty of sight while in the act of diagnostication.

It is unphilosophical to suppose that all clairvoyants are equally or similarly endowed, and, e.g., it is rarely that a genuine medical seer possesses commensurate abilities in other departments of investigation: I mean that a first rate seer of disease is seldom more than a second or third rate prescriber. This incapacity may be manifested immediately after an examination and prognosis which have been pronounced satisfactory. On the other hand, it happens in alternative cases that only the faculty to prescribe is perfect, for certain clairvoyants can detect the proper remedy for a disease, the origin, location or symptoms of which they have professed no power to discern. It is therefore frequently wise to obtain your diagnosis from one and your remedy from another. The degree of endowments, as well as the kind or class, must be taken also into account. If a mind is endowed with the power to discern objects through the mystic distance—discriminating between fancies and facts—it is a misuse of such a faculty to press it into the treatment of bodily diseases. The reverse is equally true, and the penalties of misemployment in either case are doubts and errors.

In the course of his inner life it may happen that the seer accomplishes a silent spiritual unfoldment, and immortal attributes may bloom one by one in the garden of his soul. In his clairvoyant exercises a kind of apotheosis may occur, an ascension of ordinary powers into regions of higher use. Rooting up its attachments to material things, the whole mind may be dedicated to those that are transmundane, and the seer may thus advance to the perception of great truths and principles. The investigation of disease becomes then almost impossible; the law of seership on that plane is repealed, so to speak, and any use of the inferior powers by one who is thus unfolded would be attended with penalties as a transgression of the operations and requirements of higher law. In many cases merely worldly wants, or poverty of moral faculties, have urged very high clair-voyants into unprofitable forms of the medical business, into telling of fortunes, reading the stars, psychometry, etc., to the exclusion of those spiritual exercises which expand the soul and develop its latent abilities. The consequence is loss of virtue in the spirit, retardation of the normal processes of growth, and some-times a total suspension of the clairvoyant gift. The power of comprehensive vi-sion may be impaired by mental infidelity and devotion to small things.

[1] See The Harbinger of Health, pp. 25-29.

Chapter Six - The Will in Healing

[1]

Man is an immortal self-conscious spirit, enveloped for wise purposes with matter of a grosser sort, over which he is designed to hold supreme control through intelligence and volition. His integral attitude for self-development and self-government surpasses the belief of his uneducated judgment. But he is reck-less and faithless regarding the principles of his inner life, being ignorant of the riches within his spiritual constitution, and the penalty of this is disease, with its innumerable offspring. The kindest and most skilful physicians can bring no per-fect health to those who are sick and suffering, because—in too many cases—doctor and patient know nothing of the psychological energies in the human or-ganisation, or that crude and bitter drugs can do nothing compared with the kindly offices of our own spiritual forces. The human organisation is regulated by two great positive and negative conductors, which are the sympathetic and pneumogastric nerves. Like the lesser and more delicate nerves, they take their rise in the brain, as the fount of vitality and sensibility. The sympathetic nerve transmits sensibility and life to all parts of the organism. It belongs to the great automatic hemisphere of mind. Instinct, impulse, and life are its attributes. We are concerned, however, more especially with the pneumogastric nerve, which confers energy and voluntary movement on the internal organism. It is in direct contact with the attributes and designs of will, and is a motor nerve by which volition may impose its decrees upon the whole physical economy. It is in com-munication with throat, lungs, heart and bowels—that is to say, with those or-gans which are most subject to disease. Out of the established fact that this nerve is a conductor of mental decrees arises the treatment and there may arise also the cure of these physical parts. We affirm that man can maintain his health un-der any reasonable combination of circumstances, and—with this object in view—we counsel respiration as a means of transmitting spiritual vigour to weak and debilitated organs. The heart is covered with the cardiac plexus, which arises from the pneumogastric nerve. The lungs are supplied with another plexus of nerves springing from the same conductor. Lastly, the entire digestive func-tions are provided from the same voluntary battery at the base of the brain. The organs and parts named are under the immediate control of mind.

The mode of practice is to cultivate deep, slow and uniform breathing, accompanied by a strong exercise of the will to be healthy. In cases of general weakness, concentration should be on the extremities first, working upward and inward progressively. When the brain has been reached after ten minutes of steady and deep breathing, the process should be repeated in the descending scale. By this pneumogastric self-treatment spiritual strength is received from the air. When the science of deep breathing has been attained by practice, and the will has been fixed coincidentally upon the general restoration of the system, the act of concentrating on a single diseased part will become less and less difficult. Consumptive persons may enlarge their chests and lungs beyond the possibility of disease, and so with other complaints. In acquiring this power it may be necessary to practise thrice in each twenty-four hours, the time chosen being one hour and a half or two hours after meals. The help of a sympathetic associate may, however, be indispensable at the beginning in certain cases. In conclusion, the spirit world will also lend its aid by forming a secret conjunction with the pneumogastric conductor.

And now as regards the sympathetic nerve and its wonderful system of ganglia, the automatic principles of life, motion and energy are conveyed thereby to all interior structures, lymphatic vessels and the living blood of the organism, so that all parts of the body are sympathetically related and no member can suffer without disturbing the whole. The intuition of the sympathetic nerve is wiser than the best physician, its pathological value being exhibited by the lessons which it conveys—as, e.g., the admonishment to sleep when fatigued or to rest otherwise in prostration.

[1] See The Harbinger of Health, pp. 45 et seq., extracted and condensed.

Book Eight - Philosophy of Spiritual Inter-course

Chapter One - The Philosophy of Dream

[1]

The soul in perfect sleep is folded within itself. Brain and body are weakened by the activities of the day. Hence the mind draws its faculties together—as the sensitive plant folds its leaves against human touch— and passes quietly into more interior recesses of the mental structure. The cerebellum is the dormitory of the soul, and the mind in perfect slumber retreats from all sensuous disturbances into the back portions of the brain. It is not, however, in a state of inanition but in a greater degree of harmony. Two kinds of dream may occur in this state, one of which emanates from the Land of Earth and the other from the Land of Spirits. The difference between ordinary dreaming and thinking is that the mind discriminates clearly between thought and its subsequent execution in the waking state, but not in the life of sleep. In dreaming the soul takes her wishes for granted, confuses thinking with acting and blends past experiences with present memories and emotions. There is an indiscriminate play of the will among the memories and affections of the mind.

The dreams which proceed from external or terrestrial sources are more or less rational according to the order and vividness with which the mind is accustomed to think and reason. We think and dream in accordance with our experience and habit in combining ideas, and in accordance with dispositions of mind incidental to our common nature. The mind therefore manufactures the fabric of its ordinary dreams, which is explicable upon physiological principles. For example, the peculiar quality of foods and medicines is transferred to the brain during the period of repose, and thus the mind can be impressed powerfully by the life of meat. For the rest, defective slumber, impaired health, restless thought and the influence of other disturbing causes are accountable for those dreams which are referable to the Land of Earth. [2]

In respect of those which emanate from the World of Spirits, it is a fact that spiritual dreams occur only in a state of perfect slumber. The will and faculties of thought must be in a state of complete quiescence, and as this condition is seldom enjoyed it follows that "angel's visits are few and far between." Children of earth eat too much and too often, are injudicious in their occupations, are mentally too inharmonious to permit that complete retirement of mind from cerebrum to cerebellum which is indispensable to spiritual influx during hours of

227

slumber. Such influences cannot enter when the front brain is at all positive. Only when the wind instrument is set to a high note on the spiritual scale of music can the angels awaken it to melody. Perfect slumber is nigh unto the state of death. The higher departments of mind are not occupied by thought; the holy elements of feeling are stilled; the front brain or cerebrum is a tranquil domain; there is no sentinel at the gate of the brain but the vigilant cerebellum. The mind is then ready for a high order of dream. Now if a spirit should approach and desire to impress a dream upon the sleeper's mind, it would act psychologically upon such organs in the front brain as would elaborate the dream designed. The result is not clairvoyance, though distant objects and scenery are impressed from time to time correctly on the mind. Now and then also there come our guardian spirits from a fairer home than ours and gently awaken our highest faculties to the finest thought and most serene contemplation.

The phenomena of dreams are controlled by established laws which may be applied to education and development of mind. Properly speaking, there is no such condition as absolute suspension of consciousness, only of external powers of memory. When the mind passes into a state of coma, the spirit takes up the thread of previous interior experiences. The mind has two memories, one of the body and the world without, the other a more inward scroll, on the deepest folds of which are registered those experiences which the soul has obtained from the World of Spirits. The significance of dreams depends upon their nature and derivation. There are numberless varieties of superficial or cerebral dreams—half-remembered sensations and reminiscences of the past, wrought up during imperfect slumber into uncommon shapes and phantoms. The generality of dreams among men have not the least foundation in the law of correspondence or meaning, which should alone entitle such mental phenomena to our attention. Common and disturbing dreams never emanate from the World of Spirits. Even in prophetic warnings the soul does its own work almost invariably, by extending its sensiferous faculties toward the future, and thus perceiving—reflected upon its crystal bosom—those events which laws of cause and effect are certain to develop.

The spiritual department of this subject is invested with sacred interest. Deep, lovely and positive is that philosophy which demonstrates the possibility, laws and practice of angelic intercourse. There is no matter more incontestably demonstrated than the communion of men with spiritual existences. Owing to wrong living and intemperance, no one enjoys perfect slumber except for exceedingly brief periods; but when experienced in all its fulness, and when the soul is resigned to the will of God through recognition of Nature's laws, the individual is then on the confines of the other life. True sleep is a temporary death of the body and a rest of soul. It is distinguished from imperfect slumber by the absence of all ordinary dreaming. In the deep state the soul is prepared for reception of spiritual impressions, and the influx is easy because there are no obstructions in the superior brain. The higher vessels of mind are open; the deep channels are ready for the inpouring of fresher streams than ordinary rivers of thought; and the soul unconsciously opens to angelic powers, which come at the midnight hour with sweetest salutations. It must not be supposed, however, that any spirit transmits its own thoughts to a sleeper's mind, and thus develops the dream. On the contrary, the faculties of the slumbering soul are called gradually into such action as will perfectly elaborate that dream which the guardian spirit may desire. The spiritual power steals over that portion of the front brain in which the proper faculty is located. When reached, the guardian gently brings its function into action, and thus awakens in the sleeping mind a train of thought, or generates materials for a truthful vision of some distant land. The mind is thus acted upon psychologically by spiritual beings, who breathe their influences upon it and instil their sweet discourse without disturbing its repose or exciting the least suspicion that a divine power is acting so immediately upon it. Notwithstanding, when such an impression is received from the Spirit World, its true import is undoubtedly recognised by the subject, and is never lost. Dreams generated thus may be distinguished from others by the clearness, beauty and power which characterise them.

We must not, however, depend too much upon the guardian spirit for direction and happiness. When we ascertain our duty and destiny, we should act in strict accordance with all light that we possess, and then the higher influences will pour into the soul. Let it be repeated, in conclusion, that thoughts are not deposited in the subjects' brain but are developed therein by playing upon the right faculties in a right manner, and thus the sleeper's mind is made to harmonise with that of the attending spirit.

[1] See The Great Harmonia, Vol. Ill, pp. 311-330, summarised and collated.
[2] A provisional classification of dreams belonging to this order is given in an earlier part of the work from which the text above is taken. It is affirmed that in psychology anything which disturbs the equilibrium of the mental constitution is capable—for the time being—of capturing the mind and controlling its thoughts and impressions. When disease has obtained a preponderance, deranged psychological impressions are conducted to the sensorium. It follows that dreaming deserves investigation as a precursor and accompaniment of diseases. Lively dreams are in general a sign of attenuated excitement of the nervous system. Soft or vapourish dreams denote slight cerebral irritation, or alternatively a favourable crisis in nervous fevers. Frightful dreams betoken a determination of arterial blood to the head. Dreams about blood and red objects, houses and ships on fire, imps, demons, etc., indicate an inflammatory condition of the semi-intellectual and perceptive faculties of the cerebrum. Dreams about water, rain, floods, deluges often characterise diseased mucous membranes and dropsy. Dreams in which the person sees any portion of his own body, especially in a suffering state, point to disturbance in that portion. So also dreams of food, feasts and so forth are usually traceable to impaired digestive functions. This explanation of a certain class of dreams does not pose as a solution of all such mental phenomena. I am treating here of the natural psychological science of man, which differs from the science of sympathy, somnambulism, clairvoyance and mental illumination, in this respect above all—the psychology is concerned with native positive and negative relationships and explains how equilibrium may be and is disturbed without the intervention of any fluid or cerebral element, or of another sphere, as occurs in the superior phases of this high subject.—The Great

Harmonia, Vol. Ill, pp. 96-98. It will be seen that the term psychology is used by Davis in a sense peculiar to himself. The interventions are of course those which take place in the operations of animal magnetism and in mediumship.

Chapter Two - Animal Magnetism and Clairvoyance

[1]

During hours of physical repose, while the system is recruiting and producing new energy, and while organs of sense are closed to external impressions, the mind makes imaginative excursions to different places and contemplates different things. During such journeyings the waves of sound, reflections of sight, susceptibilities of feelings, pleasures of taste are all supposed to be enjoyed. Were all this an experience of the spirit it would be distinguished by the perfection of its qualifications during the state of disconnection from the body. It is an experience of mind, still connected with the body, and the impressions are received through disturbed conditions of the nerves of sensation. It follows that there is an internal medium of sensation working upon the mind while the external medium is in a state of suspended connection with the outward world. [2] It follows also that there is another medium operating upon the internal nerves of sensation, independently of internal and external exciting causes. The nature of this medium is explained by the muscular and sympathetic nerves. Man possesses two coatings, classified as serous and mucous surfaces. One is the covering of each organ, nerve and fascia of the muscles; the other is the inner covering. They generate and sustain a positive and negative fluid, which controls the circulation. The negative expands the ventricles and attracts the blood to its reservoir; the positive contracts the ventricles and drives the blood through the system. The serous surfaces are susceptible of feeling while the mucous are not. The muscular nerves are controlled by the mind, while the sympathetic—or nerves of sensation—are the medium of actuating the mind, whose motion produces thought. The brain is composed of a sensitive congeries of fibres, to which no other part of the body bears any analogy; it is attractive or positive and receives impressions irresistibly. It has positive and negative poles, the one controlling and the other transmitting power. That ethereal substance which serves as a medium may be termed magnetism, while the muscular motion of the system is performed through the medium of electricity. When there is full and uninterrupted exercise of all organs of the body, when they are in perfect unison, the system is thoroughly magnetised. In order to demagnetise it, the equilibrium must be overcome and its positive power extracted by a power still more positive. This will produce the unconscious state which is called magnetic. The medium under consideration exists between all organic beings, for magnetism constitutes the atmosphere by which every person is surrounded. It extends through all things and man is placed thereby over the lower animal creation. His positive or subduing power renders the beasts subject, and they receive it by virtue of the same medium existing between organ and brain.

The state termed magnetic is induced by one system coming in contact with another of less positive power and attracting this from the subject. It is that power which exists upon the nerves of sensation terminating in the serous surfaces. When this fluid is withdrawn the subject is no longer susceptible of external impressions, because the medium by which they are transmitted is absent. He is then demagnetised, leaving sensation only upon the internal or mucous surfaces which produce vital action. The negative power remains; the positive has been suspended; and vital action becomes torpid and feeble. This is the magnetic state, and in this peculiar condition the patient is in sympathy with or is submissive to the will—or positive magnetic power—of the operator. It is the first state, in which the subject is negative and the operator positive. The negative phenomena observed in the subject's system stand in analogy to muscular motion. Subject and operator form one system in power, an invisible union subsisting, notwithstanding the visible distinction. The position is parallel to that which takes place in each individual, when uninterrupted in his functional capacities, one part of his system being positive, the other negative, the two one in equilibrium, and the positive mind acting upon the negative body.

There are properly four magnetic states; and further as regards the first, it is characterised by no special phenomena, save a certain dulness pervading the system because the external organs are in a measure divested of their normal share of magnetism. Persons in this state lose none of their senses but are susceptible to external impressions. They have also full power of muscular action, and midway between the first and second states they are inclined to happy feelings. Whatever takes place is of a physical nature while in higher states phenomena consist in the development of mental powers. [3] It is through the mental organisation that the second state manifests, and herein the subject is deprived of muscular power. [4] The pupil of the eye, tympanic membrane and cavity of the ear expand, but their normal actions are suspended. The extremities are somewhat cold, and in later developments all feeling ceases, so that painless surgical operations are then possible. The subject is associated with the operator mentally, and sympathetic but indefinite and incoherent accounts are received from the mind of the subject, analogous to a record of impressions obtained in dream. In the first part of the third state the subject has partial power of hearing, speech and muscular action, but unconsciousness supervenes in the middle—so far as the external world is concerned. There is strong sympathy between operator and subject, in virtue of animal electricity, which is the agent of muscular motion, and it is through this fluid that magnetic sleep is produced. The mind of the operator is concentrated on this object; the fluid passes from his own brain and nerves to the brain and system of the subject, constituting the sympathetic chain between them. All phenomena of sympathetic somnambulism are accounted for in this manner; but the subject is wholly unsusceptible to tactions and the magnetic medium is far less active than in previous states, though the negative or muscular forces are still preserved. He is, however, eminently open to the external media which connect mind with matter, so that he sees, hears and performs strange and mysterious things. The state is not clairvoyant, though often regarded as such; it is still in analogy with natural somnambulism, it being understood that the one is induced by magnetism and the other naturally by inactivity of the magnetic medium or sensation. The magnetic subject has progressed in his mental capacity toward the condition known as death, for the positive power is suspended while the negative or muscular persists, and the increased mental perception is through the medium of its own association. Still higher manifestations of the mental order will be observed in passing from the third to the fourth state. About midway between the two conditions the chain of sympathy between positive and negative is nearly disconnected. By a corresponding loss of sympathy between the mind and physical system, the former is liberated from all inclinations to which the body would render it subject: the remaining connection is in virtue of a very rare medium similar to that which connects one thought with another. So does the subject progress to the fourth state, and his mind is capable of receiving impressions from foreign or proximate objects, according to the medium with which it becomes associated. The analogy with natural death remains in this state, except that death is produced by the loss of both positive and negative forces, while in that of magnetism the positive and negative of two persons interact and are blended.

The science is thus explained, [5] with the general phenomena belonging thereto; but the particulars will vary exceedingly, according to the various dispositions and organisations upon which the magnetic condition is induced. To sum up now on the subject: (1) The magnetic state is an extension of the motive powers of organic life; and the forces which control one system in sensation, life, health and enjoyment can be united to another system and become as one; (2) the earlier states are analogous to phenomena characteristic of various conditions of natural sleep and somnambulism, while later states are in correspondence with the phenomena of physical death; the connection subsisting between the inner life or mind and the outer organisation is in virtue of a medium analogous to that between one thought and another, understood familiarly as the power of concentration; (3) to this should be added that the source of my own impressions in the magnetic and clairvoyant states is in the Second Sphere, [6] and that the knowledge which I receive is obtained by associating with those causes which lead the mind instantaneously to the effects produced by them.

[1] See The Principles of Nature, pp. 31 et seq., collated and arranged.
[2] This should be read in connection with another statement, which is remarkable for embodying a complete theory of the Astral Light, long before the revival of occult philosophy under the auspices of A. L. Constant, better known as Eliphas Levi. The statement is as follows: The entire organism of Nature is pervaded by a spiritual or vitalising medium. It is diffused throughout the realm of creation, like the medium of sensation, which permeates the human body. The recent researches of several eminent experimental philosophers have done much toward making the existence of this unseen medium a question of familiar demonstration, or at least of extreme probability. Independently of this, it is to be affirmed that there is a universal vital principle which, while

it establishes a means of communication between all bodies in Nature, and is the great sensational medium—so to speak—which pervades the illimitable nervous system of the universe, is nevertheless far inferior to and vastly different from that celestial combination of elements which constitutes the Divine Being. The fluid in question is the grand vehicle of universal influence. In pervading and traversing bodies it modifies these, and is by them modified in turn. When it circulates from one body to another, with the same quantity of power and velocity, such bodies are maintained in harmonious relations. It is also through the instrumentality of this general medium that our nerves receive sensations from surrounding objects.—The Great Harmonia, Vol. Ill, pp. 237, 238. Compare Events in the Life of a Seer, p. 87, where Davis appears to be quoting a German writer. There is reference to a rarefied active fluid which fills the whole creation. It was known to Newton, who called it Sensorium Dei.

[3] Davis has a useful distinction elsewhere on some practices which are an exercise of mere will, or of magnetism coming from the psychological power of ordinary intention. All this, so far as the subject is concerned, must be pronounced degrading to spiritual sensibilities, with everything which assails the private rights of another. It defrauds the subject of personality, when successful, and to this extent is his enemy. The best friend is he who gives you to yourself and does nothing to circumscribe or limit the natural expression and expansion of the elements and attributes of your being, though he may caution, counsel, and unfold the beauty of truth before you.—Morning Lectures, p. 293.

[4] An interesting account of some personal experiences of Davis in the magnetic state will be found in The Great Harmonia, Vol. II, pp. 28 et seq. He enumerates the following successive experiences: (1) The first effect of the operator's passes; (2) sense of electric fire moving through the entire frame; (3) great inward darkness; (4) a sense of approaching dissolution; (5) suspension of external sight and hearing; (6) loss of the power of motion; (7) accession of new and brilliant thoughts, apparently extending over the vast landscape of the Spirit Home, concerning which Davis records his persuasion that they were an influx of interior truth; (8) impression of approaching a vale of inconceivable darkness; (9) of standing on a shore lashed by waves rolling up from an ocean of eternal night; (10) immersion in uttermost darkness; (11) sense of revolution in a spiral path of darkness which contracted in descending; (12) immersion in a deep gulf of oblivion. Subsequently Davis ascribed some of the gloom which characterised this his first experience of the state as being referable to the sombre views of death and possible subsequent conditions in which he had been reared.

[5] It is claimed elsewhere that this science invests the temple of Nature with a new significance. It brings the planets nearer and begets a friendship within us for their beautiful inhabitants. Beautiful and grand realities are being disclosed thereby from the granite sides of creation, which were formerly hiding-places of innumerable mysteries; and the dark clouds that have for ages concealed from our vision the joys which pertain to our future are lifted from the face of things.—The Great Harmonia, Vol. Ill, p. 250.

[6] For this reason it is said of the interior clairvoyant senses that they can gaze upon higher worlds and reveal new worlds within the region where we now dwell. These senses address man's inward sources of knowledge, speaking to his intuition and reason. The magnificence of the spiritual universe is concealed from the limited vision of corporeal eyes, but it is visible to interior eyes.—Penetralia, p. 183.

Chapter Three - The Threshold of Deeper States

[1]

Innumerable combinations of matter are prepared to develop and complete the human organisation. A vast complexus of spiritual forces elaborates this matter, according to their specific purpose and form of action; and since the elements of man—as those of all things else—manifest tendencies to advance toward development of perfect unity, there are successive systems in his physical plan as well as in his mental structure. They are the osseous, cartilaginous, glandular, muscular, nervous, vascular and cellular, each of which, considered by itself, is perfect, though forming a part only, regarded in relation to the others. There is also a common confidence in the integrity of each and a common dependence upon the just discharge of each other's office. Moreover, that which is lower is subservient to that which is higher, together with constant communication and reception of influence and power.

The love or desire of man permeates all avenues of his being. It acts before his birth upon the osseous and kindred substances, but is manifested only in fulfilling the functions of creative motion. This accomplished, it ascends to the development of higher systems— muscles, nerves, cellular tissues—and thus becomes creative life. When birth has taken place, motion and life diffuse themselves through every membrane and become creative sensation. Furthermore, the executive will has endless ways and means of action, while the wisdom faculty has its own innumerable modes of manifestation. It follows that the matter composing the human body is not only elaborated by but is under the actual government of a spiritual oneness, which is the man internal. So does our nature typify the universe, enlivened and actuated by a Supreme Spiritual Mover. Hereof, however, is man in what has been called his normal or rudimental state. He may pass from this into the sympathetic or somnambulistic states, which have been described also previously, and this advance may happen in any one of several ways. [2] Body and mind may be inclined constitutionally thereto; long continued corporeal disturbances may render the nervous system susceptible to foreign or mental influence; and these when actively engaged—while the system is in a favourable state of health and temperature—will terminate in double consciousness. Frequently disease refines and subtilises the body to such a degree that vision and trances are induced. Sometimes a simple accident produces the same results. In such a state the body is partially under the control of mind but is subject otherwise to the direction of surrounding influences. In the former case constitutional predispositions will be exhibited; there may be extraordinary developments of distinguishing physical and mental powers, or new faculties may manifest. In the alternative case the subject will write, speak, sing, weep, laugh, contort his body and present many symptoms of monomania.

If constitutional and accidental causes are inadequate to the production of this state, the repeated influence of a second person will furnish the required degree of corporeal refinement, and the somnambulistic state will follow, but unity of desire and intention is indispensable between the persons, while, their mental structures must be not less dissimilar than are positive and negative poles. A spiritual galvanic action will then ensue, the negative body will yield, and a channel of communication will be opened between them, as between two people conversing through the mediums of speech and hearing. The agent of fulfilment is called animal magnetism, but it is really a spiritual intercourse operating throughout the organism. In this state the subject's spiritual perceptions are enlarged and improved; he can read another's memory, describe distant scenes and absent friends. [3] Occasionally he can deliver philosophic and scientific dissertations. He can also separate or combine every thought or predilection pervading the mental atmosphere of the room occupied. There are well attested instances of Latin, Greek and Hebrew words, or even whole passages, being pronounced with ease and correctness, though the subject, in his normal state, had no knowledge of these languages. But ask persons in this state respecting disease, and they will confirm only the patient's own impressions; or demand their source of information, and they will appeal to spiritual influx and prophetic power; for this is one aspect of that transitional state, already diagnosed, the phenomena of which involve long investigations to separate them from the false principles with which they have been surrounded.

The independent or clairvoyant state is seldom attained, for peculiar mental and physical qualifications are indispensable [4]—an easy and healthy mind, a simple and correct diet, a growing knowledge of God and confidence in Him, desire for refinement and goodness, a clear perception and practice of benevolence and justice, a desire for spiritual association. Two causes are engaged in the induction of clairvoyance: (1) Congenial and frequent manipulations, to tranquillise and concentrate the mind and make it susceptible of gentle influences; (2) a condition of temporary death, during which the spirit will dwell in the world of causes. During the first the subject's body becomes a passive member of the operator's active body; the spirit is held to its form by sensation, which at other times connects it with the external world; the external memory is closed and the internal is opened. During the second the spirit resides transitionally both in and out of the form at the same time; in consequence of this intercourse between sensation and thought, body and mind, the interior glides into external memory; and when out of such state the subject can recollect what was felt, heard and seen therein. In the normal condition the spirit remains within and perceives from its bodily location, but in this state it goes where it desires, and is not influenced by acquired or prevalent ideas or prejudices. It is a development of every spiritual power, the subjugation of every animal propensity, the bringing of the real man into immediate conjunction with spirits, causes and principles. [5] He utters and confirms that which man has taught and believed, if the same are true; he denounces long cherished opinions, if these are unfounded; he reveals new and vaster principles.

Those who enter the superior condition—whether through the agency of human magnetism or by constitutional and spiritual development—are subject to that universal law in virtue of which the human spirit is educated by experience. [6] If the spirit is pure in its aspirations after the interior and infinite; if it lives harmoniously among men, loving God and goodness, truth and justice; then, should it enter the clairvoyant condition, the world may repose confidence in that which it reveals. We must discriminate, however, between spiritual perceptions and spiritual impressions, the first being inferior, circumscribed and particular. In the superior condition the mind enters a vast sphere of light, or alternatively comes in contact with the electricity of the universe, an agent or medium of perception for the spiritual eyes. If I desire or pray inwardly to know the situation of some individual in the Tower of London, if such desire is good intrinsically, and if there be one therein, my spirit—yielding to its internal promptings—becomes abstracted from surrounding objects and material influences. A soft, clear light emanates from the front brain and merges into the electricity of universal Nature. Forthwith I can see from the room in which I am now writing the person whom I desire to behold. But had my desire been directed to another planet—Saturn, for example—my spiritual perceptions would then be transferred thither as readily, and I should behold those who dwell thereon.

In respect of spiritual impressions, the superior condition is induced as already described—by a kind of semi-voluntary self-abstraction. But instead of the soft, clear light radiating in straight lines from the anterior brain to some particular earthly locality it ascends, a few feet from my head, into the atmosphere and there blends with a great sphere of light, proceeding from the concentrated intelligence of the Spirit World, as from a mighty sun. This light is impregnated with that knowledge which I seek. It possesses all conceivable intelligence and flows into the mind unfolded to receive it, as light and heat flow from the visible sun into objects on earth. [7] I was in this state when The Principles of Nature was delivered to the world, and that work could not have been produced so early in my life had I not been helped by another person's supporting and congenial influence. Combined with my constitutional predisposition to spiritual illumination, the quickening power of this influence enabled me to accomplish that which, under less favourable conditions, might not have been possible earlier than my thirtieth year.

Unless a subject has attained the superior condition through the agency of magnetic influences, or unless his spirit has grown—according to progressive principles— into conjunction with the truths which animate existence, it is impossible for anyone to enter voluntarily that state in which he can see clearly the things of a higher sphere. Previous to inward development there must be the action of another system—by which the positive power, or vital magnetism, is extracted from the subject. To sustain life, such magnetism is supplied sympathetically by the operator, and so long as this is the case a bond subsists between the mind and body of the subject, so that the mind can return to its physical frame after a temporary absence, which would not be the case if this bond were severed.

The psychometrical state and superior condition are attainable by all. [8] The interior sight is not a gift bestowed upon the soul but a manifestation of harmonious mind, an inevitable development of the soul's energies. The development of these sublime powers, on this side of the Spirit Land, depends upon favourable hereditary predisposition, habits, social situation, education, moral state, and the strength and purity of the soul's aspirations. It must be remembered also that they can be weakened and rendered comparatively worthless by the misuse or perversion of their proper functions; but as much can be said of every sense or faculty belonging to man's physical and spiritual constitution. As regards development of the powers, there is that part which is not of the individual's own choice and ruling. If parents desire their children to occupy a high moral and intellectual position they must not themselves violate physiological or psychological law, nor go counter to the warnings of intuition. Hereditary predisposition is the foundation on which to base the forming of a child's character. Every human soul has an intrinsic predisposition to goodness, harmony and spiritual illumination, and they are communicated by the Father of spirits; but this predisposition must not be retarded by the transgression of progenitors. On the contrary, everything should be done to augment their manifestation. The individual, on his own part and from youth upward, should never be actuated by extreme or impulsive sensations. His habits should be consistent with harmony; he should never exercise body or mind violently and inconsiderately, for extremes disturb and retard the soul's tranquillity and development. At the same time it is very important that the body should be exercised in all its parts, because the individual must attain the fulness of the stature of a perfect man before valuable results can be reached. A state of moral goodness is not less necessary for spiritual advancement, signifying here that the mind must entertain a strong and unchanging friendship and veneration for God, truth and justice. Mental quietude is also essential to interior light. Nothing so injures and deforms the soul's powers as an uneasy, dissatisfied, impatient, combative, revengeful, unconformed disposition, especially when the individual is conscious or desires to become conscious of his relationship to the material and spiritual universe. Furthermore, aspirations should not be confined to earth, nor limited by the solar system: the soul must expand through the immeasurable *univercoelum*.

A strict adherence to rules of physical and mental discipline refines the feelings and elevates the mind. If we turn from the world of effects, through ourselves, to the inward world of causes, our knowledge of spiritual truths will be higher and greater. There is ever that counsel of wisdom, the angel of mind, which leads unto all truth: Seek and ye shall find; knock and it shall be opened unto you. Though knowing scarcely in what direction to seek, the human race is looking for important changes, for a universal demonstration of distributive justice and individual righteousness. While there are manifold evidences of a storm about to break upon the religious and political world, there is not a less general feeling of a regenerating change to come. On my part I am moved to affirm that there will be no sudden manifestation of truth, but we shall pass gradually into three kinds of realisation, being (1) the proximity of the spiritual to the natural world, (2) the possibility of spiritual intercourse, and (3) the reorganisation of society, which will be a beginning of the Kingdom of Heaven on earth. As to this, industrial harmony and individual spiritual illumination lie at the root of all general human reformation. When the interior senses are expanded, when they behold the great arcana which lie beyond the limits of external and material things, then will the vastness and music of the universe be impressed upon the inward principle. When the human mind feels the inexpressible realities of its own existence; when the principles of love, truth and wisdom shall move its fervent depths, the mind will turn from earthly imperfections, will grow into communion with the inhabitants of the Second Sphere and will so find itself but a little lower than the angels.

[1] See The Great Harmonia, Vol. Ill, pp. 191 et seq.
[2] In addition to what has been said previously on the subject, Davis terms somnambulism the first and lowest manifestation of mind in the exercise of its spiritual capacities, and especially of the eyes of the mind, which require no sunlight or artificial mediums of vision, seeing—as they do—through the agency of a high species of terrestrial electricity.—The Great Harmonia, Vol. Ill, p. 281. It follows that somnambulism, as the author says also in the same place, is clairvoyance in an incipient condition, notwithstanding the implied incertitude already quoted.
[3] We may compare what is said elsewhere respecting the clairvoyant state: Clairvoyance can see not only into kitchens, parlours and bedchambers of ordinary household life but can behold not less easily the bedchambers, parlours and kitchens of the human mind.—The Great Harmonia, Vol. IV, p. 67.
[4] So also when developed by the volition or manipulations of another, it depends very much—and inevitably—upon the particular temperament of the operator, combined with the constitutional predisposition of the subject.—The Great Harmonia, Vol. Ill, pp. 253, 254. Davis agrees with a French writer, whom he quotes without naming, that the best cases of the clairvoyant state are those which have occurred apart from artificial means.
[5] He is no longer a sensuous creature, a mind depending upon the outer senses for thought, suggestion, reason, contemplation. He is already in an interior life, where it is easy for him to behold the hidden beauties and dynamics of creation, and this within wide measures.—The Great Harmonia, Vol. Ill, p. 255.
[6] So also, in the opinion of Davis, the term clairvoyance implies a clear perception of things beyond the powers of bodily vision, but it does not imply an understanding of the things observed. However, the immediate tendency of the state is to enlarge understanding and conduct the spirit into higher spheres of contemplation.—Ibid., p. 264.
[7] The most exalted exhibition of man's mental abilities is said therefore—but in another place—to occur in the state of clairvoyance, and it reveals a sublime capacity and power to the investigator. When the body is thrown into a magnetic slumber—so deep indeed that the roaring of a battle-field could not disturb it—the spirit's beautiful sunlit eyes contemplate distant localities as though these were present. They can even fix their observation upon persons and occurrences hundreds of leagues away, with all the accuracy natural to bodily vision.—The Great Harmonia, Vol. V, pp. 319, 320.
[8] It is said further that clairvoyance is as certainly a power of the human mind as is memory or consciousness. It is not derived or borrowed but innate and natural. That clairvoyance, as to its manifestations, can be simulated I do not deny, says Davis; but I deny, with authority of knowledge, the doctrine that real power of vision can be projected by another's will into the mind of any one. It is true notwithstanding that magnetism, or some equivalent influence, is indispensable to its origin and growth. The in-

sistent materialism of the physical body acts like a clog on the feet of the interior spirit. The clouded eyes behind the bodily organs of vision must be brightened up by magnetism, but once opened truly they cannot afterwards be closed altogether. Terrestrial or celestial magnetism, sometimes even nothing beyond the refining influence of certain diseases, is required to originate clairvoyance, and when it becomes part of the mind's conscious operations, under the control of will—being the highest form of the faculty in this world—it is a power of amazing scope. Therein everything is seen from its vital points and thence outwardly, until the material form of objects is discerned fully. In this manner clairvoyance is the vision of the natural eyes reversed or inverted. The forms of the faculty are (1) a glimmering perception of things—as in somnambulism; (2) a limited vision of things terrestrial only, but including personal acts and particulars concerning diseases; (3) a discernment of personal states and emotions and thence thought-reading, psychometry, fortune-telling and prophecy. A steady progression will be likely to characterise the spiritual perceptions, and these should be exercised systematically. Then the temple of the starry heavens will swing wide its flaming doors, and the gardens of Summer Land will be as near as fields of earth to fleshly eyes, all which happens to every worthy mind a few hours after death.—Views of the Summer Land, pp. 10-14.

Chapter Four - Opening of The Spiritual Senses

[1]

Inasmuch as the physical ear is a materialisation, so to speak, of the interior spiritual ear, and as the external eye is an outer organisation evolved from the spiritual interior eye, so the experiences of the twofold special senses—outward and inward—correspond to that realm within which the exercise of each sense is natural and legitimate. Therefore spiritual things are discerned spiritually and things material are materially discerned. There is no possibility of substituting one for another, though it is true that in a temporary and inverted manner the superior senses can be used to see and hear what is external and inferior.

The opening of spiritual senses is preceded by a rapid closing in of night around the outer consciousness, for the bodily senses are deserted. Then suddenly, after the space of darkness in the temple, consciousness is stirred by the presence of a new universe and awakens or unfolds in the dawn of a new day. It is amazing that those who accept the Bible do not comprehend these great gifts of the spirit. Yet they read: "Lo, the heavens were opened unto him, and he saw the Spirit of God descending like a dove, and lighting upon him; and lo a voice from heaven, saying, This is my Beloved Son, in Whom I am well pleased." [2] And again: "It came to pass, when ye heard the voice out of the midst of the darkness that ye came near unto me. . . . Who is there of all flesh that hath heard the voice of the living God, as we have, and lived?" [3] Other passages teach the same experience: "But he . . . looked up stedfastly into heaven and saw the glory of God." [4] "He saw a man standing on the right hand of God." [5] Then he said: "Behold, I see the heavens opened." [6] Compare also: "Suddenly there shined around him a light from heaven. . . . And the Lord said unto him, Arise, and go into the city, and it shall be told thee what thou must do." [7] These psychophonic and clairvoyant examples are plain as the sun. Another instance is not less striking. "The King of Syria warred against Israel," and he instructed his officers to establish the camp "in such and such a place." But the King of Israel had a spiritual seer and a spiritual hearer with him, and was thereby kept informed of all movements of the enemy. "The heart of the King of Syria was sore troubled for this thing." So he called his servants together, to find out which one was the traitor. "And one of his servants said: None, my lord, O King, but Elisha the prophet that is in Israel, telleth the King of Israel the words that thou speakest in thy bedchamber." [8]

These innate spiritual attributes attest the immortal nature of the human spirit. It remains to say that a kind of celestial electricity unites the communicator and communicant when a spirit of the other world has intercourse in this manner with a spirit on earth. It is positive in the mind of the first and is negatively attached to the second. There is, however, a reverse current which is positive in the mind below and negative in the mind above, so that the transmission of questions and answers is practicable on both sides. The first sensation of the incarnate recipient is that of a cool, penetrating, awakening breathing, which seems to enter the inmost brain recesses and creates a *rapport* between them and the unseen world.

[1] Beyond the Valley, pp. 187-191.
[2] St. Matt. iii. 17. Davis expresses in a foot-note his belief in the literal occurrence.
[3] Cf. Deuteronomy iv. 12, 33.
[4] Acts vii. 55.
[5] Ibid., vii. 56.
[6] Ibid.
[7] St. Matt. xxvi. 18.
[8] II Kings vi. 12.

Chapter Five - The Superior Condition

[1]

In its contradistinction to our ordinary state the Superior Condition consists in a practical and conscious growth of intellectual and moral endowments. These faculties are opened and lifted to a higher degree of operation. They are then inspired by their own constitutional essences and next by contact with the life and principles of things. The result of such exercises is stamped upon the individual's character, the ultimate effects being interior elevation and education of the whole mind. The mediumistic state, on the other hand, while—as a condition—it tends to enlarge judgment and spiritualise character, is not necessarily beneficial individually to the medium. Those who receive the lessons and witness the tests of the higher powers are more likely to be permanently improved. The true mediumistic state is one of complete positiveness or isolation in respect of this world and of passive receptivity to the influences from exalted realms of intelligence and love. The faculties of the medium may be greatly excited and stimulated to extraordinary activity, but it does not follow that his mind will be developed thereby. At the same time no good-minded and loving-hearted person can exercise such gifts for a single year without experiencing considerable moral growth and intellectual refinement. On the other hand, it is possible for a medium to be a channel for the most exalted and glorious lessons and yet feel nothing higher than any other stranger to the truth. This fact, which cannot be denied, is owing to the utter indifference of some mediums to the divine lessons of which they are the bearers.

In the Superior Condition nothing of this passivity or indifference is possible. The mind is not only exalted to the fellowship of eternal principles—where it can discern the essences and properties of visible bodies—but the faculties are active and conscious of inherent energy and truth. One who enters this state methodically is like an industrious student, whose mind seeks and finds the penetralia of things. The fruits are intellectual refinement and moral growth.

[1] Answers to Ever-Recurring Questions, pp. 42-44.

Chapter Six - Intuitive Glimpses of Truth
[1]

The human spirit is framed for perception and enjoyment of heavenly realities. It longs for its native eternity. All love of the beautiful, all aspirations after wisdom, all search for the fulness of truth, all yearning after purity attest the immortal existence in store for the spirit and to which, by virtue of origin and essence, it is indissolubly allied. Our strongest passion is to possess the beautiful. In the soul's juvenile periods there is the desire after physical beauty, but the best feelings of age are moved by "the beauty of holiness." The soul swells with unutterable yearnings for a speedy fulfilment of the prayer: Thy kingdom come. This is because the elements of which the spirit is constituted are the property of the Summer Land to come, but men invest this primary existence with imperishable characteristics inseparable from our true home. Ultimately the miseries and materiality of this life become burdens. Human association no longer satisfies. The soul goes forth thirsting and hungering after righteousness, but only from that Invisible Spirit Who is God of Nature does it attain rest and hope.

The power of the soul to anticipate realities belonging to the Land of Spirit is so perfect that on its arrival there a sense of familiarity steals over the mind, as though it had many times before witnessed the same scenes. Poets and painters of landscapes colour their best thoughts with vague tints of immortal beauty. When such minds arrive at the Second Sphere they are instantly at home and content. The most physically wretched, the morally insane and crippled, even as the saint, cry naturally to heaven; and the soul's inmost fount of intuition is touched, ever and anon, by the presence of an angel. Bright and beautiful are countenances of the pure in heart, and beautiful and bright surpassingly are eyes of the higher angels. They express tender love and saving wisdom; they bring beauty and light in their garments; the aroma of their hearts mitigates pain and trouble; they give dreams of coming happiness to departing souls. How incessantly employed in deeds of friendship are the pure and noble of the Summer Land. They come down from their beautiful gardens to mingle with those on earth who pray and work for this reign of freedom. As goodness, truth and wisdom are manifestations of God, so love, purity, philanthropy come from the heart of Nature, and these attributes of humanity are displayed more fully in the world beyond. Each visitor is prompted to perform some kindly office for the sake of humanity. Of the benevolent and unselfish who once lived on earth there are millions in the adjoining world. A stream of constant philanthropy flows from them earthward: when possible, they lift the down-trodden and save the fallen from a lower depth. The selfishness of earth is not fostered in the Summer Land, and sweeter than the waters of Paradise is the breath of every one who visits mankind on missions of mercy.

Progression is the angel of our deliverance, and our heavenly visitors hasten the day of its power. While it is we always who must work out our own salvation from the causes of our unhappiness, the help of angels is with us, and it is extended in proportion as we help ourselves.

[1] See The Harbinger of Health, pp. 414 et seq., collated and arranged.

Chapter Seven - The Certainty of Spiritual Intercourse

[1]

The possibility of spiritual intercourse follows from the continued existence of the soul, with all senses and faculties, [2] after the material body is placed in the tomb. For those who believe in this it is consistent to believe also that the soul may return through affection to its native land, to the home of its childhood, and bring tidings of great joy to those who have ears. How many powers dormant before birth come out thereafter into full and perfect action; and how many powers lie hidden in the soul before death which may appear subsequently in the full force of their harmony and beauty. If the spirit is believed to be clothed with another body, and still in full possession of its present voluntary attributes, it may certainly converse when out of the natural body, as it does therein. Intercourse between minds in this world and minds in the other is just as possible as oceanic commerce between Europe and America, or the interchange of social sympathies between man and man in daily life.

Man's internal affinities yearn for corresponding ties of communion. The soul seems to ask for nourishment from an anterior source. Hence man is naturally a religious or spiritually inclined being, demanding—by virtue of strict moral necessity—the assistance of mind superior to his own. Is it not reasonable to suppose that this interior desire of the soul has its appropriate gratification? The term inspiration is surely not void of meaning. It is certain that just in proportion as the sensibilities of our minds become unfolded, so will the love and wisdom of Higher Spheres flow in to elevate the affections and intellect. Nature's Author is no respecter of persons, and so His inspiration is universal, illuminating everything according to its condition and capacity. Is it not reasonable to conclude therefore that the harmonious and virgin brain may be the medium of spiritual illumination? [3] Is there anything intrinsically unreasonable in the hypothesis that Eastern prophets, Pythagoras, Socrates, Plato, Jesus, Swedenborg received thoughts from some interior source, from spirits who once resided on earth? Do not certain instances of spiritual intercourse detailed by Daniel, Matthew and Luke seem reasonable in the light of modern analogies? If they do, a probability is established, and the next step forward takes us to the certainty of spiritual agency in the production of modern manifestations. It is grounded upon facts which occurred originally in Western New York and are now of daily occurrence in various parts of America. They are becoming familiar as household words, and no reasonable mind presumes to doubt them, any more than the actual existence of Washington City. No solution except a spiritual one can possibly cover all the phenomena which come under the denomination of sounds and movings—not to mention some other manifestations which are of vastly different order and higher import.

In the entire history of mankind no moral or social movement has so powerfully marched forward, soaring above all derision and attempts at refutation as these mysterious phenomena of our era. [4] Like the onward flow of the mountain torrent has been the march of the super-mundane manifestations. We welcome them as glimmerings of another sphere, breaking through the thin crust of ordinary experience, opening new passages in the universe. We do not look for infinite or perfect wisdom in the communications, or for instruction much superior to the mental development of the medium. When the whole field is examined carefully, it will be found that persons in this world do not—as they suppose — communicate promiscuously with Swedenborg, Washington and other illustrious minds, but always immediately with their own particular and congenial guardian spirit, who is constitutionally adapted to the earthly charge. The two are similar in organisation, inclination, desires—with this exception that the guardian is always better, wiser and more advanced, or sufficiently at least to be positive to the terrestrial mind. Hence there is a similitude between thoughts spiritually derived and those drawn from the medium's own brain. If higher spirits desire to impart thoughts they do so by attorney. A long chain of mediums is at times formed between some exalted mind in the next sphere and a person here on earth; but the spirit in closest sympathy with the earthly mind is its own congenial protector, and in almost every instance it is he who communicates immediately. If these laws of interpretation be accepted, there will be no difficulty in extricating the mind from doubts originating in contradictions.

The spirits of the various planets in our solar system [5] are in different stages of refinement, and those that are on the higher have the privilege of descending to the lower planets, of immersing their thoughts into the spirits of these at will, though the latter—in many cases—may know it not. In this manner do spirits descend to and dwell on the earth, when they have a peculiar attraction to some relative or friend. They are ever ready to introduce into his mind thoughts of higher things and pure suggestions, though—for the person concerned—these may seem to flow independently from the workings of his own spirit. Spirits from any sphere [6] may, by permission, descend to any earth in the universe and breathe sentiments into the minds of others which are pure and elevating. Hence it is that there are times when the mind appears to travel in the company of those whom it does not know. So also it experiences visions which are actually true, or which, if they are concerned with the future, may come to pass with remarkable accuracy. At other times dreams are incited by the influx of thoughts from spirits but are not defined, because they are not duly directed. There is furthermore—and it has been recognised already—a class of dreams referable only to excitement of the nervous medium or physical consciousness. These are restless thoughts, fantastic formations formulated in the guise of visions.

[1] See The Present Age and Inner Life, pp. 67 et seq.
[2] Here the term soul appears to be used in the sense established by Davis at the period of The Principles of Nature, as already noted, and in that of The Great Harmonia, Vol. IV, p. 29, where it is said in similar terms that soul, spirit and mind are used synonymously to signify the mental structure of man in general.
[3] The same interrogative mode of argument is used in one place on the question of immortality itself: Inasmuch as the aspiring progressive tendency is a universal attribute of man, may we not reasonably conclude that the soul—thus emulous—will ultimately reach the summit of immortal being? Even in his lowest condition man has desires which centre far above his body, in some higher and better individuality. Does not this longing to exceed even himself prove the workings of an interior principle which may confer immortality on the soul?—The Present Age and the Inner Life, pp. 65, 66.
[4] What is termed by Davis philosophical spiritualism is said to be a revelation of Divine Principles and of the living laws of truth which impose wholesome self-restraint, making each individual the palladium of his own progressive prosperity, combined with brotherhood and rooted in the knowledge of immortality.—The Great Harmonia, Vol. V, pp. 256, 257. And again: The works of the departed, of those we once knew and loved, shine out like angel faces, beaming with lessons of love and wisdom. Therefore, with a spirit that delights only in becoming the good we see, we cast our eyes toward the after-existence in store for each, and behold the Sun of Universal Righteousness rising with healing in its wings.—Ibid., p. 258.
[5] See The Principles of Nature, p. 675.
[6] The intention may be only to register a point of possibility, but it will be remembered that Davis does not recognise any general intervention of beings from higher spiritual spheres in the affairs of our own earth.

Chapter Eight - Philosophy and Spiritualism

[1]

All religions of the world assert the existence of a future state for man, after the death of the physical body. Seers, prophets, poets, leaders and apostles have declared the fact of a world of spirits. But we have believed these assertions long enough on mere external testimony, the authority of individuals. Now comes the era of demonstration. [2] Every man must make the pilgrimage to regions of philosophy for himself. A vast world of knowledge exists, a Spirit Land, beyond the ken of physical eyes. It is now time to roll up the curtain hung between the origin and destiny of man. When we gaze upon the scenes which lie behind and comprehend the principles which uphold the superstructure of man's immortal spirit, we shall surely conceive a new love for life and a new religion whereby to honour Deity.

The most imperative need of the world is a new philosophy, which shall destroy the hatreds of the churches, systematise the sciences and render the truths of revelation as reasonable as the growth of vegetation. The Harmonial Philosophy purports to be a revelation of the structures, laws, orders and uses of the material and spiritual universe. It is a progressive exposition of the boundless system of Nature, addressed to the human instincts and understanding—it being premised that Nature signifies the entire system of all existences, the centre and circumference, the Eternal Cause and effect of the stupendous universe.

Among the highest truths developed by the Harmonial Philosophy is that of the soul's immortality. It brings evidences of man's eternal individuality out of the very rocks and mountains of Nature, and renders the problems of the future as certain as the results of mathematical calculation. Man is immortal upon principles as plain and natural as the common laws of organism and growth. [3] The human spirit is the focal organism of Nature, because all atoms, laws and essences expend themselves in man's formation. So is the interior form rendered eternal, as it were, by a spiritual law of chemical affinity.

According to the natural laws of progress and development, the Spirit Land is revealed to our intellectual perception and harmonised with the oracles of intuition. The Harmonial Philosophy unfolds the magnificent order of the spiritual worlds with the same precision that it treats of the physical kingdoms of Nature; and so natural is this revelation that the mind accepts it, even as it concedes the existence of Jupiter and Saturn. The object is to manifest the Kingdom of Heaven on earth, to apply the laws of planets to individuals, to establish in human society the same harmonious relations that are found in the stellar world.

There is nothing in the whole realm of psychology so demonstrative of the hidden laws and slumbering forces of the human mind as the so-called Spiritual Manifestations. Man's nature is just beginning to declare its manifold resources, and there is no closing or bolting of those doors which lead to the interior nature of man, and thence to a new theology. The manifestations should be considered as a living demonstration of many truths unfolded by Harmonial Philosophy. They show, however, that the Divine cannot flow into human structures without participating in the imperfections of the latter. All revelations—though professing to descend from on high, freighted with the immaculate thoughts of the Supernal Spirit—bear the plainest evidence of having flowed from Heaven to earth—from the ideal to the actual—through imperfect and fallible channels. From a first investigation of these modern developments the sceptic returns with a persuasion that the manifestations are allied closely to the doings of jugglery. A second visit convinces him of the truths of mesmerism. The third satisfies him that psychology explains it all, and the fourth that it is referable to clairvoyance. But the fifth investigation dissipates his materialism and persuades him of the possibility of spiritual intercourse.

When the eye scans the whole ground occupied by these phenomena it is found—and is conceded by the best minds—that none but a spiritual solution can cover and explain them—even in their crude shape of sounds, vibrations and movements. [4] To affirm that the human brain can project an "odic force" sufficient to move heavy tables in such a manner that they respond intelligently to questions is to state a proposition which taxes human credulity far more than the spiritual solution of the whole matter. The simplest explanation of anything is most likely to be true, and this accepted a New Dispensation is upon us, even at the door. It has been long and very gradually coming—that good time when truth and peace, law and liberty shall reign supreme.

[1] See The Present Age and Inner Life, pp. 38-61, compared and reduced.
[2] Davis also speaks of Spiritualism as a great semi-miraculous movement, in which a divine truth is embodied. It teaches (1) that man is an organised mind or spirit, of which his physical body is a general representative; (2) that death is a physiological and chemical change, leaving the states of affection and intellect unaltered; (3) that the dynamical relations between this earth and the Spirit Land are perfect and intimate, which being so a departed person may return and hold converse with those in flesh.— The Great Harmonia, Vol. V, pp. 239, 249.
[3] But it is insisted very truly elsewhere that—to be of any practical service—man's immortality must be felt in his religious nature and not merely understood by his intellectual faculties. It is possible for every man and woman, after coming under spirit culture, to feel through all their being the sublime truth that the perfected human soul can never be extinguished. Evidences which are worth anything are not outside, are not in table-manifestations, not in spiritual stories, not in ghostly anecdotes. True evidences come through two channels—intuition and reflection, being inward sources of wisdom. Every human mind contains its own evidence and holds a note on the bank of eternal life. Individual existence is the endorsement; intuition brings forth the treasure in advance. In a word, the soul itself holds the positive proof. The riches of the future world are lodged in us. Spiritualistic manifestations are destined to become a hundredfold more desirable, but they will be sought as illustrations of immortality rather than as evidences. Let it be realised positively that a man contains within himself the power of endless continuation, and he will look naturally for some correspondence with the other world. He will be in no sense surprised when he obtains communications, nor disappointed and failing in faith when it happens that they do not come. But a person who

relies on external sources of knowledge, insensible to the inward fountains, is sure to be swept away when the sensuous evidences are wanting.—Penetralia, p. 160.

[4] Spiritualism is described elsewhere as, firstly, phenomenal or objective, and, second-ly, as subjective and philosophical—meaning that it grows from the one to the other state. When the phenomena are certified as true a philosophy is derived therefrom.— The Great Harmonia, Vol. V, p. 249.

Chapter Nine - Religious Value of Spiritualism

[1]

SPIRITUALISM is the first religion that takes facts for its foundation, rears its temples of thought on immutable principles of philosophy, recognises a Mother as well as a Father in God, and has demonstrably "brought life and im-mortality to light." [2] It is the first religion that has overcome death and the hor-rors of the grave, has sounded the gospel of freedom equally to man and woman, young and old, lord and serf. It is the first religion [3] that has satisfactorily ex-plained the phenomena of matter and mind—in and out of man. It is congenial to the true children of Nature, while it liberates mankind from slavery to creeds and gives the individual wholly to himself. It teaches that it is better for a man to think independently, even if he think wrongly, than conformably to the tyranny of social selfishnes and the dictum of ecclesiastical shams. "Where the spirit of the Lord is, there is liberty" for the individual. While it is certain that individual-ism has its own follies and fanaticisms, while it leads to isolation in some, in oth-ers to pride and tyranny, while it may set up a temporary barrier to associative efforts for the progress of the multitude, these errors will correct themselves and the positive benefits of individualism will emerge clearer, like the sun from be-hind the clouds.

Opposition to every new phase in religious development is natural, and exam-ples of folly, prejudice, hatred, condemnation and crucifixion of pioneers need not be multiplied. From an outward standpoint such opposition seems a cross too heavy to be borne.

"But truth shall conquer at the last,
For round and round we run,
And ever the right comes uppermost,
And ever is justice done."

Viewed from the harmonial standpoint, Spiritualism is the last development of the sublime relations between mankind and the next higher sphere of existence. [4] It is the grandest religion ever bestowed upon mankind. Under such blessings every being should aim to become intelligent, self-poised, intuitive, reasonable, charitable, just, progressive in all directions. Growth is the central law of our be-ing and the object of all exertion, as it will be the result of all experience. Through growth we shall overcome evil with good and straighten the crooked ways of error and injustice. Such labours and efforts will and do receive the benedictions of angel intelligences, even as good deeds attract admiration and co-operation from the generous and noble of every age and country.

[1] See Arabula, pp. 397 et seq.
[2] Herein also is said to reside its moral value, and because it furnishes a demonstration of immortal life it is affirmed that it establishes the most sublime of human aspirations. Until the objective verities of phenomenal spiritualism became known the hope of continued personal existence was enveloped in doubt.—The Great Harmonia, Vol. V, p. 249.
[3] At the same time the present exponents rightly recognise that modern spiritualism is not of the nature of religion.
[4] By the laws of cause and effect, by clairvoyance in the thinking faculties, by intuitive reasonings, it teaches that progress is "heaven's first law"; that the discords of nations will be overcome eventually by the perfect workings of God; that truth lives and will prevail everywhere; that love is the life of Nature, the presence of God in all parts of the universe, an inexhaustible fountain whereby everything lives and moves and has its being. ... It teaches also that the rule of faith and practice is that light which shines in the highest faculties of mind; that in proportion as man's affections and thoughts are harmonised, refined and exalted will the world be visited with holier conceptions of God; that individual conditions after death will be in accordance with the development of sentiments and intellect before leaving earth; and that human character will be harmonised ultimately by the spontaneous will or ever-operative laws of the Great Positive Mind.—Ibid,, pp. 253, 254.

Chapter Ten - Last Words on The Harmonial Philosophy

[1]

The central idea of the Harmonial Philosophy—which is the closing form of the present cycle of destiny—is inherent to all spirit and will be acceptable ultimately to all degrees of mind. In the opening future of this planet, it will shape and sway the interests of humanity. Its fontal inspiration and aurelian centre of attraction is the perfect love of all wisdom—meaning by wisdom the sum total of impersonal and eternal principles. Knowledge and judgment, on the other hand, are the result of accumulative sensuous observation and experience. Wisdom is thus a name given to the highest embodiment and comprehension of scientific, philosophical, spiritual and celestial principles, while knowledge is a name applied by Harmonial Philosophy to the mind's practical or available recollection of facts, things and events. It is, however, the forerunner and ordained servant of wisdom, a vestibule leading to the inner Temple of Truth.

Harmonial Philosophy recognises the existence of a First Cause, outside all human conceptions, and that its eternal attributes are power, wisdom and justice, this triad containing and implying a central attribute which is sum and crown of all—and this is goodness, the operative effect of which is that quality called mercy. Whatsoever is manifest or hidden within the universe is an expression of Divine Perfection, of an Eternal Principle of Divine Intelligence. Power, goodness, [2] wisdom, mercy, are various aspects of the Truth which is Absolute

248

Being. There are recognised also the law of progression; the science of corre-spondences; the endless chain of action, motion and development throughout Nature; the immortality of man; a purified and perfect state of existence; the uni-ty and harmony of all things. The pure love for this totality of immutable princi-ples is that unmixed and irresistible attraction which is realised by the spirit to-ward truth, for truth's immutable glory. Passion is of and from the soul, but the spirit within the soul is the fountain of love. [3] The soul is the source and play-ground of thoughts, but the spirit-essence is the sea of ideas. So will the reader comprehend that the definition of Harmonial Philosophy is this at the heart thereof: an unselfish, dispassionate, divine love of unchangeable principles.

The term Harmonial describes the quality of love which the individual must bring of necessity to the investigation of truth. Those only who seek and, having found it, impart truth with a Harmonial Love for the alpine summits of wisdom, who labour with unselfish aspiration to advance mankind in virtue and happi-ness, are worthy of the honourable title of philosopher. Whether the philosophy thus defined—which puts the human soul and spirit into harmony with God, Na-ture and Humanity—is religion or not is a question left for the intuitions of man to answer. Assuredly those who receive it are exalted above all popular infideli-ties into the realm of justice and truth; assuredly also the most spontaneous fi-delity is the characteristic of that intelligence which comprehends the truths of this philosophy. Formalities in the expression of cherished religious sentiment will give place in due season to the pleasures consequent upon spiritual harmo-ny, whereby it will be easy to accomplish each day the good that should be done.

Furthermore, it is believed and proclaimed that the same great ideas are common to all men and that nothing new in this order can be originated by any one, though certain persons may be so organised and inspired as to give certain principles their best and most useful expression. The world's history confirms this doctrine. All institutions—political and theological—are crystallised about some central principle, which some particular mind was constituted and inspired to realise and reveal. But when talented men confound private thoughts with universal ideas, and when they exalt egotistic facts and convictions as though they were eternal truths, then come the controversies and sectarian animosities which distract the world.

The world of mind, in obedience to laws of history and progress, will continue to move through cycles of conflicting modulations; but the lesson of all is this—that humanity stands now between the evening of many discordant cycles and the morning of the Harmonial Era. Yet the discord will approach more and more to a harmony, not indeed understood, but perceived and enjoyed, within measures, from least to greatest. It is an under-law of history, part of the eternal rise and fall, the ebb and flow in the mental life of man. And Nature, Reason, Intu-ition will combine to overcome evil with good, till each human being shall surely realise the high principles of truth, as he advances in the path of spiritual devel-opment.

So opens the prospect before us, and in the distance lies the spiritual temple, resplendent with God's wisdom and filled with incense from the love-gardens of eternity. There shall every soul gravitate eventually to his true position in God's harmonious universe, finding his just place in the pantheon of progress.

Hereof is the Harmonial Philosophy, the end of which is justice, nobility, freedom—for and in each and all. [4] It comes to exalt us as immortals and humble us also as creatures; to unfold a world of meaning in everything; to kindle the Divine Flame of Love on the heart's altar and make its incense ascend from the one to the many and from the universal many to that One Who is God; to unfold the universe before us, all glorious and perfect as it is, and the perfection and glory of God Who rules therein. Under such aegis there will surely come upon our world that New Birth which is the passing of an old dispensation into the new, bringing a new heaven and a new earth. It has been said that the earth with its scarred face is the symbol of the past but that air and heaven are of futurity. Meanwhile, man is a fixed fact in the universe. When once he is born into being there is no way of escape, no door to annihilation. The deaths and births, like nights and mornings, are railway junctions where passengers change trains for their several destinations. Over such changings human theories may cast gloom and dread, and so fill the soul with sad imaginings; but Nature speaks a universal language, comprehended in the heart. Nature gives us genuine births and deaths, genuine sunrises and sunsets, with beauty piled on beauty, truth on truth, joy on joy, while man is the being able to experience and appreciate it all. Creation is a vast cathedral; its various life-principles unite in a grand orchestra; and the spirit realm is vocal with shouts of joy. And man through all moves in the path of progress—he who is the middle organism, the transition type between animals and angels, bearing the image and living the life of both.

When Nature—which is God's revelation as well as God's dominion—shows her mountains piled on mountains, her imperial views, her scapes of wondrous beauty, her song-filled valleys, her curling waves which break against the shore—let those who believe in annihilation, or future misery, close eyes and deafen ears. But away with these dismal fables, and bring us the Gospel of Nature: we will read in that mighty volume and live gladly in the Creator's mansion. "It doth not yet appear what we shall be," but here and now—as by turns—we are all animal, all human, all angel—because everything centres in man.

Here now is the final message and valediction of all philosophy: Death is but a door leading to another room in the "house not made with hands." With songs of praise in our mouths, be it ours to rejoice exceedingly and attune all life to the key-note of our spiritual conviction, in view of the great hereafter and what we shall be therein.

[1] See The Great Harmonia, Vol. V, pp. 258-277, expressed in summary form.
[2] Compare The Principles of Nature, Part I, p. 1 12: "And while admiring the wisdom seen and felt in all things around and above, the mind is impressed still more deeply with an attribute still more perfect, being that of goodness."
[3] See the remarks on the distinction between soul and spirit as formulated by Davis, pp. 104 et seq., and embodying his later and altered view.
[4] See The Present Age and the Inner Life, pp. 420 et seq.

Bibliography of The Writings of Andrew Jackson Davis

I

THE PRINCIPLES OF NATURE, her Divine Revelations and a Voice to Mankind. A treatise in three parts. By and through Andrew Jackson Davis, the Poughkeepsie Seer and Clairvoyant.

Part I, The Key; Part II, The Revelation; Part III, The Application. 8vo., pp. xxii + 782. 1847. With Portrait. The work appeared concurrently in London with an analytical preface by the publisher, Mr. John Chapman. Forty-five American editions have appeared.

II

THE GREAT HARMONIA, being a Philosophical Revelation of the Natural, Spiritual and Celestial Universe. In five volumes.
Vol. I, THE PHYSICIAN, concerning the Origin and Nature of Man, the Philosophy of Health, Disease, Sleep, Death, Psychology and Healing. Crown 8vo., pp. 454. 1850.
Vol. II, THE TEACHER, concerning Spirit and its Culture, the Existence of God, etc. Crown 8vo., pp. 396. 1851.
Vol. Ill, THE SEER, concerning the Seven Mental States. Crown 8vo., pp. 401. 1852.
Vol. IV, THE REFORMER, concerning Physiological Vices and Virtues, and the Seven Phases of Marriage. Crown 8vo., pp. 446. New York, 1855, and Boston, 1856.
Vol. V, THE THINKER, a Progressive Revelation of the Eternal Principles which inspire Mind and govern Matter. Crown 8vo., pp. 438. 1855.

III

PHILOSOPHY OF SPIRITUAL INTERCOURSE: An account of Spiritual Developments at the House of Dr. Phelps and similar Cases in all parts of the Country. 8vo., pp. 176. 1851.

IV

PENETRALIA, containing Harmonial Answers. 8vo., pp. 516. 1856.

V

THE MAGIC STAFF: An Autobiography. Crown 8vo., pp. 552. 1857.

VI

THE HARBINGER OF HEALTH, containing Medical Prescriptions for the Human Body and Mind. Crown 8vo., pp. 428. 1861.

VII

ANSWERS TO EVER-RECURRING QUESTIONS FROM THE PEOPLE: A Sequel to Penetralia. Crown 8vo., pp. 417. 1862.

VIII

PROGRESSIVE TRACTS: A Series of Lectures, Nos. 1-4. 1863. N.B. — It is possible that others were issued.

IX

MORNING LECTURES: Twenty Discourses delivered before the Friends of Progress in the City of New York. Crown 8vo., pp. 434. 1864.

X

A STELLAR KEY TO THE SUMMER LAND: Illustrated with Diagrams and Engravings of Celestial Scenery. Crown 8vo., pp. viii+202. 1867.

XI

ARABULA, or THE DIVINE GUEST. Crown 8vo., pp. 403. 1867.

XII

DEATH AND THE AFTER-LIFE. Crown 8vo., pp. 210. 1868. In part a reprint of some Addresses in Morning Lectures.
XIII

THE PRESENT AGE AND INNER LIFE: Ancient and Modern Spirit Mysteries Classified and Explained. A Sequel to Spiritual Intercourse. Crown 8vo., pp. 424. 1868.

XIV

EVENTS IN THE LIFE OF A SEER: Embracing Authentic Facts, Visions, Impressions, Discoveries in Magnetism, Clairvoyance and Spiritualism. Crown 8vo., pp. 488. 1868.

XV

APPROACHING CRISIS, or Truth versus Theology. Crown 8vo., pp. 293. 1868. A review of Dr. Bushnell's lectures on the Bible, Nature, Religion, Scepticism and the Supernatural.

XVI

TALE OF A PHYSICIAN, or Seeds and Fruits of Crime. Crown 8vo., pp. 325.

1869. Described in the preface as a narrative of facts put forward under a thin veil of fiction.

XVII

THE FOUNTAIN, with Jets of New Meaning. Crown 8vo., pp. 252. 1870.

XVIII

HISTORY AND PHILOSOPHY OF EVIL, with Suggestions for more Ennobling Institutions and Philosophical Systems of Education. Crown 8vo., pp. 234. 1871.

XIX

THE TEMPLE, or Diseases of the Brain and Nerves: concerning the Origin and Philosophy of Mania, Insanity and Crime, their Treatment and Cure. Crown 8vo., pp. 487. 1 871.

XX

THE HARMONIAL MAN, or Thoughts for the Age. Crown 8vo., pp. 167. 1872.

XXI

FREE THOUGHTS CONCERNING RELIGION. Crown 8vo., pp. 215. 1872.

XXII

THE DIAKKA AND THEIR EARTHLY VICTIMS: being an explanation of much that is False and Repulsive in Spiritualism. Crown 8vo., pp. 102. 1873.

XXIII

THE GENESIS AND ETHICS OF CONJUGAL LOVE. Foolscap 8vo., pp. 142. 1874.

XXIV

VIEWS OF OUR HEAVENLY HOME: A Sequel to A Stellar Key to the Summer Land. Crown 8vo., pp. viii+290. 1877.

XXV

BEYOND THE VALLEY: A Sequel to The Magic Staff. Crown 8vo., pp. 402. 1885.

XXVI

CHILDREN'S PROGRESSIVE LYCEUM: A Divine Idea of Education. Crown 8vo., pp. 316.

N.B.—The dates given are those years in which the works were entered according to Act of Congress, and in most cases the volumes were issued at their respective places of publication in the course of the year following.

Made in the USA
Monee, IL
25 July 2025